Data Parallel C++

Mastering DPC++ for Programming of Heterogeneous Systems using C++ and SYCL

James Reinders
Ben Ashbaugh
James Brodman
Michael Kinsner
John Pennycook
Xinmin Tian

Data Parallel C++: Mastering DPC++ for Programming of Heterogeneous Systems using C++ and SYCL

James Reinders
Beaverton, OR, USA

James Brodman
Marlborough, MA, USA

John Pennycook
San Jose, CA, USA

Ben Ashbaugh
Folsom, CA, USA

Michael Kinsner
Halifax, NS, Canada

Xinmin Tian
Fremont, CA, USA

ISBN-13 (pbk): 978-1-4842-5573-5   ISBN-13 (electronic): 978-1-4842-5574-2
https://doi.org/10.1007/978-1-4842-5574-2

Copyright © 2021 by Intel Corporation

This work is subject to copyright. All rights are reserved by the Publisher, whether the whole or part of the material is concerned, specifically the rights of translation, reprinting, reuse of illustrations, recitation, broadcasting, reproduction on microfilms or in any other physical way, and transmission or information storage and retrieval, electronic adaptation, computer software, or by similar or dissimilar methodology now known or hereafter developed.

Open Access   This book is licensed under the terms of the Creative Commons Attribution 4.0 International License (http://creativecommons.org/licenses/by/4.0/), which permits use, sharing, adaptation, distribution and reproduction in any medium or format, as long as you give appropriate credit to the original author(s) and the source, provide a link to the Creative Commons license and indicate if changes were made.

The images or other third party material in this book are included in the book's Creative Commons license, unless indicated otherwise in a credit line to the material. If material is not included in the book's Creative Commons license and your intended use is not permitted by statutory regulation or exceeds the permitted use, you will need to obtain permission directly from the copyright holder.

Trademarked names, logos, and images may appear in this book. Rather than use a trademark symbol with every occurrence of a trademarked name, logo, or image we use the names, logos, and images only in an editorial fashion and to the benefit of the trademark owner, with no intention of infringement of the trademark.

The use in this publication of trade names, trademarks, service marks, and similar terms, even if they are not identified as such, is not to be taken as an expression of opinion as to whether or not they are subject to proprietary rights.

Intel, the Intel logo, Intel Optane, and Xeon are trademarks of Intel Corporation in the U.S. and/or other countries. Khronos and the Khronos Group logo are trademarks of the Khronos Group Inc. in the U.S. and/or other countries. OpenCL and the OpenCL logo are trademarks of Apple Inc. in the U.S. and/or other countries. OpenMP and the OpenMP logo are trademarks of the OpenMP Architecture Review Board in the U.S. and/or other countries. SYCL and the SYCL logo are trademarks of the Khronos Group Inc. in the U.S. and/or other countries.

Software and workloads used in performance tests may have been optimized for performance only on Intel microprocessors. Performance tests are measured using specific computer systems, components, software, operations and functions. Any change to any of those factors may cause the results to vary. You should consult other information and performance tests to assist you in fully evaluating your contemplated purchases, including the performance of that product when combined with other products. For more complete information visit www.intel.com/benchmarks. Performance results are based on testing as of dates shown in configuration and may not reflect all publicly available security updates. See configuration disclosure for details. No product or component can be absolutely secure. Intel technologies' features and benefits depend on system configuration and may require enabled hardware, software or service activation. Performance varies depending on system configuration. No computer system can be absolutely secure. Check with your system manufacturer or retailer or learn more at www.intel.com. Intel's compilers may or may not optimize to the same degree for non-Intel microprocessors for optimizations that are not unique to Intel microprocessors. These optimizations include SSE2, SSE3, and SSSE3 instruction sets and other optimizations. Intel does not guarantee the availability, functionality, or effectiveness of any optimization on microprocessors not manufactured by Intel. Microprocessor-dependent optimizations in this product are intended for use with Intel microprocessors. Certain optimizations not specific to Intel microarchitecture are reserved for Intel microprocessors. Please refer to the applicable product User and Reference Guides for more information regarding the specific instruction sets covered by this notice. Notice revision #20110804.

While the advice and information in this book are believed to be true and accurate at the date of publication, neither the authors nor the editors nor the publisher can accept any legal responsibility for any errors or omissions that may be made. The publisher makes no warranty, express or implied, with respect to the material contained herein.

Managing Director, Apress Media LLC: Welmoed Spahr
Acquisitions Editor: Natalie Pao
Development Editor: James Markham
Coordinating Editor: Jessica Vakili

Distributed to the book trade worldwide by Springer Science+Business Media New York, 1 NY Plaza, New York, NY 10004. Phone 1-800-SPRINGER, fax (201) 348-4505, e-mail orders-ny@springer-sbm.com, or visit www.springeronline.com. Apress Media, LLC is a California LLC and the sole member (owner) is Springer Science + Business Media Finance Inc (SSBM Finance). SSBM Finance Inc is a **Delaware** corporation.

For information on translations, please e-mail booktranslations@springernature.com; for reprint, paperback, or audio rights, please e-mail bookpermissions@springernature.com.

Apress titles may be purchased in bulk for academic, corporate, or promotional use. eBook versions and licenses are also available for most titles. For more information, reference our Print and eBook Bulk Sales web page at http://www.apress.com/bulk-sales.

Any source code or other supplementary material referenced by the author in this book is available to readers on GitHub via the book's product page, located at www.apress.com/978-1-4842-5573-5. For more detailed information, please visit http://www.apress.com/source-code.

Printed on acid-free paper

Table of Contents

About the Authors xvii

Preface xix

Acknowledgments xxiii

Chapter 1: Introduction 1
    Read the Book, Not the Spec 2
    SYCL 1.2.1 vs. SYCL 2020, and DPC++ 3
    Getting a DPC++ Compiler 4
    Book GitHub 4
    Hello, World! and a SYCL Program Dissection 5
    Queues and Actions 6
    It Is All About Parallelism 7
        Throughput 7
        Latency 8
        Think Parallel 8
        Amdahl and Gustafson 9
        Scaling 9
        Heterogeneous Systems 10
        Data-Parallel Programming 11
    Key Attributes of DPC++ and SYCL 12
        Single-Source 12
        Host 13
        Devices 13

TABLE OF CONTENTS

    Kernel Code 14

    Asynchronous Task Graphs 15

    C++ Lambda Functions 18

    Portability and Direct Programming 21

Concurrency vs. Parallelism 22

Summary 23

Chapter 2: Where Code Executes 25

Single-Source 26

    Host Code 27

    Device Code 28

Choosing Devices 29

Method#1: Run on a Device of Any Type 30

    Queues 31

    Binding a Queue to a Device, When Any Device Will Do 34

Method#2: Using the Host Device for Development and Debugging 35

Method#3: Using a GPU (or Other Accelerators) 38

    Device Types 38

    Device Selectors 39

Method#4: Using Multiple Devices 43

Method#5: Custom (Very Specific) Device Selection 45

    device_selector Base Class 45

    Mechanisms to Score a Device 46

Three Paths to Device Code Execution on CPU 46

Creating Work on a Device 48

    Introducing the Task Graph 48

    Where Is the Device Code? 50

TABLE OF CONTENTS

　　　Actions 53
　　　Fallback 56
　Summary 58

Chapter 3: Data Management 61
　Introduction 62
　The Data Management Problem 63
　Device Local vs. Device Remote 63
　Managing Multiple Memories 64
　　　Explicit Data Movement 64
　　　Implicit Data Movement 65
　　　Selecting the Right Strategy 66
　USM, Buffers, and Images 66
　Unified Shared Memory 67
　　　Accessing Memory Through Pointers 67
　　　USM and Data Movement 68
　Buffers 71
　　　Creating Buffers 72
　　　Accessing Buffers 72
　　　Access Modes 74
　Ordering the Uses of Data 75
　　　In-order Queues 77
　　　Out-of-Order (OoO) Queues 78
　　　Explicit Dependences with Events 78
　　　Implicit Dependences with Accessors 80
　Choosing a Data Management Strategy 86
　Handler Class: Key Members 87
　Summary 90

v

TABLE OF CONTENTS

Chapter 4: Expressing Parallelism 91

Parallelism Within Kernels 92
  Multidimensional Kernels 93
  Loops vs. Kernels 95

Overview of Language Features 97
  Separating Kernels from Host Code 97
  Different Forms of Parallel Kernels 98

Basic Data-Parallel Kernels 99
  Understanding Basic Data-Parallel Kernels 99
  Writing Basic Data-Parallel Kernels 100
  Details of Basic Data-Parallel Kernels 103

Explicit ND-Range Kernels 106
  Understanding Explicit ND-Range Parallel Kernels 107
  Writing Explicit ND-Range Data-Parallel Kernels 112
  Details of Explicit ND-Range Data-Parallel Kernels 113

Hierarchical Parallel Kernels 118
  Understanding Hierarchical Data-Parallel Kernels 119
  Writing Hierarchical Data-Parallel Kernels 119
  Details of Hierarchical Data-Parallel Kernels 122

Mapping Computation to Work-Items 124
  One-to-One Mapping 125
  Many-to-One Mapping 125

Choosing a Kernel Form 127

Summary 129

Chapter 5: Error Handling 131
Safety First 132
Types of Errors 133
Let's Create Some Errors! 135
    Synchronous Error 135
    Asynchronous Error 136
Application Error Handling Strategy 138
    Ignoring Error Handling 138
    Synchronous Error Handling 140
    Asynchronous Error Handling 141
Errors on a Device 146
Summary 147

Chapter 6: Unified Shared Memory 149
Why Should We Use USM? 150
Allocation Types 150
    Device Allocations 151
    Host Allocations 151
    Shared Allocations 151
Allocating Memory 152
    What Do We Need to Know? 153
    Multiple Styles 154
    Deallocating Memory 159
    Allocation Example 159
Data Management 160
    Initialization 160
    Data Movement 161
Queries 168
Summary 170

TABLE OF CONTENTS

Chapter 7: Buffers 173
    Buffers 174
        Creation 175
        What Can We Do with a Buffer? 181
    Accessors 182
        Accessor Creation 185
        What Can We Do with an Accessor? 191
    Summary 192

Chapter 8: Scheduling Kernels and Data Movement 195
    What Is Graph Scheduling? 196
    How Graphs Work in DPC++ 197
        Command Group Actions 198
        How Command Groups Declare Dependences 198
        Examples 199
        When Are the Parts of a CG Executed? 206
    Data Movement 206
        Explicit 207
        Implicit 208
    Synchronizing with the Host 209
    Summary 211

Chapter 9: Communication and Synchronization 213
    Work-Groups and Work-Items 214
    Building Blocks for Efficient Communication 215
        Synchronization via Barriers 215
        Work-Group Local Memory 217

TABLE OF CONTENTS

Using Work-Group Barriers and Local Memory 219
    Work-Group Barriers and Local Memory in ND-Range Kernels 223
    Work-Group Barriers and Local Memory in Hierarchical Kernels 226
Sub-Groups 230
    Synchronization via Sub-Group Barriers 230
    Exchanging Data Within a Sub-Group 231
    A Full Sub-Group ND-Range Kernel Example 233
Collective Functions 234
    Broadcast 234
    Votes 235
    Shuffles 235
    Loads and Stores 238
Summary 239

Chapter 10: Defining Kernels 241
Why Three Ways to Represent a Kernel? 242
Kernels As Lambda Expressions 244
    Elements of a Kernel Lambda Expression 244
    Naming Kernel Lambda Expressions 247
Kernels As Named Function Objects 248
    Elements of a Kernel Named Function Object 249
Interoperability with Other APIs 251
    Interoperability with API-Defined Source Languages 252
    Interoperability with API-Defined Kernel Objects 253
Kernels in Program Objects 255
Summary 257

TABLE OF CONTENTS

Chapter 11: Vectors 259
How to Think About Vectors 260
Vector Types 263
Vector Interface 264
    Load and Store Member Functions 267
    Swizzle Operations 269
Vector Execution Within a Parallel Kernel 270
Vector Parallelism 274
Summary 275

Chapter 12: Device Information 277
Refining Kernel Code to Be More Prescriptive 278
How to Enumerate Devices and Capabilities 280
    Custom Device Selector 281
    Being Curious: get_info<> 285
    Being More Curious: Detailed Enumeration Code 286
    Inquisitive: get_info<> 288
Device Information Descriptors 288
Device-Specific Kernel Information Descriptors 288
The Specifics: Those of "Correctness" 289
    Device Queries 290
    Kernel Queries 292
The Specifics: Those of "Tuning/Optimization" 293
    Device Queries 293
    Kernel Queries 294
Runtime vs. Compile-Time Properties 294
Summary 295

x

TABLE OF CONTENTS

Chapter 13: Practical Tips 297
Getting a DPC++ Compiler and Code Samples 297
Online Forum and Documentation 298
Platform Model..298
    Multiarchitecture Binaries 300
    Compilation Model..300
Adding SYCL to Existing C++ Programs 303
Debugging..305
    Debugging Kernel Code...306
    Debugging Runtime Failures 307
Initializing Data and Accessing Kernel Outputs 310
Multiple Translation Units..319
    Performance Implications of Multiple Translation Units 320
When Anonymous Lambdas Need Names 320
Migrating from CUDA to SYCL 321
Summary..322

Chapter 14: Common Parallel Patterns..323
Understanding the Patterns 324
    Map..325
    Stencil 326
    Reduction 328
    Scan...330
    Pack and Unpack..332
Using Built-In Functions and Libraries 333
    The DPC++ Reduction Library..334
    oneAPI DPC++ Library...339
    Group Functions 340

xi

TABLE OF CONTENTS

Direct Programming 341
    Map 341
    Stencil 342
    Reduction 344
    Scan 345
    Pack and Unpack 348
Summary 351
    For More Information 351

Chapter 15: Programming for GPUs 353

Performance Caveats 354
How GPUs Work 354
    GPU Building Blocks 354
    Simpler Processors (but More of Them) 356
    Simplified Control Logic (SIMD Instructions) 361
    Switching Work to Hide Latency 367
Offloading Kernels to GPUs 369
    SYCL Runtime Library 369
    GPU Software Drivers 370
    GPU Hardware 371
    Beware the Cost of Offloading! 372
GPU Kernel Best Practices 374
    Accessing Global Memory 374
    Accessing Work-Group Local Memory 378
    Avoiding Local Memory Entirely with Sub-Groups 380
    Optimizing Computation Using Small Data Types 381
    Optimizing Math Functions 382
    Specialized Functions and Extensions 382
Summary 383
    For More Information 384

xii

TABLE OF CONTENTS

Chapter 16: Programming for CPUs 387
Performance Caveats 388
The Basics of a General-Purpose CPU 389
The Basics of SIMD Hardware 391
Exploiting Thread-Level Parallelism 398
    Thread Affinity Insight 401
    Be Mindful of First Touch to Memory 405
SIMD Vectorization on CPU 406
    Ensure SIMD Execution Legality 407
    SIMD Masking and Cost 409
    Avoid Array-of-Struct for SIMD Efficiency 411
    Data Type Impact on SIMD Efficiency 413
    SIMD Execution Using single_task 415
Summary 417

Chapter 17: Programming for FPGAs 419
Performance Caveats 420
How to Think About FPGAs 420
    Pipeline Parallelism 424
    Kernels Consume Chip "Area" 427
When to Use an FPGA 428
    Lots and Lots of Work 428
    Custom Operations or Operation Widths 429
    Scalar Data Flow 430
    Low Latency and Rich Connectivity 431
    Customized Memory Systems 432
Running on an FPGA 433
    Compile Times 435

TABLE OF CONTENTS

Writing Kernels for FPGAs 440
    Exposing Parallelism 440
    Pipes 456
    Custom Memory Systems 462
Some Closing Topics 465
    FPGA Building Blocks 465
    Clock Frequency 467
Summary 468

Chapter 18: Libraries 471

Built-In Functions 472
    Use the **sycl::** Prefix with Built-In Functions 474
DPC++ Library 478
    Standard C++ APIs in DPC++ 479
    DPC++ Parallel STL 483
    Error Handling with DPC++ Execution Policies 492
Summary 492

Chapter 19: Memory Model and Atomics 495

What Is in a Memory Model? 497
    Data Races and Synchronization 498
    Barriers and Fences 501
    Atomic Operations 503
    Memory Ordering 504
The Memory Model 506
    The memory_order Enumeration Class 508
    The **memory_scope** Enumeration Class 511
    Querying Device Capabilities 512
    Barriers and Fences 514

Atomic Operations in DPC++ 515
Using Atomics in Real Life 523
    Computing a Histogram 523
    Implementing Device-Wide Synchronization 525
Summary 528
    For More Information 529

Epilogue: Future Direction of DPC++ 531
Alignment with C++20 and C++23 532
Address Spaces 534
Extension and Specialization Mechanism 536
Hierarchical Parallelism 537
Summary 538
    For More Information 539

Index 541

About the Authors

James Reinders is a consultant with more than three decades of experience in parallel computing and is an author/coauthor/editor of ten technical books related to parallel programming. He has had the great fortune to help make key contributions to two of the world's fastest computers (#1 on the TOP500 list) as well as many other supercomputers and software developer tools. James finished 10,001 days (over 27 years) at Intel in mid-2016, and he continues to write, teach, program, and consult in areas related to parallel computing (HPC and AI).

Ben Ashbaugh is a Software Architect at Intel Corporation where he has worked for over 20 years developing software drivers for Intel graphics products. For the past 10 years, Ben has focused on parallel programming models for general-purpose computation on graphics processors, including SYCL and DPC++. Ben is active in the Khronos SYCL, OpenCL, and SPIR working groups, helping to define industry standards for parallel programming, and he has authored numerous extensions to expose unique Intel GPU features.

James Brodman is a software engineer at Intel Corporation working on runtimes and compilers for parallel programming, and he is one of the architects of DPC++. He has a Ph.D. in Computer Science from the University of Illinois at Urbana-Champaign.

Michael Kinsner is a Principal Engineer at Intel Corporation developing parallel programming languages and models for a variety of architectures, and he is one of the architects of DPC++. He contributes extensively to spatial programming models and compilers, and is an Intel representative within The Khronos Group where he works on the SYCL and OpenCL

ABOUT THE AUTHORS

industry standards for parallel programming. Mike has a Ph.D. in Computer Engineering from McMaster University, and is passionate about programming models that cross architectures while still enabling performance.

John Pennycook is an HPC Application Engineer at Intel Corporation, focused on enabling developers to fully utilize the parallelism available in modern processors. He is experienced in optimizing and parallelizing applications from a range of scientific domains, and previously served as Intel's representative on the steering committee for the Intel eXtreme Performance User's Group (IXPUG). John has a Ph.D. in Computer Science from the University of Warwick. His research interests are varied, but a recurring theme is the ability to achieve application "performance portability" across different hardware architectures.

Xinmin Tian is a Senior Principal Engineer and Compiler Architect at Intel Corporation, and serves as Intel's representative on OpenMP Architecture Review Board (ARB). He is responsible for driving OpenMP offloading, vectorization, and parallelization compiler technologies for current and future Intel architectures. His current focus is on LLVM-based OpenMP offloading, DPC++ compiler optimizations for Intel oneAPI Toolkits for CPU and Xe accelerators, and tuning HPC/AI application performance. He has a Ph.D. in Computer Science, holds 27 U.S. patents, has published over 60 technical papers with over 1200 citations of his work, and has co-authored two books that span his expertise.

Preface

This book is about programming for *data parallelism* using C++. If you are new to parallel programming, that is okay. If you have never heard of SYCL or the DPC++ compiler, that is also okay.

SYCL is an industry-driven Khronos standard adding data parallelism to C++ for heterogeneous systems. DPC++ is an open source compiler project that is based on SYCL, a few extensions, and broad heterogeneous support that includes GPU, CPU, and FPGA support. All examples in this book compile and work with DPC++ compilers.

PREFACE

If you are a C programmer who is not well versed in C++, you are in good company. Several of the authors of this book happily admit that we picked up C++ by reading books that used C++ like this one. With a little patience, this book should be approachable by C programmers with a desire to write modern C++ programs.

Continuing to Evolve

When this book project began in 2019, our vision for fully supporting C++ with data parallelism required a number of extensions beyond the then-current SYCL 1.2.1 standard. These extensions, supported by the DPC++ compiler, included support for Unified Shared Memory (USM), sub-groups to complete a three-level hierarchy throughout SYCL, anonymous lambdas, and numerous programming simplifications.

At the time that this book is being published (late 2020), a provisional SYCL 2020 specification is available for public comment. The provisional specification includes support for USM, sub-groups, anonymous lambdas, and simplifications for coding (akin to C++17 CTAD). This book teaches SYCL with extensions to approximate where SYCL will be in the future. These extensions are implemented in the DPC++ compiler project. While we expect changes to be small compared to the bulk of what this book teaches, there will be changes with SYCL as the community helps refine it. Important resources for updated information include the book GitHub and errata that can be found from the web page for this book (www.apress.com/9781484255735), as well as the oneAPI DPC++ language reference (tinyurl.com/dpcppref).

PREFACE

The evolution of SYCL and DPC++ continues. Prospects for the future are discussed in the Epilogue, after we have taken a journey together to learn how to use DPC++ to create programs for heterogeneous systems using SYCL.

It is our hope that our book supports and helps grow the SYCL community, and helps promote data-parallel programming in C++.

Structure of This Book

It is hard to leap in and explain everything at once. In fact, it is impossible as far as we know. Therefore, this book is a journey that takes us through what we need to know to be an effective programmer with Data Parallel C++.

Chapter 1 lays the first foundation by covering core concepts that are either new or worth refreshing in our minds.

Chapters 2-4 lay a foundation of understanding for data-parallel programming C++. When we finish with reading Chapters 1-4, we will have a solid foundation for data-parallel programming in C++. Chapters 1-4 build on each other, and are best read in order.

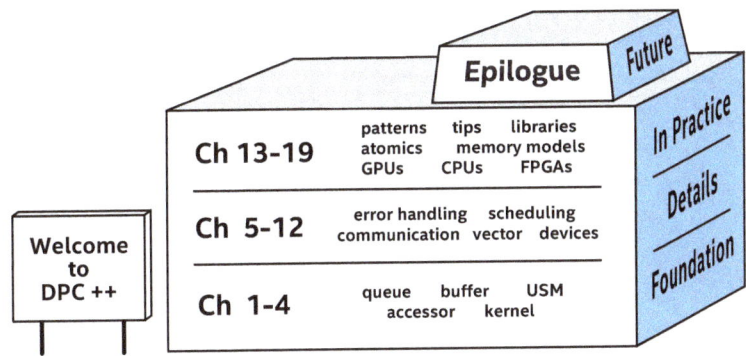

xxi

PREFACE

Chapters 5-19 fill in important details by building on each other to some degree while being easy to jump between if desired. The book concludes with an Epilogue that discusses likely and possible future directions for Data Parallel C++.

We wish you the best as you learn to use SYCL and DPC++.

James Reinders
Ben Ashbaugh
James Brodman
Michael Kinsner
John Pennycook
Xinmin Tian
October 2020

Acknowledgments

We all get to new heights by building on the work of others. Isaac Newton gave credit for his success from "standing on the shoulders of giants." We would all be in trouble if this was not allowed.

Perhaps there is no easy path to writing a new book on an exciting new developments such as SYCL and DPC++. Fortunately, there are good people who make that path easier—it is our great joy to thank them for their help!

We are deeply thankful for all those whose work has helped make this book possible, and we do wish to thank as many as we can recall by name. If we stood on your shoulders and did not call you out by name, you can know we are thankful, and please accept our apologies for any accidental forgetfulness.

A handful of people tirelessly read our early manuscripts and provided insightful feedback for which we are very grateful. These reviewers include Jefferson Amstutz, Thomas Applencourt, Alexey Bader, Gordon Brown, Konstantin Bobrovsky, Robert Cohn, Jessica Davies, Tom Deakin, Abhishek Deshmukh, Bill Dieter, Max Domeika, Todd Erdner, John Freeman, Joe Garvey, Nithin George, Milind Girkar, Sunny Gogar, Jeff Hammond, Tommy Hoffner, Zheming Jin, Paul Jurczak, Audrey Kertesz, Evgueny Khartchenko, Jeongnim Kim, Rakshith Krishnappa, Goutham Kalikrishna Reddy Kuncham, Victor Lomüller, Susan Meredith, Paul Petersen, Felipe De Azevedo Piovezan, Ruyman Reyes, Jason Sewall, Byron Sinclair, Philippe Thierry, and Peter Žužek.

We thank the entire development team at Intel who created DPC++ including its libraries and documentation, without which this book would not be possible.

ACKNOWLEDGMENTS

The Khronos SYCL working group and Codeplay are giants on which we have relied. We share, with them, the goal of bringing effective and usable data parallelism to C++. We thank all those involved in the development of the SYCL specification. Their tireless work to bring forward a truly open standard for the entire industry is to be admired. The SYCL team has been true to its mission and desire to keep this standard really open. We also highly appreciate the trailblazing work done by Codeplay, to promote and support SYCL before DPC++ was even a glimmer in our eyes. They continue to be an important resource for the entire community.

Many people within Intel have contributed extensively to DPC++ and SYCL—too many to name here. We thank all of you for your hard work, both in the evolution of the language and APIs and in the implementation of prototypes, compilers, libraries, and tools. Although we can't name everyone, we would like to specifically thank some of the key language evolution architects who have made transformative contributions to DPC++ and SYCL: Roland Schulz, Alexey Bader, Jason Sewall, Alex Wells, Ilya Burylov, Greg Lueck, Alexey Kukanov, Ruslan Arutyunyan, Jeff Hammond, Erich Keane, and Konstantin Bobrovsky.

We appreciate the patience and dedication of the DPC++ user community. The developers at Argonne National Lab have been incredibly supportive in our journey together with DPC++.

As coauthors, we cannot adequately thank each other enough. We came together in early 2019, with a vision that we would write a book to teach SYCL and DPC++. Over the next year, we became a team that learned how to teach together. We faced challenges from many commitments that tried to pull us away from book writing and reviewing, including product deadlines and standards work. Added to the mix for the entire world was COVID-19. We are a little embarrassed to admit that the *stay-at-home* orders gave us a non-trivial boost in time and focus for the book. Our thoughts and prayers extend to all those affected by this global pandemic.

ACKNOWLEDGMENTS

James Reinders: I wish to thank Jefferson Amstutz for enlightening discussions of parallelism in C++ and some critically useful help to get some C++ coding straight by using Jefferson's superpower as C++ *compiler error message whisperer*. I thank my wife, Susan Meredith, for her love, support, advice, and review. I am grateful for those in Intel who thought I would enjoy helping with this project and asked me to join in the fun! Many thanks to coauthors for their patience (with me) and hard work on this ambitious project.

Ben Ashbaugh: I am grateful for the support and encouragement of my wife, Brenna, and son, Spencer. Thank you for the uninterrupted writing time, and for excuses to go for a walk or play games when I needed a break! To everyone in the Khronos SYCL and OpenCL working groups, thank you for the discussion, collaboration, and inspiration. DPC++ and this book would not be possible without you.

James Brodman: I thank my family and friends for all their support. Thanks to all my colleagues at Intel and in Khronos for great discussions and collaborations.

Michael Kinsner: I thank my wife, Jasmine, and children, Winston and Tilly, for their support during the writing of this book and throughout the DPC++ project. Both have required a lot of time and energy, and I wouldn't have been able to do either without so much support. A thank you also goes to many people at Intel and Khronos who have poured their energy and time into SYCL and DPC++. All of you have shaped SYCL, OpenCL, and DPC++ and have been part of the countless discussions and experiments that have informed the thinking leading to DPC++ and this book.

John Pennycook: I cannot thank my wife, Louise, enough for her patience, understanding, and support in juggling book writing with care of our newborn daughter, Tamsyn. Thanks also to Roland Schulz and Jason Sewall for all of their work on DPC++ and their assistance in making sense of C++ compiler errors!

ACKNOWLEDGMENTS

Xinmin Tian: I appreciate Alice S. Chan and Geoff Lowney for their strong support during the writing of the book and throughout the DPC++ performance work. Sincere thanks to Guei-Yuan Lueh, Konstantin Bobrovsky, Hideki Saito, Kaiyu Chen, Mikhail Loenko, Silvia Linares, Pavel Chupin, Oleg Maslov, Sergey Maslov, Vlad Romanov, Alexey Sotkin, Alexey Sachkov, and the entire DPC++ compiler and runtime and tools teams for all of their great contributions and hard work in making DPC++ compiler and tools possible.

We appreciate the hard work by the entire Apress team, including the people we worked with directly the most: Natalie Pao, Jessica Vakili, C Dulcy Nirmala, and Krishnan Sathyamurthy.

We were blessed with the support and encouragement of some special managers, including Herb Hinstorff, Bill Savage, Alice S. Chan, Victor Lee, Ann Bynum, John Kreatsoulas, Geoff Lowney, Zack Waters, Sanjiv Shah, John Freeman, and Kevin Stevens.

Numerous colleagues offered information, advice, and vision. We are sure that there are more than a few people whom we have failed to mention who have positively impacted this book project. We thank all those who helped by slipping in their ingredients into our book project. We apologize to all who helped us and were not mentioned here.

Thank you all, and we hope you find this book invaluable in your endeavors.

CHAPTER 1

Introduction

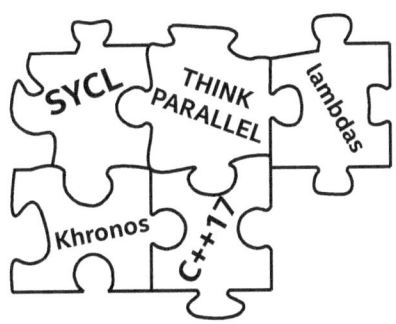

This chapter lays the foundation by covering core concepts, including terminology, that are critical to have fresh in our minds as we learn how to accelerate C++ programs using data parallelism.

Data parallelism in C++ enables access to parallel resources in a modern heterogeneous system. A single C++ application can use any combination of devices—including GPUs, CPUs, FPGAs, and AI Application-Specific Integrated Circuits (ASICs)—that are suitable to the problems at hand.

This book teaches data-parallel programming using C++ and SYCL.

SYCL (pronounced *sickle*) is an industry-driven Khronos standard that adds data parallelism to C++ for heterogeneous systems. SYCL programs perform best when paired with SYCL-aware C++ compilers such as the open source Data Parallel C++ (DPC++) compiler used in this book. SYCL is not an acronym; SYCL is simply a name.

CHAPTER 1 INTRODUCTION

DPC++ is an open source compiler project, initially created by Intel employees, committed to strong support of data parallelism in C++. The DPC++ compiler is based on SYCL, a few extensions,[1] and broad heterogeneous support that includes GPU, CPU, and FPGA devices. In addition to the open source version of DPC++, there are commercial versions available in Intel oneAPI toolkits.

Implemented features based on SYCL are supported by *both* the open source and commercial versions of the DPC++ compilers. All examples in this book compile and work with *either* version of the DPC++ compiler, and almost all will compile with recent SYCL compilers. We are careful to note where extensions are used that are DPC++ specific at the time of publication.

Read the Book, Not the Spec

No one wants to be told "Go read the spec!" Specifications are hard to read, and the SYCL specification is no different. Like every great language specification, it is full of precision and light on motivation, usage, and teaching. This book is a "study guide" to teach SYCL and use of the DPC++ compiler.

As mentioned in the Preface, this book cannot explain *everything at once*. Therefore, this chapter does what no other chapter will do: the code examples contain programming constructs that go unexplained until future chapters. We should try to not get hung up on understanding the coding examples completely in Chapter 1 and trust it will get better with each chapter.

---

[1]The DPC++ team is quick to point out that they hope all their extensions will be considered, and hopefully accepted, by the SYCL standard at some time in the future.

CHAPTER 1 INTRODUCTION

SYCL 1.2.1 vs. SYCL 2020, and DPC++

As this book goes to press, the provisional SYCL 2020 specification is available for public comments. In time, there will be a successor to the current SYCL 1.2.1 standard. That anticipated successor has been informally referred to as SYCL 2020. While it would be nice to say that this book teaches SYCL 2020, that is not possible because that standard does not yet exist.

This book teaches SYCL with extensions, to approximate where SYCL will be in the future. These extensions are implemented in the DPC++ compiler project. Almost all the extensions implemented in DPC++ exist as new features in the provisional SYCL 2020 specification. Notable new features that DPC++ supports are USM, sub-groups, syntax simplifications enabled by C++17 (known as CTAD—class template argument deduction), and the ability to use anonymous lambdas without having to name them.

At publication time, *no* SYCL compiler (including DPC++) exists that implements *all* the functionality in the SYCL 2020 provisional specification.

Some of the features used in this book are specific to the DPC++ compiler. Many of these features were originally Intel extensions to SYCL that have since been accepted into the SYCL 2020 provisional specification, and in some cases their syntax has changed slightly during the standardization process. Other features are still being developed or are under discussion for possible inclusion in future SYCL standards, and their syntax may similarly be modified. Such syntax changes are actually highly desirable during language development, as we want features to evolve and improve to address the needs of wider groups of developers and the capabilities of a wide range of devices. All of the code samples in this book use the DPC++ syntax to ensure compatibility with the DPC++ compiler.

While endeavoring to approximate where SYCL is headed, there will almost certainly need to be adjustments to information in this book to align with the standard as it evolves. Important resources for updated information include the book GitHub and errata that can be found from the web page for this book (www.apress.com/9781484255735), as well as the online oneAPI DPC++ language reference (tinyurl.com/dpcppref).

Getting a DPC++ Compiler

DPC++ is available from a GitHub repository (github.com/intel/llvm). Getting started with DPC++ instructions, including how to build the open source compiler with a clone from GitHub, can be found at intel.github.io/llvm-docs/GetStartedGuide.html.

There are also bundled versions of the DPC++ compiler, augmented with additional tools and libraries for DPC++ programming and support, available as part of a larger oneAPI project. The project brings broad support for heterogeneous systems, which include libraries, debuggers, and other tools, known as oneAPI. The oneAPI tools, including DPC++, are available freely (oneapi.com/implementations). The official oneAPI DPC++ Compiler Documentation, including a list of extensions, can be found at intel.github.io/llvm-docs.

The online companion to this book, the oneAPI DPC++ language reference online, is a great resource for more formal details building upon what is taught in this book.

Book GitHub

Shortly we will encounter code in Figure 1-1. If we want to avoid typing it all in, we can easily download all the examples in this book from a GitHub repository (www.apress.com/9781484255735—look for Services for this book: Source Code). The repository includes the complete code with build files, since most code listings omit details that are repetitive or otherwise unnecessary for illustrating a point. The repository has the latest versions of the examples, which is handy if any are updated.

```cpp
1.  #include <CL/sycl.hpp>
2.  #include <iostream>
3.  using namespace sycl;
4.
5.  const  std::string secret {
6.   "Ifmmp-!xpsme\"\012J(n!tpssz-!Ebwf/!"
7.   "J(n!bgsbje!J!dbo(u!ep!uibu/!.!IBM\01"};
8.  const auto sz = secret.size();
9.
10. int main() {
11.   queue Q;
12.
13.   char*result = malloc_shared<char>(sz, Q);
14.   std::memcpy(result,secret.data(),sz);
15.
16.   Q.parallel_for(sz,[=](auto&i) {
17.     result[i] -= 1;      device Runs
18.   }).wait();
19.
20.   std::cout << result << "\n";
21.   return 0;
22. }
```

Figure 1-1. Hello data-parallel programming

Hello, World! and a SYCL Program Dissection

Figure 1-1 shows a sample SYCL program. Compiling with the DPC++ compiler, and running it, results in the following being printed:

   Hello, world! (and some additional text left to experience by running it)

   We will completely understand this particular example by the end of Chapter 4. Until then, we can observe the single include of <CL/sycl.hpp> (line 1) that is needed to define all the SYCL constructs. All SYCL constructs live inside a namespace called sycl:

5

- Line 3 lets us avoid writing `sycl::` over and over.
- Line 11 establishes a queue for work requests directed to a particular device (Chapter 2).
- Line 13 creates an allocation for data shared with the device (Chapter 3).
- Line 16 enqueues work to the device (Chapter 4).
- Line 17 is the only line of code that will run on the device. All other code runs on the host (CPU).

Line 17 is the *kernel* code that we want to run on devices. That kernel code decrements a single character. With the power of `parallel_for()`, that kernel is run on each character in our secret string in order to decode it into the `result` string. There is no ordering of the work required, and it is actually run asynchronously relative to the main program once the `parallel_for` queues the work. It is critical that there is a wait (line 18) before looking at the result to be sure that the kernel has completed, since in this particular example we are using a convenient feature (Unified Shared Memory, Chapter 6). Without the wait, the output may occur before all the characters have been decrypted. There is much more to discuss, but that is the job of later chapters.

Queues and Actions

Chapter 2 will discuss queues and actions, but we can start with a simple explanation for now. Queues are the only connection that allows an application to direct work to be done on a device. There are two types of actions that can be placed into a queue: (a) code to execute and (b) memory operations. Code to execute is expressed via either `single_task`, `parallel_for` (used in Figure 1-1), or `parallel_for_work_group`. Memory operations perform copy operations between host and device or fill operations to initialize memory. We only need to use memory operations if we seek more control than what is done automatically for us. These are all discussed later in the book starting with Chapter 2. For now, we should be aware that queues are the connection that allows us to command a device, and we have a set of actions available to put in queues to execute code and to move around data. It is also very important to understand that requested actions are placed into a queue without waiting. The host, after submitting an action into a queue, continues to execute the program, while the device will eventually, and asynchronously, perform the action requested via the queue.

Queues connect us to devices.

We submit actions into these queues to request computational work and data movement.

Actions happen asynchronously.

It Is All About Parallelism

Since programming in C++ for data parallelism is all about parallelism, let's start with this critical concept. The goal of parallel programming is to compute something faster. It turns out there are two aspects to this: *increased throughput* and *reduced latency*.

Throughput

Increasing throughput of a program comes when we get more work done in a set amount of time. Techniques like pipelining may actually stretch out the time necessary to get a single work-item done, in order to allow overlapping of work that leads to more work-per-unit-of-time being done. Humans encounter this often when working together. The very act of sharing work involves overhead to coordinate that often slows the time to do a single item. However, the power of multiple people leads to more throughput. Computers are no different—spreading work to more processing cores adds overhead to each unit of work that likely results in some delays, but the goal is to get more total work done because we have more processing cores working together.

Latency

What if we want to get one thing done faster—for instance, analyzing a voice command and formulating a response? If we only cared about throughput, the response time might grow to be unbearable. The concept of latency reduction requires that we break up an item of work into pieces that can be tackled in parallel. For throughput, image processing might assign whole images to different processing units—in this case, our goal may be optimizing for images per second. For latency, image processing might assign each pixel within an image to different processing cores—in this case, our goal may be maximizing pixels per second from a single image.

Think Parallel

Successful parallel programmers use both techniques in their programming. This is the beginning of our quest to *Think Parallel*.

We want to adjust our minds to think first about where parallelism can be found in our algorithms and applications. We also think about how different ways of expressing the parallelism affect the performance we ultimately achieve. That is a *lot* to take in all at once. The quest to *Think Parallel* becomes a lifelong journey for parallel programmers. We can learn a few tips here.

Amdahl and Gustafson

Amdahl's Law, stated by the supercomputer pioneer Gene Amdahl in 1967, is a formula to predict the theoretical maximum speed-up when using multiple processors. Amdahl lamented that the maximum gain from parallelism is limited to (1/(1-p)) where p is the fraction of the program that runs in parallel. If we only run two-thirds of our program in parallel, then the most that program can speed up is a factor of 3. We definitely need that concept to sink in deeply! This happens because no matter how fast we make that two-thirds of our program run, the other one-third still takes the same time to complete. Even if we add one hundred GPUs, we would only get a factor of 3 increase in performance.

For many years, some viewed this as proof that parallel computing would not prove fruitful. In 1988, John Gustafson presented an article titled "Reevaluating Amdahl's Law." He observed that parallelism was not used to speed up fixed workloads, but rather it was used to allow work to be scaled up. Humans experience the same thing. One delivery person cannot deliver a single package faster with the help of many more people and trucks. However, a hundred people and trucks can deliver one hundred packages more quickly than a single driver with a truck. Multiple drivers will definitely increase throughput and will also generally reduce latency for package deliveries. Amdahl's Law tells us that a single driver cannot deliver one package faster by adding ninety-nine more drivers with their own trucks. Gustafson noticed the opportunity to deliver one hundred packages faster with these extra drivers and trucks.

Scaling

The word "scaling" appeared in our prior discussion. Scaling is a measure of how much a program speeds up (simply referred to as "speed-up") when additional computing is available. Perfect speed-up happens if one hundred packages are delivered in the same time as one package,

CHAPTER 1 INTRODUCTION

by simply having one hundred trucks with drivers instead of a single truck and driver. Of course, it does not quite work that way. At some point, there is a bottleneck that limits speed-up. There may not be one hundred places for trucks to dock at the distribution center. In a computer program, bottlenecks often involve moving data around to where it will be processed. Distributing to one hundred trucks is similar to having to distribute data to one hundred processing cores. The act of distributing is not instantaneous. Chapter 3 will start our journey of exploring how to distribute data to where it is needed in a heterogeneous system. It is critical that we know that data distribution has a cost, and that cost affects how much scaling we can expect from our applications.

Heterogeneous Systems

The phrase "heterogeneous system" snuck into the prior paragraph. For our purposes, a heterogeneous system is any system which contains multiple types of computational devices. For instance, a system with both a Central Processing Unit (CPU) and a Graphics Processing Unit (GPU) is a heterogeneous system. The CPU is often just called a processor, although that can be confusing when we speak of all the processing units in a heterogeneous system as compute processors. To avoid this confusion, SYCL refers to processing units as *devices*. Chapter 2 will begin the discussion of how to steer work (computations) to particular devices in a heterogeneous system.

GPUs have evolved to become high-performance computing devices and therefore are sometimes referred to as General-Purpose GPUs, or GPGPUs. For heterogeneous programming purposes, we can simply assume we are programming such powerful GPGPUs and refer to them as GPUs.

Today, the collection of devices in a heterogeneous system can include CPUs, GPUs, FPGAs (Field Programmable Gate Arrays), DSPs (Digital Signal Processors), ASICs (Application-Specific Integrated Circuits), and AI chips (graph, neuromorphic, etc.).

The design of such devices will generally involve duplication of compute processors (multiprocessors) and increased connections (increased bandwidth) to data sources such as memory. The first of these, multiprocessing, is particularly useful for raising throughput. In our analogy, this was done by adding additional drivers and trucks. The latter of these, higher bandwidth for data, is particularly useful for reducing latency. In our analogy, this was done with more loading docks to enable trucks to be fully loaded in parallel.

Having multiple types of devices, each with different architectures and therefore different characteristics, leads to different programming and optimization needs for each device. That becomes the motivation for SYCL, the DPC++ compiler, and the majority of what this book has to teach.

SYCL was created to address the challenges of C++ data-parallel programming for heterogeneous systems.

Data-Parallel Programming

The phrase "data-parallel programming" has been lingering unexplained ever since the title of this book. Data-parallel programming focuses on parallelism that can be envisioned as a bunch of data to operate on in parallel. This shift in focus is like Gustafson vs. Amdahl. We need one hundred packages to deliver (effectively lots of data) in order to divide up the work among one hundred trucks with drivers. The key concept comes down to what we should divide. Should we process whole images or process them in smaller tiles or process them pixel by pixel? Should we analyze a collection of objects as a single collection or a set of smaller groupings of objects or object by object?

CHAPTER 1   INTRODUCTION

Choosing the right division of work and mapping that work onto computational resources effectively is the responsibility of any parallel programmer using SYCL and DPC++. Chapter 4 starts this discussion, and it continues through the rest of the book.

Key Attributes of DPC++ and SYCL

Every DPC++ (or SYCL) program is also a C++ program. Neither SYCL nor DPC++ relies on any language changes to C++. Both can be fully implemented with templates and lambda functions.

The reason SYCL compilers[2] exist is to optimize code in a way that relies on built-in knowledge of the SYCL specification. A standard C++ compiler that lacks any built-in knowledge of SYCL cannot lead to the same performance levels that are possible with a SYCL-aware compiler.

Next, we will examine the key attributes of DPC++ and SYCL: *single-source* style, host, devices, kernel code, and asynchronous task graphs.

Single-Source

Programs can be single-source, meaning that the same translation unit[3] contains both the code that defines the compute kernels to be executed on devices and also the host code that orchestrates execution of those compute kernels. Chapter 2 begins with a more detailed look at this capability. We can still divide our program source into different files and translation units for host and device code if we want to, but the key is that we don't have to!

---

[2]It is probably more correct to call it a C++ compiler with support for SYCL.
[3]We could just say "file," but that is not entirely correct here. A translation unit is the actual input to the compiler, made from the source file after it has been processed by the C preprocessor to inline header files and expand macros.

CHAPTER 1 INTRODUCTION

Host

Every program starts by running on a host, and most of the *lines* of code in a program are usually for the host. Thus far, hosts have always been CPUs. The standard does not require this, so we carefully describe it as a host. This seems unlikely to be anything other than a CPU because the host needs to fully support C++17 in order to support all DPC++ and SYCL programs. As we will see shortly, devices do not need to support all of C++17.

Devices

Using multiple devices in a program is what makes it heterogeneous programming. That's why the word *device* has been recurring in this chapter since the explanation of heterogeneous systems a few pages ago. We already learned that the collection of devices in a heterogeneous system can include GPUs, FPGAs, DSPs, ASICs, CPUs, and AI chips, but is not limited to any fixed list.

Devices are the target for *acceleration offload* that SYCL promises. The idea of offloading computations is generally to transfer work to a device that can accelerate completion of the work. We have to worry about making up for time lost moving data—a topic that needs to constantly be on our minds.

Sharing Devices

On a system with a device, such as a GPU, we can envision two or more programs running and wanting to use a single device. They do not need to be programs using SYCL or DPC++. Programs can experience delays in processing by the device if another program is currently using it. This is really the same philosophy used in C++ programs in general for CPUs. Any system can be overloaded if we run too many active programs on our CPU (mail, browser, virus scanning, video editing, photo editing, etc.) all at once.

13

CHAPTER 1 INTRODUCTION

On supercomputers, when nodes (CPUs + all attached devices) are granted exclusively to a single application, sharing is not usually a concern. On non-supercomputer systems, we can just note that the performance of a Data Parallel C++ program may be impacted if there are multiple applications using the same devices at the same time.

Everything still works, and there is no programming we need to do differently.

Kernel Code

Code for a device is specified as kernels. This is a concept that is not unique to SYCL or DPC++: it is a core concept in other offload acceleration languages including OpenCL and CUDA.

Kernel code has certain restrictions to allow broader device support and massive parallelism. The list of features *not* supported in kernel code includes dynamic polymorphism, dynamic memory allocations (therefore no object management using new or delete operators), static variables, function pointers, runtime type information (RTTI), and exception handling. No virtual member functions, and no variadic functions, are allowed to be called from kernel code. Recursion is not allowed within kernel code.

Chapter 3 will describe how memory allocations are done before and after kernels are invoked, thereby making sure that kernels stay focused on massively parallel computations. Chapter 5 will describe handling of exceptions that arise in connection with devices.

The rest of C++ is fair game in a kernel, including lambdas, operator overloading, templates, classes, and static polymorphism. We can also share data with host (see Chapter 3) and share the read-only values of (non-global) host variables (via lambda captures).

CHAPTER 1 INTRODUCTION

Kernel: Vector Addition (DAXPY)

Kernels should feel familiar to any programmer who has work on computationally complex code. Consider implementing DAXPY, which stands for "Double-precision A times X Plus Y." A classic for decades. Figure 1-2 shows DAXPY implemented in modern Fortran, C/C++, and SYCL. Amazingly, the computation lines (line 3) are virtually identical. Chapters 4 and 10 will explain kernels in detail. Figure 1-2 should help remove any concerns that kernels are difficult to understand—they should feel familiar even if the terminology is new to us.

```
1. ! Fortran loop
2. do i = 1, n
3.   z(i) = alpha * x(i) + y(i)
4. end do
```

```
1. // C++ loop
2. for (int i=0;i<n;i++) {
3.   z[i] = alpha * x[i] + y[i];
4. }
```

EXAMPLE
IS KNOWN TO HAVE ELEMENTS NOT TAUGHT IN THIS BOOK AT ALL. PLEASE ENJOY THIS FORTRAN, SADLY THERE IS NO MORE IN THIS BOOK.

```
1. // SYCL kernel
2. myq.parallel_for(range{n},[=](id<1> i) {
3.   z[i] = alpha * x[i] + y[i];
4. }).wait();
```

Figure 1-2. DAXPY computations in Fortran, C++, and SYCL

Asynchronous Task Graphs

The asynchronous nature of programming with SYCL/DPC++ must *not* be missed. Asynchronous programming is critical to understand for two reasons: (1) proper use gives us better performance (better scaling), and (2) mistakes lead to parallel programming errors (usually race conditions) that make our applications unreliable.

15

The asynchronous nature comes about because work is transferred to devices via a "queue" of requested actions. The host program submits a requested action into a queue, and the program continues without waiting for any results. This *no waiting* is important so that we can try to keep computational resources (devices and the host) busy all the time. If we had to wait, that would tie up the host instead of allowing the host to do useful work. It would also create serial bottlenecks when the device finished, until we queued up new work. Amdahl's Law, as discussed earlier, penalizes us for time spent not doing work in parallel. We need to construct our programs to be moving data to and from devices while the devices are busy and keep all the computational power of the devices and host busy any time work is available. Failure to do so will bring the full curse of Amdahl's Law upon us.

Chapter 4 will start the discussion on thinking of our program as an asynchronous task graph, and Chapter 8 greatly expands upon this concept.

Race Conditions When We Make a Mistake

In our first code example (Figure 1-1), we specifically did a "wait" on line 18 to prevent line 20 from writing out the value from `result` before it was available. We must keep this asynchronous behavior in mind. There is another subtle thing done in that same code example—line 14 uses `std::memcpy` to load the input. Since `std::memcpy` runs on the host, line 16 and later do not execute until line 15 has completed. After reading Chapter 3, we could be tempted to change this to use `myQ.memcpy` (using SYCL). We have done exactly that in Figure 1-3 in line 8. Since that is a queue submission, there is no guarantee that it will complete before line 10. This creates a *race condition*, which is a type of parallel programming bug. A race condition exists when two parts of a program access the same data without coordination. Since we expect to write data using line 8 and then read it in line 10, we do not want a race that might have line 17 execute

CHAPTER 1 INTRODUCTION

before line 8 completes! Such a race condition would make our program unpredictable—our program could get different results on different runs and on different systems. A fix for this would be to explicitly wait for myQ.memcpy to complete before proceeding by adding .wait() to the end of line 8. That is not the best fix. We could have used event dependences to solve this (Chapter 8). Creating the queue as an ordered queue would also add an implicit dependence between the memcpy and the parallel_for. As an alternative, in Chapter 7, we will see how a buffer and accessor programming style can be used to have SYCL manage the dependences and waiting automatically for us.

```
1.  // ...we are changing one line from Figure 1-1
2.  char *result = malloc_shared<char>(sz, Q);
3.
4.  // Introduce potential data race!
5.  // We don't define a dependence
6.  // to ensure correct ordering with
7.  // later operations.
8.  Q.memcpy(result,secret.data(),sz);
9.
10. Q.parallel_for(sz,[=](auto&i) {
11.   result[i] -= 1;
12. }).wait();
13.
14. // ...
```

(handwritten annotations: "before" → line 8; "std::memcpy")

> ⚠️ **EXAMPLE** IS KNOWN TO HAVE ELEMENTS NOT TAUGHT UNTIL FUTURE CHAPTERS. EXAMINE AT YOUR OWN RISK OF CONFUSION.

Figure 1-3. Adding a race condition to illustrate a point about being asynchronous

Adding a wait() forces host synchronization between the memcpy and the kernel, which goes against the previous advice to keep the device busy all the time. Much of this book covers the different options and tradeoffs that balance program simplicity with efficient use of our systems.

For assistance with detecting data race conditions in a program, including kernels, tools such as Intel Inspector (available with the oneAPI tools mentioned previously in "Getting a DPC++ Compiler") can be helpful. The somewhat sophisticated methods used by such tools often

17

do not work on all devices. Detecting race conditions may be best done by having all the kernels run on a CPU, which can be done as a debugging technique during development work. This debugging tip is discussed as Method#2 in Chapter 2.

Chapter 4 will tell us "lambdas not considered harmful." We should be comfortable with lambda functions in order to use DPC++, SYCL, and modern C++ well. *10/7*

C++ Lambda Functions

A feature of modern C++ that is heavily used by parallel programming techniques is the lambda function. Kernels (the code to run on a device) can be expressed in multiple ways, the most common one being a lambda function. Chapter 10 discusses all the various forms that a kernel can take, including lambda functions. Here we have a refresher on C++ lambda functions plus some notes regarding use to define kernels. Chapter 10 expands on the kernel aspects after we have learned more about SYCL in the intervening chapters.

The code in Figure 1-3 has a lambda function. We can see it because it starts with the very definitive [=]. In C++, lambdas start with a square bracket, and information before the closing square bracket denotes how to *capture* variables that are used within the lambda but not explicitly passed to it as parameters. For kernels, the capture must be *by value* which is denoted by the inclusion of an equals sign within the brackets.

Support for lambda expressions was introduced in C++11. They are used to create anonymous function objects (although we can assign them to named variables) that can capture variables from the enclosing scope. The basic syntax for a C++ lambda expression is

```
[ capture-list ] ( params ) -> ret { body }
```

where

- *capture-list* is a comma-separated list of captures. We capture a variable by value by listing the variable name in the capture-list. We capture a variable by reference by prefixing it with an ampersand, for example, &v. There are also shorthands that apply to all in-scope automatic variables: [=] is used to capture all automatic variables used in the body by value and the current object by reference, [&] is used to capture all automatic variables used in the body as well as the current object by reference, and [] captures nothing. With SYCL, [=] is almost always used because no variable is allowed to be captured by reference for use in a kernel. Global variables are *not* captured in a lambda, per the C++ standard. Non-global static variables *can* be used in a kernel but *only* if they are const.

- *params* is the list of function parameters, just like for a named function. SYCL provides for parameters to identify the element(s) the kernel is being invoked to process: this can be a unique id (one-dimensional) or a 2D or 3D id. These are discussed in Chapter 4.

- *ret* is the return type. If ->*ret* is not specified, it is inferred from the return statements. The lack of a return statement, or a return with no value, implies a return type of void. SYCL kernels must *always* have a return type of void, so we should not bother with this syntax to specify a return type for kernels.

- *body* is the function body. For a SYCL kernel, the contents of this kernel have some restrictions (see earlier in this chapter in the "Kernel Code" section).

CHAPTER 1 INTRODUCTION

```cpp
int i = 1, j = 10, k = 100, l = 1000;

auto lambda = [i, &j] (int k0, int &l0) -> int {
  j = 2* j;
  k0 = 2* k0;
  l0 = 2* l0;
  return i + j + k0 + l0;
};

print_values( i, j, k, l );
std::cout << "First call returned "<< lambda( k, l ) << "\n";
print_values( i, j, k, l );
std::cout << "Second call returned "<< lambda( k, l ) << "\n";
print_values( i, j, k, l );
```

Figure 1-4. *Lambda function in C++ code*

```
i == 1
j == 10
k == 100
l == 1000
First call returned 2221
i == 1
j == 20
k == 100
l == 2000
Second call returned 4241
i == 1
j == 40
k == 100
l == 4000
```

Figure 1-5. *Output from the lambda function demonstration code in Figure 1-4*

Figure 1-4 shows a C++ lambda expression that captures one variable, i, by value and another, j, by reference. It also has a parameter k0 and another parameter l0 that is received by reference. Running the example will result in the output shown in Figure 1-5.

We can think of a lambda expression as an instance of a function object, but the compiler creates the class definition for us. For example, the lambda expression we used in the preceding example is analogous to an instance of a class as shown in Figure 1-6. Wherever we use a C++ lambda expression, we can substitute it with an instance of a function object like the one shown in Figure 1-6.

Whenever we define a function object, we need to assign it a name
(Functor in Figure 1-6). Lambdas expressed inline (as in Figure 1-4) are
anonymous because they do not need a name.

```
class Functor{
 public:
  Functor(int i, int &j) : my_i{i}, my_jRef{j}{ }

  int operator()(int k0, int &l0) {
   my_jRef = 2 * my_jRef;
   k0 = 2 * k0;
   l0 = 2 * l0;
   return my_i + my_jRef + k0 + l0;
  }

 private:
  int my_i;
  int &my_jRef;
};
```

Figure 1-6. *Function object instead of a lambda (more on this in Chapter 10)*

Portability and Direct Programming

Portability is a key objective for SYCL and DPC++; however, neither can guarantee it. All a language and compiler can do is make portability a little easier for us to achieve in our applications when we want to do so.

Portability is a complex topic and includes the concept of *functional portability* as well as *performance portability*. With functional portability, we expect our program to compile and run equivalently on a wide variety of platforms. With performance portability, we would like our program to get reasonable performance on a wide variety of platforms. While that is a pretty soft definition, the converse might be clearer—we do not want to write a program that runs superfast on one platform only to find that it is unreasonably slow on another. In fact, we'd prefer that it got the most out of any platform that it is run upon. Given the wide variety of devices in a heterogeneous system, performance portability requires non-trivial effort from us as programmers.

CHAPTER 1   INTRODUCTION

Fortunately, SYCL defines a way to code that can improve performance portability. First of all, a generic kernel can run everywhere. In a limited number of cases, this may be enough. More commonly, several versions of important kernels may be written for different types of devices. Specifically, a kernel might have a generic GPU *and* a generic CPU version. Occasionally, we may want to specialize our kernels for a specific device such as a specific GPU. When that occurs, we can write multiple versions and specialize each for a different GPU model. Or we can parameterize one version to use attributes of a GPU to modify how our GPU kernel runs to adapt to the GPU that is present.

While we are responsible for devising an effective plan for performance portability ourselves as programmers, SYCL defines constructs to allow us to implement a plan. As mentioned before, capabilities can be layered by starting with a kernel for all devices and then gradually introducing additional, more specialized kernel versions as needed. This sounds great, but the overall flow for a program can have a profound impact as well because data movement and overall algorithm choice matter. Knowing that gives insight into why no one should claim that SYCL (or other direct programming solution) solves performance portability. However, it is a tool in our toolkit to help us tackle these challenges.

Concurrency vs. Parallelism

The terms *concurrent* and *parallel* are not equivalent, although they are sometimes misconstrued as such. It is important to know that any programming consideration needed for concurrency is also important for parallelism.

The term concurrent refers to code that can be advancing but not necessarily at the same instant. On our computers, if we have a `Mail` program open and a `Web Browser`, then they are running concurrently. Concurrency can happen on systems with only one processor, through a process of time slicing (rapid switching back and forth between running each program).

> **Tip** Any programming consideration needed for concurrency is also important for parallelism.

The term parallel refers to code that can be advancing at the same instant. Parallelism requires systems that can actually do more than one thing at a time. A heterogeneous system can always do things in parallel, by its very nature of having at least two compute devices. Of course, a SYCL program does not require a heterogeneous system as it can run on a host-only system. Today, it is highly unlikely that any host system is not capable of parallel execution.

Concurrent execution of code generally faces the same issues as parallel execution of code, because any particular code sequence cannot assume that it is the only code changing the world (data locations, I/O, etc.).

Summary

This chapter provided terminology needed for SYCL and DPC++ and provided refreshers on key aspects of parallel programming and C++ that are critical to SYCL and DPC++. Chapters 2, 3, and 4 expand on three keys to SYCL programming: devices need to be given work to do (send code to run on them), be provided with data (send data to use on them), and have a method of writing code (kernels).

CHAPTER 1 INTRODUCTION

 **Open Access** This chapter is licensed under the terms of the Creative Commons Attribution 4.0 International License (http://creativecommons.org/licenses/by/4.0/), which permits use, sharing, adaptation, distribution and reproduction in any medium or format, as long as you give appropriate credit to the original author(s) and the source, provide a link to the Creative Commons license and indicate if changes were made.

The images or other third party material in this chapter are included in the chapter's Creative Commons license, unless indicated otherwise in a credit line to the material. If material is not included in the chapter's Creative Commons license and your intended use is not permitted by statutory regulation or exceeds the permitted use, you will need to obtain permission directly from the copyright holder.

CHAPTER 2

Where Code Executes

Parallel programming is not really about driving in *the* fast lane. It is actually about driving fast in *all* the lanes. This chapter is all about enabling us to put our code everywhere that we can. We choose to enable all the compute resources in a heterogeneous system whenever it makes sense. Therefore, we need to know where those compute resources are hiding (find them) and put them to work (execute our code on them).

We can control *where* our code executes—in other words, we can control which devices are used for which kernels. SYCL provides a framework for heterogeneous programming in which code can execute on a mixture of a host CPU and devices. The mechanisms which determine where code executes are important for us to understand and use.

This chapter describes where code can execute, when it will execute, and the mechanisms used to control the locations of execution. Chapter 3 will describe how to manage data so it arrives where we are executing our code, and then Chapter 4 returns to the code itself and discusses the writing of kernels.

CHAPTER 2   WHERE CODE EXECUTES

Single-Source

SYCL programs can be single-source, meaning that the same translation unit (typically a source file and its headers) contains both the code that defines the compute kernels to be executed on SYCL devices and also the host code that orchestrates execution of those kernels. Figure 2-1 shows these two code paths graphically, and Figure 2-2 provides an example application with the host and device code regions marked.

Combining both device and host code into a single-source file (or translation unit) can make it easier to understand and maintain a heterogeneous application. The combination also provides improved language type safety and can lead to more compiler optimizations of our code.

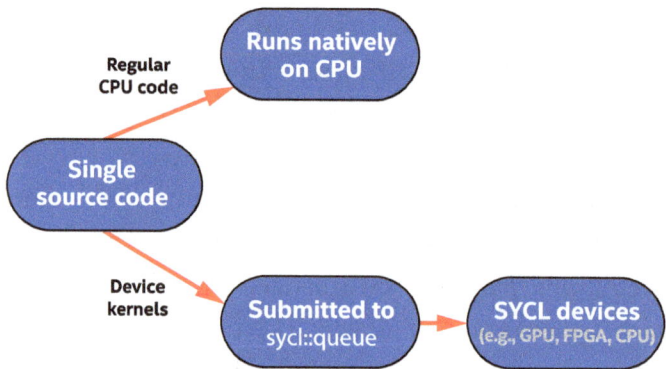

Figure 2-1. *Single-source code contains both host code (runs on CPU) and device code (runs on SYCL devices)*

CHAPTER 2 WHERE CODE EXECUTES

```
#include <CL/sycl.hpp>
#include <array>
#include <iostream>
using namespace sycl;

int main() {
  constexpr int size=16;
  std::array<int, size> data;

  // Create queue on implementation-chosen default device
  queue Q;

  // Create buffer using host allocated "data" array
  buffer B { data };

  Q.submit([&](handler& h) {
    accessor A{B, h};
    h.parallel_for(size , [=](auto& idx) {
      A[idx] = idx;
    });
  });

  // Obtain access to buffer on the host
  // Will wait for device kernel to execute to generate data
  host_accessor A{B};
  for (int i = 0; i < size; i++)
    std::cout << "data[" << i << "] = " << A[i] << "\n";

  return 0;
}
```

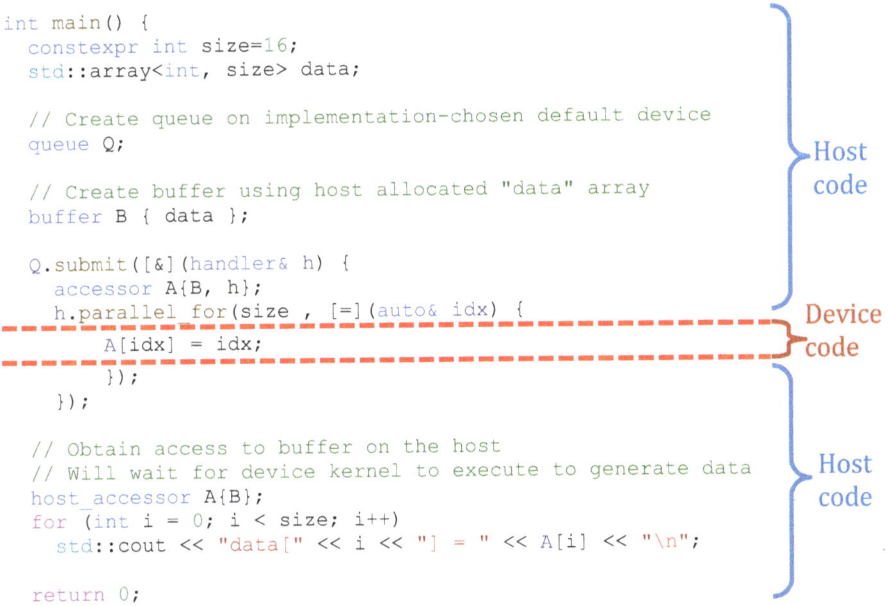

Host code

Device code

Host code

Figure 2-2. Simple SYCL program

Host Code

Applications contain C++ host code, which is executed by the CPU(s) on which the operating system has launched the application. Host code is the backbone of an application that defines and controls assignment of work to available devices. It is also the interface through which we define the data and dependences that should be managed by the runtime.

Host code is standard C++ augmented with SYCL-specific constructs and classes that are designed to be implementable as a C++ library. This makes it easier to reason about what is allowed in host code (anything that is allowed in C++) and can simplify integration with build systems.

27

CHAPTER 2 WHERE CODE EXECUTES

> SYCL applications are standard C++ augmented with constructs that can be implemented as a C++ library.
>
> A SYCL compiler may provide higher performance for a program by "understanding" these constructs.

The host code in an application orchestrates data movement and compute offload to devices, but can also perform compute-intensive work itself and can use libraries like any C++ application.

Device Code

Devices correspond to accelerators or processors that are conceptually independent from the CPU that is executing host code. An implementation must expose the host processor also as a device, as described later in this chapter, but the host processor and devices should be thought of as logically independent from each other. The host processor runs native C++ code, while devices run device code.

Queues are the mechanism through which work is submitted to a device for future execution. There are three important properties of device code to understand:

1. **It executes asynchronously from the host code.**
   The host program submits device code to a device, and the runtime tracks and starts that work only when all dependences for execution are satisfied (more on this in Chapter 3). The host program execution carries on before the submitted work is started on a device, providing the property that execution on devices is asynchronous to host program execution, unless we explicitly tie the two together.

CHAPTER 2 WHERE CODE EXECUTES

2. **There are restrictions on device code** to make it possible to compile and achieve performance on accelerator devices. For example, dynamic memory allocation and runtime type information (RTTI) are not supported within device code, because they would lead to performance degradation on many accelerators. The small set of device code restrictions is covered in detail in Chapter 10.

3. **Some functions and queries defined by SYCL are available only within device code**, because they only make sense there, for example, work-item identifier queries that allow an executing instance of device code to query its position in a larger data-parallel range (described in Chapter 4).

In general, we will refer to work including device code that is submitted to the queue as *actions*. In Chapter 3, we will learn that actions include more than device code to execute; actions also include memory movement commands. In this chapter, since we are concerned with the device code aspect of actions, we will be specific in mentioning device code much of the time.

Choosing Devices

To explore the mechanisms that let us control where device code will execute, we'll look at five use cases:

Method#1:   Running device code *somewhere*, when we don't care which device is used. This is often the first step in development because it is the simplest.

29

Method#2: Explicitly running device code on the host device, which is often used for debugging. The host device is guaranteed to be always available on any system.

Method#3: Dispatching device code to a GPU or another accelerator.

Method#4: Dispatching device code to a heterogeneous set of devices, such as a GPU and an FPGA.

Method#5: Selecting specific devices from a more general class of devices, such as a specific type of FPGA from a collection of available FPGA types.

Developers will typically debug their code as much as possible with Method#2 and only move to Methods #3–#5 when code has been tested as much as is practical with Method#2.

Method#1: Run on a Device of Any Type

When we don't care where our device code will run, it is easy to let the runtime pick for us. This automatic selection is designed to make it easy to start writing and running code, when we don't yet care about what device is chosen. This device selection does *not* take into account the code to be run, so should be considered an arbitrary choice which likely won't be optimal.

Before talking about choice of a device, even one that the implementation has selected for us, we should first cover the mechanism through which a program interacts with a device: the *queue*.

Queues

A queue is an abstraction to which actions are submitted for execution on a single device. A simplified definition of the queue class is given in Figures 2-3 and 2-4. Actions are usually the launch of data-parallel compute, although other commands are also available such as manual control of data motion for when we want more control than the automatic movement provided by the runtime. Work submitted to a queue can execute after prerequisites tracked by the runtime are met, such as availability of input data. These prerequisites are covered in Chapters 3 and 8.

```
class queue {
public:
  // Create a queue associated with the default device
  queue(const property_list = {});
  queue(const async_handler&,
        const property_list = {});

  // Create a queue associated with an explicit device
  // A device selector may be used in place of a device
  queue(const device&, const property_list = {});
  queue(const device&, const async_handler&,
        const property_list = {});

  // Create a queue associated with a device in a specific context
  // A device selector may be used in place of a device
  queue(const context&, const device&,
        const property_list = {});
  queue(const context&, const device&,
        const async_handler&,
        const property_list = {});
};
```

Figure 2-3. *Simplified definition of the constructors of the queue class*

CHAPTER 2   WHERE CODE EXECUTES

```
class queue {
public:
  // Submit a command group to this queue.
  // The command group may be a lambda or functor object.
  // Returns an event representation the action
  // performed in the command group.
  template <typename T>
  event submit(T);

  // Wait for all previously submitted actions to finish executing.
  void wait();

  // Wait for all previously submitted actions to finish executing.
  // Pass asynchronous exceptions to an async_handler if one was provided.
  void wait_and_throw();
};
```

Figure 2-4. *Simplified definition of key member functions in the queue class*

A queue is bound to a single device, and that binding occurs on construction of the queue. It is important to understand that work submitted to a queue is executed on the single device to which that queue is bound. Queues cannot be mapped to collections of devices because that would create ambiguity on which device should perform work. Similarly, a queue cannot spread the work submitted to it across multiple devices. Instead, there is an unambiguous mapping between a queue and the device on which work submitted to that queue will execute, as shown in Figure 2-5.

CHAPTER 2 WHERE CODE EXECUTES

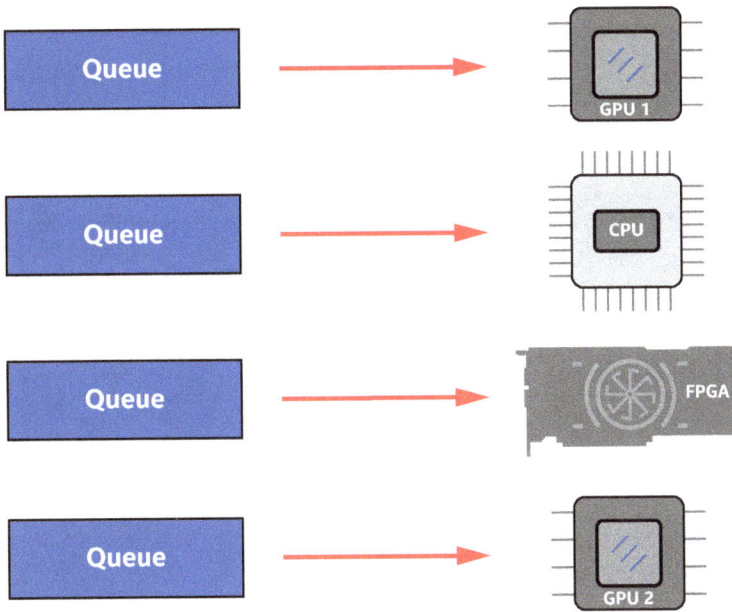

Figure 2-5. *A queue is bound to a single device. Work submitted to the queue executes on that device*

Multiple queues may be created in a program, in any way that we desire for application architecture or programming style. For example, multiple queues may be created to each bind with a different device or to be used by different threads in a host program. Multiple different queues can be bound to a single device, such as a GPU, and submissions to those different queues will result in the combined work being performed on the device. An example of this is shown in Figure 2-6. Conversely, as we mentioned previously, a queue cannot be bound to more than one device because there must not be any ambiguity on where an action is being requested to execute. If we want a queue that will load balance work across multiple devices, for example, then we can create that abstraction in our code.

33

CHAPTER 2 WHERE CODE EXECUTES

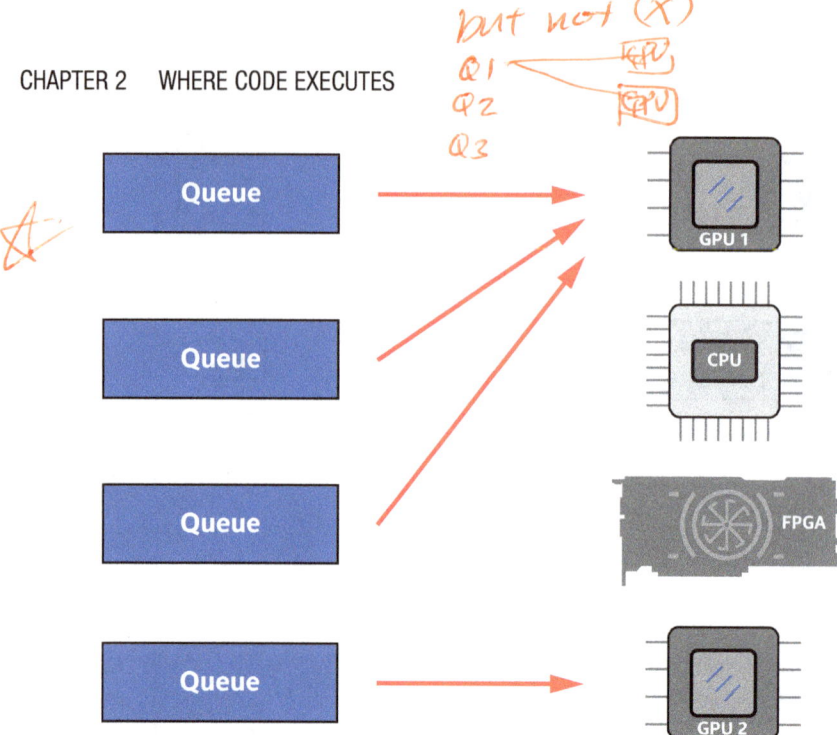

Figure 2-6. Multiple queues can be bound to a single device

Because a queue is bound to a specific device, queue construction is the most common way in code to choose the device on which actions submitted to the queue will execute. Selection of the device when constructing a queue is achieved through a device selector abstraction and associated device_selector class.

Binding a Queue to a Device, When Any Device Will Do

Figure 2-7 is an example where the device that a queue should bind to is not specified. The trivial queue constructor that does not take any arguments (as in Figure 2-7) simply chooses some available device behind the scenes. SYCL guarantees that at least one device will always be available—namely, the host device. The host device can run kernel code and is an abstraction of the processor on which the host program is executing so is always present.

34

CHAPTER 2 WHERE CODE EXECUTES

```
#include <CL/sycl.hpp>
#include <iostream>
using namespace sycl;

int main() {
  // Create queue on whatever default device that the implementation
  // chooses. Implicit use of the default_selector.
  queue Q;

  std::cout << "Selected device: " <<
  Q.get_device().get_info<info::device::name>() << "\n";

  return 0;
}
```

Possible Output:
`Device: SYCL host device`

Figure 2-7. *Implicit default device selector through trivial construction of a queue*

Using the trivial queue constructor is a simple way to begin application development and to get device code up and running. More control over selection of the device bound to a queue can be added as it becomes relevant for our application.

Method#2: Using the Host Device for Development and Debugging

The host device can be thought of as enabling the host CPU to act as if it was an independent device, allowing our device code to execute regardless of the accelerators available in a system. We always have some processor running the host program, so the host device is therefore always available to our application. The host device provides a guarantee that device code can always be run (no dependence on accelerator hardware) and has a few primary uses:

1. **Development of device code** on less capable systems that don't have any accelerators: One common use is development and testing of device code on a local system, before deploying to an HPC cluster for performance testing and optimization.

2. **Debugging of device code** with non-accelerator tooling: Accelerators are often exposed through lower-level APIs that may not have debug tooling as advanced as is available for host CPUs. With this in mind, the host device is expected to support debugging using standard tools familiar to CPU developers.

3. **Backup** if no other devices are available, to guarantee that device code can be executed functionally: The host device implementation may not have performance as a primary goal, so should be considered as a functional backup to ensure that device code can always execute in any application, but not necessarily a path to performance.

The host device is functionally like a hardware accelerator device in that a queue can bind to it and it can execute device code. Figure 2-8 shows how the host device is a peer to other accelerators that might be available in a system. It can execute device code, just like a CPU, GPU, or FPGA, and can have one or more queues constructed that bind to it.

CHAPTER 2 WHERE CODE EXECUTES

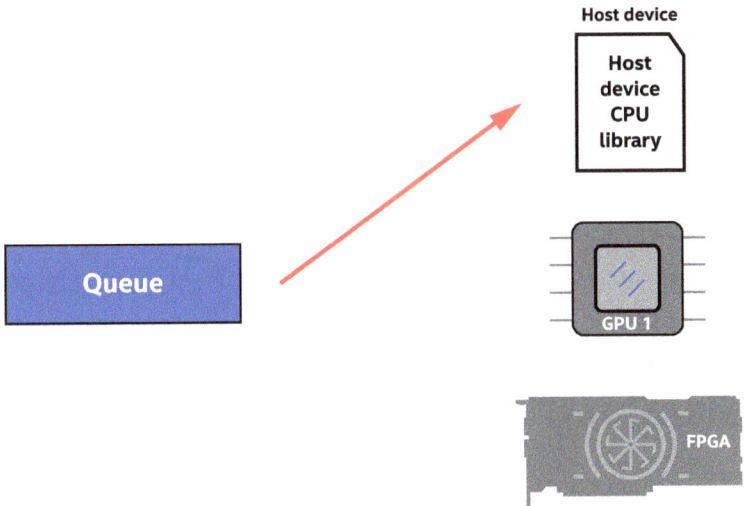

Figure 2-8. *The host device, which is always available, can execute device code like any accelerator*

An application can choose to create a queue that is bound to the host device by explicitly passing host_selector to a queue constructor, as shown in Figure 2-9.

```
#include <CL/sycl.hpp>
#include <iostream>
using namespace sycl;

int main() {
  // Create queue to use the host device explicitly
  queue Q{ host_selector{} };

  std::cout << "Selected device: " <<
    Q.get_device().get_info<info::device::name>() << "\n";
  std::cout << " -> Device vendor: " <<
    Q.get_device().get_info<info::device::vendor>() << "\n";

  return 0;
}

Possible Output:
Device: SYCL host device
```

Figure 2-9. *Selecting the host device using the* host_selector *class*

37

Even when not specifically requested (e.g., using `host_selector`), the host device might happen to be chosen by the default selector as occurred in the output in Figure 2-7.

A few variants of device selector classes are defined to make it easy for us to target a type of device. The `host_selector` is one example of these selector classes, and we'll get into others in the coming sections.

Method#3: Using a GPU (or Other Accelerators)

GPUs are showcased in the next example, but any type of accelerator applies equally. To make it easy to target common classes of accelerators, devices are grouped into several broad categories, and SYCL provides built-in selector classes for them. To choose from a broad category of device type such as "any GPU available in the system," the corresponding code is very brief, as described in this section.

Device Types

There are two main categories of devices to which a queue can be bound:

1. The host device, which has already been described.

2. Accelerator devices such as a GPU, an FPGA, or a CPU device, which are used to accelerate workloads in our applications.

Accelerator Devices

There are a few broad groups of accelerator types:

1. CPU devices

2. GPU devices

CHAPTER 2   WHERE CODE EXECUTES

3. Accelerators, which capture devices that don't identify as either a CPU device or a GPU device. This includes FPGA and DSP devices.

A device from any of these categories is easy to bind to a queue using built-in selector classes, which can be passed to queue (and some other class) constructors.

Device Selectors

Classes that must be bound to a specific device, such as the queue class, have constructors that can accept a class derived from device_selector. For example, the queue constructor is

```
queue( const device_selector &deviceSelector,
  const property_list &propList = {});
```

There are five built-in selectors for the broad classes of common devices:

default_selector	Any device of the implementation's choosing.
host_selector	Select the host device (always available).
cpu_selector	Select a device that identifies itself as a CPU in device queries.
gpu_selector	Select a device that identifies itself as a GPU in device queries.
accelerator_selector	Select a device that identifies itself as an "accelerator," which includes FPGAs.

One additional selector included in DPC++ (not available in SYCL) is available by including the header "CL/sycl/intel/fpga_extensions.hpp":

INTEL::fpga_selector	Select a device that identifies itself as an FPGA.

39

CHAPTER 2 WHERE CODE EXECUTES

A queue can be constructed using one of the built-in selectors, such as

```
queue myQueue{ cpu_selector{} };
```

Figure 2-10 shows a complete example using the cpu_selector, and Figure 2-11 shows the corresponding binding of a queue with an available CPU device.

Figure 2-12 shows an example using a variety of built-in selector classes and also demonstrates use of device selectors with another class (device) that accepts a device_selector on construction.

```cpp
#include <CL/sycl.hpp>
#include <iostream>
using namespace sycl;

int main() {
  // Create queue to use the CPU device explicitly
  queue Q{ cpu_selector{} };

  std::cout << "Selected device: " <<
    Q.get_device().get_info<info::device::name>() << "\n";
  std::cout << " -> Device vendor: " <<
    Q.get_device().get_info<info::device::vendor>() << "\n";

  return 0;
}

Possible Output:
Selected device: Intel(R) Core(TM) i5-7400 CPU @ 3.00GHz
  -> Device vendor: Intel(R) Corporation
```

Figure 2-10. *CPU device selector example*

CHAPTER 2 WHERE CODE EXECUTES

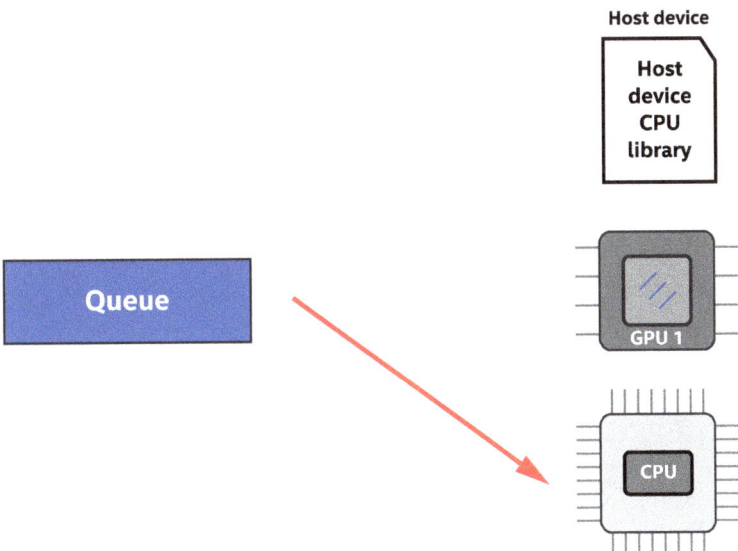

Figure 2-11. *Queue bound to a CPU device available to the application*

41

CHAPTER 2   WHERE CODE EXECUTES

```cpp
#include <CL/sycl.hpp>
#include <CL/sycl/INTEL/fpga_extensions.hpp> // For fpga_selector
#include <iostream>
#include <string>
using namespace sycl;

void output_dev_info( const device& dev,
                      const std::string& selector_name) {
  std::cout << selector_name << ": Selected device: " <<
    dev.get_info<info::device::name>() << "\n";
  std::cout << "                    -> Device vendor: " <<
    dev.get_info<info::device::vendor>() << "\n";
}

int main() {
  output_dev_info( device{ default_selector{}},
                           "default_selector" );
  output_dev_info( device{ host_selector{}},
                           "host_selector" );
  output_dev_info( device{ cpu_selector{}},
                           "cpu_selector" );
  output_dev_info( device{ gpu_selector{}},
                           "gpu_selector" );
  output_dev_info( device{ accelerator_selector{}},
                           "accelerator_selector" );
  output_dev_info( device{ INTEL::fpga_selector{}},
                           "fpga_selector" );

  return 0;
}

Possible Output:
default_selector: Selected device: Intel(R) Gen9 HD Graphics NEO
                    -> Device vendor: Intel(R) Corporation
host_selector: Selected device: SYCL host device
                    -> Device vendor:
cpu_selector: Selected device: Intel(R) Core(TM) i5-7400 CPU @ 3.00GHz
                    -> Device vendor: Intel(R) Corporation
gpu_selector: Selected device: Intel(R) Gen9 HD Graphics NEO
                    -> Device vendor: Intel(R) Corporation
accelerator_selector: Selected device: Intel(R) FPGA Emulation Device
                    -> Device vendor: Intel(R) Corporation
fpga_selector: Selected device: pac_a10 : PAC Arria 10 Platform
                    -> Device vendor: Intel Corp
```

Figure 2-12. *Example device identification output from various classes of device selectors and demonstration that device selectors can be used for construction of more than just a queue (in this case, construction of a device class instance)*

When Device Selection Fails

If a gpu_selector is used when creating an object such as a queue and if there are no GPU devices available to the runtime, then the selector throws a runtime_error exception. This is true for all device selector classes in that if no device of the required class is available, then a runtime_error exception is thrown. It is reasonable for complex applications to catch that error and instead acquire a less desirable (for the application/algorithm) device class as an alternative. Exceptions and error handling are discussed in more detail in Chapter 5.

Method#4: Using Multiple Devices

As shown in Figures 2-5 and 2-6, we can construct multiple queues in an application. We can bind these queues to a single device (the sum of work to the queues is funneled into the single device), to multiple devices, or to some combination of these. Figure 2-13 provides an example that creates one queue bound to a GPU and another queue bound to an FPGA. The corresponding mapping is shown graphically in Figure 2-14.

CHAPTER 2   WHERE CODE EXECUTES

```
#include <CL/sycl.hpp>
#include <CL/sycl/INTEL/fpga_extensions.hpp> // For fpga_selector
#include <iostream>
using namespace sycl;

int main() {
  queue my_gpu_queue( gpu_selector{} );
  queue my_fpga_queue( INTEL::fpga_selector{} );

  std::cout << "Selected device 1: " <<
    my_gpu_queue.get_device().get_info<info::device::name>() << "\n";

  std::cout << "Selected device 2: " <<
    my_fpga_queue.get_device().get_info<info::device::name>() << "\n";

  return 0;
}

Possible Output:
Selected device 1: Intel(R) Gen9 HD Graphics NEO
Selected device 2: pac_a10 : PAC Arria 10 Platform
```

Figure 2-13. Creating queues to both GPU and FPGA devices

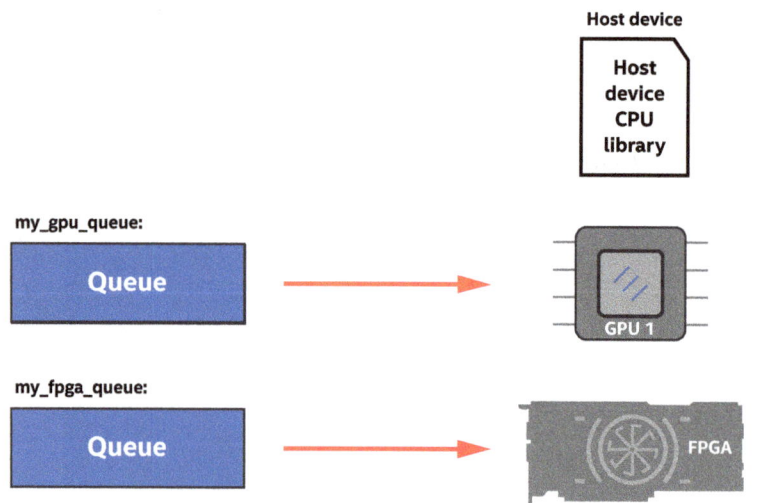

Figure 2-14. GPU + FPGA device selector example: One queue is bound to a GPU and another to an FPGA

44

Method#5: Custom (Very Specific) Device Selection

We will now look at how to write a custom selector. In addition to examples in this chapter, there are a few more examples shown in Chapter 12. The built-in device selectors are intended to let us get code up and running quickly. Real applications usually require specialized selection of a device, such as picking a desired GPU from a set of GPU types available in a system. The device selection mechanism is easily extended to arbitrarily complex logic, so we can write whatever code is required to choose the device that we prefer.

`device_selector` Base Class

All device selectors derive from the abstract `device_selector` base class and define the function call operator in the derived class:

```
virtual int operator()(const device &dev) const {
   ; /* User logic */
}
```

Defining this operator in a class that derives from `device_selector` is all that is required to define any complexity of selection logic, once we know three things:

1. The function call operator is automatically called once for each device that the runtime finds as accessible to the application, including the host device.

2. The operator returns an integer score each time that it is invoked. The highest score across all available devices is the device that the selector chooses.

3. A negative integer returned by the function call operator means that the device being considered must not be chosen.

Mechanisms to Score a Device

We have many options to create an integer score corresponding to a specific device, such as the following:

1. Return a positive value for a specific device class.

2. String match on a device name and/or device vendor strings.

3. Anything we can imagine in code leading to an integer value, based on device or platform queries.

For example, one possible approach to select an Intel Arria family FPGA device is shown in Figure 2-15.

```
class my_selector : public device_selector {
 public:
    int operator()(const device &dev) const override {
      if (
          dev.get_info<info::device::name>().find("Arria")
            != std::string::npos &&
          dev.get_info<info::device::vendor>().find("Intel")
            != std::string::npos) {
        return 1;
      }
      return -1;
    }
};
```

Figure 2-15. Custom selector for Intel Arria FPGA device

Chapter 12 has more discussion and examples for device selection (Figures 12-2 and 12-3) and discusses the `get_info` method in more depth.

Three Paths to Device Code Execution on CPU

A potential source of confusion comes from the multiple mechanisms through which a CPU can have code executed on it, as summarized in Figure 2-16.

The first and most obvious path to CPU execution is host code, which is either part of the single-source application (host code regions) or linked to and called from the host code such as a library function.

The other two available paths execute device code. The first CPU path for device code is through the host device, which was described earlier in this chapter. It is always available and is expected to execute the device code on the same CPU(s) that the host code is executing on.

A second path to execution of device code on a CPU is optional in SYCL and is a CPU accelerator device that is optimized for performance. This device is often implemented by a lower-level runtime such as OpenCL, so its availability can depend on drivers and other runtimes installed on the system. This philosophy is described by SYCL where the host device is intended to be debuggable with native CPU tools, while CPU devices may be built on implementations optimized for performance where native CPU debuggers are not available.

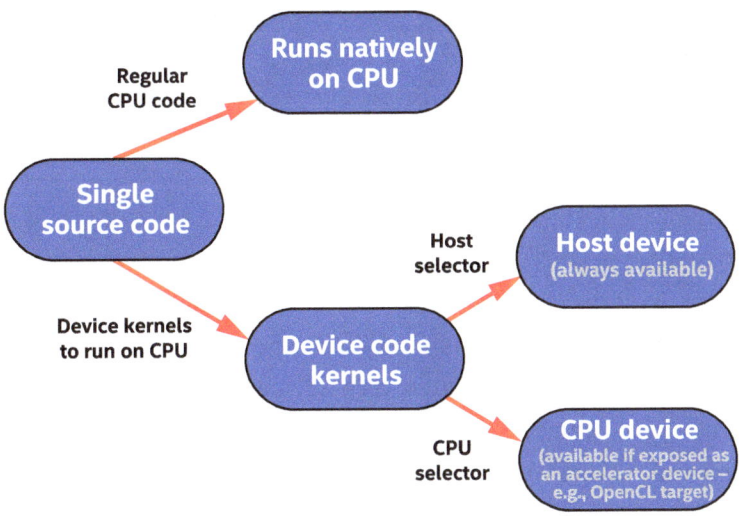

Figure 2-16. SYCL mechanisms to execute on a CPU

Although we don't cover it in this book, there is a mechanism to enqueue regular CPU code (top part of Figure 2-16) when prerequisites in the task graph are satisfied. This advanced feature can be used to execute regular CPU code alongside device code in the task graph and is known as a host task.

Creating Work on a Device

Applications usually contain a combination of both host code and device code. There are a few class members that allow us to submit device code for execution, and because these work dispatch constructs are the only way to submit device code, they allow us to easily distinguish device code from host code.

The remainder of this chapter introduces some of the work dispatch constructs, with the goal to help us understand and identify the division between device code and host code that executes natively on the host processor.

Introducing the Task Graph

A fundamental concept in the SYCL execution model is a graph of nodes. Each node (unit of work) in this graph contains an action to be performed on a device, with the most common action being a data-parallel device kernel invocation. Figure 2-17 shows an example graph with four nodes, where each node can be thought of as a device kernel invocation.

The nodes in Figure 2-17 have dependence edges defining when it is legal for a node's work to begin execution. The dependence edges are most commonly generated automatically from data dependences, although there are ways for us to manually add additional custom dependences when we want to. Node B in the graph, for example, has a dependence edge from node A. This edge means that node A must complete execution, and most likely (depending on specifics of the dependence) make generated data available on the device where node B will execute, before node B's action is started. The runtime controls resolution of dependences and triggering of node executions completely asynchronously from the host program's execution. The graph of nodes defining an application will be referred to in this book as the task graph and is covered in more detail in Chapter 3.

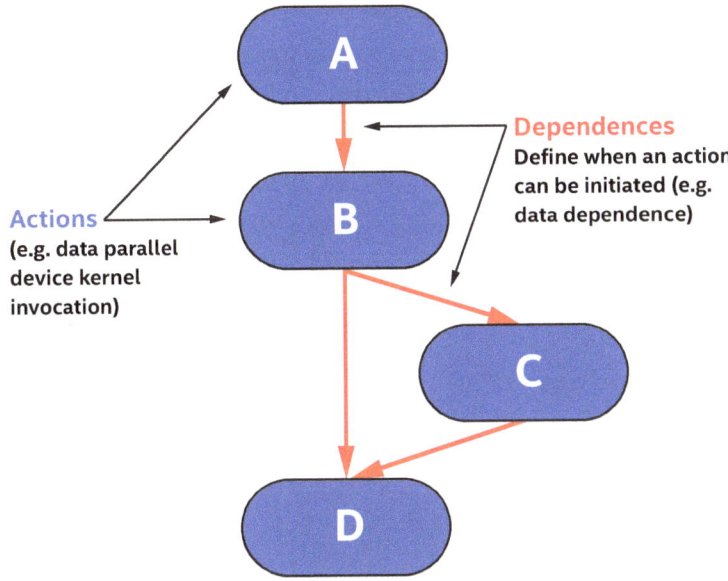

Figure 2-17. *The task graph defines actions to perform (asynchronously from the host program) on one or more devices and also dependences that determine when an action is safe to execute*

```
Q.submit([&](handler& h) {
  accessor acc{B, h};
  h.parallel_for(size , [=](auto& idx) {
    acc[idx] = idx;
  });
});
```
Device code
Command group

Figure 2-18. *Submission of device code*

Where Is the Device Code?

There are multiple mechanisms that can be used to define code that will be executed on a device, but a simple example shows how to identify such code. Even if the pattern in the example appears complex at first glance, the pattern remains the same across all device code definitions so quickly becomes second nature.

The code passed as the final argument to the parallel_for, defined as a lambda in Figure 2-18, is the device code to be executed on a device. The parallel_for in this case is the construct that lets us distinguish device code from host code. parallel_for is one of a small set of device dispatch mechanisms, all members of the handler class, that define the code to be executed on a device. A simplified definition of the handler class is given in Figure 2-19.

```
class handler {
public:
  // Specify event(s) that must be complete before the action
  // defined in this command group executes.
  void depends_on(std::vector<event>& events);

  // Guarantee that the memory object accessed by the accessor
  // is updated on the host after this action executes.
  template <typename AccessorT>
    void update_host(AccessorT acc);

  // Submit a memset operation writing to the specified pointer.
  // Return an event representing this operation.
  event memset(void *ptr, int value, size_t count);

  // Submit a memcpy operation copying from src to dest.
  // Return an event representing this operation.
  event memcpy(void *dest, const void *src, size_t count);

  // Copy to/from an accessor and host memory.
  // Accessors are required to have appropriate correct permissions.
  // Pointer can be a raw pointer or shared_ptr.
  template <typename SrcAccessorT, typename DestPointerT>
    void copy(SrcAccessorT src, DestPointerT dest);

  template <typename SrcPointerT, typename DestAccessorT>
    void copy(SrcPointerT src, DestAccessorT dest);

  // Copy between accessors.
  // Accessors are required to have appropriate correct permissions.
  template <typename SrcAccessorT, typename DestAccessorT>
    void copy(SrcAccessorT src, DestAccessorT dest);

  // Submit different forms of kernel for execution.
  template <typename KernelName, typename KernelType>
    void single_task(KernelType kernel);

  template <typename KernelName, typename KernelType, int Dims>
    void parallel_for(range<Dims> num_work_items,
                      KernelType kernel);

  template <typename KernelName, typename KernelType, int Dims>
    void parallel_for(nd_range<Dims> execution_range,
                      KernelType kernel);

  template <typename KernelName, typename KernelType, int Dims>
    void parallel_for_work_group(range<Dims> num_groups,
                                 KernelType kernel);

  template <typename KernelName, typename KernelType, int Dims>
    void parallel_for_work_group(range<Dims> num_groups,
                                 range<Dims> group_size,
                                 KernelType kernel);
};
```

Figure 2-19. Simplified definition of member functions in the handler class

In addition to calling members of the `handler` class to submit device code, there are also members of the queue class that allow work to be submitted. The queue class members shown in Figure 2-20 are shortcuts that simplify certain patterns, and we will see these shortcuts used in future chapters.

```cpp
class queue {
public:
  // Submit a memset operation writing to the specified pointer.
  // Return an event representing this operation.
  event memset(void *ptr, int value, size_t count)

  // Submit a memcpy operation copying from src to dest.
  // Return an event representing this operation.
  event memcpy(void *dest, const void *src, size_t count);

  // Submit different forms of kernel for execution.
  // Return an event representing the kernel operation.
  template <typename KernelName, typename KernelType>
    event single_task(KernelType kernel);

  template <typename KernelName, typename KernelType, int Dims>
    event parallel_for(range<Dims> num_work_items,
                       KernelType kernel);

  template <typename KernelName, typename KernelType, int Dims>
    event parallel_for(nd_range<Dims> execution_range,
                       KernelType kernel);

  // Submit different forms of kernel for execution.
  // Wait for the specified event(s) to complete
  // before executing the kernel.
  // Return an event representing the kernel operation.
  template <typename KernelName, typename KernelType>
    event single_task(const std::vector<event>& events,
                      KernelType kernel);

  template <typename KernelName, typename KernelType, int Dims>
    event parallel_for(range<Dims> num_work_items,
                       const std::vector<event>& events,
                       KernelType kernel);

  template <typename KernelName, typename KernelType, int Dims>
    event parallel_for(nd_range<Dims> execution_range,
                       const std::vector<event>& events,
                       KernelType kernel);
};
```

Figure 2-20. *Simplified definition of member functions in the queue class that act as shorthand notation for equivalent functions in the* `handler` *class*

Actions

The code in Figure 2-18 contains a `parallel_for`, which defines work to be performed on a device. The `parallel_for` is within a command group (CG) submitted to a queue, and the queue defines the device on which the work is to be performed. Within the command group, there are two categories of code:

1. **Exactly one call to an action** that either queues device code for execution or performs a manual memory operation such as `copy`.

2. **Host code** that sets up dependences defining when it is safe for the runtime to start execution of the work defined in (1), such as creation of accessors to buffers (described in Chapter 3).

The handler class contains a small set of member functions that define the action to be performed when a task graph node is executed. Figure 2-21 summarizes these actions.

Work Type	Actions (handler class methods)	Summary
Device code execution	single_task	Execute a single instance of a device function.
	parallel_for	Multiple forms are available to launch device code with different combinations of work sizes.
	parallel_for_work_group	Launch a kernel using hierarchical parallelism, described in Chapter 4.
Explicit memory operation	copy	Copy data between locations specified by accessor, pointer, and/or shared_ptr. The copy occurs as part of the DAG, including dependence tracking.
	update_host	Trigger update of host data backing of a buffer object.
	fill	Initialize data in a buffer to a specified value.

Figure 2-21. Actions that invoke device code or perform explicit memory operations

Only a single action from Figure 2-21 may be called within a command group (it is an error to call more than one), and only a single command group can be submitted to a queue per submit call. The result of this is that a single operation from Figure 2-21 exists per task graph node, to be executed when the node dependences are met and the runtime determines that it is safe to execute.

A command group must have exactly one action within it, such as a kernel launch or explicit memory operation.

The idea that code is executed asynchronously in the future is the critical difference between code that runs on the CPU as part of the host program and device code that will run in the future when dependences are satisfied. A command group usually contains code from each category, with the code that defines dependences running as part of the host program (so that the runtime knows what the dependences are) and device code running in the future once the dependences are satisfied.

```cpp
#include <CL/sycl.hpp>
#include <array>
#include <iostream>
using namespace sycl;

int main() {
  constexpr int size = 16;
  std::array<int, size> data;
  buffer B{ data };                                        // Host code

  queue Q{};  // Select any device for this queue

  std::cout << "Selected device is: " <<
    Q.get_device().get_info<info::device::name>() << "\n";

  Q.submit([&](handler& h) {                               // Immediate code to set
    accessor acc{B, h};                                    // up task graph node.

    h.parallel_for(size , [=](auto&idx){                   // Device code runs in the
                                                           // future when dependences
      acc[idx] = idx;                                      // are met.
    });
  });

  return 0;                                                // Host code
}
```

Figure 2-22. *Submission of device code*

There are three classes of code in Figure 2-22:

1. Host code: Drives the application, including creating and managing data buffers and submitting work to queues to form new nodes in the task graph for asynchronous execution.

2. Host code within a command group: This code is run on the processor that the host code is executing on and executes immediately, before the `submit` call returns. This code sets up the node dependencies by creating accessors, for example. Any arbitrary CPU code can execute here, but best practice is to restrict it to code that configures the node dependencies.

3. An action: Any action listed in Figure 2-21 can be included in a command group, and it defines the work to be performed asynchronously in the future when node requirements are met (set up by (2)).

To understand when code in an application will run, note that *anything* passed to an action listed in Figure 2-21 that initiates device code execution, or an explicit memory operation listed in Figure 2-21, will execute *asynchronously* in the future when the DAG node dependencies have been met. All other code runs as part of the host program *immediately*, as expected in typical C++ code.

Fallback

Usually a command group is executed on the command queue to which we have submitted it. However, there may be cases where the command group fails to be submitted to a queue (e.g., when the requested size of work is too large for the device's limits) or when a successfully submitted operation is unable to begin execution (e.g., when a hardware device has failed). To handle such cases, it is possible to specify a fallback queue for the command group to be executed on. The authors don't recommend this error management technique because it offers little control, and instead we recommend catching and managing the initial error as is described in Chapter 5. We briefly cover the fallback queue here because some people prefer the style and it is a well-known part of SYCL.

This style of fallback is for failed queue submissions for devices that are present on the machine. This is not a fallback mechanism to solve the problem of an accelerator not being present. On a system with no GPU device, the program in Figure 2-23 will throw an error at the Q declaration (attempted construction) indicating that "No device of requested type available."

The topic of fallback based on devices that are present will be discussed in Chapter 12.

```cpp
#include <CL/sycl.hpp>
#include <array>
#include <iostream>
using namespace sycl;

int main() {
  constexpr int global_size = 16;
  constexpr int local_size = 16;
  buffer<int,2> B{ range{ global_size, global_size }};

  queue gpu_Q{ gpu_selector{} };
  queue host_Q{ host_selector{} };

  nd_range NDR {
    range{ global_size, global_size },
    range{ local_size, local_size }};

  gpu_Q.submit([&](handler& h){
    accessor acc{B, h};

      h.parallel_for( NDR , [=](auto id) {
          auto ind = id.get_global_id();
          acc[ind] = ind[0] + ind[1];
        });
    }, host_Q); /** <<== Fallback Queue Specified **/

  host_accessor acc{B};
  for(int i=0; i < global_size; i++){
    for(int j = 0; j < global_size; j++){
      if( acc[i][j] != i+j ) {
         std::cout<<"Wrong result\n";
         return 1;
  } } }
  std::cout<<"Correct results\n";
  return 0;
}
```

Figure 2-23. *Fallback queue example*

Figure 2-23 shows code that will fail to begin execution on some GPUs, due to the requested size of the work-group. We can specify a secondary queue as a parameter to the submit function, and this secondary queue (the host device in this case) is used if the command group fails to be enqueued to the primary queue.

The fallback queue is enabled by passing a secondary queue to a `submit` call. The authors recommend catching the initial error and handling it, as described in Chapter 5, instead of using the fallback queue mechanism which offers less control.

Summary

In this chapter we provided an overview of queues, selection of the device with which a queue will be associated, and how to create custom device selectors. We also overviewed the code that executes on a device asynchronously when dependences are met vs. the code that executes as part of the C++ application host code. Chapter 3 describes how to control data movement.

 **Open Access** This chapter is licensed under the terms of the Creative Commons Attribution 4.0 International License (http://creativecommons.org/licenses/by/4.0/), which permits use, sharing, adaptation, distribution and reproduction in any medium or format, as long as you give appropriate credit to the original author(s) and the source, provide a link to the Creative Commons license and indicate if changes were made.

The images or other third party material in this chapter are included in the chapter's Creative Commons license, unless indicated otherwise in a credit line to the material. If material is not included in the chapter's Creative Commons license and your intended use is not permitted by statutory regulation or exceeds the permitted use, you will need to obtain permission directly from the copyright holder.

CHAPTER 3

Data Management

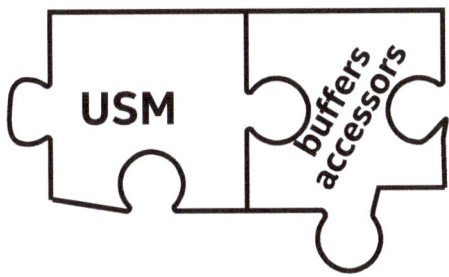

Supercomputer architects often lament that we need to "feed the beast." The phrase "feed the beast" refers to the "beast" of a computer we create when we use lots of parallelism, and feeding data to it becomes a key challenge to solve.

Feeding a Data Parallel C++ program on a heterogeneous machine requires some care to ensure data is where it needs to be when it needs to be there. In a large program, that can be a lot of work. In a preexisting C++ program, it can be a nightmare just to sort out how to manage all the data movements needed.

We will carefully explain the two ways to manage data: Unified Shared Memory (USM) and buffers. USM is pointer based, which is familiar to C++ programmers. Buffers offer a higher-level abstraction. Choice is good.

We need to control the movement of data, and this chapter covers options to do exactly that.

CHAPTER 3 DATA MANAGEMENT

In Chapter 2, we studied how to control where code executes. Our code needs data as input and produces data as output. Since our code may run on multiple devices and those devices do not necessarily share memory, we need to manage data movement. Even when data is shared, such as with USM, synchronization and coherency are concepts we need to understand and manage.

A logical question might be "Why doesn't the compiler just do everything automatically for us?" While a great deal can be handled for us automatically, performance is usually suboptimal if we do not assert ourselves as programmers. In practice, for best performance, we will need to concern ourselves with code placement (Chapter 2) and data movement (this chapter) when writing heterogeneous programs.

This chapter provides an overview of managing data, including controlling the ordering of data usage. It complements the prior chapter, which showed us how to control where code runs. This chapter helps us efficiently make our data appear where we have asked the code to run, which is important not only for correct execution of our application but also to minimize execution time and power consumption.

Introduction

Compute is nothing without data. The whole point of accelerating a computation is to produce an answer more quickly. This means that one of the most important aspects of data-parallel computations is how they access data, and introducing accelerator devices into a machine further complicates the picture. In traditional single-socket CPU-based systems, we have a single memory. Accelerator devices often have their own attached memories that cannot be directly accessed from the host. Consequently, parallel programming models that support discrete devices must provide mechanisms to manage these multiple memories and move data between them.

CHAPTER 3 DATA MANAGEMENT

In this chapter, we present an overview of the various mechanisms for data management. We introduce Unified Shared Memory and the buffer abstractions for data management and describe the relationship between kernel execution and data movement.

The Data Management Problem

Historically, one of the advantages of shared memory models for parallel programming is that they provide a single, shared view of memory. Having this single view of memory simplifies life. We are not required to do anything special to access memory from parallel tasks (aside from proper synchronization to avoid data races). While some types of accelerator devices (e.g., integrated GPUs) share memory with a host CPU, many discrete accelerators have their own local memories separate from that of the CPU as seen in Figure 3-1.

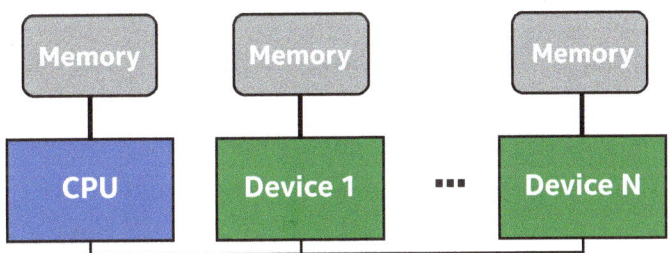

Figure 3-1. *Multiple discrete memories*

Device Local vs. Device Remote

Programs running on a device perform better when reading and writing data using memory attached directly to the device rather than remote memories. We refer to accesses to a directly attached memory as *local* accesses. Accesses to another device's memory are *remote* accesses. Remote accesses tend to be slower than local accesses because they must

63

travel over data links with lower bandwidth and/or higher latency. This means that it is often advantageous to co-locate both a computation and the data that it will use. To accomplish this, we must somehow ensure that data is copied or migrated between different memories in order to move it closer to where computation occurs.

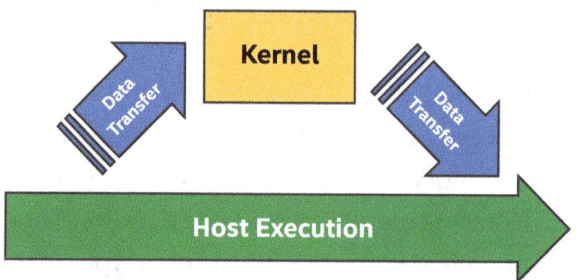

Figure 3-2. Data movement and kernel execution

Managing Multiple Memories

Managing multiple memories can be accomplished, broadly, in two ways: *explicitly* through our program or *implicitly* by the runtime. Each method has its advantages and drawbacks, and we may choose one or the other depending on circumstances or personal preference.

Explicit Data Movement

One option for managing multiple memories is to explicitly copy data between different memories. Figure 3-2 shows a system with a discrete accelerator where we must first copy any data that a kernel will require from the host memory to GPU memory. After the kernel computes results, we must copy these results back to the CPU before the host program can use that data.

The primary advantage of explicit data movement is that we have full control over when data is transferred between different memories. This is important because overlapping computation with data transfer can be essential to obtain the best performance on some hardware.

The drawback of explicit data movement is that specifying all data movements can be tedious and error prone. Transferring an incorrect amount of data or not ensuring that all data has been transferred before a kernel begins computing can lead to incorrect results. Getting all of the data movement correct from the beginning can be a very time-consuming task.

Implicit Data Movement

The alternative to program-controlled explicit data movements are implicit data movements controlled by a parallel runtime or driver. In this case, instead of requiring explicit copies between different memories, the parallel runtime is responsible for ensuring that data is transferred to the appropriate memory before it is used.

The advantage of implicit data movement is that it requires less effort to get an application to take advantage of faster memory attached directly to the device. All the heavy lifting is done automatically by the runtime. This also reduces the opportunity to introduce errors into the program since the runtime will automatically identify both when data transfers must be performed and how much data must be transferred.

The drawback of implicit data movement is that we have less or no control over the behavior of the runtime's implicit mechanisms. The runtime will provide functional correctness but may not move data in an optimal fashion that ensures maximal overlap of computation with data transfer, and this could have a negative impact on program performance.

CHAPTER 3 DATA MANAGEMENT

Selecting the Right Strategy

Picking the best strategy for a program can depend on many different factors. Different strategies might be appropriate for different phases of program development. We could even decide that the best solution is to mix and match the explicit and implicit methods for different pieces of the program. We might choose to begin using implicit data movement to simplify porting an application to a new device. As we begin tuning the application for performance, we might start replacing implicit data movement with explicit in performance-critical parts of the code. Future chapters will cover how data transfers can be overlapped with computation in order to optimize performance.

USM, Buffers, and Images

There are three abstractions for managing memory: Unified Shared Memory (USM), buffers, and images. USM is a pointer-based approach that should be familiar to C/C++ programmers. One advantage of USM is easier integration with existing C++ code that operates on pointers. Buffers, as represented by the `buffer` template class, describe one-, two-, or three-dimensional arrays. They provide an abstract view of memory that can be accessed on either the host or a device. Buffers are not directly accessed by the program and are instead used through `accessor` objects. Images act as a special type of buffer that provides extra functionality specific to image processing. This functionality includes support for special image formats, reading of images using sampler objects, and more. Buffers and images are powerful abstractions that solve many problems, but rewriting all interfaces in existing code to accept buffers or accessors can be time-consuming. Since the interface for buffers and images is largely the same, the rest of this chapter will only focus on USM and buffers.

Unified Shared Memory

USM is one tool available to us for data management. USM is a pointer-based approach that should be familiar to C and C++ programmers who use malloc or new to allocate data. USM simplifies life when porting existing C/C++ code that makes heavy use of pointers. Devices that support USM support a unified virtual address space. Having a unified virtual address space means that any pointer value returned by a USM allocation routine on the host will be a valid pointer value on the device. We do not have to manually translate a host pointer to obtain the "device version"—we see the same pointer value on both the host and device.

A more detailed description of USM can be found in Chapter 6.

Accessing Memory Through Pointers

Since not all memories are created equal when a system contains both host memory and some number of device-attached local memories, USM defines three different types of allocations: device, host, and shared. All types of allocations are performed on the host. Figure 3-3 summarizes the characteristics of each allocation type.

Allocation Type	Description	Accessible on host?	Accessible on device?	Located on
device	Allocations in device memory	✗	✓	device
host	Allocations in host memory	✓	✓	host
shared	Allocations shared between host and device	✓	✓	can migrate back and forth

Figure 3-3. USM allocation types

A `device` allocation occurs in device attached memory. Such an allocation can be read from and written to on a device but is not directly accessible from the host. We must use explicit copy operations to move data between regular allocations in host memory and `device` allocations.

A `host` allocation occurs in host memory that is accessible both on the host and on a device. This means the same pointer value is valid both in host code and in device kernels. However, when such a pointer is accessed, the data always comes from host memory. If it is accessed on a device, the data does not migrate from the host to device-local memory. Instead, data is typically sent over a bus, such as PCI-Express (PCI-E), that connects the device to the host.

A `shared` allocation is accessible on both the host and the device. In this regard, it is very similar to a host allocation, but it differs in that data can now migrate between host memory and device-local memory. This means that accesses on a device, after the migration has occurred, happen from much faster device-local memory instead of remotely accessing host memory though a higher-latency connection. Typically, this is accomplished through mechanisms inside the runtime and lower-level drivers that are hidden from us.

USM and Data Movement

USM supports both explicit and implicit data movement strategies, and different allocation types map to different strategies. Device allocations require us to explicitly move data between host and device, while host and shared allocations provide implicit data movement.

Explicit Data Movement in USM

Explicit data movement with USM is accomplished with `device` allocations and a special `memcpy()` found in the queue and handler classes. We enqueue `memcpy()` operations (actions) to transfer data either from the host to the device or from the device to the host.

CHAPTER 3 DATA MANAGEMENT

Figure 3-4 contains one kernel that operates on a device allocation. Data is copied between hostArray and deviceArray before and after the kernel executes using memcpy() operations. Calls to wait() on the queue ensure that the copy to the device has completed before the kernel executes and ensure that the kernel has completed before the data is copied back to the host. We will learn how we can eliminate these calls later in this chapter.

```cpp
#include <CL/sycl.hpp>
#include<array>
using namespace sycl;
constexpr int N = 42;

int main() {
 queue Q;

 std::array<int,N> host_array;
 int *device_array = malloc_device<int>(N, Q);

 for (int i = 0; i < N; i++)
  host_array[i] = N;

 // We will learn how to simplify this example later
 Q.submit([&](handler &h) {
   // copy hostArray to deviceArray
   h.memcpy(device_array, &host_array[0], N * sizeof(int));
  });
 Q.wait();

 Q.submit([&](handler &h) {
   h.parallel_for(N, [=](id<1> i) { device_array[i]++; });
  });
 Q.wait();

 Q.submit([&](handler &h) {
   // copy deviceArray back to hostArray
   h.memcpy(&host_array[0], device_array, N * sizeof(int));
  });
 Q.wait();

 free(device_array, Q);
 return 0;
}
```

Figure 3-4. *USM explicit data movement*

CHAPTER 3   DATA MANAGEMENT

Implicit Data Movement in USM

Implicit data movement with USM is accomplished with host and shared allocations. With these types of allocations, we do not need to explicitly insert copy operations to move data between host and device. Instead, we simply access the pointers inside a kernel, and any required data movement is performed automatically without programmer intervention (as long as your device supports these allocations). This greatly simplifies porting of existing codes: simply replace any malloc or new with the appropriate USM allocation functions (as well as the calls to free to deallocate memory), and everything should just work.

```
#include <CL/sycl.hpp>
using namespace sycl;
constexpr int N = 42;

int main() {
  queue Q;
  int *host_array = malloc_host<int>(N, Q);
  int *shared_array = malloc_shared<int>(N, Q);

  for (int i = 0; i < N; i++) {
    // Initialize hostArray on host
    host_array[i] = i;
  }

  // We will learn how to simplify this example later
  Q.submit([&](handler &h) {
      h.parallel_for(N, [=](id<1> i) {
          // access sharedArray and hostArray on device
          shared_array[i] = host_array[i] + 1;
        });
    });
  Q.wait();

  for (int i = 0; i < N; i++) {
    // access sharedArray on host
    host_array[i] = shared_array[i];
  }

  free(shared_array, Q);
  free(host_array, Q);
  return 0;
}
```

Figure 3-5.   USM implicit data movement

In Figure 3-5, we create two arrays, `hostArray` and `sharedArray`, that are host and shared allocations, respectively. While both host and shared allocations are directly accessible in host code, we only initialize `hostArray` here. Similarly, it can be directly accessed inside the kernel, performing remote reads of the data. The runtime ensures that `sharedArray` is available on the device before the kernel accesses it and that it is moved back when it is later read by the host code, all without programmer intervention.

Buffers

The other abstraction provided for data management is the buffer object. Buffers are a data abstraction that represent one or more objects of a given C++ type. Elements of a buffer object can be a scalar data type (such as an `int`, `float`, or `double`), a vector data type (Chapter 11), or a user-defined class or structure. Data structures in buffers must be C++ *trivially copyable*, which means that an object can be safely copied byte by byte where copy constructors do not need to be invoked.

While a buffer itself is a single object, the C++ type encapsulated by the buffer could be an array that contains multiple objects. Buffers represent data objects rather than specific memory addresses, so they cannot be directly accessed like regular C++ arrays. Indeed, a buffer object might map to multiple different memory locations on several different devices, or even on the same device, for performance reasons. Instead, we use *accessor* objects to read and write to buffers.

A more detailed description of buffers can be found in Chapter 7.

Creating Buffers

Buffers can be created in a variety of ways. The simplest method is to simply construct a new buffer with a range that specifies the size of the buffer. However, creating a buffer in this fashion does not initialize its data, meaning that we must first initialize the buffer through other means before attempting to read useful data from it.

Buffers can also be created from existing data on the host. This is done by invoking one of the several constructors that take either a pointer to an existing host allocation, a set of `InputIterators`, or a container that has certain properties. Data is copied during buffer construction from the existing host allocation into the buffer object's host memory. A buffer may also be created from an existing `cl_mem` object if we are using the SYCL interoperability features with OpenCL.

Accessing Buffers

Buffers may not be directly accessed by the host and device (except through advanced and infrequently used mechanisms not described here). Instead, we must create accessors in order to read and write to buffers. Accessors provide the runtime with information about how we plan to use the data in buffers, allowing it to correctly schedule data movement.

CHAPTER 3 DATA MANAGEMENT

```cpp
#include <CL/sycl.hpp>
#include <array>
using namespace sycl;
constexpr int N = 42;

int main() {
  std::array<int,N> my_data;
  for (int i = 0; i < N; i++)
    my_data[i] = 0;

  {
    queue q;
    buffer my_buffer(my_data);

    q.submit([&](handler &h) {
        // create an accessor to update
        // the buffer on the device
        accessor my_accessor(my_buffer, h);

        h.parallel_for(N, [=](id<1> i) {
            my_accessor[i]++;
          });
      });

    // create host accessor
    host_accessor host_accessor(my_buffer);

    for (int i = 0; i < N; i++) {
      // access myBuffer on host
      std::cout << host_accessor[i] << " ";
    }
    std::cout << "\n";
  }

  // myData is updated when myBuffer is
  // destroyed upon exiting scope
  for (int i = 0; i < N; i++) {
    std::cout << my_data[i] << " ";
  }
  std::cout << "\n";
}
```

Figure 3-6. Buffers and accessors

Access Mode	Description
read	Read-only access.
write	Write-only access. Previous contents not discarded.
read_write	Read and write access.

Figure 3-7. Buffer access modes

Access Modes

When creating an accessor, we can inform the runtime how we are going to use it to provide more information for optimizations. We do this by specifying an *access mode*. Access modes are defined in the access::mode enum described in Figure 3-7. In the code example shown in Figure 3-6, the accessor myAccessor is created with the default access mode, access::mode::read_write. This lets the runtime know that we intend to both read and write to the buffer through myAccessor. Access modes are how the runtime is able to optimize implicit data movement. For example, access::mode::read tells the runtime that the data needs to be available on the device before this kernel can begin executing. If a kernel only reads data through an accessor, there is no need to copy data back to the host after the kernel has completed as we haven't modified it. Likewise, access::mode::write lets the runtime know that we will modify the contents of a buffer and may need to copy the results back after computation has ended.

Creating accessors with the proper modes gives the runtime more information about how we use data in our program. The runtime uses accessors to order the uses of data, but it can also use this data to optimize scheduling of kernels and data movement. The access modes and optimization tags are described in greater detail in Chapter 7.

CHAPTER 3　DATA MANAGEMENT

Ordering the Uses of Data

Kernels can be viewed as asynchronous tasks that are submitted for execution. These tasks must be submitted to a queue where they are scheduled for execution on a device. In many cases, kernels must execute in a specific order so that the correct result is computed. If obtaining the correct result requires task A to execute before task B, we say that a *dependence*[1] exists between tasks A and B.

However, kernels are not the only form of task that must be scheduled. Any data that is accessed by a kernel needs to be available on the device before the kernel can start executing. These data dependences can create additional tasks in the form of data transfers from one device to another. Data transfer tasks may be either explicitly coded copy operations or more commonly implicit data movements performed by the runtime.

If we take all the tasks in a program and the dependences that exist between them, we can use this to visualize the information as a graph. This task graph is specifically a directed acyclic graph (DAG) where the nodes are the tasks and the edges are the dependences. The graph is *directed* because dependences are one-way: task A must happen before task B. The graph is *acyclic* because it does not contain any cycles or paths from a node that lead back to itself.

In Figure 3-8, task A must execute before tasks B and C. Likewise, B and C must execute before task D. Since B and C do not have a dependence between each other, the runtime is free to execute them

---

[1] Note that you may see "dependence" and "dependences" sometimes spelled "dependency" and "dependencies" in other texts. They mean the same thing, but we are favoring the spelling used in several important papers on data flow analysis. See https://dl.acm.org/doi/pdf/10.1145/75277.75280 and https://dl.acm.org/doi/pdf/10.1145/113446.113449.

in any order (or even in parallel) as long as task A has already executed. Therefore, the possible legal orderings of this graph are A ⇒ B ⇒ C ⇒ D, A ⇒ C ⇒ B ⇒ D, and even A ⇒ {B,C} ⇒ D if B and C can concurrently execute.

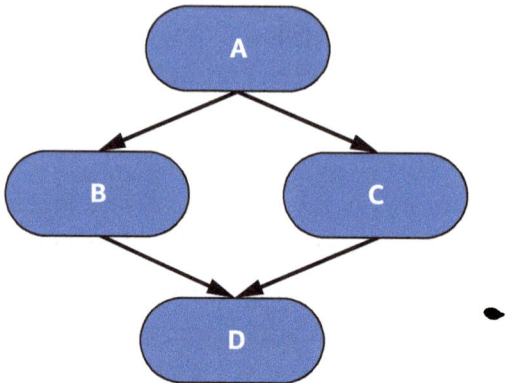

Figure 3-8. Simple task graph

Tasks may have a dependence with a subset of all tasks. In these cases, we only want to specify the dependences that matter for correctness. This flexibility gives the runtime latitude to optimize the execution order of the task graph. In Figure 3-9, we extend the earlier task graph from Figure 3-8 to add tasks E and F where E must execute before F. However, tasks E and F have no dependences with nodes A, B, C, and D. This allows the runtime to choose from many possible legal orderings to execute all the tasks.

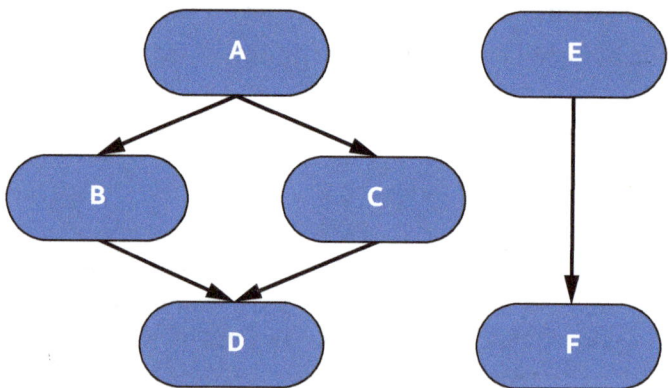

Figure 3-9. Task graph with disjoint dependences

CHAPTER 3 DATA MANAGEMENT

There are two different ways to model the execution of tasks, such as a launch of a kernel, in a queue: the queue could either execute tasks in the order of submission, or it could execute tasks in *any* order subject to any dependences that we define. There are several mechanisms for us to define the dependences needed for correct ordering.

In-order Queues

The simplest option to order tasks is to submit them to an in-order queue object. An in-order queue executes tasks in the order in which they were submitted as seen in Figure 3-10. While the intuitive task ordering of in-order queues provides an advantage in simplicity, it provides a disadvantage in that the execution of tasks will serialize even if no dependences exist between independent tasks. In-order queues are useful when bringing up applications because they are simple, intuitive, deterministic on execution ordering, and suitable for many codes.

```cpp
#include <CL/sycl.hpp>
using namespace sycl;
constexpr int N = 4;

int main() {
  queue Q{property::queue::in_order()};

  // Task A
  Q.submit([&](handler& h) {
    h.parallel_for(N, [=](id<1> i) { /*...*/ });
  });

  // Task B
  Q.submit([&](handler& h) {
    h.parallel_for(N, [=](id<1> i) { /*...*/ });
  });

  // Task C
  Q.submit([&](handler& h) {
    h.parallel_for(N, [=](id<1> i) { /*...*/ });
  });

  return 0;
}
```

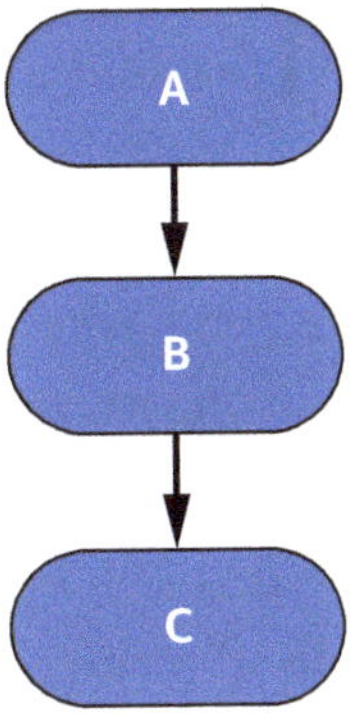

Figure 3-10. In-order queue usage

CHAPTER 3   DATA MANAGEMENT

Out-of-Order (OoO) Queues

Since queue objects are out-of-order queues (unless created with the in-order queue property), they must provide ways to order tasks submitted to them. Queues order tasks by letting us inform the runtime of dependences between them. These dependences can be specified, either explicitly or implicitly, using *command groups.*

A command group is an object that specifies a task and its dependences. Command groups are typically written as C++ lambdas passed as an argument to the submit() method of a queue object. This lambda's only parameter is a reference to a handler object. The handler object is used inside the command group to specify actions, create accessors, and specify dependences.

Explicit Dependences with Events

Explicit dependences between tasks look like the examples we have seen (Figure 3-8) where task A must execute before task B. Expressing dependences in this way focuses on explicit ordering based on the computations that occur rather than on the data accessed by the computations. Note that expressing dependences between computations is primarily relevant for codes that use USM since codes that use buffers express most dependences via accessors. In Figures 3-4 and 3-5, we simply tell the queue to wait for all previously submitted tasks to finish before we continue. Instead, we can express task dependences through *event* objects. When submitting a command group to a queue, the submit() method returns an event object. These events can then be used in two ways.

First, we can synchronize through the host by explicitly calling the wait() method on an event. This forces the runtime to wait for the task that generated the event to finish executing before host program execution may continue. Explicitly waiting on events can be very useful for debugging an application, but wait() can overly constrain the asynchronous execution of tasks since it halts all execution on the

CHAPTER 3 DATA MANAGEMENT

host thread. Similarly, one could also call wait() on a queue object, which would block execution on the host until all enqueued tasks have completed. This can be a useful tool if we do not want to keep track of all the events returned by enqueued tasks.

This brings us to the second way that events can be used. The handler class contains a method named depends_on(). This method accepts either a single event or a vector of events and informs the runtime that the command group being submitted requires the specified events to complete before the action within the command group may execute. Figure 3-11 shows an example of how depends_on() may be used to order tasks.

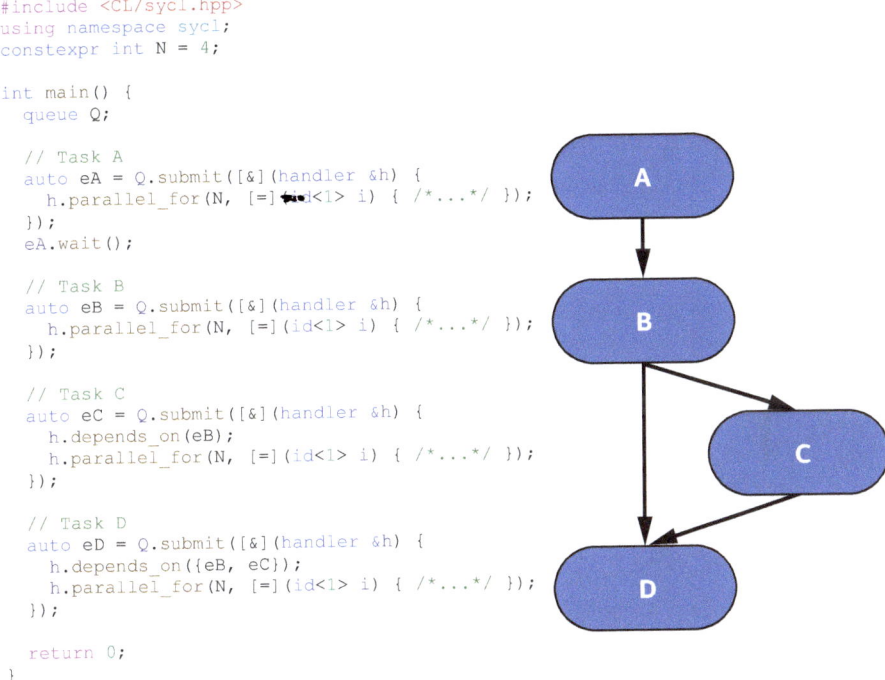

```
#include <CL/sycl.hpp>
using namespace sycl;
constexpr int N = 4;

int main() {
  queue Q;

  // Task A
  auto eA = Q.submit([&](handler &h) {
    h.parallel_for(N, [=](id<1> i) { /*...*/ });
  });
  eA.wait();

  // Task B
  auto eB = Q.submit([&](handler &h) {
    h.parallel_for(N, [=](id<1> i) { /*...*/ });
  });

  // Task C
  auto eC = Q.submit([&](handler &h) {
    h.depends_on(eB);
    h.parallel_for(N, [=](id<1> i) { /*...*/ });
  });

  // Task D
  auto eD = Q.submit([&](handler &h) {
    h.depends_on({eB, eC});
    h.parallel_for(N, [=](id<1> i) { /*...*/ });
  });

  return 0;
}
```

Figure 3-11. Using events and depends_on

Implicit Dependences with Accessors

Implicit dependences between tasks are created from data dependences. Data dependences between tasks take three forms, shown in Figure 3-12.

Dependence Type	Description
Read-after-Write (RAW)	Occurs when task B needs to read data computed by task A.
Write-after-Read (WAR)	Occurs when task B writes over data after it has been read by task A.
Write-after-Write (WAW)	Occurs when task B also writes over data written by task A.

Figure 3-12. Three forms of data dependences

Data dependences are expressed to the runtime in two ways: accessors and program order. Both must be used for the runtime to properly compute data dependences. This is illustrated in Figures 3-13 and 3-14.

```
#include <CL/sycl.hpp>
#include <array>
using namespace sycl;
constexpr int N = 42;

int main() {
  std::array<int,N> a, b, c;
  for (int i = 0; i < N; i++) {
    a[i] = b[i] = c[i] = 0;
  }

  queue Q;

  // We will learn how to simplify this example later
  buffer A{a};
  buffer B{b};
  buffer C{c};

  Q.submit([&](handler &h) {
      accessor accA(A, h, read_only);
      accessor accB(B, h, write_only);
      h.parallel_for( // computeB
        N,
        [=](id<1> i) { accB[i] = accA[i] + 1; });
    });

  Q.submit([&](handler &h) {
      accessor accA(A, h, read_only);
      h.parallel_for( // readA
        N,
        [=](id<1> i) {
          // Useful only as an example
          int data = accA[i];
        });
    });

  Q.submit([&](handler &h) {
      // RAW of buffer B
      accessor accB(B, h, read_only);
      accessor accC(C, h, write_only);
      h.parallel_for( // computeC
        N,
        [=](id<1> i) { accC[i] = accB[i] + 2; });
    });

  // read C on host
  host_accessor host_accC(C, read_only);
  for (int i = 0; i < N; i++) {
    std::cout << host_accC[i] << " ";
  }
  std::cout << "\n";
  return 0;
}
```

Figure 3-13. *Read-after-Write*

CHAPTER 3   DATA MANAGEMENT

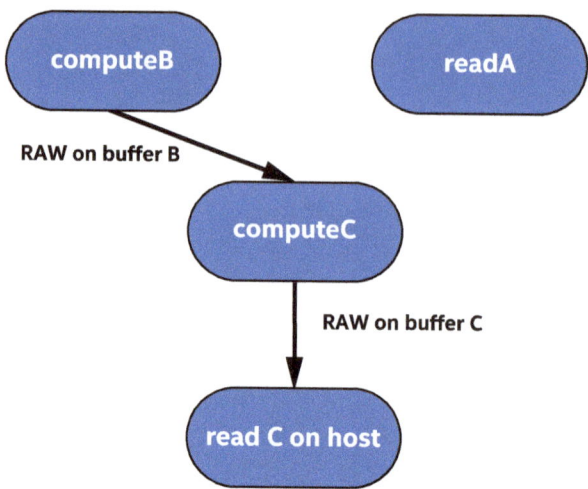

Figure 3-14. *RAW task graph*

In Figures 3-13 and 3-14, we execute three kernels—computeB, readA, and computeC–and then read the final result back on the host. The command group for kernel computeB creates two accessors, accA and accB. These accessors use access tags read_only and write_only for optimization to specify that we do not use the default access mode, access::mode::read_write. We will learn more about access tags in Chapter 7. Kernel computeB reads buffer A and writes to buffer B. Buffer A must be copied from the host to the device before the kernel begins execution.

Kernel readA also creates a read-only accessor for buffer A. Since kernel readA is submitted after kernel computeB, this creates a Read-after-Read (RAR) scenario. However, RARs do not place extra restrictions on the runtime, and the kernels are free to execute in any order. Indeed, a runtime might prefer to execute kernel readA before kernel computeB or even execute both at the same time. Both require buffer A to be copied to the device, but kernel computeB also requires buffer B to be copied in case any existing values are not overwritten by `computeB` and which might be used by later kernels. This means that the runtime could execute kernel `readA` while the data transfer for buffer B occurs and also shows that even if a kernel will only write to a buffer, the original content of the buffer may still be moved to the device because there is no guarantee that all values in the buffer will be written by a kernel (see Chapter 7 for tags that let us optimize in these cases).

Kernel `computeC` reads buffer B, which we computed in kernel `computeB`. Since we submitted kernel `computeC` after we submitted kernel `computeB`, this means that kernel `computeC` has a RAW data dependence on buffer B. RAW dependences are also called true dependences or flow dependences, as data needs to flow from one computation to another in order to compute the correct result. Finally, we also create a RAW dependence on buffer C between kernel `computeC` and the host, since the host wants to read C after the kernel has finished. This forces the runtime to copy buffer C back to the host. Since there were no writes to buffer A on devices, the runtime does not need to copy that buffer back to the host because the host has an up-to-date copy already.

CHAPTER 3   DATA MANAGEMENT

```cpp
#include <CL/sycl.hpp>
#include <array>
using namespace sycl;
constexpr int N = 42;

int main() {
  std::array<int,N> a, b;
  for (int i = 0; i < N; i++) {
    a[i] = b[i] = 0;
  }

  queue Q;
  buffer A{a};
  buffer B{b};

  Q.submit([&](handler &h) {
      accessor accA(A, h, read_only);
      accessor accB(B, h, write_only);
      h.parallel_for( // computeB
          N, [=](id<1> i) {
          accB[i] = accA[i] + 1;
          });
      });

  Q.submit([&](handler &h) {
      // WAR of buffer A
      accessor accA(A, h, write_only);
      h.parallel_for( // rewriteA
          N, [=](id<1> i) {
          accA[i] = 21 + 21;
          });
      });

  Q.submit([&](handler &h) {
      // WAW of buffer B
      accessor accB(B, h, write_only);
      h.parallel_for( // rewriteB
          N, [=](id<1> i) {
          accB[i] = 30 + 12;
          });
      });

  host_accessor host_accA(A, read_only);
  host_accessor host_accB(B, read_only);
  for (int i = 0; i < N; i++) {
    std::cout << host_accA[i] << " " << host_accB[i] << " ";
  }
  std::cout << "\n";
  return 0;
}
```

Figure 3-15. Write-after-Read and Write-after-Write

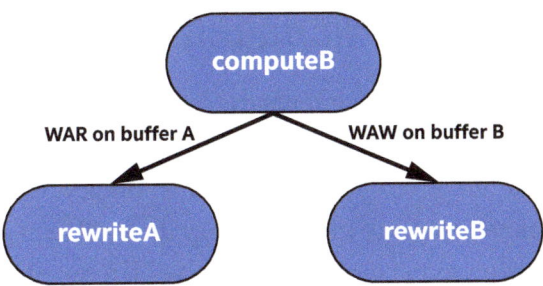

Figure 3-16. WAR and WAW task graph

In Figures 3-15 and 3-16, we again execute three kernels: computeB, rewriteA, and rewriteB. Kernel computeB once again reads buffer A and writes to buffer B, kernel rewriteA writes to buffer A, and kernel rewriteB writes to buffer B. Kernel rewriteA could theoretically execute earlier than kernel computeB since less data needs to be transferred before the kernel is ready, but it must wait until after kernel computeB finishes since there is a WAR dependence on buffer A.

In this example, kernel computeB requires the original value of A from the host, and it would read the wrong values if kernel rewriteA executed before kernel computeB. WAR dependences are also called antidependences. RAW dependences ensure that data properly flows in the correct direction, while WAR dependences ensure existing values are not overwritten before they are read. The WAW dependence on buffer B found in kernel rewrite functions similarly. If there were any reads of buffer B submitted in between kernels computeB and rewriteB, they would result in RAW and WAR dependences that would properly order the tasks. However, there is an implicit dependence between kernel rewriteB and the host in this example since the final data must be written back to the host. We will learn more about what causes this writeback in Chapter 7. The WAW dependence, also called an output dependence, ensures that the final output will be correct on the host.

CHAPTER 3   DATA MANAGEMENT

Choosing a Data Management Strategy

Selecting the right data management strategy for our applications is largely a matter of personal preference. Indeed, we may begin with one strategy and switch to another as our program matures. However, there are a few useful guidelines to help us to pick a strategy that will serve our needs.

The first decision to make is whether we want to use explicit or implicit data movement since this greatly affects what we need to do to our program. Implicit data movement is generally an easier place to start because all the data movement is handled for us, letting us focus on expression of the computation.

If we decide that we'd rather have full control over all data movement from the beginning, then explicit data movement using USM device allocations is where we want to start. We just need to be sure to add all the necessary copies between host and devices!

When selecting an implicit data movement strategy, we still have a choice of whether to use buffers or USM host or shared pointers. Again, this choice is a matter of personal preference, but there are a few questions that could help guide us to one over the other. If we're porting an existing C/C++ program that uses pointers, USM might be an easier path since most code won't need to change. If data representation hasn't guided us to a preference, another question we can ask is how we would like to express our dependences between kernels. If we prefer to think about data dependences between kernels, choose buffers. If we prefer to think about dependences as performing one computation before another and want to express that using an in-order queue or with explicit events or waiting between kernels, choose USM.

86

When using USM pointers (with either explicit or implicit data movement), we have a choice of which type of queue we want to use. In-order queues are simple and intuitive, but they constrain the runtime and may limit performance. Out-of-order queues are more complex, but they give the runtime more freedom to re-order and overlap execution. The out-of-order queue class is the right choice if our program will have complex dependences between kernels. If our program simply runs many kernels one after another, then an in-order queue will be a better option for us.

Handler Class: Key Members

We have shown a number of ways to use the handler class. Figures 3-17 and 3-18 provide a more detailed explanation of the key members of this very important class. We have not yet used all these members, but they will be used later in the book. This is as good a place as any to lay them out.

A closely related class, the queue class, is similarly explained at the end of Chapter 2. The online oneAPI DPC++ language reference provides an even more detailed explanation of both classes.

```
class handler {
  ...
  // Specifies event(s) that must be complete before the action
  //   defined in this command group executes.
  void depends_on({event / std::vector<event> & });

  // Enqueues a memset operation on the specified pointer.
  // Writes the first byte of Value into Count bytes.
  // Returns an event representing this operation.
  event memset(void *Ptr, int Value, size_t Count)

  // Enqueues a memcpy from Src to Dest.
  // Count bytes are copied.
  // Returns an event representing this operation.
  event memcpy(void *Dest, const void *Src, size_t Count);

  // Submits a kernel of one work-item for execution.
  // Returns an event representing this operation.
  template <typename KernelName, typename KernelType>
  event single_task(KernelType KernelFunc);

  // Submits a kernel with NumWork-items work-items for execution.
  // Returns an event representing this operation.
  template <typename KernelName, typename KernelType, int Dims>
  event parallel_for(range<Dims> NumWork-items, KernelType KernelFunc);

  // Submits a kernel for execution over the supplied nd_range.
  // Returns an event representing this operation.
  template <typename KernelName, typename KernelType, int Dims>
  event parallel_for(nd_range<Dims> ExecutionRange, KernelType KernelFunc);
  ...
};
```

Figure 3-17. Simplified definition of the non-accessor members of the handler class

```cpp
class handler {
  ...
  // Specifies event(s) that must be complete before the action
  // Copy to/from an accessor.
  // Valid combinations:
  // Src: accessor,    Dest: shared_ptr
  // Src: accessor,    Dest: pointer
  // Src: shared_ptr   Dest: accessor
  // Src: pointer      Dest: accessor
  // Src: accesssor    Dest: accessor
  template <typename T_Src, typename T_Dst,
            int Dims, access::mode AccessMode,
            access::target AccessTarget,
            access::placeholder IsPlaceholder =
                access::placeholder::false_t>
  void copy(accessor<T_Src, Dims, AccessMode,
                     AccessTarget, IsPlaceholder> Src,
                     shared_ptr_class<T_Dst> Dst);
  void copy(shared_ptr_class<T_Src> Src,
            accessor<T_Dst, Dims, AccessMode,
                     AccessTarget, IsPlaceholder> Dst);
  void copy(accessor<T_Src, Dims, AccessMode,
                     AccessTarget, IsPlaceholder> Src,
                     T_Dst *Dst);
  void copy(const T_Src *Src,
            accessor<T_Dst, Dims, AccessMode,
                     AccessTarget, IsPlaceholder> Dst);
  template <
     typename T_Src, int Dims_Src,
     access::mode AccessMode_Src,
     access::target AccessTarget_Src,
     typename T_Dst, int Dims_Dst,
     access::mode AccessMode_Dst,
     access::target AccessTarget_Dst,
     access::placeholder IsPlaceholder_Src =
       access::placeholder::false_t,
     access::placeholder IsPlaceholder_Dst =
       access::placeholder::false_t>
  void copy(accessor<T_Src, Dims_Src, AccessMode_Src,
                     AccessTarget_Src, IsPlaceholder_Src>
            Src,
            accessor<T_Dst, Dims_Dst, AccessMode_Dst,
                     AccessTarget_Dst, IsPlaceholder_Dst>
            Dst);

  // Provides a guarantee that the memory object accessed by the accessor
  // is updated on the host after this action executes.
  template <typename T, int Dims,
            access::mode AccessMode,
            access::target AccessTarget,
            access::placeholder IsPlaceholder =
                access::placeholder::false_t>
    void update_host(accessor<T, Dims, AccessMode,
                     AccessTarget, IsPlaceholder> Acc);
  ...
};
```

Figure 3-18. *Simplified definition of the accessor members of the handler class*

CHAPTER 3   DATA MANAGEMENT

Summary

In this chapter, we have introduced the mechanisms that address the problems of data management and how to order the uses of data. Managing access to different memories is a key challenge when using accelerator devices, and we have different options to suit our needs.

We provided an overview of the different types of dependences that can exist between the uses of data, and we described how to provide information about these dependences to queues so that they properly order tasks.

This chapter provided an overview of Unified Shared Memory and buffers. We will explore all the modes and behaviors of USM in greater detail in Chapter 6. Chapter 7 will explore buffers more deeply, including all the different ways to create buffers and control their behavior. Chapter 8 will revisit the scheduling mechanisms for queues that control the ordering of kernel executions and data movements.

 **Open Access** This chapter is licensed under the terms of the Creative Commons Attribution 4.0 International License (http://creativecommons.org/licenses/by/4.0/), which permits use, sharing, adaptation, distribution and reproduction in any medium or format, as long as you give appropriate credit to the original author(s) and the source, provide a link to the Creative Commons license and indicate if changes were made.

The images or other third party material in this chapter are included in the chapter's Creative Commons license, unless indicated otherwise in a credit line to the material. If material is not included in the chapter's Creative Commons license and your intended use is not permitted by statutory regulation or exceeds the permitted use, you will need to obtain permission directly from the copyright holder.

CHAPTER 4

Expressing Parallelism

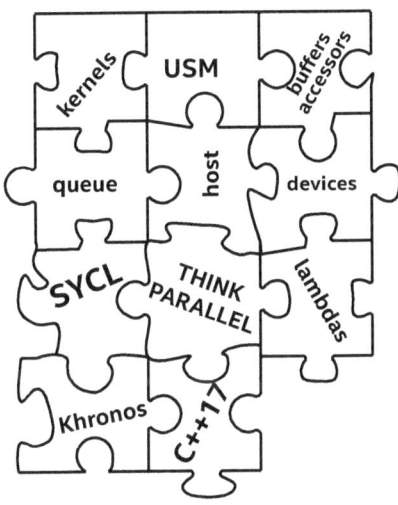

Now we can put together our first collection of puzzle pieces. We already know how to place code (Chapter 2) and data (Chapter 3) on a device—all we must do now is engage in the art of deciding what to do with it. To that end, we now shift to fill in a few things that we have conveniently left out or glossed over so far. This chapter marks the transition from simple teaching examples toward real-world parallel code and expands upon details of the code samples we have casually shown in prior chapters.

CHAPTER 4　EXPRESSING PARALLELISM

Writing our first program in a new parallel language may seem like a daunting task, especially if we are new to parallel programming. Language specifications are not written for application developers and often assume some familiarity with terminology; they do not contain answers to questions like these:

- Why is there more than one way to express parallelism?
- Which method of expressing parallelism should I use?
- How much do I really need to know about the execution model?

This chapter seeks to address these questions and more. We introduce the concept of a data-parallel kernel, discuss the strengths and weaknesses of the different kernel forms using working code examples, and highlight the most important aspects of the kernel execution model.

Parallelism Within Kernels

Parallel kernels have emerged in recent years as a powerful means of expressing data parallelism. The primary design goals of a kernel-based approach are *portability* across a wide range of devices and high programmer *productivity*. As such, kernels are typically not hard-coded to work with a specific number or configuration of hardware resources (e.g., cores, hardware threads, SIMD [Single Instruction, Multiple Data] instructions). Instead, kernels describe parallelism in terms of abstract concepts that an implementation (i.e., the combination of compiler and runtime) can then map to the hardware parallelism available on a specific target device. Although this mapping is implementation-defined, we can (and should) trust implementations to select a mapping that is sensible and capable of effectively exploiting hardware parallelism.

CHAPTER 4 EXPRESSING PARALLELISM

Exposing a great deal of parallelism in a hardware-agnostic way ensures that applications can scale up (or down) to fit the capabilities of different platforms, but...

Guaranteeing functional portability is not the same as guaranteeing high performance!

There is a significant amount of diversity in the devices supported, and we must remember that different architectures are designed and optimized for different use cases. Whenever we hope to achieve the highest levels of *performance* on a specific device, we should always expect that some additional manual optimization work will be required—regardless of the programming language we're using! Examples of such device-specific optimizations include blocking for a particular cache size, choosing a grain size that amortizes scheduling overheads, making use of specialized instructions or hardware units, and, most importantly, choosing an appropriate algorithm. Some of these examples will be revisited in Chapters 15, 16, and 17.

Striking the right balance between performance, portability, and productivity during application development is a challenge that we must all face—and a challenge that this book cannot address in its entirety. However, we hope to show that DPC++ provides all the tools required to maintain both generic portable code and optimized target-specific code using a single high-level programming language. The rest is left as an exercise to the reader!

Multidimensional Kernels

The parallel constructs of many other languages are one-dimensional, mapping work directly to a corresponding one-dimensional hardware resource (e.g., number of hardware threads). Parallel kernels are

CHAPTER 4   EXPRESSING PARALLELISM

a higher-level concept than this, and their dimensionality is more reflective of the problems that our codes are typically trying to solve (in a one-, two-, or three-dimensional space).

However, we must remember that the multidimensional indexing provided by parallel kernels is a programmer convenience implemented on top of an underlying one-dimensional space. Understanding how this mapping behaves can be an important part of certain optimizations (e.g., tuning memory access patterns).

One important consideration is which dimension is *contiguous* or *unit-stride* (i.e., which locations in the multidimensional space are next to each other in the one-dimensional space). All multidimensional quantities related to parallelism in SYCL use the same convention: dimensions are numbered from 0 to N-1, where dimension N-1 corresponds to the contiguous dimension. Wherever a multidimensional quantity is written as a list (e.g., in constructors) or a class supports multiple subscript operators, this numbering applies left to right. This convention is consistent with the behavior of multidimensional arrays in standard C++.

An example of mapping a two-dimensional space to a linear index using the SYCL convention is shown in Figure 4-1. We are of course free to break from this convention and adopt our own methods of linearizing indices, but must do so carefully—breaking from the SYCL convention may have a negative performance impact on devices that benefit from stride-one accesses.

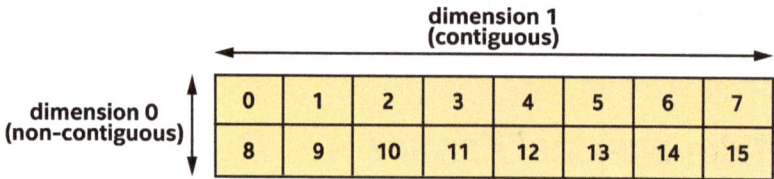

Figure 4-1. *Two-dimensional range of size (2, 8) mapped to linear indices*

CHAPTER 4 EXPRESSING PARALLELISM

If an application requires more than three dimensions, we must take responsibility for mapping between multidimensional and linear indices manually, using modulo arithmetic.

Loops vs. Kernels

An iterative loop is an inherently serial construct: each iteration of the loop is executed sequentially (i.e., in order). An optimizing compiler may be able to determine that some or all iterations of a loop can execute in parallel, but it must be conservative—if the compiler isn't smart enough or doesn't have enough information to prove that parallel execution is always safe, it must preserve the loop's sequential semantics for correctness.

```
for (int i = 0; i < N; ++i) {
  c[i] = a[i] + b[i];
}
```

Figure 4-2. Expressing a vector addition as a serial loop

Consider the loop in Figure 4-2, which describes a simple vector addition. Even in a simple case like this, proving that the loop can be executed in parallel is not trivial: parallel execution is only safe if c does not overlap a or b, which in the general case cannot be proven without a runtime check! In order to address situations like this, languages have added features enabling us to provide compilers with extra information that may simplify analysis (e.g., asserting that pointers do not overlap with `restrict`) or to override all analysis altogether (e.g., declaring that all iterations of a loop are independent or defining exactly how the loop should be scheduled to parallel resources).

The exact meaning of a *parallel loop* is somewhat ambiguous—due to overloading of the term by different parallel programming languages—but many common parallel loop constructs represent compiler transformations applied to sequential loops. Such programming models

95

enable us to write sequential loops and only later provide information about how different iterations can be executed safely in parallel. These models are very powerful, integrate well with other state-of-the-art compiler optimizations, and greatly simplify parallel programming, but do not always encourage us to think about parallelism at an early stage of development.

A parallel kernel is not a loop, and does not have iterations. Rather, a kernel describes a single operation, which can be instantiated many times and applied to different input data; when a kernel is launched in parallel, multiple instances of that operation are executed simultaneously.

```
launch N kernel instances {
  int id = get_instance_id(); // unique identifier in [0, N)
  c[id] = a[id] + b[id];
}
```

Figure 4-3. *Loop rewritten (in pseudocode) as a parallel kernel*

Figure 4-3 shows our simple loop example rewritten as a kernel using pseudocode. The opportunity for parallelism in this kernel is clear and explicit: the kernel can be executed in parallel by any number of instances, and each instance independently applies to a separate piece of data. By writing this operation as a kernel, we are asserting that it is safe to run in parallel (and ideally should be).

In short, kernel-based programming is not a way to retrofit parallelism into existing sequential codes, but a methodology for writing explicitly parallel applications.

The sooner that we can shift our thinking from parallel loops to kernels, the easier it will be to write effective parallel programs using Data Parallel C++.

Overview of Language Features

Once we've decided to write a parallel kernel, we must decide what type of kernel we want to launch and how to represent it in our program. There are a multitude of ways to express parallel kernels, and we need to familiarize ourselves with each of these options if we want to master the language.

Separating Kernels from Host Code

We have several alternative ways to separate host and device code, which we can mix and match within an application: C++ lambda expressions or function objects (functors), OpenCL C source strings, or binaries. Some of these options were already covered in Chapter 2, and all of them will be covered in more detail in Chapter 10.

The fundamental concepts of expressing parallelism are shared by all these options. For consistency and brevity, all the code examples in this chapter express kernels using C++ lambdas.

LAMBDAS NOT CONSIDERED HARMFUL

There is no need to fully understand everything that the C++ specification says about lambdas in order to get started with DPC++—all we need to know is that the body of the lambda represents the kernel and that variables captured (by value) will be passed to the kernel as arguments.

There is no performance impact arising from the use of lambdas instead of more verbose mechanisms for defining kernels. A DPC++ compiler always understands when a lambda represents the body of a parallel kernel and can optimize for parallel execution accordingly.

For a refresher on C++ lambda functions, with notes about their use in SYCL, see Chapter 1. For more specific details on using lambdas to define kernels, see Chapter 10.

CHAPTER 4 EXPRESSING PARALLELISM

Different Forms of Parallel Kernels

There are three different kernel forms, supporting different execution models and syntax. It is possible to write portable kernels using any of the kernel forms, and kernels written in any form can be tuned to achieve high performance on a wide variety of device types. However, there will be times when we may want to use a specific form to make a specific parallel algorithm easier to express or to make use of an otherwise inaccessible language feature.

The first form is used for *basic* data-parallel kernels and offers the gentlest introduction to writing kernels. With basic kernels, we sacrifice control over low-level features like scheduling in order to make the expression of the kernel as simple as possible. How the individual kernel instances are mapped to hardware resources is controlled entirely by the implementation, and so as basic kernels grow in complexity, it becomes harder and harder to reason about their performance.

The second form extends basic kernels to provide access to low-level performance-tuning features. This second form is known as *ND-range* (N-dimensional range) data parallel for historical reasons, and the most important thing to remember is that it enables certain kernel instances to be grouped together, allowing us to exert some control over data locality and the mapping between individual kernel instances and the hardware resources that will be used to execute them.

The third form provides an alternative syntax to simplify the expression of ND-range kernels using nested kernel constructs. This third form is referred to as *hierarchical* data parallel, referring to the hierarchy of the nested kernel constructs that appear in user source code.

We will revisit how to choose between the different kernel forms again at the end of this chapter, once we've discussed their features in more detail.

Basic Data-Parallel Kernels

The most basic form of parallel kernel is appropriate for operations that are *embarrassingly parallel* (i.e., operations that can be applied to every piece of data completely independently and in any order). By using this form, we give an implementation complete control over the scheduling of work. It is thus an example of a *descriptive* programming construct—we *describe* that the operation is embarrassingly parallel, and all scheduling decisions are made by the implementation.

Basic data-parallel kernels are written in a Single Program, Multiple Data (SPMD) style—a single "program" (the kernel) is applied to multiple pieces of data. Note that this programming model still permits each instance of the kernel to take different paths through the code, as a result of data-dependent branches.

One of the greatest strengths of a SPMD programming model is that it allows the same "program" to be mapped to multiple levels and types of parallelism, without any explicit direction from us. Instances of the same program could be pipelined, packed together and executed with SIMD instructions, distributed across multiple threads, or a mix of all three.

Understanding Basic Data-Parallel Kernels

The execution space of a basic parallel kernel is referred to as its execution *range*, and each instance of the kernel is referred to as an *item*. This is represented diagrammatically in Figure 4-4.

CHAPTER 4   EXPRESSING PARALLELISM

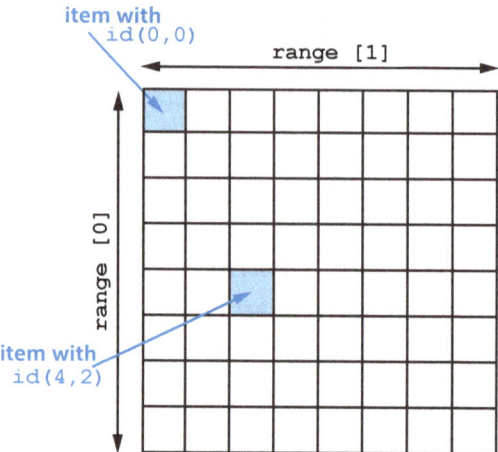

Figure 4-4. *Execution space of a basic parallel kernel, shown for a 2D range of 64 items*

The execution model of basic data-parallel kernels is very simple: it *allows* for completely parallel execution, but does not *guarantee* or *require* it. Items can be executed in any order, including sequentially on a single hardware thread (i.e., without any parallelism)! Kernels that assume that all items will be executed in parallel (e.g., by attempting to synchronize items) could therefore very easily cause programs to hang on some devices.

However, in order to guarantee correctness, we must always write our kernels under the assumption that they *could* be executed in parallel. For example, it is our responsibility to ensure that concurrent accesses to memory are appropriately guarded by atomic memory operations (see Chapter 19) in order to prevent race conditions.

Writing Basic Data-Parallel Kernels

Basic data-parallel kernels are expressed using the `parallel_for` function. Figure 4-5 shows how to use this function to express a vector addition, which is our take on "Hello, world!" for parallel accelerator programming.

```
h.parallel_for(range{N}, [=](id<1> idx) {
  c[idx] = a[idx] + b[idx];
});
```

Figure 4-5. Expressing a vector addition kernel with parallel_for

The function only takes two arguments: the first is a range specifying the number of items to launch in each dimension, and the second is a kernel function to be executed for each index in the range. There are several different classes that can be accepted as arguments to a kernel function, and which should be used depends on which class exposes the functionality required—we'll revisit this later.

Figure 4-6 shows a very similar use of this function to express a matrix addition, which is (mathematically) identical to vector addition except with two-dimensional data. This is reflected by the kernel—the only difference between the two code snippets is the dimensionality of the range and id classes used! It is possible to write the code this way because a SYCL accessor can be indexed by a multidimensional id. As strange as it looks, this can be very powerful, enabling us to write kernels templated on the dimensionality of our data.

```
h.parallel_for(range{N, M}, [=](id<2> idx) {
  c[idx] = a[idx] + b[idx];
});
```

Figure 4-6. Expressing a matrix addition kernel with parallel_for

It is more common in C/C++ to use multiple indices and multiple subscript operators to index multidimensional data structures, and this explicit indexing is also supported by accessors. Using multiple indices in this way can improve readability when a kernel operates on data of different dimensionalities simultaneously or when the memory access patterns of a kernel are more complicated than can be described by using an item's id directly.

CHAPTER 4 EXPRESSING PARALLELISM

For example, the matrix multiplication kernel in Figure 4-7 must extract the two individual components of the index in order to be able to describe the dot product between rows and columns of the two matrices. In our opinion, consistently using multiple subscript operators (e.g., [j][k]) is more readable than mixing multiple indexing modes and constructing two-dimensional id objects (e.g., id(j,k)), but this is simply a matter of personal preference.

The examples in the remainder of this chapter all use multiple subscript operators, to ensure that there is no ambiguity in the dimensionality of the buffers being accessed.

```
h.parallel_for(range{N, N}, [=](id<2> idx) {
  int j = idx[0];
  int i = idx[1];
  for (int k = 0; k < N; ++k) {
    c[j][i] += a[j][k]   * b[k][i];
//  c[idx]  += a[id(j,k) * b[id(k,i)];   <<< equivalent
  }
});
```

Figure 4-7. Expressing a naïve matrix multiplication kernel for square matrices, with parallel_for

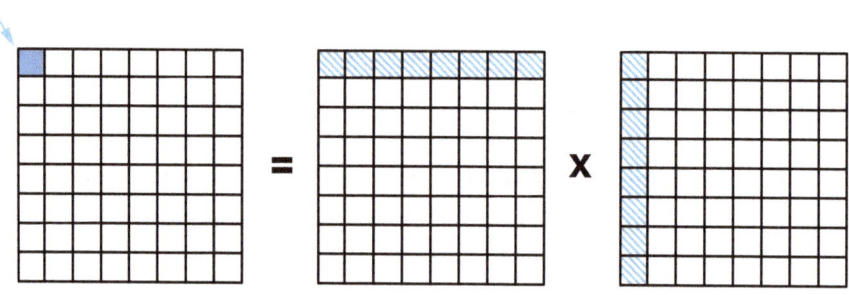

Figure 4-8. Mapping matrix multiplication work to items in the execution range

CHAPTER 4 EXPRESSING PARALLELISM

The diagram in Figure 4-8 shows how the work in our matrix multiplication kernel is mapped to individual items. Note that the number of items is derived from the size of the *output* range and that the same input values may be read by multiple items: each item computes a single value of the C matrix, by iterating sequentially over a (contiguous) row of the A matrix and a (non-contiguous) column of the B matrix.

Details of Basic Data-Parallel Kernels

The functionality of basic data-parallel kernels is exposed via three C++ classes: range, id, and item. We've already seen the range and id classes a few times in previous chapters, but we revisit them here with a different focus.

The range Class

A range represents a one-, two-, or three-dimensional range. The dimensionality of a range is a template argument and must therefore be known at compile time, but its size in each dimension is dynamic and is passed to the constructor at runtime. Instances of the range class are used to describe both the execution ranges of parallel constructs and the sizes of buffers.

A simplified definition of the range class, showing the constructors and various methods for querying its extent, is shown in Figure 4-9.

```cpp
template <int Dimensions = 1>
class range {
 public:
  // Construct a range with one, two or three dimensions
  range(size_t dim0);
  range(size_t dim0, size_t dim1);
  range(size_t dim0, size_t dim1, size_t dim2);

  // Return the size of the range in a specific dimension
  size_t get(int dimension) const;
  size_t &operator[](int dimension);
  size_t operator[](int dimension) const;

  // Return the product of the size of each dimension
  size_t size() const;

  // Arithmetic operations on ranges are also supported
};
```

Figure 4-9. Simplified definition of the range class

The `id` Class

An `id` represents an index into a one, two-, or three-dimensional range. The definition of `id` is similar in many respects to `range`: its dimensionality must also be known at compile time, and it may be used to index an individual instance of a kernel in a parallel construct or an offset into a buffer.

As shown by the simplified definition of the `id` class in Figure 4-10, an `id` is conceptually nothing more than a container of one, two, or three integers. The operations available to us are also very simple: we can query the component of an index in each dimension, and we can perform simple arithmetic to compute new indices.

Although we can construct an `id` to represent an arbitrary index, to obtain the `id` associated with a specific kernel instance, we must accept it (or an `item` containing it) as an argument to a kernel function. This `id` (or values returned by its member functions) must be forwarded to any function in which we want to query the index—there are not currently any free functions for querying the index at arbitrary points in a program, but this may be addressed by a future version of DPC++.

Each instance of a kernel accepting an `id` knows only the index in the range that it has been assigned to compute and knows nothing about the range itself. If we want our kernel instances to know about their own index *and* the range, we need to use the `item` class instead.

```
template <int Dimensions = 1>
class id {
public:
  // Construct an id with one, two or three dimensions
  id(size_t dim0);
  id(size_t dim0, size_t dim1);
  id(size_t dim0, size_t dim1, size_t dim2);

  // Return the component of the id in a specific dimension
  size_t get(int dimension) const;
  size_t &operator[](int dimension);
  size_t operator[](int dimension) const;

  // Arithmetic operations on ids are also supported
};
```

Figure 4-10. Simplified definition of the `id` class

The `item` Class

An `item` represents an individual instance of a kernel function, encapsulating both the execution range of the kernel and the instance's index within that range (using a `range` and an `id`, respectively). Like `range` and `id`, its dimensionality must be known at compile time.

A simplified definition of the `item` class is given in Figure 4-11. The main difference between `item` and `id` is that `item` exposes additional functions to query properties of the execution range (e.g., size, offset) and a convenience function to compute a linearized index. As with `id`, the only way to obtain the `item` associated with a specific kernel instance is to accept it as an argument to a kernel function.

105

```
template <int Dimensions = 1, bool WithOffset = true>
class item {
public:
  // Return the index of this item in the kernel's execution range
  id<Dimensions> get_id() const;
  size_t get_id(int dimension) const;
  size_t operator[](int dimension) const;

  // Return the execution range of the kernel executed by this item
  range<Dimensions> get_range() const;
  size_t get_range(int dimension) const;

  // Return the offset of this item (if with_offset == true)
  id<Dimensions> get_offset() const;

  // Return the linear index of this item
  // e.g. id(0) * range(1) * range(2) + id(1) * range(2) + id(2)
  size_t get_linear_id() const;
};
```

Figure 4-11. Simplified definition of the `item` *class*

Explicit ND-Range Kernels

The second form of parallel kernel replaces the flat execution range of basic data-parallel kernels with an execution range where items belong to groups and is appropriate for cases where we would like to express some notion of locality within our kernels. Different behaviors are defined and guaranteed for different types of groups, giving us more insight into and/or control over how work is mapped to specific hardware platforms.

These explicit ND-range kernels are thus an example of a more *prescriptive* parallel construct—we *prescribe* a mapping of work to each type of group, and the implementation must obey that mapping. However, it is not completely prescriptive, as the groups themselves may execute in any order and an implementation retains some freedom over how each type of group is mapped to hardware resources. This combination of prescriptive and descriptive programming enables us to design and tune our kernels for locality without impacting their portability.

Like basic data-parallel kernels, ND-range kernels are written in a SPMD style where all work-items execute the same kernel "program" applied to multiple pieces of data. The key difference is that each program

CHAPTER 4 EXPRESSING PARALLELISM

instance can query its position within the groups that contain it and can access additional functionality specific to each type of group.

Understanding Explicit ND-Range Parallel Kernels

The execution range of an ND-range kernel is divided into work-groups, sub-groups, and work-items. The ND-range represents the total execution range, which is divided into work-groups of uniform size (i.e., the work-group size must divide the ND-range size exactly in each dimension). Each work-group can be further divided by the implementation into sub-groups. Understanding the execution model defined for work-items and each type of group is an important part of writing correct and portable programs.

Figure 4-12 shows an example of an ND-range of size (8, 8, 8) divided into 8 work-groups of size (4, 4, 4). Each work-group contains 16 one-dimensional sub-groups of 4 work-items. Pay careful attention to the numbering of the dimensions: sub-groups are always one-dimensional, and so dimension 2 of the ND-range and work-group becomes dimension 0 of the sub-group.

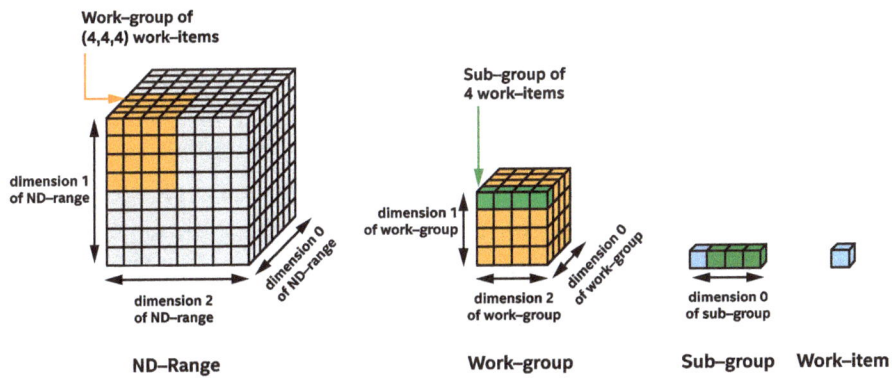

Figure 4-12. Three-dimensional ND-range divided into work-groups, sub-groups, and work-items

The exact mapping from each type of group to hardware resources is *implementation-defined*, and it is this flexibility that enables programs to execute on a wide variety of hardware. For example, work-items could be executed completely sequentially, executed in parallel by hardware threads and/or SIMD instructions, or even executed by a hardware pipeline specifically configured for a specific kernel.

In this chapter, we are focused only on the semantic guarantees of the ND-range execution model in terms of a generic target platform, and we will not cover its mapping to any one platform. See Chapters 15, 16, and 17 for details of the hardware mapping and performance recommendations for GPUs, CPUs, and FPGAs, respectively.

Work-Items

Work-items represent the individual instances of a kernel function. In the absence of other groupings, work-items can be executed in any order and cannot communicate or synchronize with each other except by way of atomic memory operations to global memory (see Chapter 19).

Work-Groups

The work-items in an ND-range are organized into work-groups. Work-groups can execute in any order, and work-items in different work-groups cannot communicate with each other except by way of atomic memory operations to global memory (see Chapter 19). However, the work-items within a work-group have concurrent scheduling guarantees when certain constructs are used, and this locality provides some additional capabilities:

1. Work-items in a work-group have access to *work-group local memory*, which may be mapped to a dedicated fast memory on some devices (see Chapter 9).

2. Work-items in a work-group can synchronize using *work-group barriers* and guarantee memory consistency using *work-group memory fences* (see Chapter 9).

3. Work-items in a work-group have access to *group functions*, providing implementations of common communication routines (see Chapter 9) and common parallel patterns such as reductions and scans (see Chapter 14).

The number of work-items in a work-group is typically configured for each kernel at runtime, as the best grouping will depend upon both the amount of parallelism available (i.e., the size of the ND-range) and properties of the target device. We can determine the maximum number of work-items per work-group supported by a specific device using the query functions of the device class (see Chapter 12), and it is our responsibility to ensure that the work-group size requested for each kernel is valid.

There are some subtleties in the work-group execution model that are worth emphasizing.

First, although the work-items in a work-group are scheduled to a single compute unit, there need not be any relationship between the number of work-groups and the number of compute units. In fact, the number of work-groups in an ND-range can be many times larger than the number of work-groups that a given device can execute concurrently! We may be tempted to try and write kernels that synchronize across work-groups by relying on very clever device-specific scheduling, but we strongly recommend against doing this—such kernels may appear to work today, but they are not guaranteed to work with future implementations and are highly likely to break when moved to a different device.

Second, although the work-items in a work-group are scheduled concurrently, they are not guaranteed to make independent *forward progress*—executing the work-items within a work-group sequentially between barriers and collectives is a valid implementation. Communication and synchronization between work-items in the same work-group is only guaranteed to be safe when performed using the barrier and collective functions provided, and hand-coded synchronization routines may deadlock.

THINKING IN WORK-GROUPS

Work-groups are similar in many respects to the concept of a task in other programming models (e.g., Threading Building Blocks): tasks can execute in any order (controlled by a scheduler); it's possible (and even desirable) to oversubscribe a machine with tasks; and it's often not a good idea to try and implement a barrier across a group of tasks (as it may be very expensive or incompatible with the scheduler). If we're already familiar with a task-based programming model, we may find it useful to think of work-groups as though they are data-parallel tasks.

Sub-Groups

On many modern hardware platforms, subsets of the work-items in a work-group known as *sub-groups* are executed with additional scheduling guarantees. For example, the work-items in a sub-group could be executed simultaneously as a result of compiler vectorization, and/or the sub-groups themselves could be executed with forward progress guarantees because they are mapped to independent hardware threads.

When working with a single platform, it is tempting to bake assumptions about these execution models into our codes, but this makes them inherently unsafe and non-portable—they may break when moving between different compilers or even when moving between different generations of hardware from the same vendor!

Defining sub-groups as a core part of the language gives us a safe alternative to making assumptions that may later prove to be device-specific. Leveraging sub-group functionality also allows us to reason about the execution of work-items at a low level (i.e., close to hardware) and is key to achieving very high levels of performance across many platforms.

As with work-groups, the work-items within a sub-group can synchronize, guarantee memory consistency, or execute common parallel patterns via group functions. However, there is no equivalent of work-group local memory for sub-groups (i.e., there is no sub-group local memory). Instead, the work-items in a sub-group can exchange data directly—without explicit memory operations—using *shuffle* operations (Chapter 9).

Some aspects of sub-groups are implementation-defined and outside of our control. However, a sub-group has a fixed (one-dimensional) size for a given combination of device, kernel, and ND-range, and we can query this size using the query functions of the `kernel` class (see Chapter 10). By default, the number of work-items per sub-group is also chosen by the implementation—we can override this behavior by requesting a particular sub-group size at compile time, but must ensure that the sub-group size we request is compatible with the device.

Like work-groups, the work-items in a sub-group are only guaranteed to execute concurrently—an implementation is free to execute each work-item in a sub-group sequentially and only switch between work-items when a sub-group collective function is encountered. Where sub-groups are special is that some devices guarantee that they make independent forward progress—on some devices, all sub-groups within a work-group are guaranteed to execute (make progress) eventually, which is a cornerstone of several producer-consumer patterns. Whether or not this independent forward progress guarantee holds can be determined using a device query.

CHAPTER 4 EXPRESSING PARALLELISM

> **THINKING IN SUB-GROUPS**
>
> If we are coming from a programming model that requires us to think about explicit vectorization, it may be useful to think of each sub-group as a set of work-items packed into a SIMD register, where each work-item in the sub-group corresponds to a SIMD lane. When multiple sub-groups are in flight simultaneously and a device guarantees they will make forward progress, this mental model extends to treating each sub-group as though it were a separate stream of vector instructions executing in parallel.

```
range global{N, N};
range local{B, B};
h.parallel_for(nd_range{global, local}, [=](nd_item<2> it) {
  int j = it.get_global_id(0);
  int i = it.get_global_id(1);

  for (int k = 0; k < N; ++k)
    c[j][i] += a[j][k] * b[k][i];
});
```

Figure 4-13. Expressing a naïve matrix multiplication kernel with ND-range parallel_for

Writing Explicit ND-Range Data-Parallel Kernels

Figure 4-13 re-implements the matrix multiplication kernel that we saw previously using the ND-range parallel kernel syntax, and the diagram in Figure 4-14 shows how the work in this kernel is mapped to the work-items in each work-group. Grouping our work-items in this way ensures locality of access and hopefully improves cache hit rates: for example, the work-group in Figure 4-14 has a local range of (4, 4) and contains 16 work-items, but only accesses four times as much data as a single work-item—in other words, each value we load from memory can be reused four times.

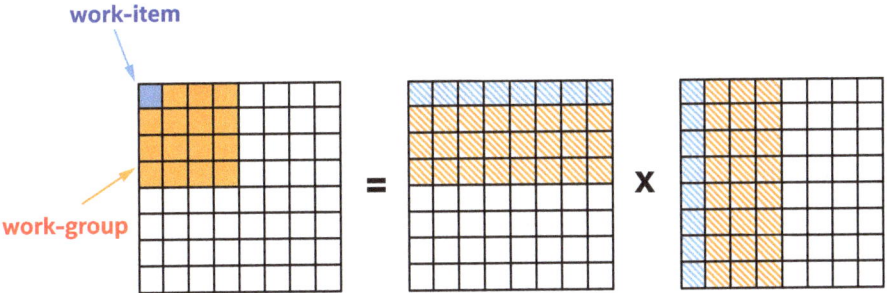

Figure 4-14. *Mapping matrix multiplication to work-groups and work-items*

So far, our matrix multiplication example has relied on a hardware cache to optimize repeated accesses to the A and B matrices from work-items in the same work-group. Such hardware caches are commonplace on traditional CPU architectures and are becoming increasingly so on GPU architectures, but there are other architectures (e.g., previous-generation GPUs, FPGAs) with explicitly managed "scratchpad" memories. ND-range kernels can use *local accessors* to describe allocations that should be placed in work-group local memory, and an implementation is then free to map these allocations to special memory (where it exists). Usage of this work-group local memory will be covered in Chapter 9.

Details of Explicit ND-Range Data-Parallel Kernels

ND-range data-parallel kernels use different classes compared to basic data-parallel kernels: range is replaced by nd_range, and item is replaced by nd_item. There are also two new classes, representing the different types of groups to which a work-item may belong: functionality tied to work-groups is encapsulated in the group class, and functionality tied to sub-groups is encapsulated in the sub_group class.

The nd_range Class

An nd_range represents a grouped execution range using two instances of the range class: one denoting the global execution range and another denoting the local execution range of each work-group. A simplified definition of the nd_range class is given in Figure 4-15.

It may be a little surprising that the nd_range class does not mention sub-groups at all: the sub-group range is not specified during construction and cannot be queried. There are two reasons for this omission. First, sub-groups are a low-level implementation detail that can be ignored for many kernels. Second, there are several devices supporting exactly one valid sub-group size, and specifying this size everywhere would be unnecessarily verbose. All functionality related to sub-groups is encapsulated in a dedicated class that will be discussed shortly.

```
template <int Dimensions = 1>
class nd_range {
public:
  // Construct an nd_range from global and work-group local ranges
  nd_range(range<Dimensions> global, range<Dimensions> local);

  // Return the global and work-group local ranges
  range<Dimensions> get_global_range() const;
  range<Dimensions> get_local_range() const;

  // Return the number of work-groups in the global range
  range<Dimensions> get_group_range() const;
};
```

Figure 4-15. Simplified definition of the nd_range class

The nd_item Class

An nd_item is the ND-range form of an item, again encapsulating the execution range of the kernel and the item's index within that range. Where nd_item differs from item is in how its position in the range is queried and represented, as shown by the simplified class definition in Figure 4-16.

For example, we can query the item's index in the (global) ND-range using the get_global_id() function or the item's index in its (local) parent work-group using the get_local_id() function.

The nd_item class also provides functions for obtaining handles to classes describing the group and sub-group that an item belongs to. These classes provide an alternative interface for querying an item's index in an ND-range. We strongly recommend writing kernels using these classes instead of relying on nd_item directly: using the group and sub_group classes is often cleaner, conveys intent more clearly, and is more aligned with the future direction of DPC++.

```
template <int Dimensions = 1>
class nd_item {
public:
  // Return the index of this item in the kernel's execution range
  id<Dimensions> get_global_id() const;
  size_t get_global_id(int dimension) const;
  size_t get_global_linear_id() const;

  // Return the execution range of the kernel executed by this item
  range<Dimensions> get_global_range() const;
  size_t get_global_range(int dimension) const;

  // Return the index of this item within its parent work-group
  id<Dimensions> get_local_id() const;
  size_t get_local_id(int dimension) const;
  size_t get_local_linear_id() const;

  // Return the execution range of this item's parent work-group
  range<Dimensions> get_local_range() const;
  size_t get_local_range(int dimension) const;

  // Return a handle to the work-group
  // or sub-group containing this item
  group<Dimensions> get_group() const;
  sub_group get_sub_group() const;
};
```

Figure 4-16. Simplified definition of the nd_item class

CHAPTER 4　EXPRESSING PARALLELISM

The group Class

The group class encapsulates all functionality related to work-groups, and a simplified definition is shown in Figure 4-17.

```
template <int Dimensions = 1>
class group {
public:
  // Return the index of this group in the kernel's execution range
  id<Dimensions> get_id() const;
  size_t get_id(int dimension) const;
  size_t get_linear_id() const;

  // Return the number of groups in the kernel's execution range
  range<Dimensions> get_group_range() const;
  size_t get_group_range(int dimension) const;

  // Return the number of work-items in this group
  range<Dimensions> get_local_range() const;
  size_t get_local_range(int dimension) const;
};
```

Figure 4-17. Simplified definition of the group class

Many of the functions that the group class provides each have equivalent functions in the nd_item class: for example, calling group.get_id() is equivalent to calling item.get_group_id(), and calling group.get_local_range() is equivalent to calling item.get_local_range(). If we're not using any of the work-group functions exposed by the class, should we still use it? Wouldn't it be simpler to use the functions in nd_item directly, instead of creating an intermediate group object? There is a tradeoff here: using group requires us to write slightly more code, but that code may be easier to read. For example, consider the code snippet in Figure 4-18: it is clear that body expects to be called by all work-items in the group, and it is clear that the range returned by get_local_range() in the body of the parallel_for is the range of the group. The same code could very easily be written using only nd_item, but it would likely be harder for readers to follow.

```
void body(group& g);

h.parallel_for(nd_range{global, local}, [=](nd_item<1> it) {
  group<1> g = it.get_group();
  range<1> r = g.get_local_range();
  ...
  body(g);
});
```

Figure 4-18. Using the group class to improve readability

The sub_group Class

The sub_group class encapsulates all functionality related to sub-groups, and a simplified definition is shown in Figure 4-19. Unlike with work-groups, the sub_group class is the only way to access sub-group functionality; none of its functions are duplicated in nd_item. The queries in the sub_group class are all interpreted relative to the calling work-item: for example, get_local_id() returns the local index of the calling work-item within its sub-group.

```
class sub_group {
public:
  // Return the index of the sub-group
  id<1> get_group_id() const;

  // Return the number of sub-groups in this item's parent work-group
  range<1> get_group_range() const;

  // Return the index of the work-item in this sub-group
  id<1> get_local_id() const;

  // Return the number of work-items in this sub-group
  range<1> get_local_range() const;

  // Return the maximum number of work-items in any
  // sub-group in this item's parent work-group
  range<1> get_max_local_range() const;
};
```

Figure 4-19. Simplified definition of the sub_group class

Note that there are separate functions for querying the number of work-items in the current sub-group and the maximum number of work-items in any sub-group within the work-group. Whether and how these differ depends on exactly how sub-groups are implemented for a specific device, but the intent is to reflect any differences between the sub-group size targeted by the compiler and the runtime sub-group size. For example, very small work-groups may contain fewer work-items than the compile-time sub-group size, or sub-groups of different sizes may be used to handle work-groups that are not divisible by the sub-group size.

Hierarchical Parallel Kernels

Hierarchical data-parallel kernels offer an experimental alternative syntax for expressing kernels in terms of work-groups and work-items, where each level of the hierarchy is programmed using a nested invocation of the parallel_for function. This *top-down* programming style is intended to be similar to writing parallel loops and may feel more familiar than the *bottom-up* programming style used by the other two kernel forms.

One complexity of hierarchical kernels is that each nested invocation of parallel_for creates a separate SPMD environment; each scope defines a new "program" that should be executed by all parallel workers associated with that scope. This complexity requires compilers to perform additional analysis and can complicate code generation for some devices; compiler technology for hierarchical parallel kernels on some platforms is still relatively immature, and performance will be closely tied to the quality of a particular compiler implementation.

Since the relationship between a hierarchical data-parallel kernel and the code generated for a specific device is compiler-dependent, hierarchical kernels should be considered a more *descriptive* construct than explicit ND-range kernels. However, since hierarchical kernels retain the ability to control the mapping of work to work-items and work-groups, they remain more *prescriptive* than basic kernels.

CHAPTER 4 EXPRESSING PARALLELISM

Understanding Hierarchical Data-Parallel Kernels

The underlying execution model of hierarchical data-parallel kernels is the same as the execution model of explicit ND-range data-parallel kernels. Work-items, sub-groups, and work-groups have identical semantics and execution guarantees.

However, the different scopes of a hierarchical kernel are mapped by the compiler to different execution resources: the outer scope is executed once per work-group (as if executed by a single work-item), while the inner scope is executed in parallel by work-items within the work-group. The different scopes also control where in memory different variables should be allocated, and the opening and closing of scopes imply work-group barriers (to enforce memory consistency).

Although the work-items in a work-group are still divided into sub-groups, the sub_group class cannot currently be accessed from a hierarchical parallel kernel; incorporating the concept of sub-groups into SYCL hierarchical parallelism requires more significant changes than introducing a new class, and work in this area is ongoing.

Writing Hierarchical Data-Parallel Kernels

In hierarchical kernels, the parallel_for function is replaced by the parallel_for_work_group and parallel_for_work_item functions, which correspond to work-group and work-item parallelism, respectively. Any code in a parallel_for_work_group scope is executed only once per work-group, and variables allocated in a parallel_for_work_group scope are visible to all work-items (i.e., they are allocated in work-group local memory). Any code in a parallel_for_work_item scope is executed in parallel by the work-items of the work-group, and variables allocated in a parallel_for_work_item scope are visible to a single work-item (i.e., they are allocated in work-item private memory).

As shown in Figure 4-20, kernels expressed using hierarchical parallelism are very similar to ND-range kernels. We should therefore view hierarchical parallelism primarily as a productivity feature; it doesn't expose any functionality that isn't already exposed via ND-range kernels, but it may improve the readability of our code and/or reduce the amount of code that we must write.

```
range num_groups{N / B, N / B}; // N is a multiple of B
range group_size{B, B};
h.parallel_for_work_group(num_groups, group_size, [=](group<2> grp) {
  int jb = grp.get_id(0);
  int ib = grp.get_id(1);
  grp.parallel_for_work_item([&](h_item<2> it) {
    int j = jb * B + it.get_local_id(0);
    int i = ib * B + it.get_local_id(1);
    for (int k = 0; k < N; ++k)
      c[j][i] += a[j][k] * b[k][i];
  });
});
```

Figure 4-20. *Expressing a naïve matrix multiplication kernel with hierarchical parallelism*

It is important to note that the ranges passed to the `parallel_for_work_group` function specify the number of groups and an optional group size, **not** the total number of work-items and group size as was the case for ND-range `parallel_for`. The kernel function accepts an instance of the group class, reflecting that the outer scope is associated with work-groups rather than individual work-items.

`parallel_for_work_item` is a member function of the group class and can only be called inside of a `parallel_for_work_group` scope. In its simplest form, its only argument is a function accepting an instance of the `h_item` class, and the number of times that the function is executed is equal to the number of work-items requested per work-group; the function is executed once per *physical* work-item. An additional productivity feature of `parallel_for_work_item` is its ability to support a *logical* range, which

CHAPTER 4   EXPRESSING PARALLELISM

is passed as an additional argument to the function. When a logical range is specified, each physical work-item executes zero or more instances of the function, and the logical items of the logical range are assigned round-robin to physical work-items.

Figure 4-21 shows an example of the mapping between a logical range consisting of 11 logical work-items and an underlying physical range consisting of 8 physical work-items. The first three work-items are assigned two instances of the function, and all other work-items are assigned only one.

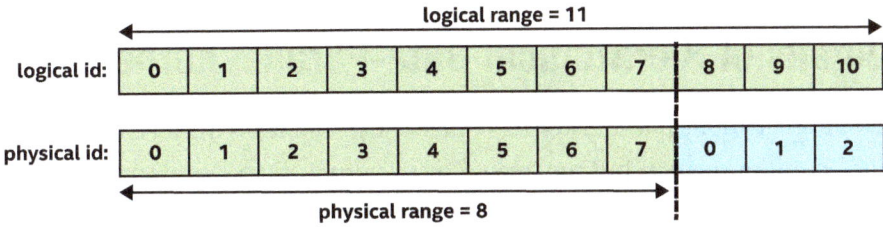

Figure 4-21. *Mapping a logical range of size 11 to a physical range of size 8*

As shown in Figure 4-22, combining the optional group size of `parallel_for_work_group` with the logical range of `parallel_for_work_item` gives an implementation the freedom to choose work-group sizes without sacrificing our ability to conveniently describe the execution range using nested parallel constructs. Note that the amount of work performed per group remains the same as in Figure 4-20, but that the amount of work has now been separated from the physical work-group size.

121

```
range num_groups{N / B, N / B}; // N is a multiple of B
range group_size{B, B};
h.parallel_for_work_group(num_groups, [=](group<2> grp) {
  int jb = grp.get_id(0);
  int ib = grp.get_id(1);
  grp.parallel_for_work_item(group_size, [&](h_item<2> it) {
    int j = jb * B + it.get_logical_local_id(0);
    int i = ib * B + it.get_logical_local_id(1);
    for (int k = 0; k < N; ++k)
      c[j][i] += a[j][k] * b[k][i];
  });
});
```

Figure 4-22. Expressing a naïve matrix multiplication kernel with hierarchical parallelism and a logical range

Details of Hierarchical Data-Parallel Kernels

Hierarchical data-parallel kernels reuse the group class from ND-range data-parallel kernels, but replace nd_item with h_item. A new private_ memory class is introduced to provide tighter control over allocations in parallel_for_work_group scope.

The h_item Class

An h_item is a variant of item that is only available within a parallel_for_work_item scope. As shown in Figure 4-23, it provides a similar interface to an nd_item, with one notable difference: the item's index can be queried relative to the physical execution range of a work-group (with get_physical_local_id()) or the logical execution range of a parallel_for_work_item construct (with get_logical_local_id()).

```cpp
template <int Dimensions>
class h_item {
public:
  // Return item's index in the kernel's execution range
  id<Dimensions> get_global_id() const;
  range<Dimensions> get_global_range() const;

  // Return the index in the work-group's execution range
  id<Dimensions> get_logical_local_id() const;
  range<Dimensions> get_logical_local_range() const;

  // Return the index in the logical execution range of the parallel_for
  id<Dimensions> get_physical_local_id() const;
  range<Dimensions> get_physical_local_range() const;
};
```

Figure 4-23. Simplified definition of the h_item class

The private_memory Class

The private_memory class provides a mechanism to declare variables that are private to each work-item, but which can be accessed across multiple parallel_for_work_item constructs nested within the same parallel_for_work_group scope.

This class is necessary because of how variables declared in different hierarchical parallelism scopes behave: variables declared at the outer scope are only private if the compiler can prove it is safe to make them so, and variables declared at the inner scope are private to a logical work-item rather than a physical one. It is impossible using scope alone for us to convey that a variable is intended to be private for each physical work-item.

To see why this is a problem, let's refer back to our matrix multiplication kernels in Figure 4-22. The ib and jb variables are declared at parallel_for_work_group scope and by default should be allocated in work-group local memory! There's a good chance that an optimizing compiler would not make this mistake, because the variables are read-only and their value is simple enough to compute redundantly on every work-item, but the language makes no such guarantees. If we want to be certain that a variable is declared in work-item private memory, we must wrap the variable declaration in an instance of the `private_memory` class, shown in Figure 4-24.

```cpp
template <typename T, int Dimensions = 1>
class private_memory {
public:
  // Construct a private variable for each work-item in the group
  private_memory(const group<Dimensions>&);

  // Return the private variable associated with this work-item
  T& operator(const h_item<Dimensions>&);
};
```

Figure 4-24. Simplified definition of the `private_memory` class

For example, if we were to rewrite our matrix multiplication kernel using the `private_memory` class, we would define the variables as `private_memory<int> ib(grp)`, and each access to these variables would become `ib[item]`. In this case, using the `private_memory` class results in code that is harder to read, and declaring the values at `parallel_for_work_item` scope is clearer.

Our recommendation is to only use the `private_memory` class if a work-item private variable is used across multiple `parallel_for_work_item` scopes within the same `parallel_for_work_group`, it is too expensive to compute repeatedly, or its computation has side effects that prevent it from being computed redundantly. Otherwise, we should rely on the abilities of modern optimizing compilers by default and declare variables at `parallel_for_work_item` scope only when their analysis fails (remembering to also report the issue to the compiler vendor).

Mapping Computation to Work-Items

Most of the code examples so far have assumed that each instance of a kernel function corresponds to a single operation on a single piece of data. This is a simple way to write kernels, but such a one-to-one mapping is not dictated by DPC++ or any of the kernel forms—we always have complete control over the assignment of data (and computation) to individual work-items, and making this assignment parameterizable can be a good way to improve performance portability.

One-to-One Mapping

When we write kernels such that there is a one-to-one mapping of work to work-items, those kernels must always be launched with a range or nd_range with a size exactly matching the amount of work that needs to be done. This is the most obvious way to write kernels, and in many cases, it works very well—we can trust an implementation to map work-items to hardware efficiently.

However, when tuning for performance on a specific combination of system and implementation, it may be necessary to pay closer attention to low-level scheduling behaviors. The scheduling of work-groups to compute resources is implementation-defined and could potentially be *dynamic* (i.e., when a compute resource completes one work-group, the next work-group it executes may come from a shared queue). The impact of dynamic scheduling on performance is not fixed, and its significance depends upon factors including the execution time of each instance of the kernel function and whether the scheduling is implemented in software (e.g., on a CPU) or hardware (e.g., on a GPU).

Many-to-One Mapping

The alternative is to write kernels with a many-to-one mapping of work to work-items. The *meaning* of the range changes subtly in this case: the range no longer describes the amount of work to be done, but rather the number of workers to use. By changing the number of workers and the amount of work assigned to each worker, we can fine-tune work distribution to maximize performance.

CHAPTER 4   EXPRESSING PARALLELISM

Writing a kernel of this form requires two changes:

1. The kernel must accept a parameter describing the total amount of work.

2. The kernel must contain a loop assigning work to work-items.

A simple example of such a kernel is given in Figure 4-25. Note that the loop inside the kernel has a slightly unusual form—the starting index is the work-item's index in the global range, and the stride is the total number of work-items. This *round-robin* scheduling of data to work-items ensures that all N iterations of the loop will be executed by a work-item, but also that linear work-items access contiguous memory locations (to improve cache locality and vectorization behavior). Work can be similarly distributed across groups or the work-items in individual groups to further improve locality.

```
size_t N = ...; // amount of work
size_t W = ...; // number of workers
h.parallel_for(range{W}, [=](item<1> it) {
  for (int i = it.get_id()[0]; i < N; i += it.get_range()[0]) {
    output[i] = function(input[i]);
  }
});
```

Figure 4-25. *Kernel with separate data and execution ranges*

These work distribution patterns are common, and they can be expressed very succinctly when using hierarchical parallelism with a logical range. We expect that future versions of DPC++ will introduce syntactic sugar to simplify the expression of work distribution in ND-range kernels.

CHAPTER 4 EXPRESSING PARALLELISM

Choosing a Kernel Form

Choosing between the different kernel forms is largely a matter of personal preference and heavily influenced by prior experience with other parallel programming models and languages.

The other main reason to choose a specific kernel form is that it is the only form to expose certain functionality required by a kernel. Unfortunately, it can be difficult to identify which functionality will be required before development begins—especially while we are still unfamiliar with the different kernel forms and their interaction with various classes.

We have constructed two guides based on our own experience in order to help us navigate this complex space. These guides should be considered rules of thumb and are definitely not intended to replace our own experimentation—the best way to choose between the different kernel forms will always be to spend some time writing in each of them, in order to learn which form is the best fit for our application and development style.

The first guide is the flowchart in Figure 4-26, which selects a kernel form based on

1. Whether we have previous experience with parallel programming

2. Whether we are writing a new code from scratch or are porting an existing parallel program written in a different language

3. Whether our kernel is embarrassingly parallel, already contains nested parallelism, or reuses data between different instances of the kernel function

4. Whether we are writing a new kernel in SYCL to maximize performance or to improve the portability of our code or because it provides a more productive means of expressing parallelism than lower-level languages

CHAPTER 4   EXPRESSING PARALLELISM

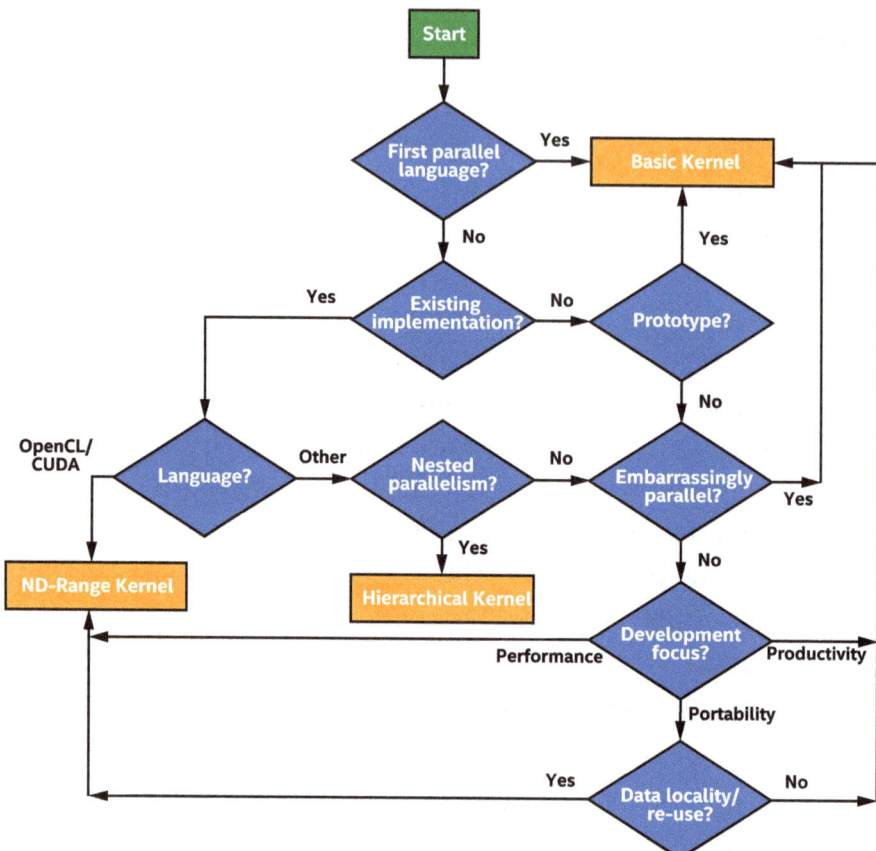

Figure 4-26. *Helping choose the right form for our kernel*

The second guide is the table in Figure 4-27, which summarizes the functionalities that are exposed to each of the kernel forms. It is important to note that this table reflects the state of DPC++ at the time of publication for this book and that the features available to each kernel form should be expected to change as the language evolves. However, we expect the basic trend to remain the same: basic data-parallel kernels will not expose locality-aware features, explicit ND-range kernels will expose all performance-enabling features, and hierarchical kernels will lag behind explicit ND-range kernels in exposing features, but their expression of those features will use higher-level abstractions.

Feature	Basic Kernel	ND-Range Kernel	Hierarchical Kernel
Work-group Local Memory	No	Yes	Yes
Work-group Barriers	No	Yes	Yes
Sub-groups	No	Yes	No
Group Functions (e.g., scan, reduce)	No	Yes	No

Figure 4-27. Features available to each kernel form

Summary

This chapter introduced the basics of expressing parallelism in DPC++ and discussed the strengths and weaknesses of each approach to writing data-parallel kernels.

DPC++ and SYCL provide support for many forms of parallelism, and we hope that we have provided enough information to prepare readers to dive in and start coding!

We have only scratched the surface, and a deeper dive into many of the concepts and classes introduced in this chapter is forthcoming: the usage of local memory, barriers, and communication routines will be covered in Chapter 9; different ways of defining kernels besides using lambda expressions will be discussed in Chapter 10; detailed mappings of the ND-range execution model to specific hardware will be explored in Chapters 15, 16, and 17; and best practices for expressing common parallel patterns using DPC++ will be presented in Chapter 14.

CHAPTER 4 EXPRESSING PARALLELISM

 **Open Access** This chapter is licensed under the terms of the Creative Commons Attribution 4.0 International License (http://creativecommons.org/licenses/by/4.0/), which permits use, sharing, adaptation, distribution and reproduction in any medium or format, as long as you give appropriate credit to the original author(s) and the source, provide a link to the Creative Commons license and indicate if changes were made.

The images or other third party material in this chapter are included in the chapter's Creative Commons license, unless indicated otherwise in a credit line to the material. If material is not included in the chapter's Creative Commons license and your intended use is not permitted by statutory regulation or exceeds the permitted use, you will need to obtain permission directly from the copyright holder.

CHAPTER 5

Error Handling

Agatha Christie wrote in 1969 that "human error is nothing to what a computer can do if it tries." It is no mystery that we, as programmers, get to clean up the mess. The mechanisms for error handling could catch programmer errors that *others* may make. Since we do not plan on making mistakes ourselves, we can focus on using error handling to handle conditions that may occur in the real world from *other* causes.

Detecting and dealing with unexpected conditions and errors can be helpful during application development (think: the *other* programmer who works on the project who *does* make mistakes), but more importantly play a critical role in stable and safe production applications and libraries.

CHAPTER 5   ERROR HANDLING

We devote this chapter to describing the error handling mechanisms available in SYCL so that we can understand what our options are and how to architect applications if we care about detecting and managing errors.

This chapter overviews synchronous and asynchronous errors in SYCL, describes the behavior of an application if we do nothing in our code to handle errors, and dives into the SYCL-specific mechanism that allows us to handle asynchronous errors.

Safety First

A core aspect of C++ error handling is that if we do nothing to handle an error that has been detected (thrown), then the application will terminate and indicate that something went wrong. This behavior allows us to write applications without focusing on error management and still be confident that errors will somehow be signaled to a developer or user. We're not suggesting that we should ignore error handling, of course! Production applications should be written with error management as a core part of the architecture, but applications often start development without such a focus. C++ aims to make code which doesn't handle errors still able to observe errors, even when they are not dealt with explicitly.

Since SYCL is Data Parallel C++, the same philosophy holds: if we do nothing in our code to manage errors and an error is detected, an abnormal termination of the program will occur to let us know that something bad happened. Production applications should of course consider error management as a core part of the software architecture, not only reporting but often also recovering from error conditions.

If we don't add any error management code and an error occurs, we will still see an abnormal program termination which is an indication to dig deeper.

Types of Errors

C++ provides a framework for notification and handling of errors through its exception mechanism. Heterogeneous programming requires an additional level of error management beyond this, because some errors occur on a device or when trying to launch work on a device. These errors are typically decoupled in time from the host program's execution, and as such they don't integrate cleanly with classic C++ exception handling mechanisms. To solve this, there are additional mechanisms to make asynchronous errors as manageable and controllable as regular C++ exceptions.

Figure 5-1 shows two components of a typical application: (1) the host code that runs sequentially and submits work to the task graph for future execution and (2) the task graph which runs asynchronously from the host program and executes kernels or other actions on devices when the necessary dependences are met. The example shows a `parallel_for` as the operation that executes asynchronously as part of the task graph, but other operations are possible as well as discussed in Chapters 3, 4, and 8.

CHAPTER 5   ERROR HANDLING

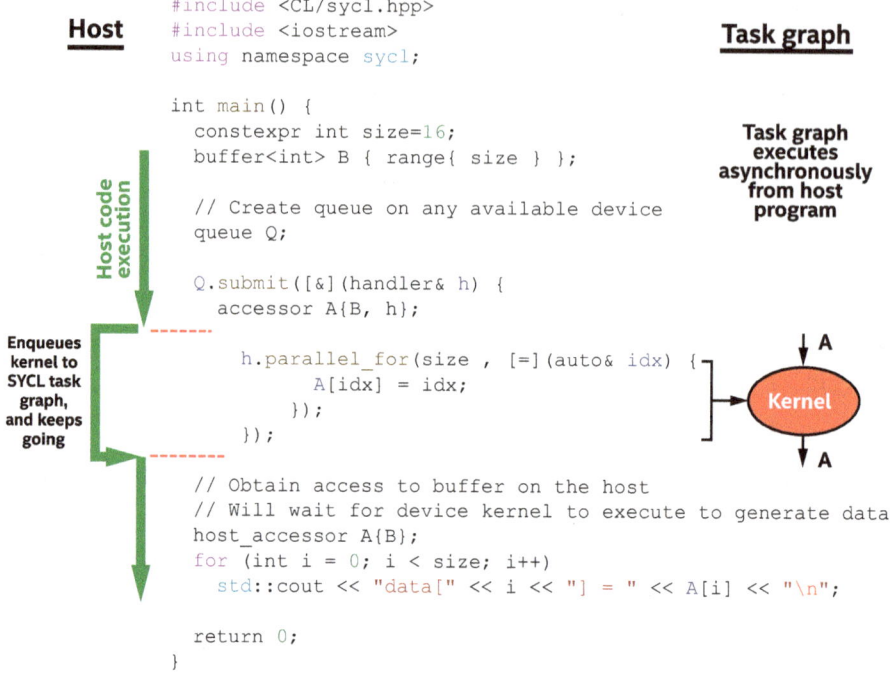

Figure 5-1. Separation of host program and task graph executions

The distinction between the left and right (host and task graph) sides of Figure 5-1 is the key to understanding the differences between *synchronous* and *asynchronous* errors.

Synchronous errors occur when an error condition can be detected as the host program executes an operation, such as an API call or object constructor. They can be detected before an instruction on the left side of the figure completes, and the error can be thrown by the operation that caused the error immediately. We can wrap specific instructions on the left side of the diagram with a try-catch construct, expecting that errors occurring as a result of operations within the try will be detected before the try block ends (and therefore caught). The C++ exception mechanism is designed to handle exactly these types of errors.

Alternatively, *asynchronous* errors occur as part of the right side of Figure 5-1, where an error is only detected when an operation in the task graph is executed. By the time that an asynchronous error is detected as part of task graph execution, the host program has typically already moved on with its execution, so there is no code to wrap with a `try-catch` construct to catch these errors. There is instead an asynchronous exception handling framework to handle these errors that occur at seemingly random times relative to host program execution.

Let's Create Some Errors!

As examples for the remainder of this chapter and to allow us to experiment, we'll create both synchronous and asynchronous errors in the following sections.

Synchronous Error

```
#include <CL/sycl.hpp>
using namespace sycl;

int main() {
  buffer<int> B{ range{16} };

  // ERROR: Create sub-buffer larger than size of parent buffer
  // An exception is thrown from within the buffer constructor
  buffer<int> B2(B, id{8}, range{16});

  return 0;
}

Example output:
terminate called after throwing an instance of
'cl::sycl::invalid_object_error'
  what():  Requested sub-buffer size exceeds the size of the parent buffer
  -30 (CL_INVALID_VALUE)
```

Figure 5-2. Creating a synchronous error

In Figure 5-2, a sub-buffer is created from a buffer but with an illegal size (larger than the original buffer). The constructor of the sub-buffer detects this error and throws an exception before the constructor's execution completes. This is a synchronous error because it occurs as part of (synchronously with) the host program's execution. The error is detectable *before the constructor returns*, so the error may be handled immediately at its point of origin or detection in the host program.

Our code example doesn't do anything to catch and handle C++ exceptions, so the default C++ uncaught exception handler calls `std::terminate` for us, signaling that something went wrong.

Asynchronous Error

Generating an asynchronous error is a bit trickier because implementations work hard to detect and report errors synchronously whenever possible. Synchronous errors are easier to debug because they occur at a specific point of origin in the host program, so are preferred whenever possible. One way to generate an asynchronous error for our demonstration purpose, though, is to add a fallback/secondary queue to our command group submission and to discard synchronous exceptions that also happen to be thrown. Figure 5-3 shows such code which invokes our `handle_async_error` function to allow us to experiment. Asynchronous errors can occur and be reported without a secondary/fallback queue, so note that the secondary queue is only part of the example and in no way a requirement for asynchronous errors.

CHAPTER 5   ERROR HANDLING

```
#include <CL/sycl.hpp>
using namespace sycl;

// Our simple asynchronous handler function
auto handle_async_error = [](exception_list elist) {
  for (auto &e : elist) {
    try{ std::rethrow_exception(e); }
    catch ( sycl::exception& e ) {
      std::cout << "ASYNC EXCEPTION!!\n";
      std::cout << e.what() << "\n";
    }
  }
};

void say_device (const queue& Q) {
  std::cout << "Device : "
    << Q.get_device().get_info<info::device::name>() << "\n";
}

int main() {
  queue Q1{ gpu_selector{}, handle_async_error };
  queue Q2{ cpu_selector{}, handle_async_error };
  say_device(Q1);
  say_device(Q2);

  try {
    Q1.submit([&] (handler &h){
        // Empty command group is illegal and generates an error
      },
      Q2); // Secondary/backup queue!
  } catch (...) {} // Discard regular C++ exceptions for this example
  return 0;
}
```

Example output:
```
Device : Intel(R) Gen9 HD Graphics NEO
Device : Intel(R) Xeon(R) E-2176G CPU @ 3.70GHz
ASYNC EXCEPTION!!
Command group submitted without a kernel or a explicit memory operation. -59
(CL_INVALID_OPERATION)
```

Figure 5-3. Creating an asynchronous error

CHAPTER 5 ERROR HANDLING

Application Error Handling Strategy

The C++ *exception* features are designed to cleanly separate the point in a program where an error is detected from the point where it may be handled, and this concept fits very well with both synchronous and asynchronous errors in SYCL. Through the throw and catch mechanisms, a hierarchy of handlers can be defined which can be important in production applications.

Building an application that can handle errors in a consistent and reliable way requires a strategy up front and a resulting software architecture built for error management. C++ provides flexible tools to implement many alternative strategies, but such architecture is beyond the scope of this chapter. There are many books and other references devoted to this topic, so we encourage looking to them for full coverage of C++ error management strategies.

This said, error detection and reporting doesn't always need to be production-scale. Errors in a program can be reliably detected and reported through minimal code if the goal is simply to detect errors during execution and to report them (but not necessarily to recover from them). The following sections cover first what happens if we ignore error handling and do nothing (the default behavior isn't all that bad!), followed by recommended error reporting that is simple to implement in basic applications.

Ignoring Error Handling

C++ and SYCL are designed to tell us that something went wrong even when we don't handle errors explicitly. The default result of unhandled synchronous or asynchronous errors is abnormal program termination which an operating system should tell us about. The following two examples mimic the behavior that will occur if we do not handle a synchronous and an asynchronous error, respectively.

CHAPTER 5 ERROR HANDLING

Figure 5-4 shows the result of an unhandled C++ exception, which could be an unhandled SYCL synchronous error, for example. We can use this code to test what a particular operating system will report in such a case.

Figure 5-5 shows example output from `std::terminate` being called, which will be the result of an unhandled SYCL asynchronous error in our application. We can use this code to test what a particular operating system will report in such a case.

Although we probably should handle errors in our programs, since uncaught errors will be caught and the program terminated, we do not need to worry about a program silently failing!

```
#include <iostream>

class something_went_wrong {};

int main() {
  std::cout << "Hello\n";

  throw(something_went_wrong{});
}

Example output in Linux:
Hello
terminate called after throwing an instance of 'something_went_wrong'

Aborted (core dumped)
```

Figure 5-4. *Unhandled exception in C++*

139

CHAPTER 5   ERROR HANDLING

```
#include <iostream>

int main() {
  std::cout << "Hello\n";

  std::terminate();
}

Example output in Linux:
Hello
terminate called without an active exception
Aborted (core dumped)
```

Figure 5-5. `std::terminate` *is called when a SYCL asynchronous exception isn't handled*

Synchronous Error Handling

We keep this section very short because SYCL synchronous errors are just C++ exceptions. Most of the additional error mechanisms added in SYCL relate to asynchronous errors which we cover in the next section, but synchronous errors are important because implementations try to detect and report as many errors synchronously as possible, since they are easier to reason about and handle.

Synchronous errors defined by SYCL are a derived class from `std::exception` of type `sycl::exception`, which allows us to catch the SYCL errors specifically though a `try-catch` structure such as what we see in Figure 5-6.

```
try{
  // Do some SYCL work
} catch (sycl::exception &e) {
  // Do something to output or handle the exceptinon
  std::cout << "Caught sync SYCL exception: " << e.what() << "\n";
  return 1;
}
```

Figure 5-6. *Pattern to catch* `sycl::exception` *specifically*

CHAPTER 5 ERROR HANDLING

On top of the C++ error handling mechanisms, SYCL adds a `sycl::exception` type for the exceptions thrown by the runtime. Everything else is standard C++ exception handling, so will be familiar to most developers.

A slightly more complete example is provided in Figure 5-7, where additional classes of exception are handled, as well as the program being ended by returning from `main()`.

```
try{
  buffer<int> B{ range{16} };

  // ERROR: Create sub-buffer larger than size of parent buffer
  // An exception is thrown from within the buffer constructor
  buffer<int> B2(B, id{8}, range{16});

} catch (sycl::exception &e) {
  // Do something to output or handle the exception
  std::cout << "Caught sync SYCL exception: " << e.what() << "\n";
  return 1;
} catch (std::exception &e) {
  std::cout << "Caught std exception: " << e.what() << "\n";
  return 2;
} catch (...) {
  std::cout << "Caught unknown exception\n";
  return 3;
}

return 0;
```

Example output:
Caught sync SYCL exception: Requested sub-buffer size exceeds the size of the parent buffer -30 (CL_INVALID_VALUE)

Figure 5-7. *Pattern to catch exceptions from a block of code*

Asynchronous Error Handling

Asynchronous errors are detected by the SYCL runtime (or an underlying backend), and the errors occur independently of execution of commands in the host program. The errors are stored in lists internal to the SYCL

141

runtime and only released for processing at specific points that the programmer can control. There are two topics that we need to discuss to cover handling of asynchronous errors:

1. **The asynchronous handler** that is invoked when there are outstanding asynchronous errors to process

2. **When** the asynchronous handler is invoked

The Asynchronous Handler

The asynchronous handler is a function that the application defines, which is registered with SYCL contexts and/or queues. At the times defined by the next section, if there are any unprocessed asynchronous exceptions that are available to be handled, then the asynchronous handler is invoked by the SYCL runtime and passed a list of these exceptions.

The asynchronous handler is passed to a context or queue constructor as a `std::function` and can be defined in ways such as a regular function, lambda, or functor, depending on our preference. The handler must accept a `sycl::exception_list` argument, such as in the example handler shown in Figure 5-8.

```
// Our simple asynchronous handler function
auto handle_async_error = [](exception_list elist) {
  for (auto &e : elist) {
    try{ std::rethrow_exception(e); }
    catch ( sycl::exception& e ) {
      std::cout << "ASYNC EXCEPTION!!\n";
      std::cout << e.what() << "\n";
    }
  }
};
```

Figure 5-8. Example asynchronous handler implementation defined as a lambda

In Figure 5-8, the `std::rethrow_exception` followed by catch of a specific exception type provides filtering of the type of exception, in this case to the only `sycl::exception`. We can also use alternative filtering approaches in C++ or just choose to handle all exceptions regardless of the type.

The handler is associated with a queue or context (low-level detail covered more in Chapter 6) at construction time. For example, to register the handler defined in Figure 5-8 with a queue that we are creating, we could write

```
queue my_queue{ gpu_selector{}, handle_async_error };
```

Likewise, to register the handler defined in Figure 5-8 with a context that we are creating, we could write

```
context my_context{ handle_async_error };
```

Most applications do not need contexts to be explicitly created or managed (they are created behind the scenes for us automatically), so if an asynchronous handler is going to be used, most developers should associate such handlers with queues that are being constructed for specific devices (and not explicit contexts).

In defining asynchronous handlers, most developers should define them on queues unless already explicitly managing contexts for other reasons.

If an asynchronous handler is not defined for a queue or the queue's parent context and an asynchronous error occurs on that queue (or in the context) that must be processed, then the default asynchronous handler is invoked. The default handler operates as if it was coded as shown in Figure 5-9.

CHAPTER 5 ERROR HANDLING

```
// Our simple asynchronous handler function
auto handle_async_error = [](exception_list elist) {
  for (auto &e : elist) {
    try{ std::rethrow_exception(e); }
    catch ( sycl::exception& e ) {
      // Print information about the asynchronous exception
    }
  }

  // Terminate abnormally to make clear to user
  // that something unhandled happened
  std::terminate();
};
```

Figure 5-9. *Example of how the default asynchronous handler behaves*

The default handler should display some information to the user on any errors in the exception list and then will terminate the application abnormally, which should also cause the operating system to report that termination was abnormal.

What we put within an asynchronous handler is up to us. It can range from logging of an error to application termination to recovery of the error condition so that an application can continue executing normally. The common case is to report any details of the error available by calling sycl::exception::what(), followed by termination of the application.

Although it's up to us to decide what an asynchronous handler does internally, a common mistake is to print an error message (that may be missed in the noise of other messages from the program), followed by completion of the handler function. Unless we have error management principles in place that allow us to recover known program state and to be confident that it's safe to continue execution, we should consider terminating the application within our asynchronous handler function(s). This reduces the chance that incorrect results will appear from a program where an error was detected, but where the application was inadvertently allowed to continue with execution regardless. In many programs, abnormal termination is the preferred result once we have experienced asynchronous exceptions.

> Consider terminating applications within an asynchronous handler, after outputting information about the error, if comprehensive error recovery and management mechanisms are not in place.

Invocation of the Handler

The asynchronous handler is called by the runtime at specific times. Errors aren't reported immediately as they occur because management of errors and safe application programming (particularly multithreaded) would become more difficult and expensive if that was the case. The asynchronous handler is instead called at the following very specific times:

1. When the host program calls **queue::throw_asynchronous()** on a specific queue
2. When the host program calls **queue::wait_and_throw()** on a specific queue
3. When the host program calls **event::wait_and_throw()** on a specific event
4. When a **queue** is destroyed
5. When a **context** is destroyed

Methods 1–3 provide a mechanism for a host program to control when asynchronous exceptions are handled, so that thread safety and other details specific to an application can be managed. They effectively provide controlled points at which asynchronous exceptions enter the host program control flow and can be processed almost as if they were synchronous errors.

If a user doesn't explicitly call one of the methods 1–3, then asynchronous errors are commonly reported during program teardown when queues and contexts are destroyed. This is often enough to signal to a user that something went wrong and that program results shouldn't be trusted.

Relying on error detection during program teardown doesn't work in all cases, though. For example, if a program will only terminate when some algorithm convergence criteria are achieved and if those criteria are only achievable by successful execution of device kernels, then an asynchronous exception may signal that the algorithm will never converge and begin the teardown (where the error would be noticed). In these cases, and also in production applications where more complete error handling strategies are in place, it makes sense to invoke `throw_asynchronous()` or `wait_and_throw()` at regular and controlled points in the program (e.g., before checking whether algorithm convergence has occurred).

Errors on a Device

The error detection and handling mechanisms discussed in this chapter have been host-based. They are mechanisms through which the host program can detect and deal with something that may have gone wrong either in the host program or potentially during execution of kernels on devices. What we have not covered is how to signal, from within the device code that we write, that something has gone wrong. This omission is not a mistake, but quite intentional.

SYCL explicitly disallows C++ exception handling mechanisms (such as `throw`) within device code, because there are performance costs for some types of device that we usually don't want to pay. If we detect that something has gone wrong within our device code, we should signal the error using existing non-exception-based techniques. For example, we could write to a buffer that logs errors or return some invalid result from our numeric calculation that we define to mean that an error occurred. The right strategy in these cases is very application specific.

Summary

In this chapter, we introduced synchronous and asynchronous errors, covered the default behavior to expect if we do nothing to manage errors that might occur, and covered the mechanisms used to handle asynchronous errors at controlled points in our application. Error management strategies are a major topic in software engineering and a significant percentage of the code written in many applications. SYCL integrates with the C++ knowledge that we already have when it comes to error handling and provides flexible mechanisms to integrate with whatever our preferred error management strategy is.

Open Access This chapter is licensed under the terms of the Creative Commons Attribution 4.0 International License (http://creativecommons.org/licenses/by/4.0/), which permits use, sharing, adaptation, distribution and reproduction in any medium or format, as long as you give appropriate credit to the original author(s) and the source, provide a link to the Creative Commons license and indicate if changes were made.

The images or other third party material in this chapter are included in the chapter's Creative Commons license, unless indicated otherwise in a credit line to the material. If material is not included in the chapter's Creative Commons license and your intended use is not permitted by statutory regulation or exceeds the permitted use, you will need to obtain permission directly from the copyright holder.

CHAPTER 6

Unified Shared Memory

The next two chapters provide a deeper look into how to manage data. There are two different approaches that complement each other: Unified Shared Memory (USM) and buffers. USM exposes a different level of abstraction for memory than buffers—USM has pointers, and buffers are a higher-level interface. This chapter focuses on USM. The next chapter will focus on buffers.

Unless we specifically know that we want to use buffers, USM is a good place to start. USM is a pointer-based model that allows memory to be read and written through regular C++ pointers.

… CHAPTER 6   UNIFIED SHARED MEMORY

Why Should We Use USM?

Since USM is based on C++ pointers, it is a natural place to start for existing pointer-based C++ codes. Existing functions that take pointers as parameters continue to work without modification. In the majority of cases, the only changes required are to replace existing calls to `malloc` or `new` with USM-specific allocation routines that we will discuss later in this chapter.

Allocation Types

While USM is based on C++ pointers, not all pointers are created equal. USM defines three different types of allocations, each with unique semantics. A device may not support all types (or even *any* type) of USM allocation. We will learn how to query what a device supports later. The three types of allocations and their characteristics are summarized in Figure 6-1.

Type	Description	Accessible on host?	Accessible on device?	Located on
device	Allocations in device memory	✗	✓	device
host	Allocations in host memory	✓	✓	host
shared	Allocations shared between host and device	✓	✓	Can migrate between host and device

Figure 6-1.   *USM allocation types*

Device Allocations

This first type of allocation is what we need in order to have a pointer into a device's attached memory, such as (G)DDR or HBM. Device allocations can be read from or written to by kernels running on a device, but they cannot be directly accessed from code executing on the host. Trying to access a device allocation on the host can result in either incorrect data or a program crashing due to an error. We must copy data between host and device using the explicit USM `memcpy` mechanisms, which specify how much data must be copied between two places, that will be covered later in this chapter.

Host Allocations

This second type of allocation is easier to use than device allocations since we do not have to manually copy data between the host and the device. Host allocations are allocations in host memory that are accessible on both the host and the device. These allocations, while accessible on the device, cannot migrate to the device's attached memory. Instead, kernels that read from or write to this memory do it *remotely*, often over a slower bus such as PCI-Express. This tradeoff between convenience and performance is something that we must take into consideration. Despite the higher access costs that host allocations can incur, there are still valid reasons to use them. Examples include rarely accessed data or large data sets that cannot fit inside device attached memory.

Shared Allocations

The final type of allocation combines attributes of both device and host allocations, combining the programmer convenience of host allocations with the greater performance afforded by device allocations. Like host allocations, shared allocations are accessible on both the host and device.

The difference between them is that shared allocations are free to migrate between host memory and device attached memory, automatically, without our intervention. If an allocation has migrated to the device, any kernel executing on that device accessing it will do so with greater performance than remotely accessing it from the host. However, shared allocations do not give us all the benefits without any drawbacks.

Automatic migration can be implemented in a variety of ways. No matter which way the runtime chooses to implement shared allocations, they usually pay a price of increased latency. With device allocations, we know exactly how much memory needs to be copied and can schedule the copy to begin as quickly as possible. The automatic migration mechanisms cannot see the future and, in some cases, do not begin moving data until a kernel tries to access it. The kernel must then wait, or block, until the data movement has completed before it can continue executing. In other cases, the runtime may not know exactly how much data the kernel will access and might conservatively move a larger amount of data than is required, also increasing latency for the kernel.

We should also note that while shared allocations *can* migrate, it does not necessarily mean that all implementations of DPC++ *will* migrate them. We expect most implementations to implement shared allocations with migration, but some devices may prefer to implement them identically to host allocations. In such an implementation, the allocation is still visible on both host and device, but we may not see the performance gains that a migrating implementation could provide.

Allocating Memory

USM allows us to allocate memory in a variety of different ways that cater to different needs and preferences. However, before we go over all the methods in greater detail, we should discuss how USM allocations differ from regular C++ allocations.

What Do We Need to Know?

Regular C++ programs can allocate memory in multiple ways: `new`, `malloc`, or allocators. No matter which syntax we prefer, memory allocation is ultimately performed by the system allocator in the host operating system. When we allocate memory in C++, the only concerns are "How much memory do we need?" and "How much memory is available to allocate?" However, USM requires extra information before an allocation can be performed.

First, USM allocation needs to specify which type of allocation is desired: device, host, or shared. It is important to request the right type of allocation in order to obtain the desired behavior for that allocation. Next, every USM allocation must specify a `context` object against which the allocation will be made. The `context` object hasn't had a lot of discussion yet, so it's worth saying a little about it here. A context represents a device or set of devices on which we can execute kernels. We can think of a context as a convenient place for the runtime to stash some state about what it's doing. Programmers are not likely to directly interact with contexts outside of passing them around in most DPC++ programs.

USM allocations are not guaranteed to be usable across different contexts—it is important that all USM allocations, queues, and kernels share the same `context` object. Typically, we can obtain this context from the queue being used to submit work to a device. Finally, `device` allocations also require that we specify which device will provide the memory for the allocation. This is important since we do not want to oversubscribe the memory of our devices (unless the device is able to support this—we will say more about that later in the chapter when we discuss migration of data). USM allocation routines can be distinguished from their C++ analogues by the addition of these extra parameters.

CHAPTER 6 UNIFIED SHARED MEMORY

Multiple Styles

Sometimes, trying to please everyone with a single option proves to be an impossible task, just as some people prefer coffee over tea, or `emacs` over `vi`. If we ask programmers what an allocation interface should look like, we will get several different answers back. USM embraces this diversity of choice and provides several different flavors of allocation interfaces. These different flavors are C-style, C++-style, and C++ allocator-style. We will now discuss each and point out their similarities and differences.

Allocations à la C

The first style of allocation functions (listed in Figure 6-2, later used in examples shown in Figures 6-6 and 6-7) is modeled after memory allocation in C: `malloc` functions that take a number of bytes to allocate and return a `void *` pointer. This style of function is type agnostic. We must specify the total number of bytes to allocate, which means if we want to allocate N objects of type X, one must ask for `N * sizeof(X)` total bytes. The returned pointer is of type `void *`, which means that we must then cast it to an appropriate pointer to type X. This style is very simple but can be verbose due to the size calculations and typecasting required.

We can further divide this style of allocation into two categories: named functions and single function. The distinction between these two flavors is how we specify the desired type of USM allocation. With the named functions (`malloc_device`, `malloc_host`, and `malloc_shared`), the type of USM allocation is encoded in the function name. The single function `malloc` requires the type of USM allocation to be specified as an additional parameter. Neither flavor is better than the other, and the choice of which to use is governed by our preference.

We cannot move on without briefly mentioning alignment. Each version of `malloc` also has an `aligned_alloc` counterpart. The `malloc` functions return memory aligned to the default behavior of our device.

CHAPTER 6 UNIFIED SHARED MEMORY

It will return a legal pointer with a valid alignment, but there may be cases where we would prefer to manually specify an alignment. In these cases, we should use one of the `aligned_alloc` variants that also require us to specify the desired alignment for the allocation. Do not expect a program to work properly if we specify an illegal alignment! Legal alignments are powers of two. It's worth noting that on many devices, allocations are maximally aligned to correspond to features of the hardware, so while we may ask for allocations to be 4-, 8-, 16-, or 32-byte aligned, we might in practice see larger alignments that give us what we ask for and then some.

```
// Named Functions
void *malloc_device(size_t size, const device &dev, const context &ctxt);
void *malloc_device(size_t size, const queue &q);
void *aligned_alloc_device(size_t alignment, size_t size,
                           const device &dev, const context &ctxt);
void *aligned_alloc_device(size_t alignment, size_t size, const queue &q);

void *malloc_host(size_t size, const context &ctxt);
void *malloc_host(size_t size, const queue &q);
void *aligned_alloc_host(size_t alignment, size_t size, const context
&ctxt);
void *aligned_alloc_host(size_t alignment, size_t size, const queue &q);

void *malloc_shared(size_t size, const device &dev, const context &ctxt);
void *malloc_shared(size_t size, const queue &q);
void *aligned_alloc_shared(size_t alignment, size_t size,
                           const device &dev, const context &ctxt);
void *aligned_alloc_shared(size_t alignment, size_t size, const queue &q);

// Single Function
void *malloc(size_t size, const device &dev, const context &ctxt,
             usm::alloc kind);
void *malloc(size_t size, const queue &q, usm::alloc kind);
void *aligned_alloc(size_t alignment, size_t size,
                    const device &dev, const context &ctxt,
                    usm::alloc kind);
void *aligned_alloc(size_t alignment, size_t size, const queue &q,
                    usm::alloc kind);
```

Figure 6-2. C-style USM allocation functions

Allocations à la C++

The next flavor of USM allocation functions (listed in Figure 6-3) is very similar to the first but with more of a C++ look and feel. We once again have both named and single function versions of the allocation routines as well as our default and user-specified alignment versions. The difference is that now our functions are C++ templated functions that allocate Count objects of type T and return a pointer of type T *. Taking advantage of modern C++ simplifies things, since we no longer need to manually calculate the total size of the allocation in bytes or cast the returned pointer to the appropriate type. This also tends to yield a more compact and less error-prone expression in code. However, we should note that unlike "new" in C++, malloc-style interfaces do not invoke constructors for the objects being allocated—we are simply allocating enough bytes to fit that type.

This flavor of allocation is a good place to start for new codes written with USM in mind. The previous C-style is a good starting point for existing C++ codes that already make heavy use of C or C++ malloc, to which we will add the use of USM.

CHAPTER 6 UNIFIED SHARED MEMORY

```
// Named Functions
template <typename T>
T *malloc_device(size_t Count, const device &Dev, const context &Ctxt);
template <typename T>
T *malloc_device(size_t Count, const queue &Q);
template <typename T>
T *aligned_alloc_device(size_t Alignment, size_t Count, const device &Dev,
                        const context &Ctxt);
template <typename T>
T *aligned_alloc_device(size_t Alignment, size_t Count, const queue &Q);

template <typename T> T *malloc_host(size_t Count, const context &Ctxt);
template <typename T> T *malloc_host(size_t Count, const queue &Q);
template <typename T>
T *aligned_alloc_host(size_t Alignment, size_t Count, const context &Ctxt);
template <typename T>
T *aligned_alloc_host(size_t Alignment, size_t Count, const queue &Q);

template <typename T>
T *malloc_shared(size_t Count, const device &Dev, const context &Ctxt);
template <typename T> T *malloc_shared(size_t Count, const queue &Q);
template <typename T>
T *aligned_alloc_shared(size_t Alignment, size_t Count, const device &Dev,
                        const context &Ctxt);
template <typename T>
T *aligned_alloc_shared(size_t Alignment, size_t Count, const queue &Q);

// Single Function
template <typename T>
T *malloc(size_t Count, const device &Dev, const context &Ctxt,
          usm::alloc Kind);
template <typename T> T *malloc(size_t Count, const queue &Q, usm::alloc Kind);
template <typename T>
T *aligned_alloc(size_t Alignment, size_t Count, const device &Dev,
                 const context &Ctxt, usm::alloc Kind);
template <typename T>
T *aligned_alloc(size_t Alignment, size_t Count, const queue &Q,
                 usm::alloc Kind);
```

Figure 6-3. *C++-style USM allocation functions*

C++ Allocators

The final flavor of USM allocation (Figure 6-4) embraces modern C++ even more than the previous flavor. This flavor is based on the C++ allocator interface, which defines objects that are used to perform memory allocations either directly or indirectly inside a container such

CHAPTER 6   UNIFIED SHARED MEMORY

as `std::vector`. This allocator flavor is most useful if our code makes heavy use of container objects that can hide the details of memory allocation and deallocation from the user, simplifying code and reducing the opportunity for bugs.

```
template <class T, usm::alloc AllocKind, size_t Alignment = 0>
class usm_allocator {
public:
  using value_type = T;
  template <typename U> struct rebind {
    typedef usm_allocator<U, AllocKind, Alignment> other;
  };

  usm_allocator() noexcept = delete;
  usm_allocator(const context &Ctxt, const device &Dev) noexcept;
  usm_allocator(const queue &Q) noexcept;
  usm_allocator(const usm_allocator &Other) noexcept;
  template <class U>
    usm_allocator(usm_allocator<U, AllocKind, Alignment> const &) noexcept;

  T *allocate(size_t NumberOfElements);
  void deallocate(T *Ptr, size_t Size);

  template <
      usm::alloc AllocT = AllocKind,
      typename std::enable_if<AllocT != usm::alloc::device, int>::type = 0,
      class U, class... ArgTs>
  void construct(U *Ptr, ArgTs &&... Args);

  template <
      usm::alloc AllocT = AllocKind,
      typename std::enable_if<AllocT == usm::alloc::device, int>::type = 0,
      class U, class... ArgTs>
  void construct(U *Ptr, ArgTs &&... Args);

  template <
      usm::alloc AllocT = AllocKind,
      typename std::enable_if<AllocT != usm::alloc::device, int>::type = 0>
  void destroy(T *Ptr);

  template <
      usm::alloc AllocT = AllocKind,
      typename std::enable_if<AllocT == usm::alloc::device, int>::type = 0>
  void destroy(T *Ptr);
};
```

Figure 6-4. *C++ allocator-style USM allocation functions*

Deallocating Memory

Whatever a program allocates must eventually be deallocated. USM defines a free method to deallocate memory allocated by one of the malloc or aligned_malloc functions. This free method also takes the context in which the memory was allocated as an extra parameter. The queue can also be substituted for the context. If memory was allocated with a C++ allocator object, it should also be deallocated using that object.

```cpp
constexpr int N = 42;

queue Q;

// Allocate N floats

// C-style
float *f1 = static_cast<float*>(malloc_shared(N*sizeof(float),Q));

// C++-style
float *f2 = malloc_shared<float>(N, Q);

// C++-allocator-style
usm_allocator<float, usm::alloc::shared> alloc(Q);
float *f3 = alloc.allocate(N);

// Free our allocations
free(f1, Q.get_context());
free(f2, Q);
alloc.deallocate(f3, N);
```

Figure 6-5. *Three styles for allocation*

Allocation Example

In Figure 6-5, we show how to perform the same allocation using the three styles just described. In this example, we allocate N single-precision floating-point numbers as shared allocations. The first allocation f1 uses the C-style void * returning malloc routines. For this allocation, we explicitly pass the device and context that we obtain from the queue.

We must also cast the result back to a `float *`. The second allocation `f2` does the same thing but using the C++-style templated malloc. Since we pass the type of our elements, `float`, to the allocation routine, we only need to specify how many floats we want to allocate, and we do not need to cast the result. We also use the form that takes the queue instead of the device and context, yielding a very simple and compact statement. The third allocation `f3` uses the USM C++ allocator class. We instantiate an allocator object of the proper type and then perform the allocation using that object. Finally, we show how to properly deallocate each allocation.

Data Management

Now that we understand how to allocate memory using USM, we will discuss how data is managed. We can look at this in two pieces: data initialization and data movement.

Initialization

Data initialization concerns filling our memory with values before we perform computations on it. One example of a common initialization pattern is to fill an allocation with zeroes before it is used. If we were to do this using USM allocations, we could do it in a variety of ways. First, we could write a kernel to do this. If our data set is particularly large or the initialization requires complex calculations, this is a reasonable way to go since the initialization can be performed in parallel (and it makes the initialized data ready to go on the device). Second, we could implement this as a loop over all the elements of an allocation that sets each to zero. However, there is potentially a problem with this approach. A loop would work fine for host and shared allocations since these are accessible on the host. However, since device allocations are *not* accessible on the host, a loop in host code would not be able to write to them. This brings us to the third option.

The `memset` function is designed to efficiently implement this initialization pattern. USM provides a version of `memset` that is a member function of both the `handler` and `queue` classes. It takes three arguments: the pointer representing the base address of the memory we want to set, a byte value representing the byte pattern to set, and the number of bytes to set to that pattern. Unlike a loop on the host, `memset` happens in parallel and also works with `device` allocations.

While `memset` is a useful operation, the fact that it only allows us to specify a byte pattern to fill into an allocation is rather limiting. USM also provides a `fill` method (as a member of the `handler` and `queue` classes) that lets us fill memory with an arbitrary pattern. The fill method is a function templated on the type of the pattern we want to write into the allocation. Template it with an `int`, and we can fill an allocation with the number "42". Similar to `memset`, `fill` takes three arguments: the pointer to the base address of the allocation to fill, the value to fill, and the number of times we want to write that value into the allocation.

Data Movement

Data movement is probably the most important aspect of USM to understand. If the right data is not in the right place at the right time, our program will produce incorrect results. USM defines two strategies that we can use to manage data: explicit and implicit. The choice of which strategy we want to use is related to the types of USM allocations our hardware supports or that we want to use.

Explicit

The first strategy USM offers is explicit data movement (Figure 6-6). Here, we must explicitly copy data between the host and device. We can do this by invoking the `memcpy` method, found on both the `handler` and `queue` classes. The `memcpy` method takes three arguments: a pointer to the

CHAPTER 6 UNIFIED SHARED MEMORY

destination memory, a pointer to the source memory, and the number of bytes to copy between host and device. We do not need to specify in which direction the copy is meant to happen—this is implicit in the source and destination pointers.

The most common usage of explicit data movement is copying to or from `device` allocations in USM since they are not accessible on the host. Having to insert explicit copying of data does require effort on our part. Additionally, it can be a source of bugs: copies could be accidentally omitted, an incorrect amount of data could be copied, or the source or destination pointer could be incorrect.

However, explicit data movement does not only come with disadvantages. It gives us large advantage: total control over data movement. Control over both how much data is copied and when the data gets copied is very important for achieving the best performance in some applications. Ideally, we can overlap computation with data movement whenever possible, ensuring that the hardware runs with high utilization.

The other types of USM allocations, `host` and `shared`, are both accessible on host and device and do not need to be explicitly copied to the device. This leads us to the other strategy for data movement in USM.

```cpp
constexpr int N = 42;

queue Q;

std::array<int,N> host_array;
int *device_array = malloc_device<int>(N, Q);
for (int i = 0; i < N; i++)
  host_array[i] = N;

Q.submit([&](handler& h) {
  // copy hostArray to deviceArray
  h.memcpy(device_array, &host_array[0], N * sizeof(int));
});

Q.wait(); // needed for now (we learn a better way later)

Q.submit([&](handler& h) {
  h.parallel_for(N, [=](id<1> i) {
    device_array[i]++;
  });
});

Q.wait(); // needed for now (we learn a better way later)

Q.submit([&](handler& h) {
  // copy deviceArray back to hostArray
  h.memcpy(&host_array[0], device_array, N * sizeof(int));
});

Q.wait(); // needed for now (we learn a better way later)

free(device_array, Q);
```

Figure 6-6. USM explicit data movement example

Implicit

The second strategy that USM provides is implicit data movement (example usage shown in Figure 6-7). In this strategy, data movement happens *implicitly*, that is, without requiring input from us. With implicit data movement, we do not need to insert calls to memcpy since we can directly access the data through the USM pointers wherever we want to use it. Instead, it becomes the job of the system to ensure that the data will be available in the correct location when it is being used.

CHAPTER 6   UNIFIED SHARED MEMORY

With host allocations, one could argue whether they really cause data movement. Since, by definition, they always remain pointers to host memory, the memory represented by a given host pointer cannot be stored on the device. However, data movement does occur as host allocations are accessed on the device. Instead of the memory being migrated to the device, the values we read or write are transferred over the appropriate interface to or from the kernel. This can be useful for streaming kernels where the data does not need to remain resident on the device.

Implicit data movement mostly concerns USM shared allocations. This type of allocation is accessible on both host and device and, more importantly, can migrate between host and device. The key point is that this migration happens automatically, or implicitly, simply by accessing the data in a different location. Next, we will discuss several things to think about when it comes to data migration for shared allocations.

```
constexpr int N = 42;

queue Q;

int* host_array = malloc_host<int>(N, Q);
int* shared_array = malloc_shared<int>(N, Q);
for (int i = 0; i < N; i++)
  host_array[i] = i;

Q.submit([&](handler& h) {
  h.parallel_for(N, [=](id<1> i) {
    // access sharedArray and hostArray on device
    shared_array[i] = host_array[i] + 1;
  });
});

Q.wait();

free(shared_array, Q);
free(host_array, Q);
```

Figure 6-7. *USM implicit data movement example*

Migration

With explicit data movement, we control how much data movement occurs. With implicit data movement, the system handles this for us, but it might not do it as efficiently. The DPC++ runtime is not an oracle—it cannot predict what data an application will access before it does it. Additionally, pointer analysis remains a very difficult problem for compilers, which may not be able to accurately analyze and identify every allocation that might be used inside a kernel. Consequently, implementations of the mechanisms for implicit data movement may make different decisions based on the capabilities of the device that supports USM, which affects both how shared allocations can be used and how they perform.

If a device is very capable, it might be able to migrate memory on demand. In this case, data movement would occur after the host or device attempts to access an allocation that is not currently in the desired location. On-demand data greatly simplifies programming as it provides the desired semantic that a USM shared pointer can be accessed anywhere and just work. If a device cannot support on-demand migration (Chapter 12 explains how to query a device for capabilities), it might still be able to guarantee the same semantics with extra *restrictions* on how shared pointers can be used.

The restricted form of USM shared allocations governs when and where shared pointers may be accessed and how big shared allocations can be. If a device cannot migrate memory on demand, that means the runtime must be conservative and assume that a kernel might access any allocation in its device attached memory. This brings a couple of consequences.

First, it means that the host and device should not try to access a shared allocation at the same time. Applications should instead alternate access in phases. The host can access an allocation, then a kernel can compute using that data, and finally the host can read the results.

Without this restriction, the host is free to access different parts of an allocation than a kernel is currently touching. Such concurrent access typically happens at the granularity of a device memory page. The host could access one page, while the device accesses another. Atomically accessing the same piece of data will be covered in Chapter 19.

The next consequence of this restricted form of shared allocations is that allocations are limited by the total amount of memory attached to a device. If a device cannot migrate memory on demand, it cannot migrate data to the host to make room to bring in different data. If a device does support on-demand migration, it is possible to *oversubscribe* its attached memory, allowing a kernel to compute on more data than the device's memory could normally contain, although this flexibility may come with a performance penalty due to extra data movement.

Fine-Grained Control

When a device supports on-demand migration of shared allocations, data movement occurs after memory is accessed in a location where it is not currently resident. However, a kernel can stall while waiting for the data movement to complete. The next statement it executes may even cause more data movement to occur and introduce additional latency to the kernel execution.

DPC++ gives us a way to modify the performance of the automatic migration mechanisms. It does this by defining two functions: `prefetch` and `mem_advise`. Figure 6-8 shows a simple utilization of each. These functions let us give hints to the runtime about how kernels will access data so that the runtime can choose to start moving data *before* a kernel tries to access it. Note that this example uses the queue shortcut methods that directly invoke `parallel_for` on the `queue` object instead of inside a lambda passed to the `submit` method (a command group).

```
// Appropriate values depend on your HW
constexpr int BLOCK_SIZE = 42;
constexpr int NUM_BLOCKS = 2500;
constexpr int N = NUM_BLOCKS * BLOCK_SIZE;

queue Q;
int *data = malloc_shared<int>(N, Q);
int *read_only_data = malloc_shared<int>(BLOCK_SIZE, Q);

// Never updated after initialization
for (int i = 0; i < BLOCK_SIZE; i++)
  read_only_data[i] = i;

// Mark this data as "read only" so the runtime can copy it
// to the device instead of migrating it from the host.
// Real values will be documented by your DPC++ backend.
int HW_SPECIFIC_ADVICE_RO = 0;

Q.mem_advise(read_only_data, BLOCK_SIZE, HW_SPECIFIC_ADVICE_RO);

event e = Q.prefetch(data, BLOCK_SIZE);

for (int b = 0; b < NUM_BLOCKS; b++) {
  Q.parallel_for(range{BLOCK_SIZE}, e, [=](id<1> i) {
    data[b * BLOCK_SIZE + i] += data[i];
  });
  if ((b + 1) < NUM_BLOCKS) {
    // Prefetch next block
    e = Q.prefetch(data + (b + 1) * BLOCK_SIZE, BLOCK_SIZE);
  }
}

Q.wait();

free(data, Q);
free(read_only_data, Q);
```

Figure 6-8. *Fine-grained control via* `prefetch` *and* `mem_advise`

The simplest way for us to do this is by invoking `prefetch`. This function is invoked as a member function of the `handler` or queue class and takes a base pointer and number of bytes. This lets us inform the runtime that certain data is about to be used on a device so that it can eagerly start migrating it. Ideally, we would issue these prefetch hints early enough such that by the time the kernel touches the data, it is already resident on the device, eliminating the latency we previously described.

The other function provided by DPC++ is mem_advise. This function allows us to provide device-specific hints about how memory will be used in kernels. An example of such possible *advice* that we could specify is that the data will only be read in a kernel, not written. In that case, the system could realize it could copy, or duplicate, the data on the device, so that the host's version does not need to be updated after the kernel is complete. However, the *advice* passed to mem_advise is specific to a particular device, so be sure to check the documentation for hardware before using this function.

Queries

Finally, not all devices support every feature of USM. We should not assume that all USM features are available if we want our programs to be portable across different devices. USM defines several things that we can query. These queries can be separated into two categories: pointer queries and device capability queries. Figure 6-9 shows a simple utilization of each.

The pointer queries in USM answer two questions. The first question is "What type of USM allocation does this pointer point to?" The get_pointer_type function takes a pointer and DPC++ context and returns a result of type usm::alloc, which can have four possible values: *host*, *device*, *shared*, or *unknown*. The second question is "What device was this USM pointer allocated against?" We can pass a pointer and a context to the function get_pointer_device and get back a device object. This is mostly used with device or shared USM allocations since it does not make much sense with host allocations.

The second type of query provided by USM concerns the capabilities of a device. USM extends the list of device information descriptors that can be queried by calling get_info on a device object. These queries can be used to test which types of USM allocations are supported by a device. Additionally, we can query if shared allocations are restricted on the

CHAPTER 6 UNIFIED SHARED MEMORY

device in the ways we previously described in this chapter. The full list of queries is shown in Figure 6-10. In Chapter 12, we will look at the query mechanism in more detail.

```
constexpr int N = 42;

template <typename T> void foo(T data, id<1> i) { data[i] = N; }

queue Q;
auto dev = Q.get_device();
auto ctxt = Q.get_context();
bool usm_shared = dev.get_info<dinfo::usm_shared_allocations>();
bool usm_device = dev.get_info<dinfo::usm_device_allocations>();
bool use_USM = usm_shared || usm_device;

if (use_USM) {
  int *data;
  if (usm_shared)
    data = malloc_shared<int>(N, Q);
  else /* use device allocations */
    data = malloc_device<int>(N, Q);

  std::cout << "Using USM with "
            << ((get_pointer_type(data, ctxt) == usm::alloc::shared)
                ? "shared"
                : "device")
            << " allocations on "
            << get_pointer_device(data, ctxt).get_info<dinfo::name>()
            << "\n";

  Q.parallel_for(N, [=](id<1> i) { foo(data, i); });
  Q.wait();
  free(data, Q);
} else /* use buffers */ {
  buffer<int, 1> data{range{N}};
  Q.submit([&](handler &h) {
    accessor a(data, h);
    h.parallel_for(N, [=](id<1> i) {
      foo(a, i); });
  });
  Q.wait();
}
```

Figure 6-9. Queries on USM pointers and devices

Device Descriptor	Type	Description
info::device::usm_device_allocations	bool	Returns true if this device supports device allocations
info::device::usm_host_allocations	bool	Returns true if this device can access host allocations
info::device::usm_shared_allocations	bool	Returns true if this device supports shared allocations
info::device::usm_restricted_shared_allocations	bool	Returns true if shared allocations are governed by the restrictions described in this chapter

Figure 6-10. USM device information descriptors

Summary

In this chapter, we've described Unified Shared Memory, a pointer-based strategy for data management. We covered the three types of allocations that USM defines. We discussed all the different ways that we can allocate and deallocate memory with USM and how data movement can be either explicitly controlled by us (the programmers) for device allocations or implicitly controlled by the system for shared allocations. Finally, we discussed how to query the different USM capabilities that a device supports and how to query information about USM pointers in a program.

Since we have not discussed synchronization in this book in detail yet, there is more on USM in later chapters when we discuss scheduling, communications, and synchronization. Specifically, we cover these additional considerations for USM in Chapters 8, 9, and 19.

In the next chapter, we will cover the second strategy for data management: buffers.

 **Open Access** This chapter is licensed under the terms of the Creative Commons Attribution 4.0 International License (http://creativecommons.org/licenses/by/4.0/), which permits use, sharing, adaptation, distribution and reproduction in any medium or format, as long as you give appropriate credit to the original author(s) and the source, provide a link to the Creative Commons license and indicate if changes were made.

The images or other third party material in this chapter are included in the chapter's Creative Commons license, unless indicated otherwise in a credit line to the material. If material is not included in the chapter's Creative Commons license and your intended use is not permitted by statutory regulation or exceeds the permitted use, you will need to obtain permission directly from the copyright holder.

CHAPTER 7

Buffers

In this chapter, we will learn about the buffer abstraction. We learned about Unified Shared Memory (USM), the pointer-based strategy for data management, in the previous chapter. USM forces us to think about where memory lives and what should be accessible where. The buffer abstraction is a higher-level model that hides this from the programmer. Buffers simply represent data, and it becomes the job of the runtime to manage how the data is stored and moved in memory.

This chapter presents an alternative approach to managing our data. The choice between buffers and USM often comes down to personal preference and the style of existing code, and applications are free to mix and match the two styles in representation of different data within the application.

CHAPTER 7   BUFFERS

USM simply exposes different abstractions for memory. USM has pointers, and buffers are a higher-level abstraction. The abstraction level of buffers allows the data contained within to be used on any device within the application, where the runtime manages whatever is needed to make that data available. Choices are good, so let's dive into buffers.

We will look more closely at how buffers are created and used. A discussion of *buffers* would not be complete without also discussing the *accessor*. While buffers abstract how we represent and store data in a program, we do not directly access the data using the buffer. Instead, we use accessor objects that inform the runtime how we intend to use the data we are accessing, and accessors are tightly coupled to the powerful data dependence mechanisms within task graphs. After we cover all the things we can do with buffers, we will also explore how to create and use accessors in our programs.

Buffers

A buffer is a high-level abstraction for data. Buffers are not necessarily tied to a single location or virtual memory address. Indeed, the runtime is free to use many different locations in memory (even across different devices) to represent a buffer, but the runtime must be sure to always give us a consistent view of the data. A buffer is accessible on the host and on any device.

```
template <typename T, int Dimensions, AllocatorT allocator>
class buffer;
```

***Figure 7-1.** Buffer class definition*

The `buffer` class is a template class with three template arguments, as shown in Figure 7-1. The first template argument is the type of the object that the buffer will contain. This type must be *trivially copyable* as defined by C++, which basically means that it is safe to copy this object byte by byte without using any special copy or move constructors. The next template argument is an integer describing the dimensionality of the buffer. The final template argument is optional, and the default value is usually what is used. This argument specifies a C++-style allocator class that is used to perform any memory allocations on the host that are needed for the buffer. First, we will examine the many ways that buffer objects can be created.

Creation

In the following figures, we show several ways in which buffer objects can be created. The choice of how to create buffers in application code is a combination of how the buffer needs to be used and personal coding preferences. Let's walk through the example and look at each instance.

```
// Create a buffer of 2x5 ints using the default allocator
buffer<int, 2, buffer_allocator> b1{range<2>{2, 5}};

// Create a buffer of 2x5 ints using the default allocator
// and CTAD for range
buffer<int, 2> b2{range{2, 5}};

// Create a buffer of 20 floats using a
// default-constructed std::allocator
buffer<float, 1, std::allocator<float>> b3{range{20}};

// Create a buffer of 20 floats using a passed-in allocator
std::allocator<float> myFloatAlloc;
buffer<float, 1, std::allocator<float>> b4{range(20), myFloatAlloc};
```

Figure 7-2. Creating buffers, Part 1

The first buffer we create in Figure 7-2, b1, is a two-dimensional buffer of ten integers. We explicitly pass all template arguments, even explicitly passing the default value of buffer_allocator as the allocator type. However, using modern C++, we can express this much more compactly. Buffer b2 is also a two-dimensional buffer of ten integers using the default allocator. Here we make use of C++17's class template argument deduction (CTAD) to automatically infer template arguments we have to express.

CTAD is an all-or-none tool—it must either infer every template argument for a class or infer none of them. In this case, we use the fact that we are initializing b2 with a range that takes two arguments to infer that it is a two-dimensional range. The allocator template argument has a default value, so we do not need to explicitly list it when creating the buffer.

With buffer b3, we create a buffer of 20 floats and use a default-constructed std::allocator<float> to allocate any necessary memory on the host. When using a custom allocator type with a buffer, we often want to pass an actual allocator object to the buffer to use instead of the default-constructed one. Buffer b4 shows how to do this, taking the allocator object after the range in the call to its constructor.

For the first four buffers in our example, we let the buffer allocate any memory it needs and do not initialize that data with any values at the time of their creation. It is a common pattern to use buffers to effectively wrap existing C++ allocations, which may already have been initialized with data. We can do this by passing a source of initial values to the buffer constructor. Doing so allows us to do several things, which we will see with the next example.

```
// Create a buffer of 4 doubles and initialize it from a host pointer
double myDoubles[4] = {1.1, 2.2, 3.3, 4.4};
buffer b5{myDoubles, range{4}};

// Create a buffer of 5 doubles and initialize it from a host pointer
// to const double
const double myConstDbls[5] = {1.0, 2.0, 3.0, 4.0, 5.0};
buffer b6{myConstDbls, range{5}};

// Create a buffer from a shared pointer to int
auto sharedPtr = std::make_shared<int>(42);
buffer b7{sharedPtr, range{1}};
```

Figure 7-3. Creating buffers, Part 2

In Figure 7-3, buffer b5 creates a one-dimensional buffer of four doubles. We pass the host pointer to the C array myDoubles to the buffer constructor in addition to the range that specifies the size of the buffer. Here we can make full use of CTAD to infer all the template arguments of our buffer. The host pointer we pass points to doubles, which gives us the data type of our buffer. The number of dimensions is automatically inferred from the one-dimensional range, which itself is inferred because it is created with only one number. Finally, the default allocator is used, so we do not have to specify that.

Passing a host pointer has a few ramifications of which we should be aware. By passing a pointer to host memory, we are promising the runtime that we will not try to access the host memory during the lifetime of the buffer. This is not (and cannot be) enforced by a SYCL implementation—it is our responsibility to ensure that we do not break this contract. One reason that we should not try to access this memory while the buffer is alive is that the buffer may choose to use different memory on the host to represent the buffer content, often for optimization reasons. If it does so, the values will be copied into this new memory from the host pointer. If subsequent kernels modify the buffer, the original host pointer will not reflect the updated values until certain specified synchronization points. We will talk more about when data gets written back to a host pointer later in this chapter.

Buffer b6 is very similar to buffer b5 with one major difference. This time, we are initializing the buffer with a pointer to `const double`. This means that we can only read values through the host pointer and not write them. However, the type for our buffer in this example is still `double`, not `const double` since the deduction guides do not take `const`-ness into consideration. This means that the buffer may be written to by a kernel, but we must use a different mechanism to update the host after the buffer has outlived its use (covered later in this chapter).

Buffers can also be initialized using C++ shared pointer objects. This is useful if our application already uses shared pointers, as this method of initialization will properly count the reference and ensure that the memory is not deallocated. Buffer b7 initializes a buffer from a single integer and initializes it using a shared pointer.

Chapter 7 Buffers

```
// Create a buffer of ints from an input iterator
std::vector<int> myVec;
buffer b8{myVec.begin(), myVec.end()};
buffer b9{myVec};

// Create a buffer of 2x5 ints and 2 non-overlapping
// sub-buffers of 5 ints.
buffer<int, 2> b10{range{2, 5}};
buffer b11{b10, id{0, 0}, range{1, 5}};
buffer b12{b10, id{1, 0}, range{1, 5}};
```

Figure 7-4. Creating buffers, Part 3

Containers are commonly used in modern C++ applications, with examples including std::array, std::vector, std::list, or std::map. We can initialize one-dimensional buffers using containers in two different ways. The first way, as shown in Figure 7-4 by buffer b8, uses input iterators. Instead of a host pointer, we pass two iterators to the buffer constructor, one representing the beginning of the data and another representing the end. The size of the buffer is computed as the number of elements returned by incrementing the start iterator until it equals the end iterator. This is useful for any data type that implements the C++ InputIterator interface. If the container object that provides the initial values for a buffer is also contiguous, then we can use an even simpler form to create the buffer. Buffer b9 creates a buffer from a vector simply by passing the vector to the constructor. The size of the buffer is determined by the size of the container being used to initialize it, and the type for the buffer data comes from the type of the container data. Creating buffers using this approach is common and recommended from containers such as std::vector and std::array.

The final example of buffer creation illustrates another feature of the buffer class. It is possible to create a view of a buffer from another buffer, or a sub-buffer. A sub-buffer requires three things: a reference to a parent buffer, a base index, and the range of the sub-buffer. A sub-buffer cannot be created from a sub-buffer. Multiple sub-buffers can be created from the same buffer, and they are free to overlap. Buffer b10 is created exactly like buffer b2, a two-dimensional buffer of integers with five integers per row. Next, we create two sub-buffers from buffer b10, sub-buffers b11 and b12. Sub-buffer b11 starts at index (0,0) and contains every element in the first row. Similarly, sub-buffer b12 starts at index (1,0) and contains every element in the second row. This yields two disjoint sub-buffers. Since the sub-buffers do not overlap, different kernels could operate on the different sub-buffers concurrently, but we will talk more about scheduling execution graphs and dependences in the next chapter.

```
queue Q;
int my_ints[42];

// create a buffer of 42 ints
buffer<int> b{range(42)};

// create a buffer of 42 ints, initialize
// with a host pointer, and add the
// use_host_pointer property
buffer b1{my_ints, range(42),
  {property::buffer::use_host_ptr{}}};

// create a buffer of 42 ints, initialize pointer,
// with a host and add the use_mutex property
std::mutex myMutex;
buffer b2{my_ints, range(42),
  {property::buffer::use_mutex{myMutex}}};

// Retrive a pointer to the mutex used by this buffer
auto mutexPtr =
  b2.get_property<property::buffer::use_mutex>().
    get_mutex_ptr();

// lock the mutex until we exit scope
std::lock_guard<std::mutex> guard{*mutexPtr};

// create a context-bound buffer of 42 ints,
// initialized from a host pointer
buffer b3{my_ints, range(42),
  {property::buffer::context_bound{Q.get_context()}}};
```

Figure 7-5. *Buffer properties*

CHAPTER 7 BUFFERS

Buffer Properties

Buffers can also be created with special properties that alter their behavior. In Figure 7-5, we will walk through an example of the three different optional buffer properties and discuss how they might be used. Note that these properties are relatively uncommon in most codes.

use_host_ptr

The first property that may be optionally specified during buffer creation is use_host_ptr. When present, this property requires the buffer to not allocate any memory on the host, and any allocator passed or specified on buffer construction is effectively ignored. Instead, the buffer must use the memory pointed to by a host pointer that is passed to the constructor. Note that this does not require the device to use the same memory to hold the buffer's data. A device is free to cache the contents of a buffer in its attached memory. Also note that this property may only be used when a host pointer is passed to the constructor. This option can be useful when the program wants full control over all host memory allocations.

In our example in Figure 7-5, we create a buffer b as we saw in our previous examples. We next create buffer b1 and initialize it with a pointer to myInts. We also pass the property use_host_ptr, which means that buffer b1 will only use the memory pointed to by myInts and not allocate any additional temporary storage.

use_mutex

The next property, use_mutex, concerns fine-grained sharing of memory between buffers and host code. Buffer b2 is created using this property. The property takes a reference to a mutex object that can later be queried from the buffer as we see in the example. This property also requires a host pointer be passed to the constructor, and it lets the runtime determine when it is safe to access updated values in host code through the provided host pointer. We cannot lock the mutex until the runtime guarantees that the host pointer sees the latest value of the buffer. While this could be combined with the use_host_ptr property, it is not required. use_mutex is a mechanism that allows host code to access data within a buffer while the buffer is still alive and without using the host accessor mechanism (described later). In general, the host accessor mechanism should be preferred unless we have a specific reason to use a mutex, particularly because there are no guarantees on how long it will take before the mutex will be successfully locked and the data ready for use by host code.

context_bound

The final property is shown in the creation of buffer b3 in our example. Here, our buffer of 42 integers is created with the context_bound property. The property takes a reference to a context object. Normally, a buffer is free to be used on any device or context. However, if this property is used, it locks the buffer to the specified context. Attempting to use the buffer on another context will result in a runtime error. This could be useful for debugging programs by identifying cases where a kernel might be submitted to the wrong queue, for instance. In practice, we do not expect to see this property used in many programs, and the ability for buffers to be accessed on any device in any context is one of the most powerful properties of the buffer abstraction (which this property undoes).

What Can We Do with a Buffer?

Many things can be done with buffer objects. We can query characteristics of a buffer, determine if and where any data is written back to host memory after the buffer is destroyed, or reinterpret a buffer as one with different characteristics. One thing that cannot be done, however, is to directly access the data that a buffer represents. Instead, we must create accessor objects to access the data, and we will learn all about this later in the chapter.

Examples of things that can be queried about a buffer include its range, the total number of data elements it represents, and the number of bytes required to store its elements. We can also query which allocator object is being used by the buffer and whether the buffer is a sub-buffer or not.

Updating host memory when a buffer is destroyed is an important aspect to consider when using buffers. Depending on how a buffer is created, host memory may or may not be updated with the results of a computation after buffer destruction. If a buffer is created and initialized from a host pointer to non-`const` data, that same pointer is updated with the updated data when the buffer is destroyed. However, there is also a way to update host memory regardless of how a buffer was created. The `set_final_data` method is a template method of `buffer` that can accept either a raw pointer, a C++ `OutputIterator`, or a `std::weak_ptr`. When the buffer is destroyed, data contained by the buffer will be written to the host using the supplied location. Note that if the buffer was created and initialized from a host pointer to non-`const` data, it's as if `set_final_data` was called with that pointer. Technically, a raw pointer is a special case of an `OutputIterator`. If the parameter passed to `set_final_data` is a `std::weak_ptr`, the data is not written to the host if the pointer has expired or has already been deleted. Whether or not writeback occurs can also be controlled by the `set_write_back` method.

Accessors

Data represented by a buffer cannot be directly accessed through the buffer object. Instead, we must create accessor objects that allow us to safely access a buffer's data. Accessors inform the runtime where and how we want to access data, allowing the runtime to ensure that the right data is in the right place at the right time. This is a very powerful concept, especially when combined with the task graph that schedules kernels for execution based in part on data dependences.

CHAPTER 7 BUFFERS

Accessor objects are instantiated from the templated `accessor` class. This class has five template parameters. The first parameter is the type of the data being accessed. This should be the same as the type of data being stored by the corresponding buffer. Similarly, the second parameter describes the dimensionality of the data and buffer and defaults to a value of one.

Mode	Description
read	Read-only access
Write	Write-only access preserving previous contents
read_Write	Read and write access

Figure 7-6. *Access modes*

The next three template parameters are unique to accessors. The first of these is the *access mode*. The access mode describes how we intend to use an accessor in a program. The possible modes are listed in Figure 7-6. We will learn how these modes are used to order the execution of kernels and perform data movement in Chapter 8. The access mode parameter does have a default value if none is specified or automatically inferred. If we do not specify otherwise, accessors will default to read_write access mode for non-const data types and read for const data types. These defaults are always correct, but providing more accurate information may improve a runtime's ability to perform optimizations. When starting application development, it is safe and concise to simply not specify an access mode, and we can then refine the access modes based on profiling of performance-critical regions of the application.

CHAPTER 7 BUFFERS

Target	Description
global_buffer	Access a buffer through global memory
constant_buffer	Access a buffer through constant memory
local	Access work-group local memory
unsampled_image	Access an unsampled_image
sampled_image	Access a sampled_image
host_buffer	Access a buffer on the host
host_unsampled_image	Access an unsampled_image on the host
host_sampled_image	Access a sample_image on the host

Figure 7-7. Access targets

The next template parameter is the *access target*. Buffers are an abstraction of data and do not describe where and how data is stored. The access target describes both what type of data, broadly speaking, we are accessing and which memory will contain that data. The possible access targets are listed in Figure 7-7. The type of data is one of two types: a buffer or an image. Images are discussed in this book, but we can think of them as special-purpose buffers that provide domain-specific operations for image processing.

The other aspect of an access target is what we should focus on. Devices may have different types of memories available. These memories are represented by different address spaces. The most commonly used type of memory will be a device's global memory. Most accessors inside kernels will use this target, so global is the default target (if we specify nothing). Constant and local buffers use special-purpose memories. Constant memory, as its name implies, is used to store values that are constant during the lifetime of a kernel invocation. Local memory is special memory available to a work-group that is not accessible to other work-groups. We will learn how to use local memory in Chapter 9.

The other target of note is the host buffer, which is the target used when accessing a buffer on the host. The default value for this template parameter is `global_buffer`, so in most cases we do not need to specify a target within our code.

The final template parameter governs whether an accessor is a *placeholder* accessor or not. This is not a parameter that a programmer is likely to ever directly set. A placeholder accessor is one that is declared outside of a command group but meant to be used to access data on a device inside a kernel. We will see what differentiates a placeholder accessor from one that is not once we look at examples of accessor creation.

While accessors can be extracted from a buffer object using its `get_access` method, it's simpler to directly create (construct) them. This is the style we will use in upcoming examples since it is very simple to understand and is compact.

Accessor Creation

Figure 7-8 shows an example program with everything that we need to get started with accessors. In this example, we have three buffers, A, B, and C. The first task we submit to the queue creates accessors to each buffer and defines a kernel that uses these accessors to initialize the buffers with some values. Each accessor is constructed with a reference to the buffer it will access as well as the handler object defined by the command group we're submitting to the queue. This effectively binds the accessor to the kernel we're submitting as part of the command group. Regular accessors are device accessors since they, by default, target global buffers stored in device memory. This is the most common use case.

```
constexpr int N = 42;

queue Q;

// create 3 buffers of 42 ints
buffer<int> A{range{N}};
buffer<int> B{range{N}};
buffer<int> C{range{N}};
accessor pC{C};

Q.submit([&](handler &h) {
  accessor aA{A, h};
  accessor aB{B, h};
  accessor aC{C, h};
  h.parallel_for(N, [=](id<1> i) {
    aA[i] = 1;
    aB[i] = 40;
    aC[i] = 0;
  });
});

Q.submit([&](handler &h) {
  accessor aA{A, h};
  accessor aB{B, h};
  accessor aC{C, h};
  h.parallel_for(N, [=](id<1> i) {
    aC[i] += aA[i] + aB[i]; });
});

Q.submit([&](handler &h) {
  h.require(pC);
  h.parallel_for(N, [=](id<1> i) {
    pC[i]++; });
});

host_accessor result{C};
for (int i = 0; i < N; i++)
  assert(result[i] == N);
```

Figure 7-8. *Simple accessor creation*

The second task we submit also defines three accessors to the buffers. We then use those accessors in the second kernel to add the elements of buffers A and B into buffer C. Since this second task operates on the same data as the first one, the runtime will execute this task after the first one is complete. We will learn about this in detail in the next chapter.

The third task shows how we can use a placeholder accessor. The accessor pC is declared at the beginning of the example in Figure 7-8 after we create our buffers. Note that the constructor is not passed a handler object since we don't have one to pass. This lets us create a reusable accessor object ahead of time. However, in order to use this accessor inside a kernel, we need to bind it to a command group during submission. We do this using the handler object's `require` method. Once we have bound our placeholder accessor to a command group, we can then use it inside a kernel as we would any other accessor.

Finally, we create a `host_accessor` object in order to read the results of our computations back on the host. Note that this is a different type than we used inside our kernels. Host accessors use a separate `host_accessor` class to allow proper inference of template arguments, providing a simple interface. Note that the host accessor `result` in this example also does not take a handler object since we once again do not have one to pass. The special type for host accessors also lets us disambiguate them from placeholders. An important aspect of host accessors is that the constructor only completes when the data is available for use on the host, which means that construction of a host accessor can appear to take a long time. The constructor must wait for any kernels to finish executing that produce the data to be copied as well as for the copy itself to finish. Once the host accessor construction is complete, it is safe to use the data that it accesses directly on the host, and we are guaranteed that the latest version of the data is available to us on the host.

While this example is perfectly correct, we don't say anything about how we intend to use our accessors when we create them. Instead, we use the default access mode, which is `read-write`, for the non-`const int` data in our buffers. This is potentially overconservative and may create unnecessary dependences between operations or superfluous data movement. A runtime may be able to do a better job if it has more information about how we plan to use the accessors we create. However, before we go through an example where we do this, we should first introduce one more tool—the access tag.

CHAPTER 7 BUFFERS

Access tags are a compact way to express the desired combination of access mode and target for an accessor. Access tags, when used, are passed as a parameter to an accessor's constructor. The possible tags are shown in Figure 7-9. When an accessor is constructed with a tag parameter, C++ CTAD can then properly deduce the desired access mode and target, providing an easy way to override the default values for those template parameters. We could also manually specify the desired template parameters, but tags provide a simpler, more compact way to get the same result without spelling out fully templated accessors.

Tag type	Tag value	Access mode	Access target
mode_tag_t	read_write	read_write	default
mode_tag_t	read_only	read	default
mode_tag_t	write_only	write	default
mode_target_tag_t	read_constant	read	constant_buffer

Figure 7-9. Access tags

Let's take our previous example and rewrite it to add access tags. This new and improved example is shown in Figure 7-10.

```
constexpr int N = 42;

queue Q;

// Create 3 buffers of 42 ints
buffer<int> A{range{N}};
buffer<int> B{range{N}};
buffer<int> C{range{N}};

accessor pC{C};

Q.submit([&](handler &h) {
  accessor aA{A, h, write_only, noinit};
  accessor aB{B, h, write_only, noinit};
  accessor aC{C, h, write_only, noinit};
  h.parallel_for(N, [=](id<1> i) {
    aA[i] = 1;
    aB[i] = 40;
    aC[i] = 0;
  });
});

Q.submit([&](handler &h) {
  accessor aA{A, h, read_only};
  accessor aB{B, h, read_only};
  accessor aC{C, h, read_write};
  h.parallel_for(N, [=](id<1> i) {
    aC[i] += aA[i] + aB[i]; });
  });

Q.submit([&](handler &h) {
  h.require(pC);
  h.parallel_for(N, [=](id<1> i) {
    pC[i]++; });
});

host_accessor result{C, read_only};

for (int i = 0; i < N; i++)
  assert(result[i] == N);
```

Figure 7-10. *Accessor creation with specified usage*

We begin by declaring our buffers as we did in Figure 7-8. We also create our placeholder accessor that we'll use later. Let's now look at the first task we submit to the queue. Previously, we created our accessors by passing a reference to a buffer and the handler object for the command group. Now, we add two extra parameters to our constructor calls. The first new parameter is an access tag. Since this kernel is writing the initial values for our buffers, we use the `write_only` access tag. This lets the runtime know that this kernel is producing new data and will not read from the buffer.

The second new parameter is an optional accessor property, similar to the optional properties for buffers that we saw earlier in the chapter. The property we pass, `noinit`, lets the runtime know that the previous contents of the buffer can be discarded. This is useful because it can let the runtime eliminate unnecessary data movement. In this example, since the first task is writing the initial values for our buffers, it's unnecessary for the runtime to copy the uninitialized host memory to the device before the kernel executes. The `noinit` property is useful for this example, but it should not be used for read-modify-write cases or kernels where only some values in a buffer may be updated.

The second task we submit to our queue is identical to before, but now we add access tags to our accessors. Here, we add the tags `read_only` to accessors aA and aB to let the runtime know that we will only read the values of buffers A and B through these accessors. The third accessor, aC, gets the `read_write` access tag since we accumulate the sum of the elements of A and B into C. We explicitly use the tag in the example to be consistent, but this is unnecessary since the default access mode is `read_write`.

The default usage is retained in the third task where we use our placeholder accessor. This remains unchanged from the simplified example we saw in Figure 7-8. Our final accessor, the host accessor `result`, now receives an access tag when we create it. Since we only read the final values on the host, we pass the `read_only` tag to the constructor. If we rewrote the program in such a way that the host accessor was destroyed, launching another kernel that operated on buffer C would not require it to be written back to the device since the `read_only` tag lets the runtime know that it will not be modified by the host.

What Can We Do with an Accessor?

Many things can be done with an accessor object. However, the most important thing we can do is spelled out in the accessor's name—access data. This is usually done through one of the accessor's [] operators. We use the [] operator in our examples in Figures 7-8 and 7-10. This operator takes either an id object that can properly index multidimensional data or a single size_t. The second case is used when an accessor has more than one dimension. It returns an object that is then meant to be indexed again with [] until we arrive at a scalar value, and this would be of the form a[i][j] in a two-dimensional case. Remember that the ordering of accessor dimensions follows the convention of C++ where the rightmost dimension is the unit-stride dimension (iterates "fastest").

An accessor can also return a pointer to the underlying data. This pointer can be accessed directly following normal C++ rules. Note that there can be additional complexity involved with respect to the address space of this pointer. Address spaces and their quirks will be discussed in a later chapter.

Many things can also be queried from an accessor object. Examples include the number of elements accessible through the accessor, the size in bytes of the region of the buffer it covers, or the range of data accessible.

Accessors provide a similar interface to C++ containers and may be used in many situations where containers may be passed. The container interface supported by accessors includes the data method, which is equivalent to get_pointer, and several flavors of forward and backward iterators.

CHAPTER 7 BUFFERS

Summary

In this chapter, we have learned about buffers and accessors. Buffers are an abstraction of data that hides the underlying details of memory management from the programmer. They do this in order to provide a simpler, higher-level abstraction. We went through several examples that showed us the different ways to construct buffers as well as the different optional properties that can be specified to alter their behavior. We learned how to initialize a buffer with data from host memory as well as how to write data back to host memory when we are done with a buffer.

Since we should not access buffers directly, we learned how to access the data in a buffer by using accessor objects. We learned the difference between device accessors and host accessors. We discussed the different access modes and targets and how they inform the runtime how and where an accessor will be used by the program. We showed the simplest way to use accessors using the default access modes and targets, and we learned how to distinguish between a placeholder accessor and one that is not. We then saw how to further optimize the example program by giving the runtime more information about our accessor usage by adding access tags to our accessor declarations. Finally, we covered many of the different ways that accessors can be used in a program.

In the next chapter, we will learn in greater detail how the runtime can use the information we give it through accessors to schedule the execution of different kernels. We will also see how this information informs the runtime about when and how the data in buffers needs to be copied between the host and a device. We will learn how we can explicitly control data movement involving buffers—and USM allocations too.

CHAPTER 7   BUFFERS

 **Open Access** This chapter is licensed under the terms of the Creative Commons Attribution 4.0 International License (http://creativecommons.org/licenses/by/4.0/), which permits use, sharing, adaptation, distribution and reproduction in any medium or format, as long as you give appropriate credit to the original author(s) and the source, provide a link to the Creative Commons license and indicate if changes were made.

The images or other third party material in this chapter are included in the chapter's Creative Commons license, unless indicated otherwise in a credit line to the material. If material is not included in the chapter's Creative Commons license and your intended use is not permitted by statutory regulation or exceeds the permitted use, you will need to obtain permission directly from the copyright holder.

193

CHAPTER 8

Scheduling Kernels and Data Movement

We need to discuss our role as the concert master for our parallel programs. The proper orchestration of a parallel program is a thing of beauty—code running full speed without waiting for data, because we have arranged for all data to arrive and depart at the proper times. Code well-decomposed to keep the hardware maximally busy. It is the thing that dreams are made of!

Life in the fast lanes—not just one lane!—demands that we take our work as the conductor seriously. In order to do that, we can think of our job in terms of task graphs.

Therefore, in this chapter, we will cover task graphs, the mechanism that is used to run complex sequences of kernels correctly and efficiently. There are two things that need sequencing in an application: kernels and data movement. Task graphs are the mechanism that we use to achieve proper sequencing.

First, we will quickly review how we can use dependences to order tasks from Chapter 3. Next, we will cover how the DPC++ runtime builds graphs. We will discuss the basic building block of DPC++ graphs, the command group. We will then illustrate the different ways we can build graphs of common patterns. We will also discuss how data movement, both explicit and implicit, is represented in graphs. Finally, we will discuss the various ways to synchronize our graphs with the host.

What Is Graph Scheduling?

In Chapter 3, we discussed data management and ordering the uses of data. That chapter described the key abstraction behind graphs in DPC++: dependences. Dependences between kernels are fundamentally based on what data a kernel accesses. A kernel needs to be certain that it reads the correct data before it can compute its output.

We described the three types of data dependences that are important for ensuring correct execution. The first, Read-after-Write (RAW), occurs when one task needs to read data produced by a different task. This type of dependence describes the flow of data between two kernels. The second type of dependence happens when one task needs to update data after another task has read it. We call that type of dependence a Write-after-Read (WAR) dependence. The final type of data dependence occurs when two tasks try to write the same data. This is known as a Write-after-Write (WAW) dependence.

Data dependences are the building blocks we will use to build graphs. This set of dependences is all we need to express both simple linear chains of kernels and large, complex graphs with hundreds of kernels with elaborate dependences. No matter which types of graph a computation needs, DPC++ graphs ensure that a program will execute correctly based on the expressed dependences. However, it is up to the programmer to make sure that a graph correctly expresses all the dependences in a program.

How Graphs Work in DPC++

A command group can contain three different things: an action, its dependences, and miscellaneous host code. Of these three things, the one that is always required is the action since without it, the command group really doesn't do anything. Most command groups will also express dependences, but there are cases where they may not. One such example is the first action submitted in a program. It does not depend on anything to begin execution; therefore, we would not specify any dependence. The other thing that can appear inside a command group is arbitrary C++ code that executes on the host. This is perfectly legal and can be useful to help specify the action or its dependences, and this code is executed while the command group is created (not later when the action is performed based on dependences having been met).

Command groups are typically expressed as a C++ lambda expression passed to the submit method. Command groups can also be expressed through shortcut methods on queue objects that take a kernel and set of event-based dependences.

Command Group Actions

There are two types of actions that may be performed by a command group: kernels and explicit memory operations. A command group may only perform a single action. As we've seen in earlier chapters, kernels are defined through calls to a `parallel_for` or `single_task` method and express computations that we want to perform on our devices. Operations for explicit data movement are the second type of action. Examples from USM include `memcpy`, `memset`, and `fill` operations. Examples from buffers include `copy`, `fill`, and `update_host`.

How Command Groups Declare Dependences

The other main component of a command group is the set of dependences that must be satisfied before the action defined by the group can execute. DPC++ allows these dependences to be specified in several ways.

If a program uses in-order DPC++ queues, the in-order semantics of the queue specify implicit dependences between successively enqueued command groups. One task cannot execute until the previously submitted task has completed.

Event-based dependences are another way to specify what must be complete before a command group may execute. These event-based dependences may be specified in two ways. The first way is used when a command group is specified as a lambda passed to a queue's `submit` method. In this case, the programmer invokes the `depends_on` method of the command group handler object, passing either an event or vector of events as parameter. The other way is used when a command group is created from the shortcut methods defined on the queue object. When the programmer directly invokes `parallel_for` or `single_task` on a queue, an event or vector of events may be passed as an extra parameter.

CHAPTER 8   SCHEDULING KERNELS AND DATA MOVEMENT

The last way that dependences may be specified is through the creation of accessor objects. Accessors specify how they will be used to read or write data in a buffer object, letting the runtime use this information to determine the data dependences that exist between different kernels. As we reviewed in the beginning of this chapter, examples of data dependences include one kernel reading data that another produces, two kernels writing the same data, or one kernel modifying data after another kernel reads it.

Examples

Now we will illustrate everything we've just learned with several examples. We will present how one might express two different dependence patterns in several ways. The two patterns we will illustrate are linear dependence chains where one task executes after another and a "Y" pattern where two independent tasks must execute before successive tasks.

Graphs for these dependence patterns can be seen in Figures 8-1 and 8-2. Figure 8-1 depicts a linear dependence chain. The first node represents the initialization of data, while the second node presents the reduction operation that will accumulate the data into a single result. Figure 8-2 depicts a "Y" pattern where we independently initialize two different pieces of data. After the data is initialized, an addition kernel will sum the two vectors together. Finally, the last node in the graph accumulates the result into a single value.

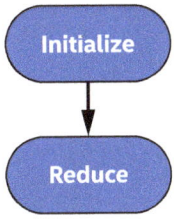

Figure 8-1. *Linear dependence chain graph*

For each pattern, we will show three different implementations. The first implementation will use in-order queues. The second will use event-based dependences. The last implementation will use buffers and accessors to express data dependences between command groups.

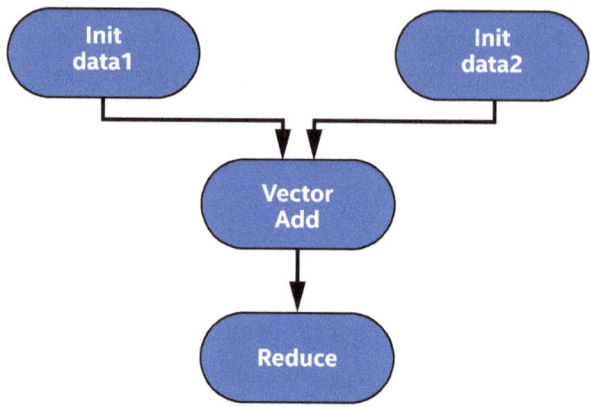

Figure 8-2. *"Y" pattern dependence graph*

```
constexpr int N = 42;

queue Q{property::queue::in_order()};

int *data = malloc_shared<int>(N, Q);

Q.parallel_for(N, [=](id<1> i) { data[i] = 1; });

Q.single_task([=]() {
  for (int i = 1; i < N; i++)
    data[0] += data[i];
});

Q.wait();

assert(data[0] == N);
```

Figure 8-3. *Linear dependence chain with in-order queues*

CHAPTER 8 SCHEDULING KERNELS AND DATA MOVEMENT

Figure 8-3 shows how to express a linear dependence chain using in-order queues. This example is very simple because the semantics of in-order queues already guarantee a sequential order of execution between command groups. The first kernel we submit initializes the elements of an array to 1. The next kernel then takes those elements and sums them together into the first element. Since our queue is in order, we do not need to do anything else to express that the second kernel should not execute until the first kernel has completed. Finally, we wait for the queue to finish executing all its tasks, and we check that we obtained the expected result.

```
constexpr int N = 42;
queue Q;

int *data = malloc_shared<int>(N, Q);

auto e = Q.parallel_for(N, [=](id<1> i) { data[i] = 1; });

Q.submit([&](handler &h) {
  h.depends_on(e);
  h.single_task([=]() {
    for (int i = 1; i < N; i++)
      data[0] += data[i];
  });
});

Q.wait();
assert(data[0] == N);
```

Figure 8-4. *Linear dependence chain with events*

Figure 8-4 shows the same example using an out-of-order queue and event-based dependences. Here, we capture the event returned by the first call to `parallel_for`. The second kernel is then able to specify a dependence on that event and the kernel execution it represents by passing it as a parameter to `depends_on`. We will see in Figure 8-6 how we could shorten the expression of the second kernel using one of the shortcut methods for defining kernels.

CHAPTER 8   SCHEDULING KERNELS AND DATA MOVEMENT

```
constexpr int N = 42;
queue Q;

buffer<int> data{range{N}};

Q.submit([&](handler &h) {
  accessor a{data, h};
  h.parallel_for(N, [=](id<1> i) { a[i] = 1; });
});

Q.submit([&](handler &h) {
  accessor a{data, h};
  h.single_task([=]() {
    for (int i = 1; i < N; i++)
      a[0] += a[i];
  });
});

host_accessor h_a{data};
assert(h_a[0] == N);
```

***Figure 8-5.** Linear dependence chain with buffers and accessors*

Figure 8-5 rewrites our linear dependence chain example using buffers and accessors instead of USM pointers. Here we once again use an out-of-order queue but use data dependences specified through accessors instead of event-based dependences to order the execution of the command groups. The second kernel reads the data produced by the first kernel, and the runtime can see this because we declare accessors based on the same underlying buffer object. Unlike the previous examples, we do not wait for the queue to finish executing all its tasks. Instead, we declare a host accessor that defines a data dependence between the output of the second kernel and our assertion that we computed the correct answer on the host. Note that while a host accessor gives us an up-to-date view of data on the host, it does not guarantee that the original host memory has been updated if any was specified when the buffer was created. We can't safely access the original host memory unless the buffer is first destroyed or unless we use a more advanced mechanism like the mutex mechanism described in Chapter 7.

CHAPTER 8 SCHEDULING KERNELS AND DATA MOVEMENT

```cpp
constexpr int N = 42;

queue Q{property::queue::in_order()};

int *data1 = malloc_shared<int>(N, Q);
int *data2 = malloc_shared<int>(N, Q);

Q.parallel_for(N, [=](id<1> i) { data1[i] = 1; });

Q.parallel_for(N, [=](id<1> i) { data2[i] = 2; });

Q.parallel_for(N, [=](id<1> i) { data1[i] += data2[i]; });

Q.single_task([=]() {
  for (int i = 1; i < N; i++)
    data1[0] += data1[i];

  data1[0] /= 3;
});

Q.wait();
assert(data1[0] == N);
```

Figure 8-6. *"Y" pattern with in-order queues*

Figure 8-6 shows how to express a "Y" pattern using in-order queues. In this example, we declare two arrays, data1 and data2. We then define two kernels that will each initialize one of the arrays. These kernels do not depend on each other, but because the queue is in order, the kernels must execute one after the other. Note that it would be perfectly legal to swap the order of these two kernels in this example. After the second kernel has executed, the third kernel adds the elements of the second array to those of the first array. The final kernel sums up the elements of the first array to compute the same result we did in our examples for linear dependence chains. This summation kernel depends on the previous kernel, but this linear chain is also captured by the in-order queue. Finally, we wait for all kernels to complete and validate that we successfully computed our magic number.

CHAPTER 8 SCHEDULING KERNELS AND DATA MOVEMENT

```
constexpr int N = 42;
queue Q;

int *data1 = malloc_shared<int>(N, Q);
int *data2 = malloc_shared<int>(N, Q);

auto e1 = Q.parallel_for(N,
            [=](id<1> i) { data1[i] = 1; });

auto e2 = Q.parallel_for(N,
            [=](id<1> i) { data2[i] = 2; });

auto e3 = Q.parallel_for(range{N}, {e1, e2},
            [=](id<1> i) { data1[i] += data2[i]; });

Q.single_task(e3, [=]() {
  for (int i = 1; i < N; i++)
    data1[0] += data1[i];

  data1[0] /= 3;
});

Q.wait();
assert(data1[0] == N);
```

Figure 8-7. *"Y" pattern with events*

Figure 8-7 shows our "Y" pattern example with out-of-order queues instead of in-order queues. Since the dependences are no longer implicit due to the order of the queue, we must explicitly specify the dependences between command groups using events. As in Figure 8-6, we begin by defining two independent kernels that have no initial dependences. We represent these kernels by two events, e1 and e2. When we define our third kernel, we must specify that it depends on the first two kernels. We do this by saying that it depends on events e1 and e2 to complete before it may execute. However, in this example, we use a shortcut form to specify these dependences instead of the handler's depends_on method. Here, we pass the events as an extra parameter to parallel_for. Since we want to pass multiple events at once, we use the form that accepts a std::vector of events, but luckily modern C++ simplifies this for us by automatically converting the expression {e1, e2} into the appropriate vector.

CHAPTER 8 SCHEDULING KERNELS AND DATA MOVEMENT

```cpp
constexpr int N = 42;
queue Q;

buffer<int> data1{range{N}};
buffer<int> data2{range{N}};

Q.submit([&](handler &h) {
  accessor a{data1, h};
  h.parallel_for(N, [=](id<1> i) { a[i] = 1; });
});

Q.submit([&](handler &h) {
  accessor b{data2, h};
  h.parallel_for(N, [=](id<1> i) { b[i] = 2; });
});

Q.submit([&](handler &h) {
  accessor a{data1, h};
  accessor b{data2, h, read_only};
  h.parallel_for(N, [=](id<1> i) { a[i] += b[i]; });
});

Q.submit([&](handler &h) {
  accessor a{data1, h};
  h.single_task([=]() {
    for (int i = 1; i < N; i++)
      a[0] += a[i];
    a[0] /= 3;
  });
});

host_accessor h_a{data1};
assert(h_a[0] == N);
```

Figure 8-8. *"Y" pattern with accessors*

In our final example, seen in Figure 8-8, we again replace USM pointers and events with buffers and accessors. This example represents the two arrays data1 and data2 as buffer objects. Our kernels no longer use the shortcut methods for defining kernels since we must associate accessors with a command group handler. Once again, the third kernel must capture the dependence on the first two kernels. Here this is accomplished by declaring accessors for our buffers. Since we have previously declared accessors for these buffers, the runtime is able to properly order the execution of these kernels. Additionally, we also provide extra information to the runtime here when we declare accessor b. We add the access tag read_only to let the runtime know that we're only going to read this data, not produce new values. As we saw in our buffer and accessor example for linear dependence chains, our final kernel orders itself by updating the values produced in the third kernel. We retrieve the final value of our computation by declaring a host accessor that will wait for the final kernel to finish executing before moving the data back to the host where we can read it and assert we computed the correct result.

When Are the Parts of a CG Executed?

Since task graphs are asynchronous, it makes sense to wonder when exactly command groups are executed. By now, it should be clear that kernels may be executed as soon as their dependences have been satisfied, but what happens with the host portion of a command group?

When a command group is submitted to a queue, it is executed immediately on the host (before the submit call returns). This host portion of the command group is executed only once. Any kernel or explicit data operation defined in the command group is enqueued for execution on the device.

Data Movement

Data movement is another very important aspect of graphs in DPC++ that is essential for understanding application performance. However, it can often be accidentally overlooked if data movement happens implicitly in a program, either using buffers and accessors or using USM shared allocations. Next, we will examine the different ways that data movement can affect graph execution in DPC++.

Explicit

Explicit data movement has the advantage that it appears *explicitly* in a graph, making it obvious for programmers what goes on within execution of a graph. We will separate explicit data operations into those for USM and those for buffers.

As we learned in Chapter 6, explicit data movement in USM occurs when we need to copy data between device allocations and the host. This is done with the memcpy method, found in both the queue and handler classes. Submitting the action or command group returns an event that can be used to order the copy with other command groups.

Explicit data movement with buffers occurs by invoking either the copy or update_host method of the command group handler object. The copy method can be used to manually exchange data between host memory and an accessor object on a device. This can be done for a variety of reasons. A simple example is checkpointing a long-running sequence of computations. With the copy method, data can be written from the device to arbitrary host memory in a one-way fashion. If this were done using buffers, most cases (i.e., those where the buffer was not created with use_host_ptr) would require the data to first be copied to the host and then from the buffer's memory to the desired host memory.

The update_host method is a very specialized form of copy. If a buffer was created around a host pointer, this method will copy the data represented by the accessor back to the original host memory. This can be useful if a program manually synchronizes host data with a buffer that was created with the special use_mutex property. However, this use case is not likely to occur in most programs.

CHAPTER 8 SCHEDULING KERNELS AND DATA MOVEMENT

Implicit

Implicit data movement can have hidden consequences for command groups and task graphs in DPC++. With implicit data movement, data is copied between host and device either by the DPC++ runtime or by some combination of hardware and software. In either case, copying occurs without explicit input from the user. Let's again look separately at the USM and buffer cases.

With USM, implicit data movement occurs with host and shared allocations. As we learned in Chapter 6, host allocations do not really move data so much as access it remotely, and shared allocations may migrate between host and device. Since this migration happens automatically, there is really nothing to think about with USM implicit data movement and command groups. However, there are some nuances with shared allocations worth keeping in mind.

The prefetch operation works in a similar fashion to memcpy in order to let the runtime begin migrating shared allocations before a kernel attempts to use them. However, unlike memcpy where data must be copied in order to ensure correct results, prefetches are often treated as *hints* to the runtime to increase performance, and prefetches do not invalidate pointer values in memory (as a copy would when copying to a new address range). The program will still execute correctly if a prefetch has not completed before a kernel begins executing, and so many codes may choose to make command groups in a graph not depend on prefetch operations since they are not a functional requirement.

Buffers also carry some nuance. When using buffers, command groups must construct accessors for buffers that specify how the data will be used. These data dependences express the ordering between different command groups and allow us to construct task graphs. However, command groups with buffers sometimes fill another purpose: they specify the requirements on data movement.

Accessors specify that a kernel will read or write to a buffer. The corollary from this is that the data must also be available on the device, and if it is not, the runtime must move it there before the kernel may begin executing. Consequently, the DPC++ runtime must keep track of where the current version of a buffer resides so that data movement operations can be scheduled. Accessor creation effectively creates an extra, hidden node in the graph. If data movement is necessary, the runtime must perform it first. Only then may the kernel being submitted execute.

Let us take another look at Figure 8-8. In this example, our first two kernels will require buffers `data1` and `data2` to be copied to the device; the runtime implicitly creates extra graph nodes to perform the data movement. When the third kernel's command group is submitted, it is likely that these buffers will still be on the device, so the runtime will not need to perform any extra data movement. The fourth kernel's data is also likely to not require any extra data movement, but the creation of the host accessor requires the runtime to schedule a movement of buffer `data1` back to the host before the accessor is available for use.

Synchronizing with the Host

The last topic we will discuss is how to synchronize graph execution with the host. We have already touched on this throughout the chapter, but we will now examine all the different ways a program can do this.

The first method for host synchronization is one we've used in many of our previous examples: waiting on a queue. Queue objects have two methods, `wait` and `wait_and_throw`, that block execution until every command group that was submitted to the queue has completed. This is a very simple method that handles many common cases. However, it is worth pointing out that this method is very coarse-grained. If finer-grained synchronization is desired, one of the other approaches we will discuss may be better suit an application's needs.

The next method for host synchronization is to synchronize on events. This gives more flexibility over synchronizing on a queue since it lets an application only synchronize on specific actions or command groups. This is done by either invoking the `wait` method on an event or invoking the static method `wait` on the event class, which can accept a vector of events.

We have seen the next method used in Figures 8-5 and 8-8: host accessors. Host accessors perform two functions. First, they make data available for access on the host, as their name implies. Second, they synchronize with the host by defining a new dependence between the currently accessing graph and the host. This ensures that the data that gets copied back to the host is the correct value of the computation the graph was performing. However, we once again note that if the buffer was constructed from existing host memory, this original memory is not guaranteed to contain the updated values.

Note that host accessors are blocking. Execution on the host may not proceed past the creation of the host accessor until the data is available. Likewise, a buffer cannot be used on a device while a host accessor exists and keeps its data available. A common pattern is to create host accessors inside additional C++ scopes in order to free the data once the host accessor is no longer needed. This is an example of the next method for host synchronization.

Certain objects in DPC++ have special behaviors when they are destroyed, and their destructors are invoked. We just learned how host accessors can make data remain on the host until they are destroyed. Buffers and images also have special behavior when they are destroyed or leave scope. When a buffer is destroyed, it waits for all command groups that use that buffer to finish execution. Once a buffer is no longer being used by any kernel or memory operation, the runtime may have to copy data back to the host. This copy occurs either if the buffer was initialized with a host pointer or if a host pointer was passed to the method `set_final_data`. The runtime will then copy back the data for that buffer and update the host pointer before the object is destroyed.

The final option for synchronizing with the host involves an uncommon feature first described in Chapter 7. Recall that the constructors for buffer objects optionally take a property list. One of the valid properties that may be passed when creating a buffer is use_mutex. When a buffer is created in this fashion, it adds the requirement that the memory owned by the buffer can be shared with the host application. Access to this memory is governed by the mutex used to initialize the buffer. The host is able to obtain the lock on the mutex when it is safe to access the memory shared with the buffer. If the lock cannot be obtained, the user may need to enqueue memory movement operations to synchronize the data with the host. This use is very specialized and unlikely to be found in the majority of DPC++ applications.

Summary

In this chapter, we have learned about graphs and how they are built, scheduled, and executed in DPC++. We went into detail on what command groups are and what function they serve. We discussed the three things that can be within a command group: dependences, an action, and miscellaneous host code. We reviewed how to specify dependences between tasks using events as well as through data dependences described by accessors. We learned that the single action in a command group may be either a kernel or an explicit memory operation, and we then looked at several examples that showed the different ways we can construct common execution graph patterns. Next, we reviewed how data movement is an important part of DPC++ graphs, and we learned how it can appear either explicitly or implicitly in a graph. Finally, we looked at all the ways to synchronize the execution of a graph with the host.

Understanding the program flow can enable us to understand the sort of debug information that can be printed if we have runtime failures to debug. Chapter 13 has a table in the section "Debugging Runtime Failures" that will make a little more sense given the knowledge we have gained by this point in the book. However, this book does not attempt to discuss these advanced compiler dumps in detail.

Hopefully this has left you feeling like a graph expert who can construct graphs that range in complexity from linear chains to enormous graphs with hundreds of nodes and complex data and task dependences! In the next chapter, we'll begin to dive into low-level details that are useful for improving the performance of an application on a specific device.

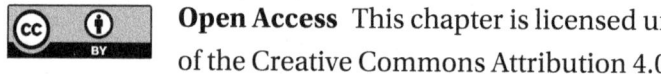

Open Access This chapter is licensed under the terms of the Creative Commons Attribution 4.0 International License (http://creativecommons.org/licenses/by/4.0/), which permits use, sharing, adaptation, distribution and reproduction in any medium or format, as long as you give appropriate credit to the original author(s) and the source, provide a link to the Creative Commons license and indicate if changes were made.

The images or other third party material in this chapter are included in the chapter's Creative Commons license, unless indicated otherwise in a credit line to the material. If material is not included in the chapter's Creative Commons license and your intended use is not permitted by statutory regulation or exceeds the permitted use, you will need to obtain permission directly from the copyright holder.

CHAPTER 9

Communication and Synchronization

In Chapter 4, we discussed ways to express parallelism, either using basic data-parallel kernels, explicit ND-range kernels, or hierarchical parallel kernels. We discussed how basic data-parallel kernels apply the same operation to every piece of data independently. We also discussed how explicit ND-range kernels and hierarchical parallel kernels divide the execution range into work-groups of work-items.

In this chapter, we will revisit the question of how to break up a problem into bite-sized chunks in our continuing quest to *Think Parallel*. This chapter provides more detail regarding explicit ND-range kernels and hierarchical parallel kernels and describes how groupings of work-items may be used to improve the performance of some types of algorithms. We will describe how groups of work-items provide additional guarantees for

Chapter 9 Communication and Synchronization

how parallel work is executed, and we will introduce language features that support groupings of work-items. Many of these ideas and concepts will be important when optimizing programs for specific devices in Chapters 15, 16, and 17 and to describe common parallel patterns in Chapter 14.

Work-Groups and Work-Items

Recall from Chapter 4 that explicit ND-range and hierarchical parallel kernels organize work-items into work-groups and that the work-items in a work-group are guaranteed to execute concurrently. This property is important, because when work-items are guaranteed to execute concurrently, the work-items in a work-group can cooperate to solve a problem.

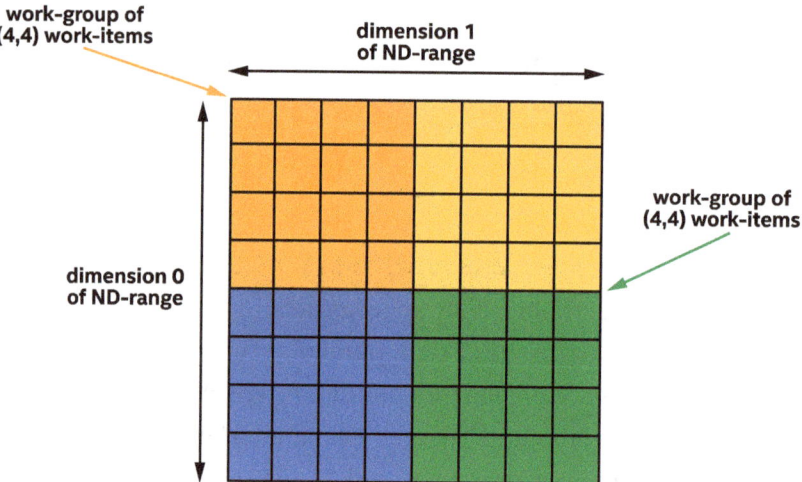

Figure 9-1. Two-dimensional ND-range of size (8, 8) divided into four work-groups of size (4,4)

Figure 9-1 shows an ND-range divided into work-groups, where each work-group is represented by a different color. The work-items in each work-group are guaranteed to execute concurrently, so a work-item may communicate with other work-items that share the same color.

Because the work-items in different work-groups are not guaranteed to execute concurrently, a work-item with one color cannot reliably communicate with a work-item with a different color, and a kernel may deadlock if one work-item attempts to communicate with another work-item that is not currently executing. Since we want our kernels to complete execution, we must ensure that when one work-item communicates with another work-item, they are in the same work-group.

Building Blocks for Efficient Communication

This section describes building blocks that support efficient communication between work-items in a group. Some are fundamental building blocks that enable construction of custom algorithms, whereas others are higher level and describe common operations used by many kernels.

Synchronization via Barriers

The most fundamental building block for communication is the *barrier* function. The barrier function serves two key purposes:

First, the barrier function synchronizes execution of work-items in a group. By synchronizing execution, one work-item can ensure that another work-item has completed an operation before using the result of that operation. Alternatively, one work-item is given time to complete its operation before another work-item uses the result of the operation.

Second, the barrier function synchronizes how each work-item views the state of memory. This type of synchronization operation is known as enforcing *memory consistency* or *fencing* memory (more details in Chapter 19). Memory consistency is at least as important as synchronizing execution since it ensures that the results of memory operations performed before the barrier are visible to other work-items after the barrier. Without memory consistency, an operation in one work-item is like a tree falling in a forest, where the sound may or may not be heard by other work-items!

Figure 9-2 shows four work-items in a group that synchronize at a barrier function. Even though the execution time for each work-item may differ, no work-items can execute past the barrier until all work-items execute the barrier. After executing the barrier function, all work-items have a consistent view of memory.

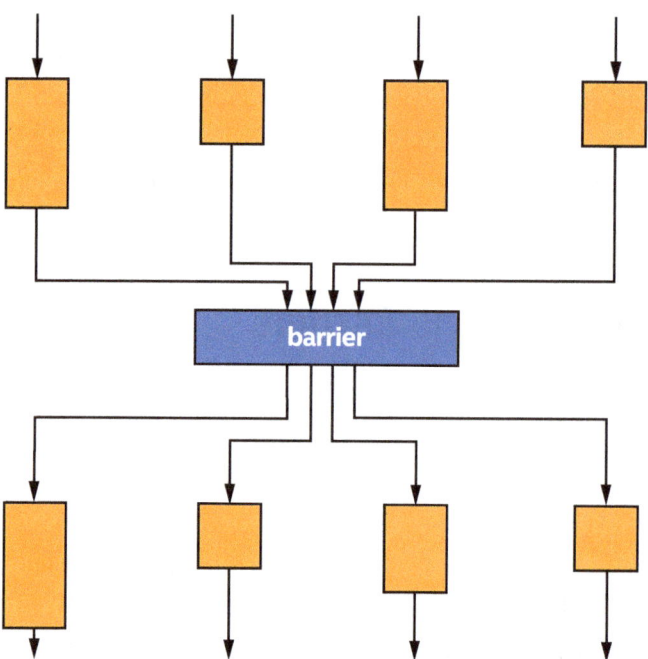

Figure 9-2. Four work-items in a group synchronize at a barrier function

> **WHY ISN'T MEMORY CONSISTENT BY DEFAULT?**
>
> For many programmers, the idea of memory consistency—and that different work-items can have different views of memory—can feel very strange. Wouldn't it be easier if all memory was consistent for all work-items by default? The short answer is that it would, but it would also be very expensive to implement. By allowing work-items to have inconsistent views of memory and only requiring memory consistency at defined points during program execution, accelerator hardware may be cheaper, may perform better, or both.

Because barrier functions synchronize execution, it is critically important that either all work-items in the group execute the barrier or no work-items in the group execute the barrier. If some work-items in the group branch around any barrier function, the other work-items in the group may wait at the barrier forever—or at least until the user gives up and terminates the program!

> **COLLECTIVE FUNCTIONS**
>
> When a function is required to be executed by all work-items in a group, it may be called a *collective function*, since the operation is performed by the group and not by individual work-items in the group. Barrier functions are not the only collective functions available in SYCL. Other collective functions are described later in this chapter.

Work-Group Local Memory

The work-group barrier function is sufficient to coordinate communication among work-items in a work-group, but the communication itself must occur through memory. Communication may occur through either

USM or buffers, but this can be inconvenient and inefficient: it requires a dedicated allocation for communication and requires partitioning the allocation among work-groups.

To simplify kernel development and accelerate communication between work-items in a work-group, SYCL defines a special *local memory* space specifically for communication between work-items in a work-group.

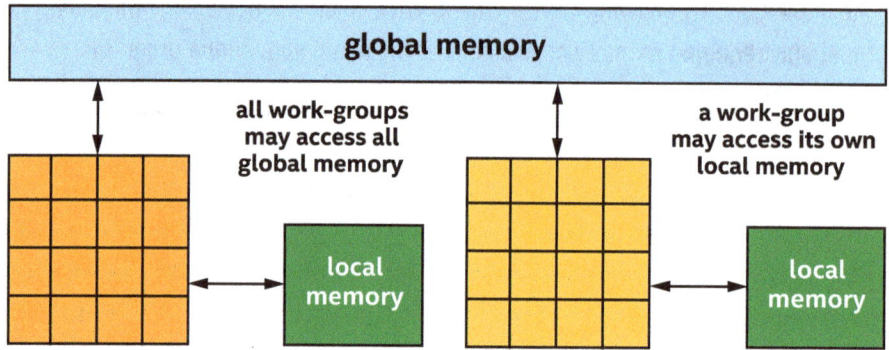

Figure 9-3. *Each work-group may access all global memory, but only its own local memory*

In Figure 9-3, two work-groups are shown. Both work-groups may access USM and buffers in the *global memory* space. Each work-group may access variables in its own *local memory* space, but cannot access variables in another work-group's local memory.

When a work-group begins, the contents of its local memory are uninitialized, and local memory does not persist after a work-group finishes executing. Because of these properties, local memory may only be used for temporary storage while a work-group is executing.

For some devices, such as for many CPU devices, local memory is a software abstraction and is implemented using the same memory subsystems as global memory. On these devices, using local memory is primarily a convenience mechanism for communication. Some compilers may use the memory space information for compiler optimizations, but otherwise using local memory for communication will not fundamentally perform better than communication via global memory on these devices.

For other devices though, such as many GPU devices, there are dedicated resources for local memory, and on these devices, communicating via local memory will perform better than communicating via global memory.

Communication between work-items in a work-group can be more convenient and faster when using local memory!

We can use the device query `info::device::local_mem_type` to determine whether an accelerator has dedicated resources for local memory or whether local memory is implemented as a software abstraction of global memory. Please refer to Chapter 12 for more information about querying properties of a device and to Chapters 15, 16, and 17 for more information about how local memory is typically implemented for CPUs, GPUs, and FPGAs.

Using Work-Group Barriers and Local Memory

Now that we have identified the basic building blocks for efficient communication between work-items, we can describe how to express work-group barriers and local memory in kernels. Remember that communication between work-items requires a notion of work-item grouping, so these concepts can only be expressed for ND-range kernels and hierarchical kernels and are not included in the execution model for basic data-parallel kernels.

This chapter will build upon the naïve matrix multiplication kernel examples introduced in Chapter 4 by introducing communication between the work-items in the work-groups executing the matrix multiplication. On many devices—but not necessarily all!—communicating through local memory will improve the performance of the matrix multiplication kernel.

A NOTE ABOUT MATRIX MULTIPLICATION

In this book, matrix multiplication kernels are used to demonstrate how changes in a kernel affect performance. Although matrix multiplication performance may be improved on some devices using the techniques described in this chapter, matrix multiplication is such an important and common operation that many vendors have implemented highly tuned versions of matrix multiplication. Vendors invest significant time and effort implementing and validating functions for specific devices and in some cases may use functionality or techniques that are difficult or impossible to use in standard parallel kernels.

USE VENDOR-PROVIDED LIBRARIES!

When a vendor provides a library implementation of a function, it is almost always beneficial to use it rather than re-implementing the function as a parallel kernel! For matrix multiplication, one can look to oneMKL as part of Intel's oneAPI toolkits for solutions appropriate for DPC++ programmers.

Figure 9-4 shows the naïve matrix multiplication kernel we will be starting from, taken from Chapter 4.

```
h.parallel_for(range{M, N}, [=](id<2> id) {
  int m = id[0];
  int n = id[1];

  T sum = 0;
  for (int k = 0; k < K; k++)
    sum += matrixA[m][k] * matrixB[k][n];

  matrixC[m][n] = sum;
});
```

Figure 9-4. *The naïve matrix multiplication kernel from Chapter 4*

In Chapter 4, we observed that the matrix multiplication algorithm has a high degree of reuse and that grouping work-items may improve locality of access which may improve cache hit rates. In this chapter, instead of relying on *implicit* cache behavior to improve performance, our modified matrix multiplication kernels will instead use local memory as an *explicit cache*, to guarantee locality of access.

For many algorithms, it is helpful to think of local memory as an explicit cache.

Figure 9-5 is a modified diagram from Chapter 4 showing a work-group consisting of a single row, which makes the algorithm using local memory easier to understand. Observe that for elements in a row of the result matrix, every result element is computed using a unique column of data from one of the input matrices, shown in blue and orange. Because there is no data sharing for this input matrix, it is not an ideal candidate for local memory. Observe, though, that every result element in the row accesses the exact same data in the other input matrix, shown in green. Because this data is reused, it is an excellent candidate to benefit from work-group local memory.

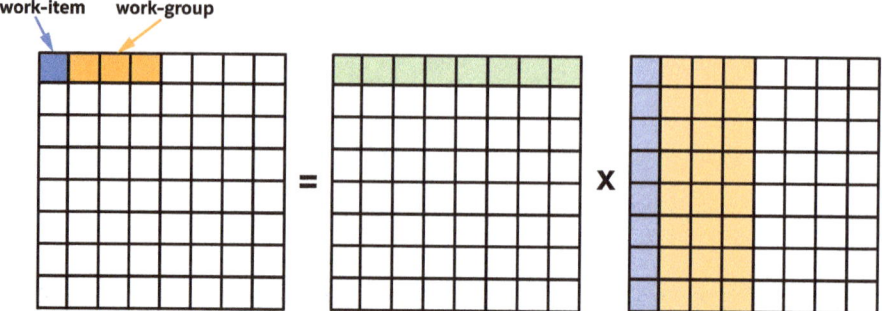

Figure 9-5. Mapping of matrix multiplication to work-groups and work-items

Because we want to multiply matrices that are potentially very large and because work-group local memory may be a limited resource, our modified kernels will process subsections of each matrix, which we will refer to as a matrix *tile*. For each tile, our modified kernel will load data for the tile into local memory, synchronize the work-items in the group, and then load the data from local memory rather than global memory. The data that is accessed for the first tile is shown in Figure 9-6.

In our kernels, we have chosen the tile size to be equivalent to the work-group size. This is not required, but because it simplifies transfers into or out of local memory, it is common and convenient to choose a tile size that is a multiple of the work-group size.

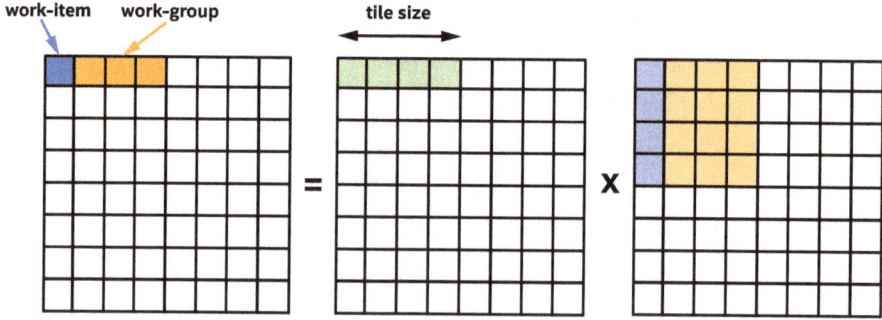

Figure 9-6. Processing the first tile: the green input data (left of X) is reused and is read from local memory, the blue and orange input data (right of X) is read from global memory

Work-Group Barriers and Local Memory in ND-Range Kernels

This section describes how work-group barriers and local memory are expressed in ND-range kernels. For ND-range kernels, the representation is explicit: a kernel declares and operates on a local accessor representing an allocation in the local address space and calls a barrier function to synchronize the work-items in a work-group.

Local Accessors

To declare local memory for use in an ND-range kernel, use a *local accessor*. Like other accessor objects, a local accessor is constructed within a command group handler, but unlike the accessor objects discussed in Chapters 3 and 7, a local accessor is not created from a buffer object. Instead, a local accessor is created by specifying a type and a range describing the number of elements of that type. Like other accessors, local accessors may be one-dimensional, two-dimensional, or three-dimensional. Figure 9-7 demonstrates how to declare local accessors and use them in a kernel.

Remember that local memory is uninitialized when each work-group begins and does not persist after each work-group completes. This means that a local accessor must always be `read_write`, since otherwise a kernel would have no way to assign the contents of local memory or view the results of an assignment. Local accessors may optionally be atomic though, in which case accesses to local memory via the accessor are performed atomically. Atomic accesses are discussed in more detail in Chapter 19.

CHAPTER 9   COMMUNICATION AND SYNCHRONIZATION

```
// This is a typical global accessor.
accessor dataAcc {dataBuf, h};

// This is a 1D local accessor consisting of 16 ints:
local_accessor<int> localIntAcc{16, h};

// This is a 2D local accessor consisting of 4 x 4 floats:
local_accessor<float,2> localFloatAcc{{4,4}, h};

h.parallel_for(nd_range<1>{{size}, {16}}, [=](nd_item<1> item) {
  auto index = item.get_global_id();
  auto local_index = item.get_local_id();

  // Within a kernel, a local accessor may be read from
  // and written to like any other accessor.
  localIntAcc[local_index] = dataAcc[index] + 1;
  dataAcc[index] = localIntAcc[local_index];
});
```

Figure 9-7. Declaring and using local accessors

Synchronization Functions

To synchronize the work-items in an ND-range kernel work-group, call the barrier function in the nd_item class. Because the barrier function is a member of the nd_item class, it is only available to ND-range kernels and is not available to basic data-parallel kernels or hierarchical kernels.

The barrier function currently accepts one argument to describe the memory spaces to synchronize or *fence*, but the arguments to the barrier function may change in the future as the memory model evolves in SYCL and DPC++. In all cases though, the arguments to the barrier function provide additional control regarding the memory spaces that are synchronized or the *scope* of the memory synchronization.

When no arguments are passed to the barrier function, the barrier function will use functionally correct and conservative defaults. The code examples in this chapter use this syntax for maximum portability and readability. For highly optimized kernels, it is recommended to precisely describe which memory spaces or which work-items must be synchronized, which may improve performance.

CHAPTER 9 COMMUNICATION AND SYNCHRONIZATION

A Full ND-Range Kernel Example

Now that we know how to declare a local memory accessor and synchronize access to it using a barrier function, we can implement an ND-range kernel version of matrix multiplication that coordinates communication among work-items in the work-group to reduce traffic to global memory. The complete example is shown in Figure 9-8.

```
// Traditional accessors, representing matrices in global memory:
accessor matrixA{bufA, h};
accessor matrixB{bufB, h};
accessor matrixC{bufC, h};

// Local accessor, for one matrix tile:
constexpr int tile_size = 16;
local_accessor<int> tileA{tile_size, h};

h.parallel_for(
  nd_range<2>{{M, N}, {1, tile_size}}, [=](nd_item<2> item) {
    // Indices in the global index space:
    int m = item.get_global_id()[0];
    int n = item.get_global_id()[1];

    // Index in the local index space:
    int i = item.get_local_id()[1];

    T sum = 0;
    for (int kk = 0; kk < K; kk += tile_size) {
      // Load the matrix tile from matrix A, and synchronize
      // to ensure all work-items have a consistent view
      // of the matrix tile in local memory.
      tileA[i] = matrixA[m][kk + i];
      item.barrier();

      // Perform computation using the local memory tile, and
      // matrix B in global memory.
      for (int k = 0; k < tile_size; k++)
        sum += tileA[k] * matrixB[kk + k][n];

      // After computation, synchronize again, to ensure all
      // reads from the local memory tile are complete.
      item.barrier();
    }

    // Write the final result to global memory.
    matrixC[m][n] = sum;
});
```

Figure 9-8. Expressing a tiled matrix multiplication kernel with an ND-range parallel_for *and work-group local memory*

The main loop in this kernel can be thought of as two distinct phases: in the first phase, the work-items in the work-group collaborate to load shared data from the A matrix into work-group local memory; and in the second, the work-items perform their own computations using the shared data. In order to ensure that all work-items have completed the first phase before moving onto the second phase, the two phases are separated by a call to barrier to synchronize all work-items and to provide a memory fence. This pattern is a common one, and the use of work-group local memory in a kernel almost always necessitates the use of work-group barriers.

Note that there must also be a call to barrier to synchronize execution between the computation phase for the current tile and the loading phase for the next matrix tile. Without this synchronization operation, part of the current matrix tile may be overwritten by one work-item in the work-group before another work-item is finished computing with it. In general, any time that one work-item is reading or writing data in local memory that was read or written by another work-item, synchronization is required. In Figure 9-8, the synchronization is done at the end of the loop, but it would be equally correct to synchronize at the beginning of each loop iteration instead.

Work-Group Barriers and Local Memory in Hierarchical Kernels

This section describes how work-group barriers and local memory are expressed in hierarchical kernels. Unlike ND-range kernels, local memory and barriers in hierarchical kernels are implicit, requiring no special syntax or function calls. Some programmers will find the hierarchical kernel representation more intuitive and easier to use, whereas other programmers will appreciate the direct control provided by ND-range kernels. In most cases, the same algorithms may be described using both representations, so we can choose the representation that we find easiest to develop and maintain.

Scopes for Local Memory and Barriers

Recall from Chapter 4 that hierarchical kernels express two levels of parallel execution through use of the parallel_for_work_group and parallel_for_work_item functions. These two levels, or scopes, of parallel execution are used to express whether a variable is in work-group local memory and shared across all work-items in the work-group or whether a variable is in per-work-item private memory that is not shared among work-items. The two scopes are also used to synchronize the work-items in a work-group and to enforce memory consistency.

Figure 9-9 shows an example hierarchical kernel that declares a variable at work-group scope in local memory, loads into it, and then uses that variable in work-item scope. There is an implicit barrier between the write into local memory at work-group scope and the read from local memory at work-item scope.

```
range group_size{16};
range num_groups = size / group_size;

h.parallel_for_work_group(num_groups, group_size, [=](group<1> group) {
  // This variable is declared at work-group scope, so
  // it is allocated in local memory and accessible to
  // all work-items.
  int localIntArr[16];

  // There is an implicit barrier between code and variables
  // declared at work-group scope and the code and variables
  // at work-item scope.

  group.parallel_for_work_item([&](h_item<1> item) {
    auto index = item.get_global_id();
    auto local_index = item.get_local_id();

    // The code at work-item scope can read and write the
    // variables declared at work-group scope.
    localIntArr[local_index] = index + 1;
    data_acc[index] = localIntArr[local_index];
  });
});
```

Figure 9-9. Hierarchical kernel with a local memory variable

CHAPTER 9   COMMUNICATION AND SYNCHRONIZATION

The main advantage of the hierarchical kernel representation is that it looks very similar to standard C++ code, where some variables may be assigned in one scope and used in a nested scope. Of course, this also may be considered a disadvantage, since it is not immediately obvious which variables are in local memory and when barriers must be inserted by the hierarchical kernel compiler. This is especially true for devices where barriers are expensive!

A Full Hierarchical Kernel Example

Now that we know how to express local memory and barriers in hierarchical kernels, we can write a hierarchical kernel that implements the same algorithm as the ND-range kernel in Figure 9-7. This kernel is shown in Figure 9-10.

Although the hierarchical kernel is very similar to the ND-range kernel, there is one key difference: in the ND-range kernel, the results of the matrix multiplication are accumulated into the per-work-item variable sum before writing to the output matrix in memory, whereas the hierarchical kernel accumulates into memory. We could accumulate into a per-work-item variable in the hierarchical kernel as well, but this requires a special private_memory syntax to declare per-work-item data at work-group scope, and one of the reasons we chose to use the hierarchical kernel syntax was to avoid special syntax!

Hierarchical kernels do not require special syntax to declare variables in work-group local memory, but they require special syntax to declare some variables in work-item private memory!

To avoid the special per-work-item data syntax, it is a common pattern for work-item loops in hierarchical kernels to write intermediate results to either work-group local memory or global memory.

CHAPTER 9   COMMUNICATION AND SYNCHRONIZATION

```cpp
const int tileSize = 16;
range group_size{1, tileSize};
range num_groups{M, N / tileSize};

h.parallel_for_work_group(num_groups, group_size, [=](group<2> group) {
  // Because this array is declared at work-group scope
  // it is in local memory
  T tileA[16];

  for (int kk = 0; kk < K; kk += tileSize) {
    // A barrier may be inserted between scopes here
    // automatically, unless the compiler can prove it is
    // not required

    // Load the matrix tile from matrix A
    group.parallel_for_work_item([&](h_item<2> item) {
      int m = item.get_global_id()[0];
      int i = item.get_local_id()[1];
      tileA[i] = matrixA[m][kk + i];
    });

    // A barrier gets inserted here automatically, so all
    // work items have a consistent view of memory

    group.parallel_for_work_item([&](h_item<2> item) {
      int m = item.get_global_id()[0];
      int n = item.get_global_id()[1];
      for (int k = 0; k < tileSize; k++)
        matrixC[m][n] += tileA[k] * matrixB[kk + k][n];
    });

    // A barrier gets inserted here automatically, too

  }
});
```

Figure 9-10. *A tiled matrix multiplication kernel implemented as a hierarchical kernel*

One final interesting property of the kernel in Figure 9-10 concerns the loop iteration variable kk: since the loop is at work-group scope, the loop iteration variable kk could be allocated out of work-group local memory, just like the `tileA` array. In this case though, since the value of kk is the same for all work-items in the work-group, a smart compiler may choose to allocate kk from per-work-item memory instead, especially for devices where work-group local memory is a scarce resource.

229

CHAPTER 9 COMMUNICATION AND SYNCHRONIZATION

Sub-Groups

So far in this chapter, work-items have communicated with other work-items in the work-group by exchanging data through work-group local memory and by synchronizing via implicit or explicit barrier functions, depending on how the kernel is written.

In Chapter 4, we discussed another grouping of work-items. A sub-group is an implementation-defined subset of work-items in a work-group that execute together on the same hardware resources or with additional scheduling guarantees. Because the implementation decides how to group work-items into sub-groups, the work-items in a sub-group may be able to communicate or synchronize more efficiently than the work-items in an arbitrary work-group.

This section describes the building blocks for communication among work-items in a sub-group. Note that sub-groups are currently implemented only for ND-range kernels and sub-groups are not expressible through hierarchical kernels.

Synchronization via Sub-Group Barriers

Just like how the work-items in a work-group in an ND-range kernel may synchronize using a work-group barrier function, the work-items in a sub-group may synchronize using a sub-group barrier function. Whereas the work-items in a work-group synchronize by calling a group_barrier function or the barrier function in the nd_item class, the work-items in a sub-group synchronize by calling a group_barrier function or the barrier function in a special sub_group class that may be queried from the nd_item class, as shown in Figure 9-11.

```
h.parallel_for(nd_range{{size}, {16}}, [=](nd_item<1> item) {
  auto sg = item.get_sub_group();
  ...
  sg.barrier();
  ...
});
```

Figure 9-11. Querying and using the sub_group *class*

Like the work-group barrier, the sub-group barrier may accept optional arguments to more precisely control the barrier operation. Regardless of whether the sub-group barrier function is synchronizing global memory or local memory, synchronizing only the work-items in the sub-group is likely cheaper than synchronizing all of the work-items in the work-group.

Exchanging Data Within a Sub-Group

Unlike work-groups, sub-groups do not have a dedicated memory space for exchanging data. Instead, work-items in the sub-group may exchange data through work-group local memory, through global memory, or more commonly by using sub-group *collective functions*.

As described previously, a *collective function* is a function that describes an operation performed by a group of work-items, not an individual work-item, and because a barrier synchronization function is an operation performed by a group of work-items, it is one example of a collective function.

Other collective functions express common communication patterns. We will describe the semantics for many collective functions in detail later in this chapter, but for now, we will briefly describe the broadcast collective function that we will use to implement matrix multiplication using sub-groups.

The broadcast collective function takes a value from one work-item in the group and communicates it to all other work-items in the group. An example is shown in Figure 9-12. Notice that the semantics of the broadcast function require that the local_id identifying which value in the group to communicate must be the same for all work-items in the group, ensuring that the result of the broadcast function is also the same for all work-items in the group.

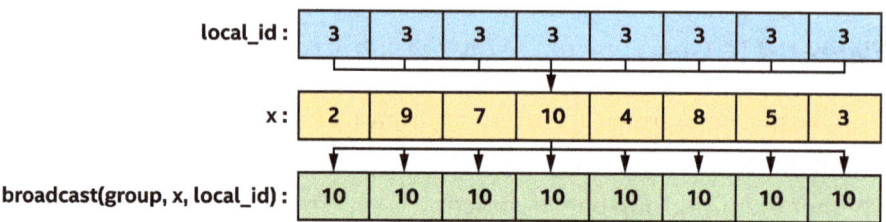

Figure 9-12. Processing by the broadcast function

If we look at the innermost loop of our local memory matrix multiplication kernel, shown in Figure 9-13, we can see that the access to the matrix tile is a broadcast, since each work-item in the group reads the same value out of the matrix tile.

```
h.parallel_for<class MatrixMultiplication>(
    nd_range<2>{ {M, N}, {1, tileSize} }, [=](nd_item<2> item) {
    ...
    // Perform computation using the local memory tile, and
    // matrix B in global memory.
    for( size_t k = 0; k < tileSize; k++ ) {
        // Because the value of k is the same for all work-items
        // in the group, these reads from tileA are broadcast
        // operations.
        sum += tileA[k] * matrixB[kk + k][n];
    }
    ...
});
```

Figure 9-13. Matrix multiplication kernel includes a broadcast operation

We will use the sub-group broadcast function to implement a matrix multiplication kernel that does not require work-group local memory or barriers. On many devices, sub-group broadcasts are faster than broadcasting with work-group local memory and barriers.

CHAPTER 9   COMMUNICATION AND SYNCHRONIZATION

A Full Sub-Group ND-Range Kernel Example

Figure 9-14 is a complete example that implements matrix multiplication using sub-groups. Notice that this kernel requires no work-group local memory or explicit synchronization and instead uses a sub-group broadcast collective function to communicate the contents of the matrix tile among work-items.

```
// Note: This example assumes that the sub-group size is
// greater than or equal to the tile size!
static const int tileSize = 4;

h.parallel_for(
  nd_range<2>{{M, N}, {1, tileSize}}, [=](nd_item<2> item) {
    auto sg = item.get_sub_group();

    // Indices in the global index space:
    int m = item.get_global_id()[0];
    int n = item.get_global_id()[1];

    // Index in the local index space:
    int i = item.get_local_id()[1];

    T sum = 0;
    for (int_fast64_t kk = 0; kk < K; kk += tileSize) {
      // Load the matrix tile from matrix A.
      T tileA = matrixA[m][kk + i];

      // Perform computation by broadcasting from the matrix
      // tile and loading from matrix B in global memory.  The loop
      // variable k describes which work-item in the sub-group to
      // broadcast data from.
      for (int k = 0; k < tileSize; k++)
        sum += intel::broadcast(sg, tileA, k) * matrixB[kk + k][n];
    }

    // Write the final result to global memory.
    matrixC[m][n] = sum;
  });
});
```

Figure 9-14. *Tiled matrix multiplication kernel expressed with ND-range* `parallel_for` *and sub-group collective functions*

CHAPTER 9 COMMUNICATION AND SYNCHRONIZATION

Collective Functions

In the "Sub-Groups" section of this chapter, we described collective functions and how collective functions express common communication patterns. We specifically discussed the broadcast collective function, which is used to communicate a value from one work-item in a group to the other work-items in the group. This section describes additional collective functions.

Although the collective functions described in this section can be implemented directly in our programs using features such as atomics, work-group local memory, and barriers, many devices include dedicated hardware to accelerate collective functions. Even when a device does not include specialized hardware, vendor-provided implementations of collective functions are likely tuned for the device they are running on, so calling a built-in collective function will usually perform better than a general-purpose implementation that we might write.

Use collective functions for common communication patterns to simplify code and increase performance!

Many collective functions are supported for both work-groups and sub-groups. Other collective functions are supported only for sub-groups.

Broadcast

The broadcast function enables one work-item in a group to share the value of a variable with all other work-items in the group. A diagram showing how the broadcast function works can be found in Figure 9-12. The broadcast function is supported for both work-groups and sub-groups.

CHAPTER 9   COMMUNICATION AND SYNCHRONIZATION

Votes

The any_of and all_of functions (henceforth referred to collectively as "vote" functions) enable work-items to compare the result of a Boolean condition across their group: any_of returns true if the condition is true for at least one work-item in the group, and all_of returns true only if the condition is true for all work-items in the group. A comparison of these two functions for an example input is shown in Figure 9-15.

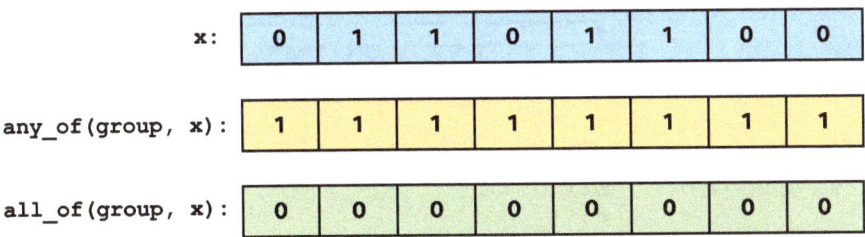

Figure 9-15. Comparison of the any_of and all_of functions

The any_of and all_of vote functions are supported for both work-groups and sub-groups.

Shuffles

One of the most useful features of sub-groups is the ability to communicate directly between individual work-items without explicit memory operations. In many cases, such as the sub-group matrix multiplication kernel, these *shuffle* operations enable us to remove work-group local memory usage from our kernels and/or to avoid unnecessary repeated accesses to global memory. There are several flavors of these shuffle functions available.

The most general of the shuffle functions is called shuffle, and as shown in Figure 9-16, it allows for arbitrary communication between any pair of work-items in the sub-group. This generality may come at a performance cost, however, and we strongly encourage making use of the more specialized shuffle functions wherever possible.

CHAPTER 9 COMMUNICATION AND SYNCHRONIZATION

In Figure 9-16, a generic shuffle is used to sort the x values of a sub-group using pre-computed permutation indices. Arrows are shown for one work-item in the sub-group, where the result of the shuffle is the value of x for the work-item with `local_id` equal to 7.

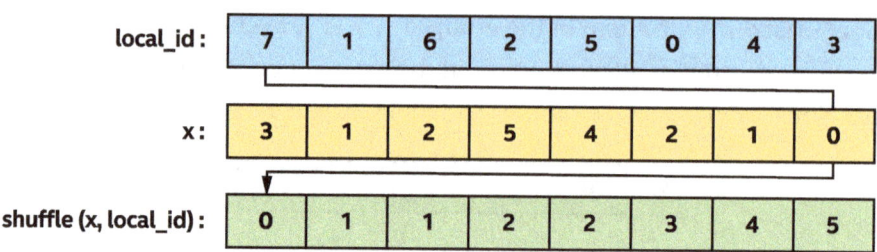

Figure 9-16. Using a generic shuffle to sort x values based on pre-computed permutation indices

Note that the sub-group broadcast function can be thought of as a specialized version of the general-purpose shuffle function, where the shuffle index is the same for all work-items in the sub-group. When the shuffle index is known to be the same for all work-items in the sub-group, using broadcast instead of shuffle provides the compiler additional information and may increase performance on some implementations.

The shuffle_up and shuffle_down functions effectively *shift* the contents of a sub-group by a fixed number of elements in a given direction, as shown in Figure 9-17. Note that the values returned to the last five work-items in the sub-group are undefined and are shown as blank in Figure 9-17. Shifting can be useful for parallelizing loops with loop-carried dependences or when implementing common algorithms such as exclusive or inclusive scans.

CHAPTER 9 COMMUNICATION AND SYNCHRONIZATION

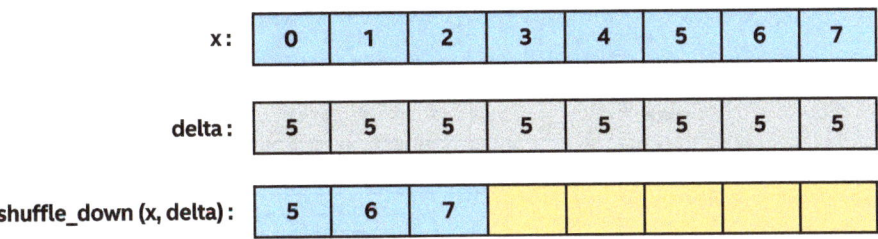

Figure 9-17. Using `shuffle_down` *to shift* x *values of a sub-group by five items*

The `shuffle_xor` function swaps the values of two work-items, as specified by the result of an XOR operation applied to the work-item's sub-group local id and a fixed constant. As shown in Figures 9-18 and 9-19, several common communication patterns can be expressed using an XOR: for example, swapping pairs of neighboring values

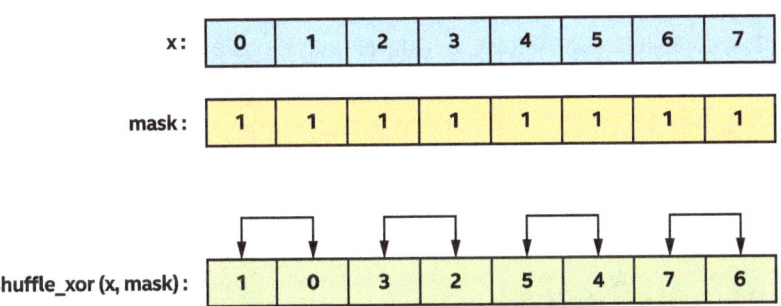

Figure 9-18. Swapping neighboring pairs of x *using a* `shuffle_xor`

or reversing the sub-group values.

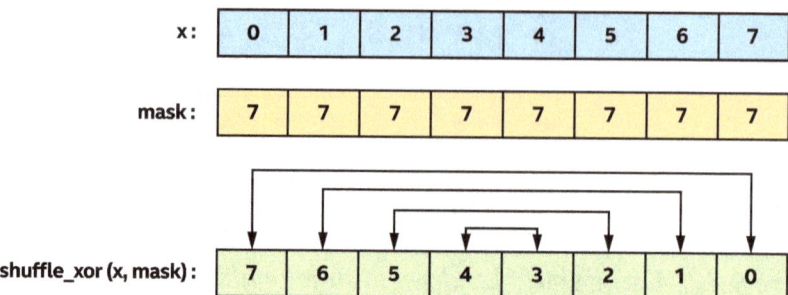

Figure 9-19. *Reverse the values of x using a shuffle_xor*

SUB-GROUP OPTIMIZATIONS USING BROADCAST, VOTE, AND COLLECTIVES

The behavior of broadcast, vote, and other collective functions applied to sub-groups is identical to when they are applied to work-groups, but they deserve additional attention because they may enable aggressive optimizations in certain compilers. For example, a compiler may be able to reduce register usage for variables that are broadcast to all work-items in a sub-group or may be able to reason about control flow divergence based on usage of the any_of and all_of functions.

Loads and Stores

The sub-group load and store functions serve two purposes: first, informing the compiler that all work-items in the sub-group are loading contiguous data starting from the same (uniform) location in memory and, second, enabling us to request optimized loads/stores of large amounts of contiguous data.

For an ND-range parallel_for, it may not be clear to the compiler how addresses computed by different work-items relate to one another. For example, as shown in Figure 9-20, accessing a contiguous block of

CHAPTER 9 COMMUNICATION AND SYNCHRONIZATION

memory from indices [0, 32) appears to have a strided access pattern from the perspective of each work-item.

item 0						item 7	
0	1	2	3	4	5	6	7
8	9	10	11	12	13	14	15
16	17	18	19	20	21	22	23
24	25	26	27	28	29	30	31

```
for(int b = 0; <4; ++b)
{
    int offset = b * sg.get_max_local_range ();
    array [offset + sg.get_local_id ()];
    ...
}
```

Figure 9-20. *Memory access pattern of a sub-group accessing four contiguous blocks*

Some architectures include dedicated hardware to detect when work-items in a sub-group access contiguous data and combine their memory requests, while other architectures require this to be known ahead of time and encoded in the load/store instruction. Sub-group loads and stores are not required for correctness on any platform, but may improve performance on some platforms and should therefore be considered as an optimization hint.

Summary

This chapter discussed how work-items in a group may communicate and cooperate to improve the performance of some types of kernels.

We first discussed how ND-range kernels and hierarchical kernels support grouping work-items into work-groups. We discussed how grouping work-items into work-groups changes the parallel execution model, guaranteeing that the work-items in a work-group execute concurrently and enabling communication and synchronization.

Next, we discussed how the work-items in a work-group may synchronize using barriers and how barriers are expressed explicitly for ND-range kernels or implicitly between work-group and work-item scopes for hierarchical kernels. We also discussed how communication between work-items in a work-group can be performed via work-group local memory, both to simplify kernels and to improve performance, and we discussed how work-group local memory is represented using local accessors for ND-range kernels or allocations at work-group scope for hierarchical kernels.

We discussed how work-groups in ND-range kernels may be further divided into sub-groupings of work-items, where the sub-groups of work-items may support additional communication patterns or scheduling guarantees.

For both work-groups and sub-groups, we discussed how common communication patterns may be expressed and accelerated through use of collective functions.

The concepts in this chapter are an important foundation for understanding the common parallel patterns described in Chapter 14 and for understanding how to optimize for specific devices in Chapters 15, 16, and 17.

Open Access This chapter is licensed under the terms of the Creative Commons Attribution 4.0 International License (http://creativecommons.org/licenses/by/4.0/), which permits use, sharing, adaptation, distribution and reproduction in any medium or format, as long as you give appropriate credit to the original author(s) and the source, provide a link to the Creative Commons license and indicate if changes were made.

The images or other third party material in this chapter are included in the chapter's Creative Commons license, unless indicated otherwise in a credit line to the material. If material is not included in the chapter's Creative Commons license and your intended use is not permitted by statutory regulation or exceeds the permitted use, you will need to obtain permission directly from the copyright holder.

CHAPTER 10

Defining Kernels

Thus far in this book, our code examples have represented kernels using C++ lambda expressions. Lambda expressions are a concise and convenient way to represent a kernel right where it is used, but they are not the only way to represent a kernel in SYCL. In this chapter, we will explore various ways to define kernels in detail, helping us to choose a kernel form that is most natural for our C++ coding needs.

This chapter explains and compares three ways to represent a kernel:

- Lambda expressions
- Named function objects (functors)
- Interoperability with kernels created via other languages or APIs

CHAPTER 10 DEFINING KERNELS

This chapter closes with a discussion of how to explicitly manipulate kernels in a program object to control when and how kernels are compiled.

Why Three Ways to Represent a Kernel?

Before we dive into the details, let's start with a summary of why there are three ways to define a kernel and the advantages and disadvantages of each method. A useful summary is given in Figure 10-1.

Bear in mind that a kernel is used to express a unit of computation and that many instances of a kernel will usually execute in parallel on an accelerator. SYCL supports multiple ways to express a kernel to integrate naturally and seamlessly into a variety of codebases while executing efficiently on a wide diversity of accelerator types.

CHAPTER 10 DEFINING KERNELS

Kernel Representation	Description
Lambda Expression	Pros: • Lambda expressions are a concise way to represent a kernel right where it is used. • Lambda expressions are a familiar way to represent kernel-like operations in modern C++ codebases. • Lambda capture rules automatically pass data to kernels. Cons: • Kernels represented as lambda expressions cannot be templated, cannot easily be reused, and cannot be shipped as a library. • The lambda syntax may be unfamiliar to some C++ codebases.
Named Function Object (Functor)	Pros: • Functors can be templated, reused, and shipped as a part of a library, just like any other C++ class. • Functors provide more control over the data that gets passed into a kernel. Cons: • Kernels represented as functors require more code than kernels represented as lambda expressions. • Kernel arguments must be explicitly passed to functors and are not captured automatically.
Interoperability with Other Languages or APIs	Pros: • Enables re-use of previously written kernels or libraries. • Enables large application codebases to incrementally add support for SYCL. • Kernel languages from other APIs may support features that have not been added or are difficult to express with SYCL. Cons: • Interoperability is an optional feature that may not be supported by all SYCL implementations or by all SYCL devices in an implementation. • Kernels written in other APIs are not compiled by the SYCL device compiler, which may limit compile-time syntax checking, type checking for kernel arguments, and optimization opportunities. • Kernels written in other APIs may not support the latest C++ features.

Figure 10-1. Three ways to represent a kernel

CHAPTER 10 DEFINING KERNELS

Kernels As Lambda Expressions

C++ lambda expressions, also referred to as *anonymous function objects, unnamed function objects, closures,* or simply *lambdas,* are a convenient way to express a kernel right where it is used. This section describes how to represent a kernel as a C++ lambda expression. This expands on the introductory refresher on C++ lambda functions, in Chapter 1, which included some coding samples with output.

C++ lambda expressions are very powerful and have an expressive syntax, but only a specific subset of the full C++ lambda expression syntax is required (and supported) when expressing a kernel.

```
h.parallel_for(size,
   // This is the start of a kernel lambda expression:
   [=](id<1> i) {
      data_acc[i] = data_acc[i] + 1;
   }
   // This is the end of the kernel lambda expression.
);
```

Figure 10-2. *Kernel defined using a lambda expression*

Elements of a Kernel Lambda Expression

Figure 10-2 shows a kernel written as a typical lambda expression—the code examples so far in this book have used this syntax.

The illustration in Figure 10-3 shows more elements of a lambda expression that may be used with kernels, but many of these elements are not typical. In most cases, the lambda defaults are sufficient, so a typical kernel lambda expression looks more like the lambda expression in Figure 10-2 than the more complicated lambda expression in Figure 10-3.

```
accessor data_acc {data_buf, h};
h.parallel_for(size,
  ① ② ④⑤                    ⑥                          ⑦
  [=](id<1> i) noexcept [[cl::reqd_work_group_size(8,1,1)]] -> void {
    data_acc[i] = data_acc[i] + 1;   ③
});
```

Figure 10-3. More elements of a kernel lambda expression, including optional elements

1. The first part of a lambda expression describes the lambda *captures*. *Capturing* a variable from a surrounding scope enables it to be used within the lambda expression, without explicitly passing it to the lambda expression as a parameter.

   C++ lambda expressions support capturing a variable by copying it or by creating a reference to it, but for kernel lambda expressions, variables may only be captured by copy. General practice is to simply use the default capture mode [=], which implicitly captures all variables by value, although it is possible to explicitly name each captured variable as well. Any variable used within a kernel that is not captured by value will cause a compile-time error.

2. The second part of a lambda expression describes parameters that are passed to the lambda expression, just like parameters that are passed to named functions.

For kernel lambda expressions, the parameters depend on how the kernel was invoked and usually identify the index of the work-item in the parallel execution space. Please refer to Chapter 4 for more details about the various parallel execution spaces and how to identify the index of a work-item in each execution space.

3. The last part of the lambda expression defines the lambda function body. For a kernel lambda expression, the function body describes the operations that should be performed at each index in the parallel execution space.

There are other parts of a lambda expression that are supported for kernels, but are either optional or infrequently used:

4. Some *specifiers* (such as mutable) may be supported, but their use is not recommended, and support may be removed in future versions of SYCL (it is gone in the provisional SYCL 2020) or DPC++. None is shown in the example code.

5. The *exception specification* is supported, but must be noexcept if provided, since exceptions are not supported for kernels.

6. Lambda *attributes* are supported and may be used to control how the kernel is compiled. For example, the reqd_work_group_size attribute can be used to require a specific work-group size for a kernel.

7. The *return type* may be specified, but must be void if provided, since non-void return types are not supported for kernels.

CHAPTER 10   DEFINING KERNELS

> **LAMBDA CAPTURES: IMPLICIT OR EXPLICIT?**
>
> Some C++ style guides recommend against implicit (or default) captures for lambda expressions due to possible dangling pointer issues, especially when lambda expressions cross scope boundaries. The same issues may occur when lambdas are used to represent kernels, since kernel lambdas execute asynchronously on the device, separately from host code.
>
> Because implicit captures are useful and concise, it is common practice for SYCL kernels and a convention we use in this book, but it is ultimately our decision whether to prefer the brevity of implicit captures or the clarity of explicit captures.

Naming Kernel Lambda Expressions

There is one more element that must be provided in some cases when a kernel is written as a lambda expression: because lambda expressions are *anonymous*, at times SYCL requires an explicit kernel name template parameter to uniquely identify a kernel written as a lambda expression.

```
// In this example, "class Add" names the kernel lambda:
h.parallel_for<class Add>(size, [=](id<1> i) {
  data_acc[i] = data_acc[i] + 1;
});
```

Figure 10-4. Naming kernel lambda expressions

Naming a kernel lambda expression is a way for a host code compiler to identify which kernel to invoke when the kernel was compiled by a separate device code compiler. Naming a kernel lambda also enables runtime introspection of a compiled kernel or building a kernel by name, as shown in Figure 10-9.

To support more concise code when the kernel name template parameter is not required, the DPC++ compiler supports omitting the kernel name template parameter for a kernel lambda via the -fsycl-unnamed-lambda compiler option. When using this option, no explicit kernel name template parameter is required, as shown in Figure 10-5.

```
// In many cases the explicit kernel name template parameter
// is not required.
h.parallel_for(size, [=](id<1> i) {
  data_acc[i] = data_acc[i] + 1;
});
```

Figure 10-5. Using unnamed kernel lambda expressions

Because the kernel name template parameter for lambda expressions is not required in most cases, we can usually start with an unnamed lambda and only add a kernel name in specific cases when the kernel name template parameter is required.

When the kernel name template parameter is not required, using unnamed kernel lambdas is preferred to reduce verbosity.

Kernels As Named Function Objects

Named function objects, also known as *functors*, are an established pattern in C++ that allows operating on an arbitrary collection of data while maintaining a well-defined interface. When used to represent a kernel, the member variables of a named function object define the state that the kernel may operate on, and the overloaded function call operator() is invoked for each work-item in the parallel execution space.

Named function objects require more code than lambda expressions to express a kernel, but the extra verbosity provides more control and additional capabilities. It may be easier to analyze and optimize kernels expressed as named function objects, for example, since any buffers and data values used by the kernel must be explicitly passed to the kernel, rather than captured automatically.

Finally, because named function objects are just like any other C++ class, kernels expressed as named function objects may be templated, unlike kernels expressed as lambda expressions. Kernels expressed as named function objects may also be easier to reuse and may be shipped as part of a separate header file or library.

Elements of a Kernel Named Function Object

The code in Figure 10-6 describes the elements of a kernel represented as a named function object.

CHAPTER 10   DEFINING KERNELS

```cpp
class Add {
public:
  Add(accessor<int> acc) : data_acc(acc) {}
  void operator()(id<1> i) {
    data_acc[i] = data_acc[i] + 1;
  }

private:
  accessor<int> data_acc;
};

int main() {
  constexpr size_t size = 16;
  std::array<int, size> data;

  for (int i = 0; i < size; i++)
    data[i] = i;

  {
    buffer data_buf{data};

    queue Q{ host_selector{} };
    std::cout << "Running on device: "
              << Q.get_device().get_info<info::device::name>() << "\n";

    Q.submit([&](handler& h) {
      accessor data_acc {data_buf, h};
      h.parallel_for(size, Add(data_acc));
    });
  }
});
```

Figure 10-6. *Kernel as a named function object*

When a kernel is expressed as a named function object, the named function object type must follow C++11 rules to be trivially copyable. Informally, this means that the named function objects may be safely copied byte by byte, enabling the member variables of the named function object to be passed to and accessed by kernel code executing on a device.

The arguments to the overloaded function call `operator()` depend on how the kernel is launched, just like for kernels expressed as lambda expressions.

Because the function object is named, the host code compiler can use the function object type to associate with the kernel code produced by the device code compiler, even if the function object is templated. As a result, no additional kernel name template parameter is needed to name a kernel function object.

Interoperability with Other APIs

When a SYCL implementation is built on top of another API, the implementation may be able to interoperate with kernels defined using mechanisms of the underlying API. This allows an application to easily and incrementally integrate SYCL into existing codebases.

Because a SYCL implementation may be layered on top of many other APIs, the functionality described in this section is optional and may not be supported by all implementations. The underlying API may even differ depending on the specific device type or device vendor!

Broadly speaking, an implementation may support two interoperability mechanisms: from an API-defined source or intermediate representation (IR) or from an API-specific handle. Of these two mechanisms, the ability to create a kernel from an API-defined source or intermediate representation is more portable, since some source or IR formats are supported by multiple APIs. For example, OpenCL C kernels may be directly consumed by many APIs or may be compiled into some form understood by an API, but it is unlikely that an API-specific kernel handle from one API will be understood by a different API.

Remember that all forms of interoperability are optional!

Different SYCL implementations may support creating kernels from different API-specific handles—or not at all.

Always check the documentation for details!

CHAPTER 10 DEFINING KERNELS

Interoperability with API-Defined Source Languages

With this form of interoperability, the contents of the kernel are described as source code or using an intermediate representation that is not defined by SYCL, but the kernel objects are still created using SYCL API calls. This form of interoperability allows reuse of kernel libraries written in other source languages or use of domain-specific languages (DSLs) that generate code in an intermediate representation.

An implementation must understand the kernel source code or intermediate representation to utilize this form of interoperability. For example, if the kernel is written using OpenCL C in source form, the implementation must support building SYCL programs from OpenCL C kernel source code.

Figure 10-7 shows how a SYCL kernel may be written as OpenCL C kernel source code.

```
// Note: This must select a device that supports interop!
queue Q{ cpu_selector{} };

program p{Q.get_context()};

p.build_with_source(R"CLC(
      kernel void add(global int* data) {
        int index = get_global_id(0);
        data[index] = data[index] + 1;
      }
    )CLC",
    "-cl-fast-relaxed-math");

std::cout << "Running on device: "
          << Q.get_device().get_info<info::device::name>() << "\n";

Q.submit([&](handler& h) {
  accessor data_acc {data_buf, h};

  h.set_args(data_acc);
  h.parallel_for(size, p.get_kernel("add"));
});
```

Figure 10-7. Kernel created from OpenCL C kernel source

In this example, the kernel source string is represented as a C++ raw string literal in the same file as the SYCL host API calls, but there is no requirement that this is the case, and some applications may read the kernel source string from a file or even generate it just-in-time.

Because the SYCL compiler does not have visibility into a SYCL kernel written in an API-defined source language, any kernel arguments must explicitly be passed using the set_arg() or set_args() interface. The SYCL runtime and the API-defined source language must agree on a convention to pass objects as kernel arguments. In this example, the accessor dataAcc is passed as the global pointer kernel argument data.

The build_with_source() interface supports passing optional API-defined build options to precisely control how the kernel is compiled. In this example, the program build options -cl-fast-relaxed-math are used to indicate that the kernel compiler can use a faster math library with relaxed precision. The program build options are optional and may be omitted if no build options are required.

Interoperability with API-Defined Kernel Objects

With this form of interoperability, the kernel objects themselves are created in another API and then imported into SYCL. This form of interoperability enables one part of an application to directly create and use kernel objects using underlying APIs and another part of the application to reuse the same kernels using SYCL APIs. The code in Figure 10-8 shows how a SYCL kernel may be created from an OpenCL kernel object.

CHAPTER 10　DEFINING KERNELS

```
// Note: This must select a device that supports interop
// with OpenCL kernel objects!
queue Q{ cpu_selector{} };
context sc = Q.get_context();

const char* kernelSource =
    R"CLC(
        kernel void add(global int* data) {
            int index = get_global_id(0);
            data[index] = data[index] + 1;
        }
    )CLC";
cl_context c = sc.get();
cl_program p =
    clCreateProgramWithSource(c, 1, &kernelSource, nullptr, nullptr);
clBuildProgram(p, 0, nullptr, nullptr, nullptr, nullptr);
cl_kernel k = clCreateKernel(p, "add", nullptr);

std::cout << "Running on device: "
          << Q.get_device().get_info<info::device::name>() << "\n";

Q.submit([&](handler& h) {
  accessor data_acc{data_buf, h};

  h.set_args(data_acc);
  h.parallel_for(size, kernel{k, sc});
});

clReleaseContext(c);
clReleaseProgram(p);
clReleaseKernel(k);
```

Figure 10-8. Kernel created from an OpenCL kernel object

As with other forms of interoperability, the SYCL compiler does not have visibility into an API-defined kernel object. Therefore, kernel arguments must be explicitly passed using the set_arg() or set_args() interface, and the SYCL runtime and the underlying API must agree on a convention to pass kernel arguments.

CHAPTER 10 DEFINING KERNELS

Kernels in Program Objects

In prior sections, when kernels were either created from an API-defined representation or from API-specific handles, the kernels were created in two steps: first by creating a *program object* and then by creating the kernel from the program object. A program object is a collection of kernels and the functions they call that are compiled as a unit.

For kernels represented as lambda expressions or named function objects, the program object containing the kernel is usually implicit and invisible to an application. For applications that require more control, an application can explicitly manage kernels and the program objects that encapsulate them. To describe why this may be beneficial, it is helpful to take a brief look at how many SYCL implementations manage just-in-time (JIT) kernel compilation.

While not required by the specification, many implementations compile kernels "lazily." This is usually a good policy since it ensures fast application startup and does not unnecessarily compile kernels that are never executed. The disadvantage of this policy is that the first use of a kernel usually takes longer than subsequent uses, since it includes the time needed to compile the kernel, plus the time needed to submit and execute the kernel. For some complex kernels, the time needed to compile the kernel can be significant, making it desirable to shift compilation to a different point during application execution, such as when the application is loading, or in a separate background thread.

Some kernels may also benefit from implementation-defined "build options" to precisely control how the kernel is compiled. For example, for some implementations, it may be possible to instruct the kernel compiler to use a math library with lower precision and better performance.

To provide more control over when and how a kernel is compiled, an application can explicitly request that a kernel be compiled before the kernel is used, using specific build options. Then, the pre-compiled kernel can be submitted into a queue for execution, like usual. Figure 10-9 shows how this works.

255

CHAPTER 10 DEFINING KERNELS

```
// This compiles the kernel named by the specified template
// parameter using the "fast relaxed math" build option.
program p(Q.get_context());

p.build_with_kernel_type<class Add>("-cl-fast-relaxed-math");

Q.submit([&](handler& h) {
  accessor data_acc {data_buf, h};

  h.parallel_for<class Add>(
    // This uses the previously compiled kernel.
    p.get_kernel<class Add>(),
    range{size},
    [=](id<1> i) {
       data_acc[i] = data_acc[i] + 1;
  });
});
```

Figure 10-9. *Compiling kernel lambdas with build options*

In this example, a program object is created from a SYCL context, and the kernel defined by the specified template parameter is built using the build_with_kernel_type function. For this example, the program build options -cl-fast-relaxed-math indicate that the kernel compiler can use a faster math library with relaxed precision, but the program build options are optional and may be omitted if no special program build options are required. The template parameter naming the kernel lambda is required in this case, to identify which kernel to compile.

A program object may also be created from a context and a specific list of devices, rather than all the devices in the context, allowing a program object for one set of devices to be compiled with different build options than those of another program object for a different set of devices.

The previously compiled kernel is passed to the `parallel_for` using the get_kernel function in addition to the usual kernel lambda expression. This ensures that the previously compiled kernel that was built using the relaxed math library gets used. If the previously compiled kernel is not passed to the `parallel_for`, then the kernel will be compiled again, without any special build options. This may be functionally correct, but it is certainly not the intended behavior!

CHAPTER 10 DEFINING KERNELS

In many cases, such as in the simple example shown earlier, these additional steps are unlikely to produce a noticeable change in application behavior and may be omitted for clarity, but they should be considered when tuning an application for performance.

> **IMPROVING INTEROPERABILITY AND PROGRAM OBJECT MANAGEMENT**
>
> Although the SYCL interfaces for interoperability and program object management described in this chapter are useful and functional, they are likely to be improved and enhanced in future versions of SYCL and DPC++. Please refer to the latest SYCL and DPC++ documentation to find updates that were not available or not stable enough to include in this book!

Summary

In this chapter, we explored different ways to define kernels. We described how to seamlessly integrate into existing C++ codebases by representing kernels as C++ lambda expressions or named function objects. For new codebases, we also discussed the pros and cons of the different kernel representations, to help choose the best way to define kernels based on the needs of the application or library.

We also described how to interoperate with other APIs, either by creating a kernel from an API-defined source language or intermediate representation or by creating a kernel object from a handle to an API representation of the kernel. Interoperability enables an application to migrate from lower-level APIs to SYCL over time or to interface with libraries written for other APIs.

Finally, we described how kernels are typically compiled in a SYCL application and how to directly manipulate kernels in program objects to control the compilation process. Even though this level of control will not be required for most applications, it is a useful technique to be aware of when tuning an application.

Open Access This chapter is licensed under the terms of the Creative Commons Attribution 4.0 International License (http://creativecommons.org/licenses/by/4.0/), which permits use, sharing, adaptation, distribution and reproduction in any medium or format, as long as you give appropriate credit to the original author(s) and the source, provide a link to the Creative Commons license and indicate if changes were made.

The images or other third party material in this chapter are included in the chapter's Creative Commons license, unless indicated otherwise in a credit line to the material. If material is not included in the chapter's Creative Commons license and your intended use is not permitted by statutory regulation or exceeds the permitted use, you will need to obtain permission directly from the copyright holder.

CHAPTER 11

Vectors

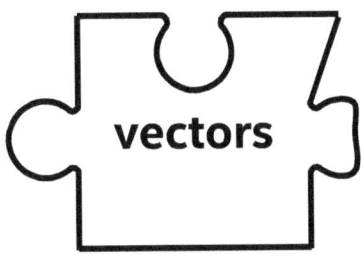

Vectors are collections of data. These can be useful because parallelism in our computers comes from collections of compute hardware, and data is often processed in related groupings (e.g., the color channels in an RGB pixel). Sound like a marriage made in heaven? It is so important, we'll spend a chapter discussing the merits of vector types and how to utilize them. We will not dive into *vectorization* in this chapter, since that varies based on device type and implementations. Vectorization is covered in Chapters 15 and 16.

This chapter seeks to address the following questions:

- What are vector types?

- How much do I really need to know about the vector interface?

- Should vector types be used to express parallelism?

- When should I use vector types?

CHAPTER 11   VECTORS

We discuss the strengths and weaknesses of available vector types using working code examples and highlight the most important aspects of exploiting vector types.

How to Think About Vectors

Vectors are a surprisingly controversial topic when we talk with parallel programming experts, and in the authors' experience, this is because different people define and think about the term in different ways.

There are two broad ways to think about vector data types (a collection of data):

1. **As a convenience type**, which groups data that you might want to refer to and operate on as a group, for example, grouping the color channels of a pixel (e.g., RGB, YUV) into a single variable (e.g., float3), which could be a vector. We could define a pixel class or struct and define math operators like + on it, but vector types conveniently do this for us out of the box. Convenience types can be found in many shader languages used to program GPUs, so this way of thinking is already common among many GPU developers.

2. As a mechanism to describe how code **maps to a SIMD instruction set** in hardware. For example, in some languages and implementations, operations on a float8 could in theory map to an eight-lane SIMD instruction in hardware. Vector types are used in multiple languages as a convenient high-level alternative to CPU-specific SIMD intrinsics for specific instruction sets, so this way of thinking is already common among many CPU developers.

CHAPTER 11 VECTORS

Although these two interpretations are very different, they unintentionally became combined and muddled together as SYCL and other languages became applicable to both CPUs and GPUs. A vector in the SYCL 1.2.1 specification is compatible with either interpretation (we will revisit this later), so we need to clarify our recommended thinking in DPC++ before going any further.

Throughout this book, we talk about how work-items can be grouped together to expose powerful communication and synchronization primitives, such as sub-group barriers and shuffles. For these operations to be efficient on vector hardware, there is an assumption that different work-items in a sub-group combine and map to SIMD instructions. Said another way, multiple work-items are grouped together by the compiler, at which point they can map to SIMD instructions in the hardware. Remember from Chapter 4 that this is a basic premise of SPMD programming models that operate on top of vector hardware, where a single work-item constitutes a *lane* of what *might* be a SIMD instruction in hardware, instead of a work-item defining the *entire* operation that will be a SIMD instruction in the hardware. You can think of the compiler as always vectorizing across work-items when mapping to SIMD instructions in hardware, when programming in a SPMD style with the DPC++ compiler.

For the features and hardware described in this book, vectors are useful primarily for the first interpretation in this section—vectors are convenience types that should not be thought of as mapping to SIMD instructions in hardware. Work-items are grouped together to form SIMD instructions in hardware, on the platforms where that applies (CPUs, GPUs). Vectors should be thought of as providing convenient operators such as swizzles and math functions that make common operations on groups of data concise within our code (e.g., adding two RGB pixels).

For developers coming from languages that don't have vectors or from GPU shading languages, we can think of SYCL vectors as local to a work-item in that if there is an addition of two four-element vectors, that addition might take four instructions in the hardware (it would be

261

scalarized from the perspective of the work-item). Each element of the vector would be added through a different instruction/clock cycle in the hardware. With this interpretation, vectors are a convenience in that we can add two vectors in a single operation in our source code, as opposed to performing four scalar operations in the source.

For developers coming from a CPU background, we should know that implicit vectorization to SIMD hardware occurs by default in the compiler in a few ways independent of the vector types. The compiler performs this implicit vectorization across work-items, extracts the vector operations from well-formed loops, or honors vector types when mapping to vector instructions—see Chapter 16 for more information.

OTHER IMPLEMENTATIONS POSSIBLE!

Different compilers and implementations of SYCL and DPC++ can in theory make different decisions on how vector data types in code map to vector hardware instructions. We should read a vendor's documentation and optimization guides to understand how to write code that will map to efficient SIMD instructions. This book is written principally against the DPC++ compiler, so documents the thinking and programming patterns that it is built around.

CHANGES ARE ON THE HORIZON

We have just said to consider vector types as convenience types and to expect vectorization across work-items when thinking about the mapping to hardware on devices where that makes sense. This is expected to be the default interpretation in the DPC++ compiler and toolchain going forward. However, there are two additional future-looking changes to be aware of.

First, we can expect some future DPC++ features that *will* allow us to write explicit vector code that maps directly to SIMD instructions in the hardware, particularly for experts who want to tune details of code for a specific architecture and take control from the compiler vectorizers. This is a niche feature that will be used by very few developers, but we can expect programming mechanisms to exist eventually where this is possible. Those programming mechanisms will make it very clear which code is written in an explicit vector style, so that there isn't confusion between the code we write today and that new more explicit (and less portable) style.

Second, the need for this section of the book (talking about interpretations of vectors) highlights that there is confusion on what a vector means, and that will be solved in SYCL in the future. There is a hint of this in the SYCL 2020 provisional specification where a math array type (marray) has been described, which is explicitly the first interpretation from this section—a convenience type unrelated to vector hardware instructions. We should expect another type to also eventually appear to cover the second interpretation, likely aligned with the C++ std::simd templates. With these two types being clearly associated with specific interpretations of a vector data type, our intent as programmers will be clear from the code that we write. This will be less error prone and less confusing and may even reduce the number of heated discussions between expert developers when the question arises "What *is* a vector?"

Vector Types

Vector types in SYCL are cross-platform class templates that work efficiently on devices as well as in host C++ code and allow sharing of vectors between the host and its devices. Vector types include methods that allow construction of a new vector from a swizzled set of component elements, meaning that elements of the new vector can be picked in an arbitrary order from elements of the old vector. vec is a vector type that compiles down to the built-in vector types on target device backends, where possible, and provides compatible support on the host.

The vec class is templated on its number of elements and its element type. The number of elements parameter, numElements, can be one of 1,

2, 3, 4, 8, or 16. Any other value will produce a compilation failure. The element type parameter, dataT, must be one of the basic scalar types supported in device code.

The SYCL vec class template provides interoperability with the underlying vector type defined by vector_t which is available only when compiled for the device. The vec class can be constructed from an instance of vector_t and can implicitly convert to an instance of vector_t in order to support interoperability with native SYCL backends from a kernel function (e.g., OpenCL backends). An instance of the vec class template can also be implicitly converted to an instance of the data type when the number of elements is 1 in order to allow single-element vectors and scalars to be easily interchangeable.

For our programming convenience, SYCL provides a number of type aliases of the form using <type><elems> = vec<<storage-type>, <elems>>, where <elems> is 2, 3, 4, 8, and 16 and pairings of <type> and <storage-type> for integral types are char ⇔ int8_t, uchar ⇔ uint8_t, short ⇔ int16_t, ushort ⇔ uint16_t, int ⇔ int32_t, uint ⇔ uint32_t, long ⇔ int64_t, and ulong ⇔ uint64_t and for floating-point types half, float, and double. For example, uint4 is an alias to vec<uint32_t, 4> and float16 is an alias to vec<float, 16>.

Vector Interface

The functionality of vector types is exposed through the class vec. The vec class represents a set of data elements that are grouped together. The interfaces of the constructors, member functions, and non-member functions of the vec class template are described in Figures 11-1, 11-4, and 11-5.

The XYZW members listed in Figure 11-2 are available only when numElements <= 4. RGBA members are available only when numElements == 4.

The members lo, hi, odd, and even shown in Figure 11-3 are available only when numElements > 1.

```
vec Class declaration
template <typename dataT, int numElements> class vec;
vec Class Members
using element_type = dataT;
vec();
explicit vec(const dataT &arg);
template <typename ... argTN> vec(const argTN&... args);
vec(const vec<dataT, numElements> &rhs);

#ifdef __SYCL_DEVICE_ONLY__           // available on device only
vec(vector_t openclVector);
operator vector_t() const;
#endif

operator dataT() const; // Available only if numElements == 1
size_t get_count() const;
size_t get_size() const;

template <typename convertT, rounding_mode roundingMode>
vec<convertT, numElements> convert() const;
template <typename asT> asT as() const;
```

Figure 11-1. vec *class declaration and member functions*

```
template<int... swizzleindexes>
 __swizzled_vec__ swizzle() const;
 __swizzled_vec__ XYZW_ACCESS() const;
 __swizzled_vec__ RGBA_ACCESS() const;
 __swizzled_vec__ INDEX_ACCESS() const;

#ifdef SYCL_SIMPLE_SWIZZLES
// Available only when numElements <= 4
// XYZW_SWIZZLE is all permutations with repetition of:
// x, y, z, w, subject to numElements
 __swizzled_vec__ XYZW_SWIZZLE() const;

// Available only when numElements == 4
// RGBA_SWIZZLE is all permutations with repetition of: r, g, b, a.
 __swizzled_vec__ RGBA_SWIZZLE() const;
#endif
```

Figure 11-2. swizzled_vec *member functions*

CHAPTER 11 VECTORS

```
__swizzled_vec__ lo() const;
__swizzled_vec__ hi() const;
__swizzled_vec__ odd() const;
__swizzled_vec__ even() const;

template <access::address_space addressSpace>
  void load(size_t offset, multi_ptr ptr<dataT, addressSpace> ptr);
template <access::address_space addressSpace>
  void store(size_t offset, multi_ptr ptr<dataT, addressSpace> ptr) const;

vec<dataT, numElements> &operator=(const vec<dataT, numElements> &rhs);
vec<dataT, numElements> &operator=(const dataT &rhs);
vec<RET, numElements>  operator!();

// Not available for floating point types:
vec<dataT, numElements> operator~();
```

Figure 11-3. vec operator interface

Member function with OP variable	For all types, OP may be	For integral types, OP may be
vec<dataT, numElements> **operatorOP**(const **vec**<dataT, numElements> &rhs) const;	+, -, *, /	%, &, |, ^, <<, >>
vec<dataT, numElements> **operatorOP**(const dataT &rhs) const;		
vec<dataT, numElements> **&operatorOP**(const **vec**<dataT, numElements> &rhs) const;	+=, -=, *=, /=	%=, &=, |=, ^=, <<=, >>=
vec<dataT, numElements> **&operatorOP**(const dataT &rhs) const;		
vec<RET, numElements> **operatorOP**(const **vec**<dataT, numElements> &rhs) const;	&&, ||, ==, !=, <, >, <=, >=	
vec<RET, numElements> **operatorOP**(const dataT &rhs) const;		
vec<dataT, numElements> **&operatorOP**() const;	++, --	
vec<dataT, numElements> **operatorOP**(int) const;		

Figure 11-4. vec member functions

Non-member function with OP variable	For all types, OP may be	For non floating-point types, OP may be
template <typename dataT, int numElements> **vec**<dataT, numElements> **operatorOP**(const dataT, &*lhs*) const *vec*<dataT, numElements> &*rhs*);	+, -, *, /	%, &, |, ^, <<, >>
template <typename dataT, int numElements> **vec**<RET, numElements> **operatorOP**(const dataT &*lhs*, const **vec**<dataT, numElements> &rhs);	&&, ||, ==, !=, <, >, <=, >=	

Figure 11-5. vec non-member functions

Load and Store Member Functions

Vector load and store operations are members of the vec class for loading and storing the elements of a vector. These operations can be to or from an array of elements of the same type as the channels of the vector. An example is shown in Figure 11-6.

CHAPTER 11 VECTORS

```
buffer fpBuf(fpData);
queue Q;
Q.submit([&](handler& h) {
  accessor buf{fpBuf, h};

  h.parallel_for(size, [=](id<1> idx){
    size_t offset = idx[0]/16;
    float16 inpf16;
    inpf16.load(offset, buf.get_pointer());
    float16 result = inpf16 * 2.0f;
    result.store(offset, buf.get_pointer());
  });
});
```

***Figure 11-6.** Use of load and store member functions.*

In the vec class, dataT and numElements are template parameters that reflect the component type and dimensionality of a vec.

The load() member function template will read values of type dataT from the memory at the address of the multi_ptr, offset in elements of dataT by numElements*offset, and write those values to the channels of the *vec*.

The store() member function template will read channels of the *vec* and write those values to the memory at the address of the multi_ptr, offset in elements of dataT by numElements*offset.

The parameter is a multi_ptr rather than an accessor so that locally created pointers can also be used as well as pointers passed from the host.

The data type of the multi_ptr is dataT, the data type of the components of the vec class specialization. This requires that the pointer passed to either load() or store() must match the type of the vec instance itself.

Swizzle Operations

In graphics applications, *swizzling* means rearranging the data elements of a vector. For example, if a = {1, 2, 3, 4,}, and knowing that the components of a four-element vector can be referred to as {x, y, z, w}, we could write b = a.wxyz(). The result in the variable b would be {4, 1, 2, 3}. This form of code is common in GPU applications where there is efficient hardware for such operations. Swizzles can be performed in two ways:

- By calling the swizzle member function of a vec, which takes a variadic number of integer template arguments between 0 and numElements-1, specifying swizzle indices

- By calling one of the simple swizzle member functions such as XYZW_SWIZZLE and RGBA_SWIZZLE

Note that the simple swizzle functions are only available for up to four-element vectors and are only available when the macro SYCL_SIMPLE_SWIZZLES is defined before including sycl.hpp. In both cases, the return type is always an instance of __swizzled_vec__, an implementation-defined temporary class representing a swizzle of the original vec instance. Both the swizzle member function template and the simple swizzle member functions allow swizzle indexes to be repeated. Figure 11-7 shows a simple usage of __swizzled_vec__.

CHAPTER 11 VECTORS

```
constexpr int size = 16;

std::array<float4, size> input;
for (int i = 0; i < size; i++)
  input[i] = float4(8.0f, 6.0f, 2.0f, i);

buffer B(input);

queue Q;
Q.submit([&](handler& h) {
  accessor A{B, h};

  // We can access the individual elements of a vector by using
  // the functions x(), y(), z(), w() and so on.
  //
  // "Swizzles" can be used by calling a vector member equivalent
  // to the swizzle order that we need, for example zyx() or any
  // combination of the elements. The swizzle need not be the same
  // size as the original vector.
  h.parallel_for(size, [=](id<1> idx) {
    auto   b  = A[idx];
    float  w  = b.w();
    float4 sw = b.xyzw();
    sw = b.xyzw() * sw.wzyx();;
    sw = sw + w;
    A[idx] = sw.xyzw();
  });
});
```

Figure 11-7. Example of using the __swizzled_vec__ class

Vector Execution Within a Parallel Kernel

As described in Chapters 4 and 9, a work-item is the leaf node of the parallelism hierarchy and represents an individual instance of a kernel function. Work-items can be executed in any order and cannot communicate or synchronize with each other except through atomic memory operations to local and global memory or through group collective functions (e.g., `shuffle`, `barrier`).

As described at the start of this chapter, a vector in DPC++ should be interpreted as a convenience for us when writing code. Each vector is local to a single work-item (instead of relating to vectorization in hardware) and

CHAPTER 11   VECTORS

can therefore be thought of as equivalent to a private array of numElements in our work-item. For example, the storage of a "float4 y4" declaration is equivalent to float y4[4]. Consider the example shown in Figure 11-8.

```
Q.parallel_for(8, [=](id<1> i){
  ... ...
  float   x  = a[i];       // i = 0, 1, 2, ..., 7
  float4  y4 = b[i];       // i = 0, 1, 2, ..., 7
  ... ...
});
```

Figure 11-8. *Vector execution example*

For the scalar variable x, the result of kernel execution with multiple work-items on hardware that has SIMD instructions (e.g., CPUs, GPUs) might use a vector register and SIMD instructions, but the vectorization is across work-items and unrelated to any vector type in our code. Each work-item could operate on a different location in the implicit vec_x, as shown in Figure 11-9. The scalar data in a work-item can be thought of as being implicitly vectorized (combined into SIMD hardware instructions) across work-items that happen to execute at the same time, in some implementations and on some hardware, but the work-item code that we write does not encode this in any way—this is at the core of the SPMD style of programming.

work-item ID	w0	w1	w2	w3	w4	w5	w6	w7
vec_x	a0	a1	a2	a3	a4	a5	a6	a7

Figure 11-9. *Vector expansion from scalar variable x to* vec_x[8]

With the implicit vector expansion from scalar variable x to vec_x[8] by the compiler as shown in Figure 11-9, the compiler creates a SIMD operation in hardware from a scalar operation that occurs in multiple work-items.

CHAPTER 11 VECTORS

For the vector variable y4, the result of kernel execution for multiple work-items, for example, eight work-items, does not process the vec4 by using vector operations in hardware. Instead each work-item independently sees its own vector, and the operations on elements on that vector occur across multiple clock cycles/instructions (the vector is scalarized by the compiler), as shown in Figure 11-10.

work-item ID	vec_y0	vec_y1	vec_y2	vec_y3
w0	b0	b0	b0	b0
w1	b1	b1	b1	b1
w2	b2	b2	b2	b2
w3	b3	b3	b3	b4
w4	b4	b4	b4	b5
w5	b5	b5	b5	b6
w6	b6	b6	b6	b6
w7	b7	b7	b7	b7

Figure 11-10. Vertical expansion to equivalent of vec_y[8][4] of y4 across eight work-items

Each work-item sees the original data layout of y4, which provides an intuitive model to reason about and tune. The performance downside is that the compiler has to generate gather/scatter memory instructions for both CPUs and GPUs, as shown in Figure 11-11, (the vectors are contiguous in memory and neighboring work-items operating on different vectors in parallel), so scalars are often an efficient approach over explicit vectors when a compiler will vectorize across work-items (e.g., across a sub-group). See Chapters 15 and 16 for more details.

```
Q.parallel_for(8, [=](id<1> i){
  ... ...
  float4 y4 = b[i];      // i = 0, 1, 2, ..., 7
  ... ...
  // "dowork" expects y4 with vec_y[8][4] data layout
  float x = dowork(&y4);
});
```

Figure 11-11. *Vector code example with address escaping*

When the compiler is able to prove that the address of y4 does not escape from the current kernel work-item or all callee functions are to be inlined, then the compiler may perform optimizations that act as if there was a horizontal unit-stride expansion to vec_y[4][8] from y4 using a set of vector registers, as shown in Figure 11-12. In this case, compilers can achieve optimal performance without generating gather/scatter SIMD instructions for both CPUs and GPUs. The compiler optimization reports provide information to programmers about this type of transformation, whether it occurred or not, and can provide hints on how to tweak our code for increased performance.

work-item ID	w0	w1	w2	w3	w4	w5	w6	w7
y0	b0	b1	b2	b3	b4	b5	b6	b7
y1	b0	b1	b2	b3	b4	b5	b6	b7
y2	b0	b1	b2	b3	b4	b5	b6	b7
y3	b0	b1	b2	b3	b4	b5	b6	b7

Figure 11-12. *Horizontal unit-stride expansion to vec_y[4][8] of y4*

CHAPTER 11　VECTORS

Vector Parallelism

Although vectors in source code within DPC++ should be interpreted as convenience tools that are local to only a single work-item, this chapter on vectors would not be complete without some mention of how SIMD instructions in hardware operate. This discussion is not coupled to vectors within our source code, but provides orthogonal background that will be useful as we progress to the later chapters of this book that describe specific device types (GPU, CPU, FPGA).

Modern CPUs and GPUs contain SIMD instruction hardware that operate on multiple data values contained in one vector register or a register file. For example, with Intel x86 AVX-512 and other modern CPU SIMD hardware, SIMD instructions can be used to exploit data parallelism. On CPUs and GPUs that provide SIMD hardware, we can consider a vector addition operation, for example, on an eight-element vector, as shown in Figure 11-13.

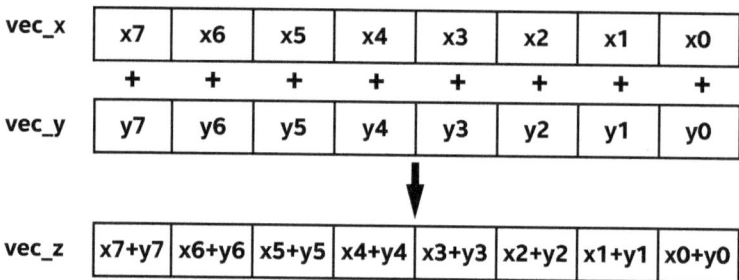

Figure 11-13. SIMD addition with eight-way data parallelism

The vector addition in this example could execute in a single instruction on vector hardware, adding the vector registers vec_x and vec_y in parallel with that SIMD instruction.

Exposing potential parallelism in a hardware-agnostic way ensures that our applications can scale up (or down) to fit the capabilities of different platforms, including those with vector hardware instructions.

Striking the right balance between work-item and other forms of parallelism during application development is a challenge that we must all engage with, and that is covered more in Chapters 15, 16, and 17.

Summary

There are multiple interpretations of the term *vector* within programming languages, and understanding the interpretation that a particular language or compiler has been built around is important when we want to write performant and scalable code. DPC++ and the DPC++ compiler have been built around the idea that vectors in source code are convenience functions local to a work-item and that implicit vectorization by the compiler across work-items may map to SIMD instructions in the hardware. When we want to write code which maps directly to vector hardware explicitly, we should look to vendor documentation and future extensions to SYCL and DPC++. Writing our kernels using multiple work-items (e.g., ND-range) and relying on the compiler to vectorize across work-items should be how most applications are written because doing so leverages the powerful abstraction of SPMD, which provides an easy-to-reason-about programming model, and that provides scalable performance across devices and architectures.

This chapter has described the vec interface, which offers convenience out of the box when we have groupings of similarly typed data that we want to operate on (e.g., a pixel with multiple color channels). It has also touched briefly on SIMD instructions in hardware, to prepare us for more detailed discussions in Chapters 15 and 16.

CHAPTER 11 VECTORS

 **Open Access** This chapter is licensed under the terms of the Creative Commons Attribution 4.0 International License (http://creativecommons.org/licenses/by/4.0/), which permits use, sharing, adaptation, distribution and reproduction in any medium or format, as long as you give appropriate credit to the original author(s) and the source, provide a link to the Creative Commons license and indicate if changes were made.

The images or other third party material in this chapter are included in the chapter's Creative Commons license, unless indicated otherwise in a credit line to the material. If material is not included in the chapter's Creative Commons license and your intended use is not permitted by statutory regulation or exceeds the permitted use, you will need to obtain permission directly from the copyright holder.

CHAPTER 12

Device Information

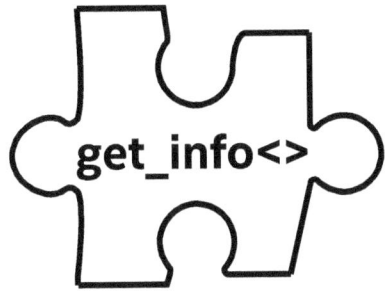

Chapter 2 introduced us to the mechanisms that direct work to a particular device—controlling *where code executes.* In this chapter, we explore how to adapt to the devices that are present at runtime.

We want our programs to be portable. In order to be portable, we need our programs to adapt to the capabilities of the device. We can parameterize our programs to only use features that are present and to tune our code to the particulars of devices. If our program is not designed to adapt, then bad things can happen including slow execution or program failures.

Fortunately, the creators of the SYCL specification thought about this and gave us interfaces to let us solve this problem. The SYCL specification defines a device class that encapsulates a device on which kernels may be executed. The ability to query the device class, so that our program can adapt to the device characteristics and capabilities, is the heart of what this chapter teaches.

CHAPTER 12   DEVICE INFORMATION

Many of us will start with having logic to figure out "Is there a GPU present?" to inform the choices our program will make as it executes. That is the start of what this chapter covers. As we will see, there is much more information available to help us make our programs robust and performant.

Parameterizing a program can help with correctness, portability, performance portability, and future proofing.

This chapter dives into the most important queries and how to use them effectively in our programs.

Device-specific properties are queryable using `get_info`, but DPC++ diverges from SYCL 1.2.1 in that it fully overloads `get_info` to alleviate the need to use `get_work_group_info` for work-group information that is really device-specific information. DPC++ does not support use of `get_work_group_info`. This change means that device-specific kernel and work-group properties are properly found as queries for device-specific properties (`get_info`). This corrects a confusing historical anomaly still present in SYCL 1.2.1 that was inherited from OpenCL.

Refining Kernel Code to Be More Prescriptive

It is useful to consider that our coding, kernel by kernel, will fall broadly into one of three categories:

- Generic kernel code: Run anywhere, not tuned to a specific class of device.

- Device type–specific kernel code: Run on a type of device (e.g., GPU, CPU, FPGA), not tuned to specific *models* of a device type. This is very useful because many device types share common features, so it's safe to make some assumptions that would not apply to fully general code written for all devices.

- Tuned device-specific kernel code: Run on a type of device, with tuning that reacts to specific parameters of a device—this covers a broad range of possibilities from a small amount of tuning to very detailed optimization work.

It is our job as programmers to determine when different patterns (Chapter 14) are needed for different device types. We dedicate Chapters 14, 15, 16, and 17 to illuminating this important thinking.

It is most common to start by implementing generic kernel code to get it working. Chapter 2 specifically talks about what methods are easiest to debug when getting started with a kernel implementation. Once we have a kernel working, we may evolve it to target the capabilities of a specific device type or device model.

Chapter 14 offers a framework of thinking to consider parallelism first, before we dive into device considerations. It is our choice of pattern (aka algorithm) that dictates our code, and it is our job as programmers to determine when different patterns are needed for different devices. Chapters 15 (GPU), 16 (CPU), and 17 (FPGA) dive more deeply into the qualities that distinguish these device types and motivate a choice in pattern to use. It is these qualities that motivate us to consider writing distinct versions of kernels for different devices when the approaches (pattern choice) on different device types differ.

When we have a kernel written for a specific type of device (e.g., a specific CPU, GPU, FPGA, etc.), it is logical to adapt it to specific vendors or even models of such devices. Good coding style is to parameterize code based on features (e.g., item size support found from a device query).

We should write code to query parameters that describe the actual capabilities of a device instead of its marketing information; it is very bad programming practice to query the model number of a device and react to that—such code is less portable.

It is common to write a different kernel for each device type that we want to support (a GPU version of a kernel and an FPGA version of a kernel and maybe a generic version of a kernel). When we get more specific, to support a specific device vendor or even device model, we may benefit when we can parameterize a kernel rather than duplicate it. We are free to do either, as we see fit. Code cluttered with too many parameter adjustments may be hard to read or excessively burdened at runtime. It is common however that parameters can fit neatly into a single version of a kernel.

Parameterizing makes the most sense when the algorithm is broadly the same but has been tuned for the capabilities of a specific device. Writing a different kernel is much cleaner when using a completely different approach, pattern, or algorithm.

How to Enumerate Devices and Capabilities

Chapter 2 enumerates and explains five methods for choosing a device on which to execute. Essentially, Method#1 was the least prescriptive *run it somewhere*, and we evolve to the most prescriptive Method#5 which considered executing on a fairly precise model of a device from a family of devices. The enumerated methods in between gave a mix of flexibility and prescriptiveness. Figures 12-1, 12-2, and 12-3 help to illustrate how we can select a device.

Figure 12-1 shows that even if we allow the implementation to select a default device for us (Method#1 in Chapter 2), we can still query for information about the selected device.

Figure 12-2 shows how we can try to set up a queue using a specific device (in this case, a GPU), but fall back explicitly on the host if no GPU is available. This gives us some control of our device choice. If we simply used a default queue, we could end up with an unexpected device type (e.g., a DSP, FPGA). If we explicitly want to use the host device if there is no GPU device, this code does that for us. Recall that the host device is always guaranteed to exist, so we do not need to worry about using the host_selector.

It is not recommended that we use the solution shown in Figure 12-2. In addition to appearing a little scary and error prone, Figure 12-2 does not give us control over what GPU is selected because it is implementation dependent which GPU we get if more than one is available. Despite being both instructive and functional, there is a better way. It is recommended that we write custom device selectors as shown in the next code example (Figure 12-3).

Custom Device Selector

Figure 12-3 uses a custom device selector. Custom device selectors were first discussed in Chapter 2 as Method#5 for choosing where our code runs (Figure 2-15). The custom device selector causes its operator(), shown in Figure 12-3, to be invoked for each device available to the application. The device selected is the one that receives the highest score.[1] In this example, we will have a little fun with our selector:

---

[1] If our device selector returned only negative values, then the my_selector() would throw a runtime_error exception as expected on non-GPU systems in Figure 12-2. Since we return a positive value for the host, that cannot happen in Figure 12-3.

- Reject GPUs with a vendor name including the word "Martian" (return –1).
- Favor GPUs with a vendor name including the word "ACME" (return 824).
- Any other GPU is a good one (return 799).
- We pick the host device if no GPU is present (return 99).
- All other devices are ignored (return –1).

The next section, "Being Curious: get_info<>," dives into the rich information that get_devices(), get_platforms(), and get_info<> offer. Those interfaces open up any type of logic we might want to utilize to pick our devices, including the simple vendor name checks shown in Figures 2-15 and 12-3.

```
queue Q;
std::cout << "By default, we are running on "
  << Q.get_device().get_info<info::device::name>() << "\n";
// sample output:
// By default, we are running on Intel(R) Gen9 HD Graphics NEO.
```

Figure 12-1. Device we have been assigned by default

Queries about devices rely on installed software (special user-level drivers), to respond regarding a device. SYCL and DPC++ rely on this, just as an operating system needs drivers to access hardware—it is not sufficient that the hardware simply be installed in a machine.

CHAPTER 12 DEVICE INFORMATION

```
auto GPU_is_available = false;

try {
  device testForGPU((gpu_selector()));
  GPU_is_available = true;
} catch (exception const& ex) {
  std::cout << "Caught this SYCL exception: " << ex.what() << std::endl;
}

auto Q = GPU_is_available ? queue(gpu_selector()) : queue(host_selector());

std::cout << "After checking for a GPU, we are running on:\n "
          << Q.get_device().get_info<info::device::name>() << "\n";

// sample output using a system with a GPU:
// After checking for a GPU, we are running on:
//   Intel(R) Gen9 HD Graphics NEO.
//
// sample output using a system with an FPGA accelerator, but no GPU:
// Caught this SYCL exception: No device of requested type available.
// ...(CL_DEVICE_NOT_FOUND)
// After checking for a GPU, we are running on:
//   SYCL host device.
```

Figure 12-2. *Using try-catch to select a GPU device if possible, host device if not*

283

```cpp
class my_selector : public device_selector {
 public:
  int operator()(const device &dev) const {
    int score = -1;

    // We prefer non-Martian GPUs, especially ACME GPUs
    if (dev.is_gpu()) {
      if (dev.get_info<info::device::vendor>().find("ACME")
          != std::string::npos) score += 25;

      if (dev.get_info<info::device::vendor>().find("Martian")
          == std::string::npos) score += 800;
    }

    // Give host device points so it is used if no GPU is available.
    // Without these next two lines, systems with no GPU would select
    // nothing, since we initialize the score to a negative number above.
    if (dev.is_host()) score += 100;

    return score;
  }
};

int main() {
  auto Q = queue{ my_selector{} };

  std::cout << "After checking for a GPU, we are running on:\n "
    << Q.get_device().get_info<info::device::name>() << "\n";

  // Sample output using a system with a GPU:
  // After checking for a GPU, we are running on:
  //   Intel(R) Gen9 HD Graphics NEO.
  //
  // Sample output using a system with an FPGA accelerator, but no GPU:
  // After checking for a GPU, we are running on:
  //   SYCL host device.

  return 0;
}
```

Figure 12-3. Custom device selector—our preferred solution

CHAPTER 12   DEVICE INFORMATION

Being Curious: get_info<>

In order for our program to "know" what devices are available at runtime, we can have our program query available devices from the device class, and then we can learn more details using get_info<> to inquire about a specific device. We provide a simple program, called *curious* (see Figure 12-4), that uses these interfaces to dump out information for us to look at directly. This can be very useful for doing a sanity check when developing or debugging a program that uses these interfaces. Failure of this program to work as expected can often tell us that the software drivers we need are not installed correctly. Figure 12-5 shows sample output from this program, with the high-level information about the devices that are present.

```cpp
// Loop through available platforms
for (auto const& this_platform : platform::get_platforms() ) {
  std::cout << "Found platform: "
    << this_platform.get_info<info::platform::name>() << "\n";

  // Loop through available devices in this platform
  for (auto const& this_device : this_platform.get_devices() ) {
    std::cout << " Device: "
      << this_device.get_info<info::device::name>() << "\n";
  }
  std::cout << "\n";
}
```

Figure 12-4. *Simple use of device query mechanisms: curious.cpp*

```
% make curious
dpcpp curious.cpp -o curious

% ./curious
Found platform 1...
Platform: Intel(R) FPGA Emulation Platform for OpenCL(TM)
Device: Intel(R) FPGA Emulation Device

Found platform 2...
Platform: Intel(R) OpenCL HD Graphics
Device: Intel(R) Gen9 HD Graphics NEO

Found platform 3...
Platform: Intel(R) OpenCL
Device: Intel(R) Xeon(R) E-2176G CPU @ 3.70GHz

Found platform 4...
Platform: SYCL host platform
Device: SYCL host device
```

Figure 12-5. *Sample output from curious.cpp*

Being More Curious: Detailed Enumeration Code

We offer a program, which we have named verycurious.cpp (Figure 12-6), to illustrate some of the detailed information available using get_info<>. Again, we find ourselves writing code like this to help when developing or debugging a program. Figure 12-5 shows sample output from this program, with the lower-level information about the devices that are present.

Now that we have shown how to access the information, we will discuss the information fields that prove the most important to query and act upon in applications.

```cpp
template <auto query, typename T>
void do_query( const T& obj_to_query, const std::string& name, int indent=4)
{
  std::cout << std::string(indent, ' ') << name << " is '"
    << obj_to_query.template get_info<query>() << "'\n";
}

// Loop through the available platforms
for (auto const& this_platform : platform::get_platforms() ) {
  std::cout << "Found Platform:\n";
  do_query<info::platform::name>(this_platform,
      "info::platform::name");
  do_query<info::platform::vendor>(this_platform,
      "info::platform::vendor");
  do_query<info::platform::version>(this_platform,
      "info::platform::version");
  do_query<info::platform::profile>(this_platform,
      "info::platform::profile");

  // Loop through the devices available in this plaform
  for (auto &dev : this_platform.get_devices() ) {
    std::cout << "  Device: "
              << dev.get_info<info::device::name>() << "\n";
    std::cout << "    is_host(): "
              << (dev.is_host() ? "Yes" : "No") << "\n";
    std::cout << "    is_cpu(): "
              << (dev.is_cpu() ? "Yes" : "No") << "\n";
    std::cout << "    is_gpu(): "
              << (dev.is_gpu() ? "Yes" : "No") << "\n";
    std::cout << "    is_accelerator(): "
              << (dev.is_accelerator() ? "Yes" : "No") << "\n";

    do_query<info::device::vendor>(dev, "info::device::vendor");
    do_query<info::device::driver_version>(dev,
              "info::device::driver_version");
    do_query<info::device::max_work_item_dimensions>(dev,
              "info::device::max_work_item_dimensions");
    do_query<info::device::max_work_group_size>(dev,
              "info::device::max_work_group_size");
    do_query<info::device::mem_base_addr_align>(dev,
              "info::device::mem_base_addr_align");
    do_query<info::device::partition_max_sub_devices>(dev,
              "info::device::partition_max_sub_devices");

    std::cout << "   Many more queries are available than shown here!\n";
  }
  std::cout << "\n";
}
```

Figure 12-6. More detailed use of device query mechanisms: verycurious.cpp

Inquisitive: get_info<>

The `has_extension()` interface allows a program to test directly for a feature, rather than having to walk through a list of extensions from `get_info <info::platform::extensions>` as printed out by the previous code examples. The SYCL 2020 provisional specification has defined new mechanisms to query extensions and detailed aspects of devices, but we don't cover those features (which are just being finalized) in this book. Consult the online oneAPI DPC++ language reference for more information.

Device Information Descriptors

Our "curious" program examples, used earlier in this chapter, utilize the most used SYCL device class member functions (i.e., `is_host`, `is_cpu`, `is_gpu`, `is_accelerator`, `get_info`, `has_extension`). These member functions are documented in the SYCL specification in a table titled "Member functions of the SYCL device class" (in SYCL 1.2.1, it is Table 4.18).

The "curious" program examples also queried for information using the `get_info` member function. There is a set of queries that must be supported by all SYCL devices, including a host device. The complete list of such items is described in the SYCL specification in a table titled "Device information descriptors" (in SYCL 1.2.1, it is Table 4.20).

Device-Specific Kernel Information Descriptors

Like platforms and devices, we can query information about our kernels using a `get_info` function. Such information (e.g., supported work-group sizes, preferred work-group size, the amount of private memory required per work-item) is device-specific, and so the `get_info` member function of the `kernel` class accepts a `device` as an argument.

CHAPTER 12 DEVICE INFORMATION

> **DEVICE-SPECIFIC KERNEL INFORMATION IN SYCL 1.2.1**
>
> For historical reasons dating back to OpenCL naming, SYCL inherited a combination of queries named `kernel::get_info` and `kernel::get_work_group_info`, returning information about a kernel object and information pertaining to a kernel's execution on a specific device, respectively.
>
> Use of overloading in DPC++ and SYCL (as of 2020 provisional) allows for both types of information to be supported through a single `get_info` API.

The Specifics: Those of "Correctness"

We will divide the specifics into information about necessary conditions (correctness) and information useful for tuning but not necessary for correctness.

In this first correctness category, we will enumerate conditions that should be met in order for kernels to launch properly. Failure to abide by these device limitations will lead to program failures. Figure 12-7 shows how we can fetch a few of these parameters in a way that the values are available for use in host code and in kernel code (via lambda capture). We can modify our code to utilize this information; for instance, it could guide our code on buffer sizing or work-group sizing.

> Submitting a kernel that does not satisfy these conditions will generate an error.

289

CHAPTER 12 DEVICE INFORMATION

```
std::cout << "We are running on:\n"
          << dev.get_info<info::device::name>() << "\n";

// Query results like the following can be used to calculate how
// large our kernel invocations should be.
auto maxWG = dev.get_info<info::device::max_work_group_size>();
auto maxGmem = dev.get_info<info::device::global_mem_size>();
auto maxLmem = dev.get_info<info::device::local_mem_size>();

std::cout << "Max WG size is " << maxWG
          << "\nMax Global memory size is " << maxGmem
          << "\nMax Local memory size is "  << maxLmem << "\n";
```

Figure 12-7. Fetching parameters that can be used to shape a kernel

Device Queries

device_type: cpu, gpu, accelerator, custom,[2] automatic, host, all. These are most often tested by is_host(), is_cpu, is_gpu(), and so on (see Figure 12-6):

> max_work_item_sizes: The maximum number of work-items that are permitted in each dimension of the work-group of the nd_range. The minimum value is (1, 1, 1) for non-custom devices.
>
> max_work_group_size: The maximum number of work-items that are permitted in a work-group executing a kernel on a single compute unit. The minimum value is 1.
>
> global_mem_size: The size of global memory in bytes.
>
> local_mem_size: The size of local memory in bytes. Except for custom devices, the minimum size is 32 K.

---

[2]Custom devices are not discussed in this book. If we find ourselves programming a device that identifies itself using the *custom* type, we will need to study the documentation for that device to learn more.

extensions: Device-specific information not specifically detailed in the SYCL specification, often vendor-specific, as illustrated in our verycurious program (Figure 12-6).

max_compute_units: Indicative of the amount of parallelism available on a device—implementation-defined, interpret with care!

sub_group_sizes: Returns the set of sub-group sizes supported by the device.

usm_device_allocations: Returns true if this device supports device allocations as described in explicit USM.

usm_host_allocations: Returns true if this device can access host allocations.

usm_shared_allocations: Returns true if this device supports shared allocations.

usm_restricted_shared_allocations: Returns true if this device supports shared allocations as governed by the restrictions of "restricted USM" on the device. This property requires that property usm_shared_allocations returns true for this device.

usm_system_allocator: Returns true if the system allocator may be used instead of USM allocation mechanisms for shared allocations on this device.

We advise avoiding max_compute_units in program logic.

We have found that querying the maximum number of compute units should be avoided, in part because the definition isn't crisp enough to be useful in code tuning. Instead of using `max_compute_units`, most programs should express their parallelism and let the runtime map it onto available parallelism. Relying on `max_compute_units` for correctness only makes sense when augmented with implementation- and device-specific information. Experts might do that, but most developers do not and do not need to do so! Let the runtime do its job in this case!

Kernel Queries

The mechanisms discussed in Chapter 10, under "Kernels in Program Objects," are needed to perform these kernel queries:

> `work_group_size`: Returns the maximum work-group size that can be used to execute a kernel on a specific device
>
> `compile_work_group_size`: Returns the work-group size specified by a kernel if applicable; otherwise returns (0, 0, 0)
>
> `compile_sub_group_size`: Returns the sub-group size specified by a kernel if applicable; otherwise returns 0
>
> `compile_num_sub_groups`: Returns the number of sub-groups specified by a kernel if applicable; otherwise returns 0
>
> `max_sub_group_size`: Returns the maximum sub-group size for a kernel launched with the specified work-group size
>
> `max_num_sub_groups`: Returns the maximum number of sub-groups for a kernel

The Specifics: Those of "Tuning/ Optimization"

There are a few additional parameters that can be considered as fine-tuning parameters for our kernels. These can be ignored without jeopardizing the correctness of a program. These allow our kernels to really utilize the particulars of the hardware for performance.

> Paying attention to the results of these queries can help when tuning for a cache (if it exists).

Device Queries

> global_mem_cache_line_size: Size of global memory cache line in bytes.
>
> global_mem_cache_size: Size of global memory cache in bytes.
>
> local_mem_type: The type of local memory supported. This can be info::local_mem_type::local implying dedicated local memory storage such as SRAM or info::local_mem_type::global. The latter type means that local memory is just implemented as an abstraction on top of global memory with no performance gains. For custom devices (only), the local memory type can also be info::local_mem_type::none, indicating local memory is not supported.

Kernel Queries

> preferred_work_group_size: The preferred work-group size for executing a kernel on a specific device.
>
> preferred_work_group_size_multiple: The preferred work-group size for executing a kernel on a specific device

Runtime vs. Compile-Time Properties

The queries described in this chapter are performed through runtime APIs (get_info), meaning that the results are not known until runtime. This covers many use cases, but the SYCL specification is also undergoing work to provide compile-time querying of properties, when they can be known by a toolchain, to allow more advanced programming techniques such as templating of kernels based on properties of devices. Compile-time adaptation of code based on queries is not possible with the existing runtime queries, and this ability can be important for advanced optimizations or when writing kernels that use some extensions. The interfaces were not defined well enough yet at the time of writing to describe those interfaces in this book, but we can look forward to much more powerful query and code adaptation mechanisms that are coming soon in SYCL and DPC++! Look to the online oneAPI DPC++ language reference and the SYCL specifications for updates.

Summary

The most portable programs will query the devices that are available in a system and adjust their behavior based on runtime information. This chapter opens the door to the rich set of information that is available to allow such tailoring of our code to adjust to the hardware that is present at runtime.

Our programs can be made more portable, more performance portable, and more future-proof by parameterizing our application to adjust to the characteristics of the hardware. We can also test that the hardware present falls within the bounds of any assumptions we have made in the design of our program and either warn or abort when hardware is found that lies outside the bounds of our assumptions.

 **Open Access** This chapter is licensed under the terms of the Creative Commons Attribution 4.0 International License (http://creativecommons.org/licenses/by/4.0/), which permits use, sharing, adaptation, distribution and reproduction in any medium or format, as long as you give appropriate credit to the original author(s) and the source, provide a link to the Creative Commons license and indicate if changes were made.

The images or other third party material in this chapter are included in the chapter's Creative Commons license, unless indicated otherwise in a credit line to the material. If material is not included in the chapter's Creative Commons license and your intended use is not permitted by statutory regulation or exceeds the permitted use, you will need to obtain permission directly from the copyright holder.

CHAPTER 13

Practical Tips

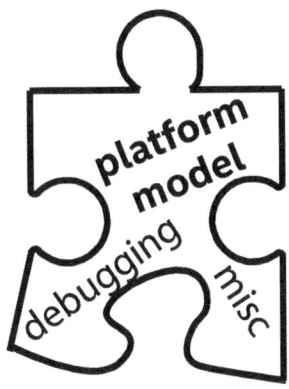

This chapter is home to a number of pieces of useful information, practical tips, advice, and techniques that have proven useful when programming SYCL and using DPC++. None of these topics are covered exhaustively, so the intent is to raise awareness and encourage learning more as needed.

Getting a DPC++ Compiler and Code Samples

Chapter 1 covers how to get the DPC++ compiler (oneapi.com/implementations or github.com/intel/llvm) and where to get the code samples (www.apress.com/9781484255735—look for Services for this book: Source Code). This is mentioned again to emphasize how useful it can be to try the examples (including making modifications!) to gain hands-on experience. Join the club of those who know what the code in Figure 1-1 actually prints out!

Online Forum and Documentation

The Intel Developer Zone hosts a forum for discussing the DPC++ compiler, DPC++ Library (Chapter 18), DPC++ Compatibility Tool (for CUDA migration—discussed later in this chapter), and gdb included in the oneAPI toolkit (this chapter touches on debugging too). This is an excellent place to post questions about writing code, including suspected compiler bugs. You will find posts from some of the book authors on this forum doing exactly that, especially while writing this book. The forum is available online at https://software.intel.com/en-us/forums/oneapi-data-parallel-c-compiler.

The online oneAPI DPC++ language reference is a great resource to find a complete list of the classes and member definitions, details on compiler options, and more.

Platform Model

A SYCL or DPC++ compiler is designed to act and feel like any other C++ compiler we have ever used. A notable difference is that a regular C++ compiler produces code only for a CPU. It is worth understanding the inner workings, at a high level, that enable a compiler to produce code for a host CPU *and* devices.

The platform model (Figure 13-1), used by SYCL and DPC++, specifies a host that coordinates and controls the compute work that is performed on the devices. Chapter 2 describes how to assign work to devices, and Chapter 4 dives into how to program devices. Chapter 12 describes using the platform model at various levels of specificity.

CHAPTER 13   PRACTICAL TIPS

As we discussed in Chapter 2, there is always a device corresponding to the host, known as the *host device*. Providing this guaranteed-to-be-available target for device code allows device code to be written assuming that at least one device is available, even if it is the host itself! The choice of the devices on which to run device code is under program control—it is entirely our choice as programmers if, and how, we want to execute code on specific devices.

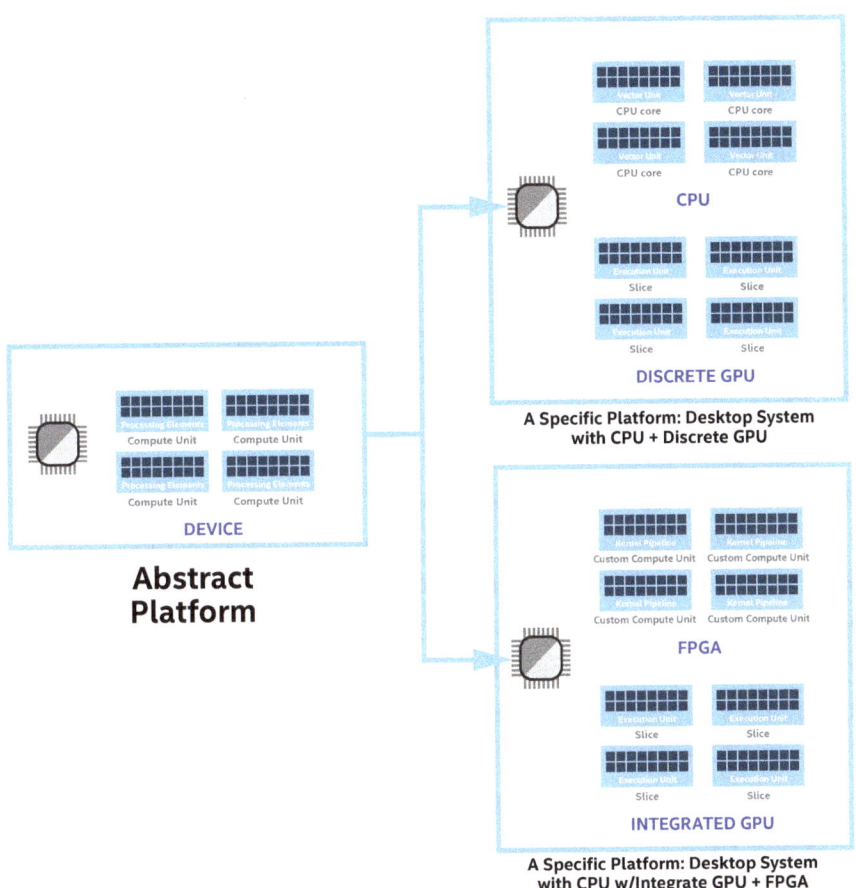

Figure 13-1. *Platform model: Can be used abstractly or with specificity*

Multiarchitecture Binaries

Since our goal is to have a single-source code to support a heterogeneous machine, it is only natural to want a single executable file to be the result.

A multiarchitecture binary (aka *fat binary*) is a single binary file that has been expanded to include all the compiled and intermediate code needed for our heterogeneous machine. The concept of multiarchitecture binaries is not new. For example, some operating systems support multiarchitecture 32-bit and 64-bit libraries and executables. A multiarchitecture binary acts like any other a.out or A.exe we are used to—but it contains everything needed for a heterogeneous machine. This helps to automate the process of picking the right code to run for a particular device. As we discuss next, one possible form of the device code in a fat binary is an intermediate format that defers the final creation of device instructions until runtime.

Compilation Model

The single-source nature of SYCL and DPC++ allows compilations to act and feel like regular C++ compilations. There is no need for us to invoke additional passes for devices or deal with bundling device and host code. That is all handled automatically for us by the compiler. Of course, understanding the details of what is happening can be important for several reasons. This is useful knowledge if we want to target specific architectures more effectively, and it is important to understand if we need to debug a failure happening in the compilation process.

We will review the compilation model so that we are educated for when that knowledge is needed. Since the compilation model supports code that executes on both a host and potentially several devices simultaneously, the commands issued by the compiler, linker, and other supporting tools are more complicated than the C++ compilations we are used to (targeting only one architecture). Welcome to the heterogeneous world!

This heterogeneous complexity is intentionally hidden from us by the DPC++ compiler and "just works."

The DPC++ compiler can generate target-specific executable code similar to traditional C++ compilers (*ahead-of-time* (AOT) compilation, sometimes referred to as offline kernel compilation), or it can generate an intermediate representation that can be *just-in-time* (JIT) compiled to a specific target at runtime.

The compiler can only compile ahead of time if the device target is known ahead of time (at the time when we compile our program). Deferring for just-in-time compilation gives more flexibility, but requires the compiler and the runtime to perform additional work while our application is running.

DPC++ compilation can be "ahead-of-time" or "just-in-time."

By default, when we compile our code for most devices, the output for device code is stored in an intermediate form. At runtime, the device handler on the system will *just-in-time* compile the intermediate form into code to run on the device(s) to match what is available on the system.

We can ask the compiler to compile ahead-of-time for specific devices or classes of devices. This has the advantage of saving runtime, but it has the disadvantage of added compile time and fatter binaries! Code that is compiled ahead-of-time is not as portable as just-in-time because it cannot adjust at runtime. We can include both in our binary to get the benefits of both.

Compiling for a specific device ahead-of-time also helps us to check at build time that our program should work on that device. With just-in-time compilation, it is possible that a program will fail to compile at runtime (which can be caught using the mechanisms in Chapter 5). There are a few debugging tips for this in the upcoming "Debugging" section of this chapter, and Chapter 5 details how these errors can be caught at runtime to avoid requiring that our applications abort.

Figure 13-2 illustrates the DPC++ compilation process from source code to fat binary (executable). Whatever combinations we choose are combined into a fat binary. The fat binary is employed by the runtime when the application executes (and it is the binary that we execute on the host!). At times, we may want to compile device code for a particular device in a separate compile. We would want the results of such a separate compilation to eventually be combined into our fat binary. This can be very useful for FPGA development when full compile (doing a full synthesis place-and-route) times can be very long and is in fact a requirement for FPGA development to avoid requiring the synthesis tools to be installed on a runtime system. Figure 13-3 shows the flow of the bundling/unbundling activity supported for such needs. We always have the option to compile everything at once, but during development, the option to break up compilation can be very useful.

Every SYCL and DPC++ compiler has a compilation model with the same goal, but the exact implementation details will vary. The diagrams shown here are for the DPC++ compiler toolchain.

One DPC++-specific component is shown in Figure 13-2 as the *integration header generator* that will not be mentioned again in this book. We can program without ever needing to know what it is or what it does. Nevertheless, to satisfy the curious, here is a little information: The integration header generator generates a header file providing information about SYCL kernels found in the translation unit. This includes how the names of SYCL kernel types map to symbolic names and information about kernel parameters and their locations within the corresponding lambda or functor object created by the compiler to capture them. The integration header is the mechanism used to implement the convenient style of kernel invocation from host code via C++ lambda/functor objects, which frees us from the time-consuming task of setting individual arguments, resolving kernels by name, and so on.

CHAPTER 13　PRACTICAL TIPS

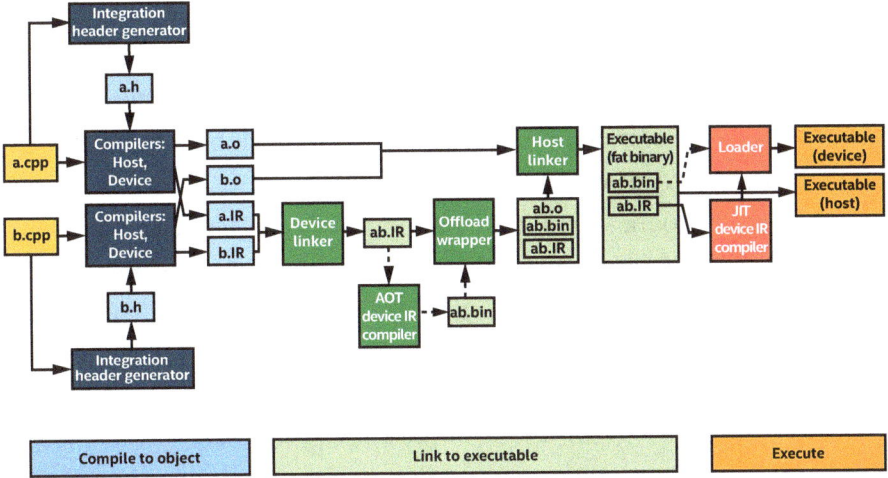

Figure 13-2. *Compilation process: Ahead-of-time and just-in-time options*

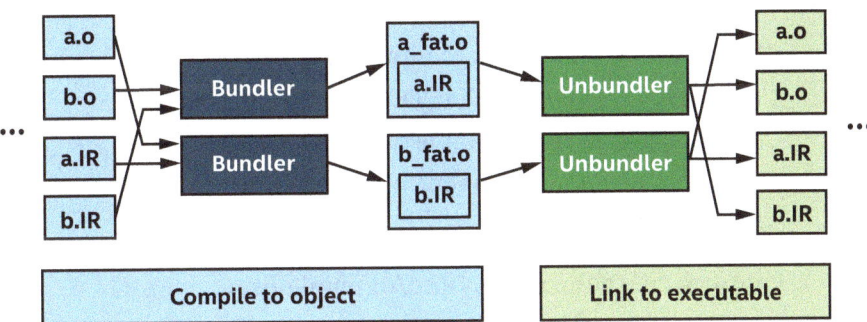

Figure 13-3. *Compilation process: Offload bundler/unbundler*

Adding SYCL to Existing C++ Programs

Adding the appropriate exploitation of parallelism to an existing C++ program is the first step to using SYCL. If a C++ application is already exploiting parallel execution, that may be a bonus, or it may be a headache. That is because the way we divide the work of an application into parallel execution greatly affects what we can do with it. When programmers talk about *refactoring* a program, they are referring to rearranging the flow of execution and data within a program to get it ready to exploit parallelism. This is a complex topic that we will only touch briefly upon. There is no *one-size-fits-all* answer on how to prepare an application for parallelism, but there are some tips worth noting.

When adding parallelism to a C++ application, an easy approach to consider is to find an isolated point in the program where the opportunity for parallelism is the greatest. We can start our modification there and then continue to add parallelism in other areas as needed. A complicating factor is that refactoring (e.g., rearranging the program flow and redesigning data structures) may improve the opportunity for parallelism.

Once we find an isolated point in the program where the opportunity for parallelism is the greatest, we will need to consider how to use SYCL at that point in the program. That is what the rest of the book teaches.

At a high level, the key steps for introducing parallelism consist of

1. Safety with concurrency (commonly called *thread safety* in conventional CPU programming): Adjusting all shared mutable data (data that can change and is shared concurrently) to be used concurrently

2. Introducing concurrency and/or parallelism

3. Tuning for parallelism (best scaling, optimizing for throughput or latency)

It is important to consider step #1 first. Many applications have already been refactored for concurrency, but many have not. With SYCL as the sole source of parallelism, we focus on safety for the data being used within kernels and possibly shared with the host. If we have other techniques in our program (OpenMP, MPI, TBB, etc.) that introduce parallelism, that is an additional concern on top of our SYCL programming. It is important to note that it is okay to use multiple techniques inside a single program—SYCL does not need to be the only source of parallelism within a program. This book does not cover the advanced topic of mixing with other parallelism techniques.

Debugging

This section conveys some modest debugging advice, to ease the challenges unique to debugging a parallel program, especially one targeting a heterogeneous machine.

We should never forget that we have the option to debug our applications while they are running on the host device. This debugging tip is described as Method#2 in Chapter 2. Because the architectures of devices often include fewer debugging hooks, tools can often probe code on a host more precisely. Another advantage of running *everything* on the host is that many errors relating to synchronization will disappear, including moving memory back and forth between the host and devices. While we eventually need to debug all such errors, this can allow incremental debugging so we can resolve some bugs before others.

Debugging tip Running on the host device is a powerful debugging tool.

Parallel programming errors, specifically data races and deadlocks, are generally easier for tools to detect and eliminate when running all code on the host. Much to our chagrin, we will most often see program failures from such parallel programming errors when running on a combination of host and devices. When such issues strike, it is very useful to remember that pulling back to host-only is a powerful debugging tool. Thankfully, SYCL and DPC++ are carefully designed to keep this option available to us and easy to access.

> **Debugging tip** If a program is deadlocking, check that the host accessors are being destroyed properly.

The following DPC++ compiler options are a good idea when we start debugging:

- `-g`: Put debug information in the output.
- `-ferror-limit=1`: Maintain sanity when using C++ with template libraries such as SYCL/DPC++.
- `-Werror -Wall -Wpedantic`: Have the compiler enforce good coding to help avoid producing incorrect code to debug at runtime.

We really do not need to get bogged down fixing pedantic warnings just to use DPC++, so choosing to not use `-Wpedantic` is understandable.

When we leave our code to be compiled just-in-time during runtime, there is code we can inspect. This is *highly dependent* on the layers used by our compiler, so looking at the compiler documentation for suggestions is a good idea.

Debugging Kernel Code

While debugging kernel code, start by running on the host device (as advised in Chapter 2). The code for device selectors in Chapter 2 can easily be modified to accept runtime options, or compiler-time options, to redirect work to the host device when we are debugging.

When debugging kernel code, SYCL defines a C++-style `stream` that can be used within a kernel (Figure 13-4). DPC++ also offers an experimental implementation of a C-style `printf` that has useful capabilities, with some restrictions. Additional details are in the online oneAPI DPC++ language reference.

```
Q.submit([&](handler &h){
  stream out(1024, 256, h);
  h.parallel_for(range{8}, [=](id<1> idx){
    out << "Testing my sycl stream (this is work-item ID:" << idx << ")\n";
  });
});
```

Figure 13-4. sycl::stream

When debugging kernel code, experience encourages that we put breakpoints before `parallel_for` or inside `parallel_for`, but not actually on the `parallel_for`. A breakpoint placed on a `parallel_for` can trigger a breakpoint multiple times even after performing the next operation. This C++ debugging advice applies to many template expansions like those in SYCL, where a breakpoint on the template call will translate into a complicated set of breakpoints when it is expanded by the compiler. There may be ways that implementations can ease this, but the key point here is that we can avoid some confusion on all implementations by not setting the breakpoint precisely on the `parallel_for` itself.

Debugging Runtime Failures

When a runtime error occurs while compiling just-in-time, we are either dealing with a compiler/runtime bug, or we have accidentally programmed nonsense that was not detected until it tripped up the runtime and created difficult-to-understand runtime error messages. It can be a bit intimidating to dive into these bugs, but even a cursory look may allow us to get a better idea of what caused a particular issue. It might yield some additional knowledge that will guide us to avoid the issue, or it may just help us submit a short bug report to the compiler team. Either way, knowing that some tools exist to help can be important.

CHAPTER 13   PRACTICAL TIPS

Output from our program that indicates a runtime failure may look like this:

```
origin>: error: Invalid record (Producer: 'LLVM9.0.0' Reader: 'LLVM 9.0.0')
terminate called after throwing an instance of 'cl::sycl::compile_program_error'
```

Seeing this throw noted here lets us know that our host program could have been constructed to catch this error. While that may not solve our problem, it does mean that runtime compiler failures do not need to abort our application. Chapter 5 dives into this topic.

When we see a runtime failure and have any difficulty debugging it quickly, it is worth simply trying a rebuild using ahead-of-time compilations. If the device we are targeting has an ahead-of-time compilation option, this can be an easy thing to try that may yield easier-to-understand diagnostics. If our errors can be seen at compile time instead of JIT or runtime, often much more useful information will be found in the error messages from the compiler instead of the small amount of error information we usually see from a JIT or the runtime. For specific options, check the online oneAPI DPC++ documentation for *ahead-of-time compilation*.

When our SYCL programs are running on top of an OpenCL runtime and using the OpenCL backend, we can run our programs with the OpenCL Intercept Layer: github.com/intel/opencl-intercept-layer. This is a tool that can inspect, log, and modify OpenCL commands that an application (or higher-level runtime) is generating. It supports a lot of controls, but good ones to set initially are `ErrorLogging`, `BuildLogging`, and maybe `CallLogging` (though it generates a lot of output). Useful dumps are possible with `DumpProgramSPIRV`. The OpenCL Intercept Layer is a separate utility and is not part of any specific OpenCL implementation, so it works with many SYCL compilers.

For suspected compiler issues on Linux systems with Intel GPUs, we can dump intermediate compiler output from the Intel Graphics Compiler. We do this by setting the environment variable IGC_ShaderDumpEnable equal to 1 (for some output) or the environment variable IGC_ShaderDumpEnableAll to 1 (for lots and lots of output). The dumped output goes in /tmp/IntelIGC. This technique may not apply to all builds of the graphics drivers, but it is worth a try to see if it applies to our system.

Figure 13-5 lists these and a few additional environment variables (supported on Windows and Linux) supported by compilers or runtimes to aid in advanced debugging. These are DPC++ implementation-dependent advanced debug options that exist to inspect and control the compilation model. They are not discussed or utilized in this book. The online oneAPI DPC++ language reference is a good place to learn more.

These options are not described more within this book, but they are mentioned here to open up this avenue of advanced debugging as needed. These options *may* give us insight into how to work around an issue or bug. It is possible that our source code is inadvertently triggering an issue that can be resolved by correcting the source code. Otherwise, the use of these options is for very advanced debugging of the compiler itself. Therefore, they are associated more with compiler developers than with users of the compiler. Some advanced users find these options useful; therefore, they are mentioned here and never again in this book. To dig deeper, the GitHub for DPC++ has a document for all environment variables under llvm / sycl / doc / EnvironmentVariables.md.

Debugging tip When other options are exhausted and we need to debug a runtime issue, we look for dump tools that might give us hints toward the cause.

Environment variables	Value	Description
SYCL_PI_TRACE	1 (basic), 2 (advanced), -1 (all)	Runtime: Value of 1 enables tracing of Runtime Plugin Interface (PI) for plugin and device discovery; Value of 2 enables tracing of all PI calls. Value of -1 unleashes all levels of tracing.
SYCL_PRINT_EXECUTION_GRAPH	always (or ask to dump only select files by specifying: before_addCG, after_addCG, before_addCopyBack, after_addCopyBack, before_addHostAcc, or after_addHostAcc)	Runtime: create text files (with DOT extension) tracing the execution graph. Relatively easy to browse traces of what is happening during runtime.
CL_CONFIG_USE_VECTORIZER	true or false	Runtime: ask the Intel CPU compiler to enable or disable vectorizer.
CL_CONFIG_CPU_TARGET_ARCH	skx,core-avx2	Runtime: ask the Intel CPU compiler to generate code for processors that support Intel Advanced Vector Extensions (Intel AVX512 and AVX2),
CL_CONFIG_DUMP_ASM	true or false	Runtime: ask the Intel CPU compiler to dump CPU assembly code.
IGC_ShaderDumpEnable	0 or 1	Linux only. Runtime: ask the Intel Graphics Compiler (JIT) to dump some information.
IGC_ShaderDumpEnableAll	0 or 1	Linux only. Runtime: ask the Intel Graphics Compiler (JIT) to dump *lots* of information.
SYCL_DUMP_IMAGES	true or false	Compile time: Request via SYCL_DUMP_IMAGES=1 that compiler to dump a SPV file containing the intermediate code which is passed to JIT compiler during execution.
SYCL_USE_KERNEL_SPV	<device binary>	Runtime: Load device image from the specified file. If runtime is unable to read the file, cl::sycl::runtime_error exception is thrown.

Figure 13-5. *DPC++ advanced debug options*

Initializing Data and Accessing Kernel Outputs

In this section, we dive into a topic that causes confusion for new users of SYCL and that leads to the most common (in our experience) first bugs that we encounter as new SYCL developers.

Put simply, when we create a buffer from a host memory allocation (e.g., array or vector), we can't access the host allocation directly until the buffer has been destroyed. The buffer owns any host allocation passed to

CHAPTER 13　PRACTICAL TIPS

it at construction time, for the buffer's entire lifetime. There are rarely used mechanisms that *do* let us access the host allocation while a buffer is still alive (e.g., buffer mutex), but those advanced features don't help with the early bugs described here.

If we construct a buffer from a host memory allocation, we must not directly access the host allocation until the buffer has been destroyed! While it is alive, the buffer owns the allocation.

A common bug appears when the host program accesses a host allocation while a buffer still owns that allocation. All bets are off once this happens, because we don't know what the buffer is using the allocation for. Don't be surprised if the data is incorrect—the kernels that we're trying to read the output from may not have even started running yet! As described in Chapters 3 and 8, SYCL is built around an asynchronous task graph mechanism. Before we try to use output data from task graph operations, we need to be sure that we have reached synchronization points in the code where the graph has executed and made data available to the host. Both buffer destruction and creation of host accessors are operations that cause this synchronization.

Figure 13-6 shows a common pattern of code that we often write, where we cause a buffer to be destroyed by closing the block scope that it was defined within. By causing the buffer to go out of scope and be destroyed, we can then safely read kernel results through the original host allocation that was passed to the buffer constructor.

CHAPTER 13 PRACTICAL TIPS

```
constexpr size_t N = 1024;

// Set up queue on any available device
queue q;

// Create host containers to initialize on the host
std::vector<int> in_vec(N), out_vec(N);

// Initialize input and output vectors
for (int i=0; i < N; i++) in_vec[i] = i;
std::fill(out_vec.begin(), out_vec.end(), 0);

// Nuance: Create new scope so that we can easily cause
// buffers to go out of scope and be destroyed
{

  // Create buffers using host allocations (vector in this case)
  buffer in_buf{in_vec}, out_buf{out_vec};

  // Submit the kernel to the queue
  q.submit([&](handler& h) {
    accessor in{in_buf, h};
    accessor out{out_buf, h};

    h.parallel_for(range{N}, [=](id<1> idx) {
      out[idx] = in[idx];
    });
  });

// Close the scope that buffer is alive within!  Causes
// buffer destruction which will wait until the kernels
// writing to buffers have completed, and will copy the
// data from written buffers back to host allocations (our
// std::vectors in this case).  After the buffer destructor
// runs, caused by this closing of scope, then it is safe
// to access the original in_vec and out_vec again!
}

// Check that all outputs match expected value
// WARNING: The buffer destructor must have run for us to safely
// use in_vec and out_vec again in our host code.  While the buffer
// is alive it owns those allocations, and they are not safe for us
// to use!  At the least they will contain values that are not up to
// date.  This code is safe and correct because the closing of scope
// above has caused the buffer to be destroyed before this point
// where we use the vectors again.
for (int i=0; i<N; i++)
  std::cout << "out_vec[" << i << "]=" << out_vec[i] << "\n";
```

Figure 13-6. Common pattern—buffer creation from a host allocation

There are two common reasons to associate a buffer with existing host memory like in Figure 13-6:

1. To simplify initialization of data in a buffer. We can just construct the buffer from host memory that we (or another part of the application) have already initialized.

2. To reduce the characters typed because closing scope with a '}' is slightly more concise (though more error prone) than creating a `host_accessor` to the buffer.

If we use a host allocation to dump or verify the output values from a kernel, we need to put the buffer allocation into a block scope (or other scopes) so that we can control when it is destroyed. We must then make sure that the buffer is destroyed before we access the host allocation to obtain the kernel output. Figure 13-6 shows this done correctly, while Figure 13-7 shows a common bug where the output is accessed while the buffer is still alive.

Advanced users may prefer to use buffer destruction to return result data from kernels into a host memory allocation. But for most users, and especially new developers, it is recommended to use scoped host accessors.

CHAPTER 13 PRACTICAL TIPS

```
constexpr size_t N = 1024;

// Set up queue on any available device
queue q;

// Create host containers to initialize on the host
std::vector<int> in_vec(N), out_vec(N);

// Initialize input and output vectors
for (int i=0; i < N; i++) in_vec[i] = i;
std::fill(out_vec.begin(), out_vec.end(), 0);

// Create buffers using host allocations (vector in this case)
buffer in_buf{in_vec}, out_buf{out_vec};

// Submit the kernel to the queue
q.submit([&](handler& h) {
  accessor in{in_buf, h};
  accessor out{out_buf, h};

  h.parallel_for(range{N}, [=](id<1> idx) {
    out[idx] = in[idx];
  });
});

// BUG!!! We're using the host allocation out_vec, but the buffer out_buf
// is still alive and owns that allocation!  We will probably see the
// initialiation value (zeros) printed out, since the kernel probably
// hasn't even run yet, and the buffer has no reason to have copied
// any output back to the host even if the kernel has run.
for (int i=0; i<N; i++)
  std::cout << "out_vec[" << i << "]=" << out_vec[i] << "\n";
```

Figure 13-7. *Common bug: Reading data directly from host allocation during buffer lifetime*

Prefer to use host accessors instead of scoping of buffers, especially when getting started.

To avoid these bugs, we recommend using host accessors instead of buffer scoping when getting started with SYCL and DPC++. Host accessors provide access to a buffer from the host, and once their constructor has

CHAPTER 13 PRACTICAL TIPS

finished running, we are guaranteed that any previous writes (e.g., from kernels submitted before the host_accessor was created) to the buffer have executed and are visible. This book uses a mixture of both styles (i.e., host accessors and host allocations passed to the buffer constructor) to provide familiarity with both. Using host accessors tends to be less error prone when getting started. Figure 13-8 shows how a host accessor can be used to read output from a kernel, without destroying the buffer first.

```
constexpr size_t N = 1024;

// Set up queue on any available device
queue q;

// Create host containers to initialize on the host
std::vector<int> in_vec(N), out_vec(N);

// Initialize input and output vectors
for (int i=0; i < N; i++) in_vec[i] = i;
std::fill(out_vec.begin(), out_vec.end(), 0);

// Create buffers using host allocations (vector in this case)
buffer in_buf{in_vec}, out_buf{out_vec};

// Submit the kernel to the queue
q.submit([&](handler& h) {
  accessor in{in_buf, h};
  accessor out{out_buf, h};

  h.parallel_for(range{N}, [=](id<1> idx) {
    out[idx] = in[idx];
  });
});

// Check that all outputs match expected value
// Use host accessor!  Buffer is still in scope / alive
host_accessor A{out_buf};

for (int i=0; i<N; i++) std::cout << "A[" << i << "]=" << A[i] << "\n";
```

Figure 13-8. Recommendation: Use a host accessor to read kernel results

315

Host accessors can be used whenever a buffer is alive, such as at both ends of a typical buffer lifetime—for initialization of the buffer content and for reading of results from our kernels. Figure 13-9 shows an example of this pattern.

```
constexpr size_t N = 1024;

// Set up queue on any available device
queue q;

// Create buffers of size N
buffer<int> in_buf{N}, out_buf{N};

// Use host accessors to initialize the data
{ // CRITICAL: Begin scope for host_accessor lifetime!
  host_accessor in_acc{ in_buf }, out_acc{ out_buf };
  for (int i=0; i < N; i++) {
    in_acc[i] = i;
    out_acc[i] = 0;
  }
} // CRITICAL: Close scope to make host accessors go out of scope!

// Submit the kernel to the queue
q.submit([&](handler& h) {
  accessor in{in_buf, h};
  accessor out{out_buf, h};

  h.parallel_for(range{N}, [=](id<1> idx) {
    out[idx] = in[idx];
  });
});

// Check that all outputs match expected value
// Use host accessor!  Buffer is still in scope / alive
host_accessor A{out_buf};

for (int i=0; i<N; i++) std::cout << "A[" << i << "]=" << A[i] << "\n";
```

Figure 13-9. *Recommendation: Use host accessors for buffer initialization and reading of results*

One final detail to mention is that host accessors sometime cause an opposite bug in applications, because they also have a lifetime. While a host_accessor to a buffer is alive, the runtime will not allow that buffer to be used by any devices! The runtime does not analyze our host programs to determine when they *might* access a host accessor, so the only way for it to know that the host program has finished accessing a buffer is for the host_accessor destructor to run. As shown in Figure 13-10, this can cause applications to appear to hang if our host program is waiting for some kernels to run (e.g., queue::wait() or acquiring another host accessor) and if the DPC++ runtime is waiting for our earlier host accessor(s) to be destroyed before it can run kernels that use a buffer.

When using host accessors, be sure that they are destroyed when no longer needed to unlock use of the buffer by kernels or other host accessors.

```cpp
constexpr size_t N = 1024;

// Set up queue on any available device
queue q;

// Create buffers using host allocations (vector in this case)
buffer<int> in_buf{N}, out_buf{N};

// Use host accessors to initialize the data
host_accessor in_acc{ in_buf }, out_acc{ out_buf };
for (int i=0; i < N; i++) {
  in_acc[i] = i;
  out_acc[i] = 0;
}

// BUG: Host accessors in_acc and out_acc are still alive!
// Later q.submits will never start on a device, because the
// runtime doesn't know that we've finished accessing the
// buffers via the host accessors. The device kernels
// can't launch until the host finishes updating the buffers,
// since the host gained access first (before the queue submissions).
// This program will appear to hang! Use a debugger in that case.

// Submit the kernel to the queue
q.submit([&](handler& h) {
  accessor in{in_buf, h};
  accessor out{out_buf, h};

  h.parallel_for(range{N}, [=](id<1> idx) {
    out[idx] = in[idx];
  });
});

std::cout <<
  "This program will deadlock here!!!  Our host_accessors used\n"
  " for data initialization are still in scope, so the runtime won't\n"
  " allow our kernel to start executing on the device (the host could\n"
  " still be initializing the data that is used by the kernel). "
  " The next line\n of code is acquiring a host accessor for"
  " the output, which will wait for\n the kernel to run first. "
  " Since in_acc and out_acc have not been\n"
  " destructed, the kernel is not safe for the runtime to run, "
  " and we deadlock.\n";

// Check that all outputs match expected value
// Use host accessor! Buffer is still in scope / alive
host_accessor A{out_buf};

for (int i=0; i<N; i++) std::cout << "A[" << i << "]=" << A[i] << "\n";
```

Figure 13-10. Bug (hang!) from improper use of host_accessors

Multiple Translation Units

When we want to call functions inside a kernel that are defined in a different translational unit, those functions need to be labeled with SYCL_EXTERNAL. Without this attribute, the compiler will only compile a function for use outside of device code (making it illegal to call that external function from within device code).

There are a few restrictions on SYCL_EXTERNAL functions that do not apply if we define the function within the same translation unit:

- SYCL_EXTERNAL can only be used on functions.

- SYCL_EXTERNAL functions cannot use raw pointers as parameter or return types. Explicit pointer classes must be used instead.

- SYCL_EXTERNAL functions cannot call a parallel_for_work_item method.

- SYCL_EXTERNAL functions cannot be called from within a parallel_for_work_group scope.

If we try to compile a kernel that is calling a function that is not inside the same translation unit and is not declared with SYCL_EXTERNAL, then we can expect a compile error similar to

```
error: SYCL kernel cannot call an undefined function
without SYCL_EXTERNAL attribute
```

If the function itself is compiled without a SYCL_EXTERNAL attribute, we can expect to see either a link or runtime failure such as

```
terminate called after throwing an instance of
'cl::sycl::compile_program_error'
...error: undefined reference to ...
```

CHAPTER 13 PRACTICAL TIPS

DPC++ supports SYCL_EXTERNAL. SYCL does not require compilers to support SYCL_EXTERNAL; it is an *optional* feature in general.

Performance Implications of Multiple Translation Units

An implication of the compilation model (see earlier in this chapter) is that if we scatter our device code into multiple translation units, that may trigger more invocations of just-in-time compilation than if our device code is co-located. This is highly implementation dependent and is subject to changes over time as implementations mature.

Such effects on performance are minor enough to ignore through most of our development work, but when we get to fine-tuning to maximize code performance, there are two things we can consider to mitigate these effects: (1) group device code together in the same translation unit, and (2) use ahead-of-time compilation to avoid just-in-time compilation effects entirely. Since both of these require some effort on our part, we only do this when we have finished our development and are trying to squeeze every ounce of performance out of our application. When we do resort to this detailed tuning, it is worth testing changes to observe their effect on the exact SYCL implementation that we are using.

When Anonymous Lambdas Need Names

SYCL provides for assigning names defined as lambdas in case tools need it and for debugging purposes (e.g., to enable displays in terms of user-defined names). Throughout most of this book, anonymous lambdas have been used for kernels because names are not needed when using DPC++ (except for passing of compile options as described with lambda naming discussion in Chapter 10). They are also made optional as of the SYCL 2020 provisional.

When we have an advanced need to mix SYCL tools from multiple vendors on a codebase, the tooling may require that we name lambdas. This is done by adding a `<class uniquename>` to the SYCL action construct in which the lambda is used (e.g., `parallel_for`). This naming allows tools from multiple vendors to interact in a defined way within a single compilation and can also help by displaying kernel names that we define within debug tools and layers.

Migrating from CUDA to SYCL

Migrating CUDA code to SYCL or DPC++ is not covered in detail in this book. There are tools and resources available that explore doing this. Migrating CUDA code is relatively straightforward since it is a kernel-based approach to parallelism. Once written in SYCL or DPC++, the new program is enhanced by its ability to target more devices than supported by CUDA alone. The newly enhanced program can still be targeted to NVIDIA GPUs using SYCL compilers with NVIDIA GPU support.

Migrating to SYCL opens the door to the diversity of devices supported by SYCL, which extends far beyond just GPUs.

When using the DPC++ Compatibility Tool, the `--report-type=value` option provides very useful statistics about the migrated code. One of the reviewers of this book called it a "beautiful flag provided by Intel `dpct`." The `--in-root` option can prove very useful when migrating CUDA code depending on source code organization of a project.

CHAPTER 13   PRACTICAL TIPS

To learn more about CUDA migration, two resources are a good place to start:

- Intel's DPC++ Compatibility Tool transforms CUDA applications into DPC++ code (tinyurl.com/CUDAtoDPCpp).

- Codeplay tutorial "Migrating from CUDA to SYCL" (tinyurl.com/codeplayCUDAtoSYCL).

Summary

Popular culture today often refers to tips as *life hacks*. Unfortunately, programming culture often assigns a negative connotation to *hack*, so the authors refrained from naming this chapter "SYCL Hacks." Undoubtedly, this chapter has just touched the surface of what practical tips can be given for using SYCL and DPC++. More tips can be shared by all of us on the online forum as we learn together how to make the most out of SYCL with DPC++.

 **Open Access** This chapter is licensed under the terms of the Creative Commons Attribution 4.0 International License (http://creativecommons.org/licenses/by/4.0/), which permits use, sharing, adaptation, distribution and reproduction in any medium or format, as long as you give appropriate credit to the original author(s) and the source, provide a link to the Creative Commons license and indicate if changes were made.

The images or other third party material in this chapter are included in the chapter's Creative Commons license, unless indicated otherwise in a credit line to the material. If material is not included in the chapter's Creative Commons license and your intended use is not permitted by statutory regulation or exceeds the permitted use, you will need to obtain permission directly from the copyright holder.

CHAPTER 14

Common Parallel Patterns

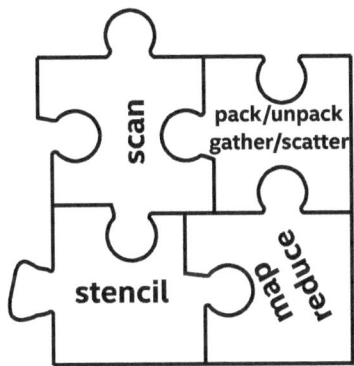

When we are at our best as programmers, we recognize patterns in our work and apply techniques that are time proven to be the best solution. Parallel programming is no different, and it would be a serious mistake not to study the patterns that have proven to be useful in this space. Consider the MapReduce frameworks adopted for Big Data applications; their success stems largely from being based on two simple yet effective parallel patterns—*map* and *reduce*.

There are a number of common patterns in parallel programming that crop up time and again, independent of the programming language that we're using. These patterns are versatile and can be employed at any level of parallelism (e.g., sub-groups, work-groups, full devices) and on any device (e.g., CPUs, GPUs, FPGAs). However, certain properties of the patterns (such as their scalability) may affect their suitability for different devices. In some cases, adapting an application to a new device may simply require choosing appropriate parameters or fine-tuning an implementation of a pattern; in others, we may be able to improve performance by selecting a different pattern entirely.

Developing an understanding of how, when, and where to use these common parallel patterns is a key part of improving our proficiency in DPC++ (and parallel programming in general). For those with existing parallel programming experience, seeing how these patterns are expressed in DPC++ can be a quick way to spin up and gain familiarity with the capabilities of the language.

This chapter aims to provide answers to the following questions:

- Which patterns are the most important to understand?
- How do the patterns relate to the capabilities of different devices?
- Which patterns are already provided as DPC++ functions and libraries?
- How would the patterns be implemented using direct programming?

Understanding the Patterns

The patterns discussed here are a subset of the parallel patterns described in the book *Structured Parallel Programming* by McCool et al. We do not cover the patterns related to *types* of parallelism (e.g., fork-join, branch-and-bound) but focus on the algorithmic patterns most useful for writing data-parallel kernels.

CHAPTER 14 COMMON PARALLEL PATTERNS

We wholeheartedly believe that understanding this subset of parallel patterns is critical to becoming an effective DPC++ programmer. The table in Figure 14-1 presents a high-level overview of the different patterns, including their primary use cases, their key attributes, and how their attributes impact their affinity for different hardware devices.

Pattern	Useful For	Key Attributes	Device Affinity
Map	Simple parallel kernels	No data dependences and high scalability	All
Stencil	Structured data dependences	Data dependences and data re-use	Depends on stencil size
Reduction	Combining partial results	Data dependences	All
Scan Pack/Unpack	Filtering and restructuring data	Limited scalability	Depends on problem size

Figure 14-1. *Parallel patterns and their affinity for different device types*

Map

The map pattern is the simplest parallel pattern of all and will be immediately familiar to readers with experience of functional programming languages. As shown in Figure 14-2, each input element of a range is independently *mapped* to an output by applying some function. Many data-parallel operations can be expressed as instances of the map pattern (e.g., vector addition).

CHAPTER 14 COMMON PARALLEL PATTERNS

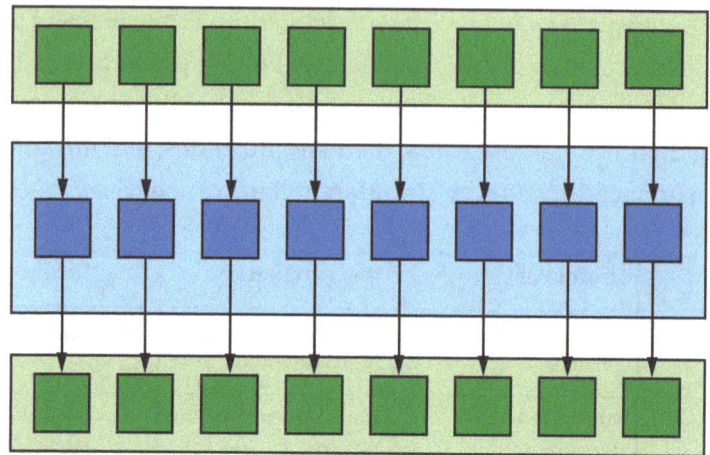

Figure 14-2. Map pattern

Since every application of the function is completely independent, expressions of map are often very simple, relying on the compiler and/or runtime to do most of the hard work. We should expect kernels written to the map pattern to be suitable for any device and for the performance of those kernels to scale very well with the amount of available hardware parallelism.

However, we should think carefully before deciding to rewrite entire applications as a series of map kernels! Such a development approach is highly productive and guarantees that an application will be portable to a wide variety of device types but encourages us to ignore optimizations that may significantly improve performance (e.g., improving data reuse, fusing kernels).

Stencil

The stencil pattern is closely related to the map pattern. As shown in Figure 14-3, a function is applied to an input and a set of neighboring inputs described by a *stencil* to produce a single output. Stencil patterns appear frequently in many domains, including scientific/engineering applications (e.g., finite difference codes) and computer vision/machine learning applications (e.g., image convolutions).

CHAPTER 14   COMMON PARALLEL PATTERNS

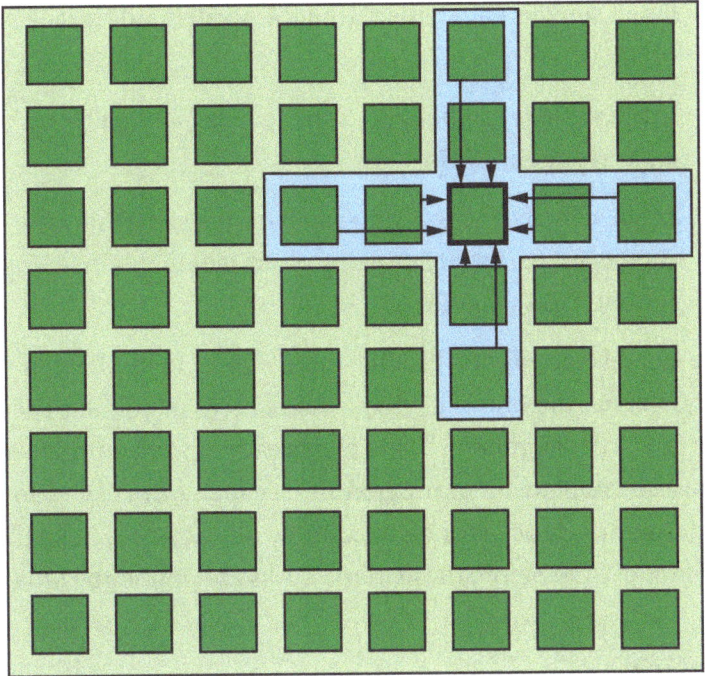

Figure 14-3. Stencil pattern

When the stencil pattern is executed out-of-place (i.e., writing the outputs to a separate storage location), the function can be applied to every input independently. Scheduling stencils in the real world is often more complicated than this: computing neighboring outputs requires the same data, and loading that data from memory multiple times will degrade performance; and we may wish to apply the stencil in-place (i.e., overwriting the original input values) in order to decrease an application's memory footprint.

The suitability of a stencil kernel for different devices is therefore highly dependent on properties of the stencil and the input problem. As a rule of thumb:

- Small stencils can benefit from the scratchpad storage of GPUs.

- Large stencils can benefit from the (comparatively) large caches of CPUs.

- Small stencils operating on small inputs can achieve significant performance gains via implementation as systolic arrays on FPGAs.

Since stencils are easy to describe but complex to implement efficiently, stencils are one of the most active areas of domain-specific language (DSL) development. There are already several embedded DSLs leveraging the template meta-programming capabilities of C++ to generate high-performance stencil kernels at compile time, and we hope that it is only a matter of time before these frameworks are ported to DPC++.

Reduction

A reduction is a common parallel pattern which *combines* partial results from each instance of a kernel invocation using an operator that is typically *associative* and *commutative* (e.g., addition). The most ubiquitous examples of reductions are computing a sum (e.g., while computing a dot product) or computing the minimum/maximum value (e.g., using maximum velocity to set time-step size).

CHAPTER 14 COMMON PARALLEL PATTERNS

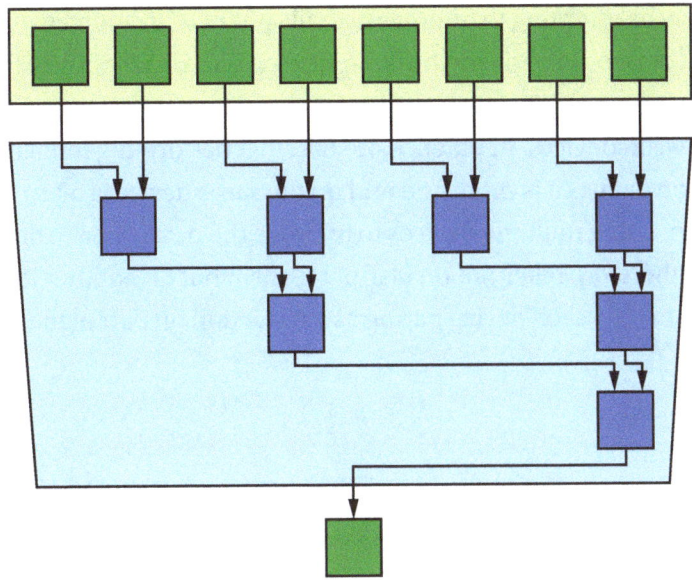

Figure 14-4. *Reduction pattern*

Figure 14-4 shows the reduction pattern implemented by way of a tree reduction, which is a popular implementation requiring $\log_2(N)$ combination operations for a range of *N* input elements. Although tree reductions are common, other implementations are possible—in general, we should not assume that a reduction combines values in a specific order.

Kernels are rarely embarrassingly parallel in real life, and even when they are, they are often paired with reductions (as in MapReduce frameworks) to summarize their results. This makes reductions one of the most important parallel patterns to understand and one that we *must* be able to execute efficiently on any device.

Tuning a reduction for different devices is a delicate balancing act between the time spent computing partial results and the time spent combining them; using too little parallelism increases computation time, whereas using too much parallelism increases combination time.

It may be tempting to improve overall system utilization by using different devices to perform the computation and combination steps, but such tuning efforts must pay careful attention to the cost of moving data between devices. In practice, we find that performing reductions directly on data as it is produced and on the same device is often the best approach. Using multiple devices to improve the performance of reduction patterns therefore relies not on task parallelism but on another level of data parallelism (i.e., each device performs a reduction on part of the input data).

Scan

The scan pattern computes a generalized prefix sum using a binary associative operator, and each element of the output represents a partial result. A scan is said to be *inclusive* if the partial sum for element i is the sum of all elements in the range $[0, i]$ (i.e., the sum *including i*). A scan is said to be *exclusive* if the partial sum for element i is the sum of all elements in the range $[0, i])$ (i.e., the sum *excluding i*).

At first glance, a scan appears to be an inherently serial operation, since the value of each output depends on the value of the previous output! While it is true that scan has less opportunities for parallelism than other patterns (and may therefore be less scalable), Figure 14-5 shows that it is possible to implement a parallel scan using multiple sweeps over the same data.

CHAPTER 14 COMMON PARALLEL PATTERNS

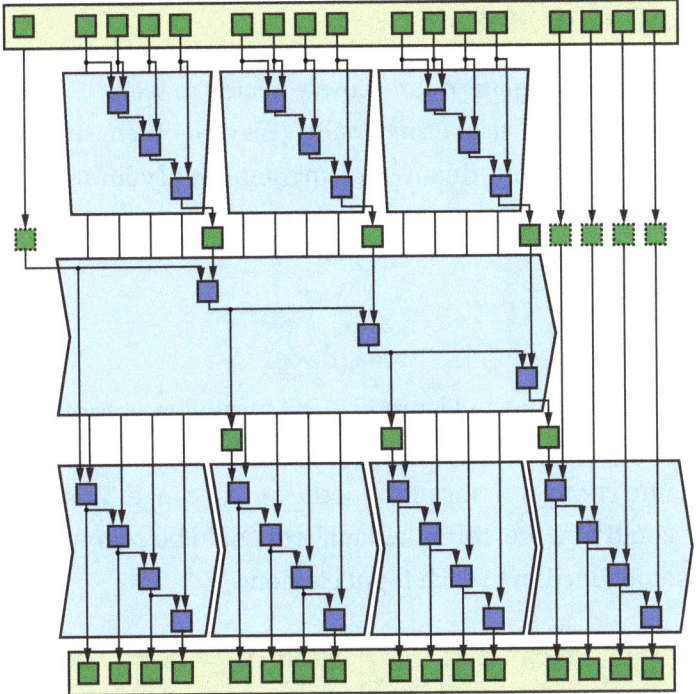

Figure 14-5. Scan pattern

Because the opportunities for parallelism within a scan operation are limited, the best device on which to execute a scan is highly dependent on problem size: smaller problems are a better fit for a CPU, since only larger problems will contain enough data parallelism to saturate a GPU. Problem size is less of a concern for FPGAs and other spatial architectures, since scans naturally lend themselves to pipeline parallelism. As in the case of a reduction, a good rule of thumb is to execute the scan operation on the same device that produced the data—considering where and how scan operations fit into an application during optimization will typically produce better results than focusing on optimizing the scan operations in isolation.

331

CHAPTER 14   COMMON PARALLEL PATTERNS

Pack and Unpack

The pack and unpack patterns are closely related to scans and are often implemented on top of scan functionality. We cover them separately here because they enable performant implementations of common operations (e.g., appending to a list) that may not have an obvious connection to prefix sums.

Pack

The pack pattern, shown in Figure 14-6, discards elements of an input range based on a Boolean condition, *packing* the elements that are not discarded into contiguous locations of the output range. This Boolean condition could be a pre-computed mask or could be computed online by applying some function to each input element.

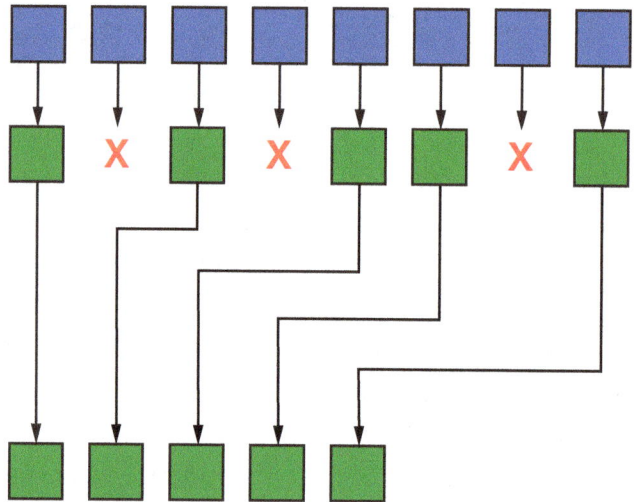

Figure 14-6. *Pack pattern*

Like with scan, there is an inherently serial nature to the pack operation. Given an input element to pack/copy, computing its location in the output range requires information about how many prior elements were also packed/copied into the output. This information is equivalent to an exclusive scan over the Boolean condition driving the pack.

Unpack

As shown in Figure 14-7 (and as its name suggests), the unpack pattern is the opposite of the pack pattern. Contiguous elements of an input range are *unpacked* into non-contiguous elements of an output range, leaving other elements untouched. The most obvious use case for this pattern is to unpack data that was previously packed, but it can also be used to fill in "gaps" in data resulting from some previous computation.

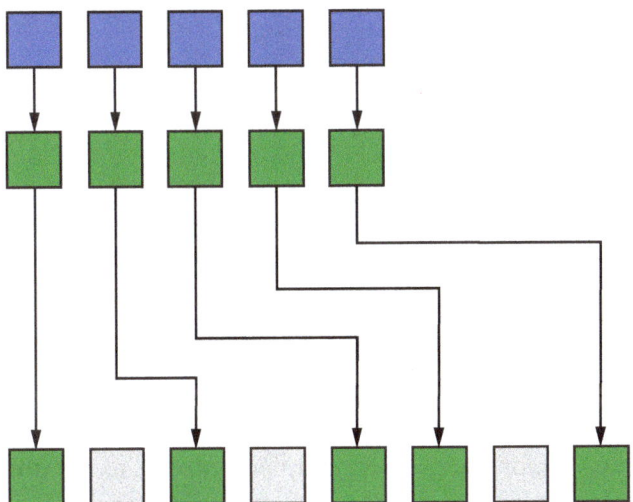

Figure 14-7. Unpack pattern

Using Built-In Functions and Libraries

Many of these patterns can be expressed directly using built-in functionality of DPC++ or vendor-provided libraries written in DPC++. Leveraging these functions and libraries is the best way to balance performance, portability, and productivity in real large-scale software engineering projects.

The DPC++ Reduction Library

Rather than require that each of us maintain our own library of portable and highly performant reduction kernels, DPC++ provides a convenient abstraction for describing variables with reduction semantics. This abstraction simplifies the expression of reduction kernels and makes the fact that a reduction is being performed explicit, allowing implementations to select between different reduction algorithms for different combinations of device, data type, and reduction operation.

```
h.parallel_for(
  nd_range<1>{N, B},
  reduction(sum, plus<>()),
  [=](nd_item<1> it, auto& sum) {
    int i = it.get_global_id(0);
    sum += data[i];
});
```

Figure 14-8. Reduction expressed as an ND-range data-parallel kernel using the reduction library

The kernel in Figure 14-8 shows an example of using the reduction library. Note that the kernel body doesn't contain any reference to reductions—all we must specify is that the kernel contains a reduction which combines instances of the sum variable using the plus functor. This provides enough information for an implementation to automatically generate an optimized reduction sequence.

At the time of writing, the reduction library only supports kernels with a single reduction variable. Future versions of DPC++ are expected to support kernels which perform more than one reduction simultaneously, by specifying multiple reductions between the nd_range and functor arguments passed into parallel_for and taking multiple reducers as arguments to the kernel functor.

The result of a reduction is not guaranteed to be written back to the original variable until the kernel has completed. Apart from this restriction, accessing the result of a reduction behaves identically to accessing any other variable in SYCL: accessing a reduction result stored in a buffer requires the creation of an appropriate device or host accessor, and accessing a reduction result stored in a USM allocation may require explicit synchronization and/or memory movement.

One important way in which the DPC++ reduction library differs from reduction abstractions found in other languages is that it restricts our access to the reduction variable during kernel execution—we cannot inspect the intermediate values of a reduction variable, and we are forbidden from updating the reduction variable using anything other than the specified combination function. These restrictions prevent us from making mistakes that would be hard to debug (e.g., adding to a reduction variable while trying to compute the maximum) and ensure that reductions can be implemented efficiently on a wide variety of different devices.

The `reduction` Class

The `reduction` class is the interface we use to describe the reductions present in a kernel. The only way to construct a reduction object is to use one of the functions shown in Figure 14-9.

```
template <typename T, typename BinaryOperation>
unspecified reduction(T* variable, BinaryOperation combiner);

template <typename T, typename BinaryOperation>
unspecified reduction(T* variable, T identity, BinaryOperation combiner);
```

Figure 14-9. *Function prototypes of the `reduction` function*

The first version of the function allows us to specify the reduction variable and the operator used to combine the contributions from each work-item. The second version allows us to provide an optional identity value associated with the reduction operator—this is an optimization for user-defined reductions, which we will revisit later.

Note that the return type of the `reduction` function is unspecified, and the `reduction` class itself is completely implementation-defined. Although this may appear slightly unusual for a C++ class, it permits an implementation to use different classes (or a single class with any number of template arguments) to represent different reduction algorithms. Future versions of DPC++ may decide to revisit this design in order to enable us to explicitly request specific reduction algorithms in specific execution contexts.

The `reducer` Class

An instance of the `reducer` class encapsulates a reduction variable, exposing a limited interface ensuring that we cannot update the reduction variable in any way that an implementation could consider to be unsafe. A simplified definition of the `reducer` class is shown in Figure 14-10. Like the `reduction` class, the precise definition of the `reducer` class is implementation-defined—a reducer's type will depend on how the reduction is being performed, and it is important to know this at compile time in order to maximize performance. However, the functions and operators that allow us to update the reduction variable are well-defined and are guaranteed to be supported by any DPC++ implementation.

```
template <typename T,
          typename BinaryOperation,
          /* implementation-defined */>
class reducer {
  // Combine partial result with reducer's value
  void combine(const T& partial);
};

// Other operators are available for standard binary operations
template <typename T>
auto& operator +=(reducer<T,plus::<T>>&, const T&);
```

Figure 14-10. Simplified definition of the `reducer` class

Specifically, every reducer provides a `combine()` function which combines the partial result (from a single work-item) with the value of the reduction variable. How this combine function behaves is implementation-defined but is not something that we need to worry about when writing a kernel. A reducer is also required to make other operators available depending on the reduction operator; for example, the += operator is defined for `plus` reductions. These additional operators are provided only as a programmer convenience and to improve readability; where they are available, these operators have identical behavior to calling `combine()` directly.

User-Defined Reductions

Several common reduction algorithms (e.g., a tree reduction) do not see each work-item directly update a single shared variable, but instead accumulate some partial result in a private variable that will be combined at some point in the future. Such private variables introduce a problem: how should the implementation initialize them? Initializing variables to the first contribution from each work-item has potential performance ramifications, since additional logic is required to detect and handle uninitialized variables. Initializing variables to the identity of the reduction operator instead avoids the performance penalty but is only possible when the identity is known.

DPC++ implementations can only automatically determine the correct identity value to use when a reduction is operating on simple arithmetic types and the reduction operator is a standard functor (e.g., `plus`). For user-defined reductions (i.e., those operating on user-defined types and/or using user-defined functors), we may be able to improve performance by specifying the identity value directly.

CHAPTER 14 COMMON PARALLEL PATTERNS

```cpp
template <typename T, typename I>
struct pair {
  bool operator<(const pair& o) const {
    return val <= o.val || (val == o.val && idx <= o.idx);
  }
  T val;
  I idx;
};

template <typename T, typename I>
using minloc = minimum<pair<T, I>>;

constexpr size_t N = 16;
constexpr size_t L = 4;

queue Q;
float* data = malloc_shared<float>(N, Q);
pair<float, int>* res = malloc_shared<pair<float, int>>(1, Q);
std::generate(data, data + N, std::mt19937{});

pair<float, int> identity = {
    std::numeric_limits<float>::max(), std::numeric_limits<int>::min()
};
*res = identity;

auto red = reduction(res, identity, minloc<float, int>());

Q.submit([&](handler& h) {
  h.parallel_for(nd_range<1>{N, L}, red, [=](nd_item<1> item, auto& res) {
    int i = item.get_global_id(0);
    pair<float, int> partial = {data[i], i};
    res.combine(partial);
  });
}).wait();

std::cout << "minimum value = " << res->val << " at " << res->idx << "\n";
```

Figure 14-11. Using a user-defined reduction to find the location of the minimum value with an ND-range kernel

CHAPTER 14 COMMON PARALLEL PATTERNS

Support for user-defined reductions is limited to trivially copyable types and combination functions with no side effects, but this is enough to enable many real-life use cases. For example, the code in Figure 14-11 demonstrates the usage of a user-defined reduction to compute both the minimum element in a vector and its location.

oneAPI DPC++ Library

The C++ Standard Template Library (STL) contains several algorithms which correspond to the parallel patterns discussed in this chapter. The algorithms in the STL typically apply to sequences specified by pairs of iterators and—starting with C++17—support an *execution policy* argument denoting whether they should be executed sequentially or in parallel.

The oneAPI DPC++ Library (oneDPL) leverages this execution policy argument to provide a high-productivity approach to parallel programming that leverages kernels written in DPC++ under the hood. If an application can be expressed solely using functionality of the STL algorithms, oneDPL makes it possible to make use of the accelerators in our systems without writing a single line of DPC++ kernel code!

The table in Figure 14-12 shows how the algorithms available in the STL relate to the parallel patterns described in this chapter and to legacy serial algorithms (available before C++17) where appropriate. A more detailed explanation of how to use these algorithms in a DPC++ application can be found in Chapter 18.

Pattern	Serial Algorithm(s)	Parallel Algorithm(s)
Map	transform	transform
Stencil	transform	transform
Reduction	accumulate	reduce transform_reduce
Scan	partial_sum	inclusive_scan exclusive_scan transform_inclusive_scan transform_exclusive_scan
Pack	N/A	copy_if
Unpack	N/A	N/A

Figure 14-12. Relating parallel patterns with the C++17 algorithm library

Group Functions

Support for parallel patterns in DPC++ device code is provided by a separate library of *group functions*. These group functions exploit the parallelism of a specific group of work-items (i.e., a work-group or a sub-group) to implement common parallel algorithms at limited scope and can be used as building blocks to construct other more complex algorithms.

Like oneDPL, the syntax of the group functions in DPC++ is based on that of the algorithm library in C++. The first argument to each function accepts a group or sub_group object in place of an execution policy, and any restrictions from the C++ algorithms apply. Group functions are performed collaboratively by all the work-items in the specified group and so must be treated similarly to a group barrier—all work-items in the group must encounter the same algorithm in converged control flow (i.e., all work-items in the group must similarly encounter or not encounter the algorithm call), and all work-items must provide the same function arguments in order to ensure that they agree on the operation being performed.

At the time of writing, the reduce, exclusive_scan, and inclusive_scan functions are limited to supporting only primitive data types and the most common reduction operators (e.g., plus, minimum, and maximum). This is enough for many use cases, but future versions of DPC++ are expected to extend collective support to user-defined types and operators.

Direct Programming

Although we recommend leveraging libraries wherever possible, we can learn a lot by looking at how each pattern *could* be implemented using "native" DPC++ kernels.

The kernels in the remainder of this chapter should not be expected to reach the same level of performance as highly tuned libraries but are useful in developing a greater understanding of the capabilities of DPC++—and may even serve as a starting point for prototyping new library functionality.

> **USE VENDOR-PROVIDED LIBRARIES!**
>
> When a vendor provides a library implementation of a function, it is almost always beneficial to use it rather than re-implementing the function as a kernel!

Map

Owing to its simplicity, the map pattern can be implemented directly as a basic parallel kernel. The code shown in Figure 14-13 shows such an implementation, using the map pattern to compute the square root of each input element in a range.

CHAPTER 14 COMMON PARALLEL PATTERNS

```
Q.parallel_for(N, [=](id<1> i) {
  output[i] = sqrt(input[i]);
}).wait();
```

Figure 14-13. *Implementing the map pattern in a data-parallel kernel*

Stencil

Implementing a stencil directly as a multidimensional basic data-parallel kernel with multidimensional buffers, as shown in Figure 14-14, is straightforward and easy to understand.

```
id<2> offset(1, 1);
h.parallel_for(stencil_range, offset, [=](id<2> idx) {
  int i = idx[0];
  int j = idx[1];

  float self  = input[i][j];
  float north = input[i - 1][j];
  float east  = input[i][j + 1];
  float south = input[i + 1][j];
  float west  = input[i][j - 1];
  output[i][j] = (self + north + east + south + west) / 5.0f;
});
```

Figure 14-14. *Implementing the stencil pattern in a data-parallel kernel*

However, this expression of the stencil pattern is very naïve and should not be expected to perform very well. As mentioned earlier in the chapter, it is well-known that leveraging locality (via spatial or temporal blocking) is required to avoid repeated reads of the same data from memory. A simple example of spatial blocking, using work-group local memory, is shown in Figure 14-15.

CHAPTER 14 COMMON PARALLEL PATTERNS

```
range<2> local_range(B, B);
// Includes boundary cells
range<2> tile_size = local_range + range<2>(2, 2);
auto tile = local_accessor<float, 2>(tile_size, h);

// Compute the average of each cell and its immediate neighbors
id<2> offset(1, 1);

h.parallel_for(
  nd_range<2>(stencil_range, local_range, offset), [=](nd_item<2> it) {
    // Load this tile into work-group local memory
    id<2> lid = it.get_local_id();
    range<2> lrange = it.get_local_range();
    for (int ti = lid[0]; ti < B + 2; ti += lrange[0]) {
      int gi = ti + B * it.get_group(0);
      for (int tj = lid[1]; tj < B + 2; tj += lrange[1]) {
        int gj = tj + B * it.get_group(1);
        tile[ti][tj] = input[gi][gj];
      }
    }
    it.barrier(access::fence_space::local_space);

    // Compute the stencil using values from local memory
    int gi = it.get_global_id(0);
    int gj = it.get_global_id(1);

    int ti = it.get_local_id(0) + 1;
    int tj = it.get_local_id(1) + 1;

    float self  = tile[ti][tj];
    float north = tile[ti - 1][tj];
    float east  = tile[ti][tj + 1];
    float south = tile[ti + 1][tj];
    float west  = tile[ti][tj - 1];
    output[gi][gj] = (self + north + east + south + west) / 5.0f;
});
```

Figure 14-15. *Implementing the stencil pattern in an ND-range kernel, using work-group local memory*

Selecting the best optimizations for a given stencil requires compile-time introspection of block size, the neighborhood, and the stencil function itself, requiring a much more sophisticated approach than discussed here.

Reduction

It is possible to implement reduction kernels in DPC++ by leveraging language features that provide synchronization and communication capabilities between work-items (e.g., atomic operations, work-group and sub-group functions, sub-group shuffles). The kernels in Figures 14-16 and 14-17 show two possible reduction implementations: a naïve reduction using a basic `parallel_for` and an atomic operation for every work-item; and a slightly smarter reduction that exploits locality using an ND-range `parallel_for` and a work-group reduce function, respectively. We will revisit these atomic operations in more detail in Chapter 19.

```
Q.parallel_for(N, [=](id<1> i) {
   atomic_ref<
     int,
     memory_order::relaxed,
     memory_scope::system,
     access::address_space::global_space>(*sum) += data[i];
}).wait();
```

Figure 14-16. Implementing a naïve reduction expressed as a data-parallel kernel

```
Q.parallel_for(nd_range<1>{N, B}, [=](nd_item<1> it) {
  int i = it.get_global_id(0);
  int group_sum = reduce(it.get_group(), data[i], plus<>());
  if (it.get_local_id(0) == 0) {
    atomic_ref<
      int,
      memory_order::relaxed,
      memory_scope::system,
      access::address_space::global_space>(*sum) += group_sum;
  }
}).wait();
```

Figure 14-17. Implementing a naïve reduction expressed as an ND-range kernel

There are numerous other ways to write reduction kernels, and different devices will likely prefer different implementations, owing to differences in hardware support for atomic operations, work-group local memory size, global memory size, the availability of fast device-wide barriers, or even the availability of dedicated reduction instructions. On some architectures, it may even be faster (or necessary!) to perform a tree reduction using $\log_2(N)$ separate kernel calls.

We strongly recommend that manual implementations of reductions be considered only for cases that are not supported by the DPC++ reduction library or when fine-tuning a kernel for the capabilities of a specific device—and even then, only after being 100% sure that the reduction library is underperforming!

Scan

As we saw earlier in this chapter, implementing a parallel scan requires multiple sweeps over the data, with synchronization occurring between each sweep. Since DPC++ does not provide a mechanism for synchronizing all work-items in an ND-range, a direct implementation of a device-wide scan must be implemented using multiple kernels that communicate partial results through global memory.

The code, shown in Figures 14-18, 14-19, and 14-20, demonstrates an inclusive scan implemented using several kernels. The first kernel distributes the input values across work-groups, computing work-group local scans in work-group local memory (note that we could have used the work-group `inclusive_scan` function instead). The second kernel computes a local scan using a single work-group, this time over the final value from each block. The third kernel combines these intermediate results to finalize the prefix sum. These three kernels correspond to the three layers of the diagram in Figure 14-5.

```
// Phase 1: Compute local scans over input blocks
q.submit([&](handler& h) {
  auto local = local_accessor<int32_t, 1>(L, h);
  h.parallel_for(nd_range<1>(N, L), [=](nd_item<1> it) {
    int i = it.get_global_id(0);
    int li = it.get_local_id(0);

    // Copy input to local memory
    local[li] = input[i];
    it.barrier();

    // Perform inclusive scan in local memory
    for (int32_t d = 0; d <= log2((float)L) - 1; ++d) {
      uint32_t stride = (1 << d);
      int32_t update = (li >= stride) ? local[li - stride] : 0;
      it.barrier();
      local[li] += update;
      it.barrier();
    }

    // Write the result for each item to the output buffer
    // Write the last result from this block to the temporary buffer
    output[i] = local[li];
    if (li == it.get_local_range()[0] - 1)
      tmp[it.get_group(0)] = local[li];
  });
}).wait();
```

Figure 14-18. Phase 1 for implementing a global inclusive scan in an ND-range kernel: Computing across each work-group

```
// Phase 2: Compute scan over partial results
q.submit([&](handler& h) {
  auto local = local_accessor<int32_t, 1>(G, h);
  h.parallel_for(nd_range<1>(G, G), [=](nd_item<1> it) {
    int i = it.get_global_id(0);
    int li = it.get_local_id(0);

    // Copy input to local memory
    local[li] = tmp[i];
    it.barrier();

    // Perform inclusive scan in local memory
    for (int32_t d = 0; d <= log2((float)G) - 1; ++d) {
      uint32_t stride = (1 << d);
      int32_t update = (li >= stride) ? local[li - stride] : 0;
      it.barrier();
      local[li] += update;
      it.barrier();
    }

    // Overwrite result from each work-item in the temporary buffer
    tmp[i] = local[li];
  });
}).wait();
```

Figure 14-19. Phase 2 for implementing a global inclusive scan in an ND-range kernel: Scanning across the results of each work-group

```
// Phase 3: Update local scans using partial results
q.parallel_for(nd_range<1>(N, L), [=](nd_item<1> it) {
  int g = it.get_group(0);
  if (g > 0) {
    int i = it.get_global_id(0);
    output[i] += tmp[g - 1];
  }
}).wait();
```

Figure 14-20. Phase 3 (final) for implementing a global inclusive scan in an ND-range kernel

Figures 14-18 and 14-19 are very similar; the only differences are the size of the range and how the input and output values are handled. A real-life implementation of this pattern could use a single function taking different arguments to implement these two phases, and they are only presented as distinct code here for pedagogical reasons.

Pack and Unpack

Pack and unpack are also known as gather and scatter operations. These operations handle differences in how data is arranged in memory and how we wish to present it to the compute resources.

Pack

Since pack depends on an exclusive scan, implementing a pack that applies to all elements of an ND-range must also take place via global memory and over the course of several kernel enqueues. However, there is a common use case for pack that does not require the operation to be applied over all elements of an ND-range—namely, applying a pack only across items in a specific work-group or sub-group.

The snippet in Figure 14-21 shows how to implement a group pack operation on top of an exclusive scan.

```
uint32_t index = exclusive_scan(g, (uint32_t) predicate, plus<>());
if (predicate)
  dst[index] = value;
```

Figure 14-21. *Implementing a group pack operation on top of an exclusive scan*

The code in Figure 14-22 demonstrates how such a pack operation could be used in a kernel to build a list of elements which require some additional postprocessing (in a future kernel). The example shown is based on a real kernel from molecular dynamics simulations: the work-items in the sub-group assigned to particle *i* cooperate to identify all other particles within a fixed distance of *i*, and only the particles in this "neighbor list" will be used to calculate the force acting on each particle.

```
range<2> global(N, 8);
range<2> local(1, 8);
Q.parallel_for(
  nd_range<2>(global, local),
  [=](nd_item<2> it) [[cl::intel_reqd_sub_group_size(8)]] {
    int i = it.get_global_id(0);
    sub_group sg = it.get_sub_group();
    int sglid = sg.get_local_id()[0];
    int sgrange = sg.get_max_local_range()[0];

    uint32_t k = 0;
    for (int j = sglid; j < N; j += sgrange) {

      // Compute distance between i and neighbor j
      float r = distance(position[i], position[j]);

      // Pack neighbors that require post-processing into a list
      uint32_t pack = (i != j) and (r <= CUTOFF);
      uint32_t offset = exclusive_scan(sg, pack, plus<>());
      if (pack)
        neighbors[i * MAX_K + k + offset] = j;

      // Keep track of how many neighbors have been packed so far
      k += reduce(sg, pack, plus<>());
    }
    num_neighbors[i] = reduce(sg, k, maximum<>());
}).wait();
```

Figure 14-22. *Using a sub-group pack operation to build a list of elements needing additional postprocessing*

Note that the pack pattern never re-orders elements—the elements that are packed into the output array appear in the same order as they did in the input. This property of pack is important and enables us to use pack functionality to implement other more abstract parallel algorithms (such as `std::copy_if` and `std::stable_partition`). However, there are other parallel algorithms that can be implemented on top of pack functionality where maintaining order is not required (such as `std::partition`).

Unpack

As with pack, we can implement unpack using scan. Figure 14-23 shows how to implement a sub-group unpack operation on top of an exclusive scan.

```
uint32_t index = exclusive_scan(sg, (uint32_t) predicate, plus<>());
return (predicate) ? new_value[index] : original_value;
```

Figure 14-23. Implementing a sub-group unpack operation on top of an exclusive scan

The code in Figure 14-24 demonstrates how such a sub-group unpack operation could be used to improve load balancing in a kernel with divergent control flow (in this case, computing the Mandelbrot set). Each work-item is assigned a separate pixel to compute and iterates until convergence or a maximum number of iterations is reached. An unpack operation is then used to replace completed pixels with new pixels.

```
// Keep iterating as long as one work-item has work to do
while (any_of(sg, i < Nx)) {
  uint32_t converged =
    next_iteration(params, i, j, count, cr, ci, zr, zi, mandelbrot);
  if (any_of(sg, converged)) {

    // Replace pixels that have converged using an unpack
    // Pixels that haven't converged are not replaced
    uint32_t index = exclusive_scan(sg, converged, plus<>());
    i = (converged) ? iq + index : i;
    iq += reduce(sg, converged, plus<>());

    // Reset the iterator variables for the new i
    if (converged)
      reset(params, i, j, count, cr, ci, zr, zi);
  }
}
```

Figure 14-24. Using a sub-group unpack operation to improve load balancing for kernels with divergent control flow

The degree to which an approach like this improves efficiency (and decreases execution time) is highly application- and input-dependent, since checking for completion and executing the unpack operation both introduce some overhead! Successfully using this pattern in realistic applications will therefore require some fine-tuning based on the amount of divergence present and the computation being performed (e.g., introducing a heuristic to execute the unpack operation only if the number of active work-items falls below some threshold).

Summary

This chapter has demonstrated how to implement some of the most common parallel patterns using DPC++ and SYCL features, including built-in functions and libraries.

The SYCL and DPC++ ecosystems are still developing, and we expect to uncover new best practices for these patterns as developers gain more experience with the language and from the development of production-grade applications and libraries.

For More Information

- *Structured Parallel Programming: Patterns for Efficient Computation* by Michael McCool, Arch Robison, and James Reinders, © 2012, published by Morgan Kaufmann, ISBN 978-0-124-15993-8

- Intel oneAPI DPC++ Library Guide, https://software.intel.com/en-us/oneapi-dpcpp-library-guide

- Algorithms library, C++ Reference, https://en.cppreference.com/w/cpp/algorithm

CHAPTER 14 COMMON PARALLEL PATTERNS

 **Open Access** This chapter is licensed under the terms of the Creative Commons Attribution 4.0 International License (http://creativecommons.org/licenses/by/4.0/), which permits use, sharing, adaptation, distribution and reproduction in any medium or format, as long as you give appropriate credit to the original author(s) and the source, provide a link to the Creative Commons license and indicate if changes were made.

The images or other third party material in this chapter are included in the chapter's Creative Commons license, unless indicated otherwise in a credit line to the material. If material is not included in the chapter's Creative Commons license and your intended use is not permitted by statutory regulation or exceeds the permitted use, you will need to obtain permission directly from the copyright holder.

CHAPTER 15

Programming for GPUs

Over the last few decades, Graphics Processing Units (GPUs) have evolved from specialized hardware devices capable of drawing images on a screen to general-purpose devices capable of executing complex parallel kernels. Nowadays, nearly every computer includes a GPU alongside a traditional CPU, and many programs may be accelerated by offloading part of a parallel algorithm from the CPU to the GPU.

In this chapter, we will describe how a typical GPU works, how GPU software and hardware execute a SYCL application, and tips and techniques to keep in mind when we are writing and optimizing parallel kernels for a GPU.

CHAPTER 15 PROGRAMMING FOR GPUS

Performance Caveats

As with any processor type, GPUs differ from vendor to vendor or even from product generation to product generation; therefore, best practices for one device may not be best practices for a different device. The advice in this chapter is likely to benefit many GPUs, both now and in the future, but...

To achieve optimal performance for a particular GPU, always consult the GPU vendor's documentation!

Links to documentation from many GPU vendors are provided at the end of this chapter.

How GPUs Work

This section describes how typical GPUs work and how GPUs differ from other accelerator types.

GPU Building Blocks

Figure 15-1 shows a very simplified GPU consisting of three high-level building blocks:

1. Execution resources: A GPU's execution resources are the processors that perform computational work. Different GPU vendors use different names for their execution resources, but all modern GPUs consist of multiple programmable processors. The processors may be *heterogeneous* and specialized for particular tasks, or they may be *homogeneous* and interchangeable. Processors for most modern GPUs are *homogeneous* and interchangeable.

CHAPTER 15 PROGRAMMING FOR GPUS

2. Fixed functions: GPU fixed functions are hardware units that are less programmable than the execution resources and are specialized for a single task. When a GPU is used for graphics, many parts of the graphics pipeline such as rasterization or raytracing are performed using fixed functions to improve power efficiency and performance. When a GPU is used for data-parallel computation, fixed functions may be used for tasks such as workload scheduling, texture sampling, and dependence tracking.

3. Caches and memory: Like other processor types, GPUs frequently have caches to store data accessed by the execution resources. GPU caches may be *implicit*, in which case they require no action from the programmer, or may be *explicit* scratchpad memories, in which case a programmer must purposefully move data into a cache before using it. Many GPUs also have a large pool of memory to provide fast access to data used by the execution resources.

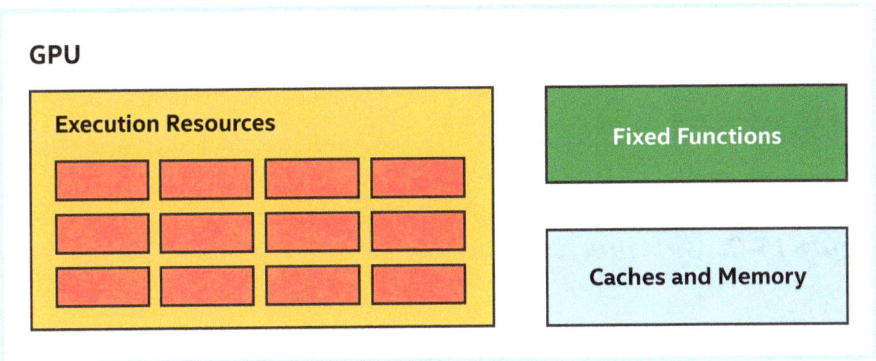

Figure 15-1. *Typical GPU building blocks—not to scale!*

CHAPTER 15   PROGRAMMING FOR GPUS

Simpler Processors (but More of Them)

Traditionally, when performing graphics operations, GPUs process large batches of data. For example, a typical game frame or rendering workload involves thousands of vertices that produce millions of pixels per frame. To maintain interactive frame rates, these large batches of data must be processed as quickly as possible.

A typical GPU design tradeoff is to eliminate features from the processors forming the execution resources that accelerate single-threaded performance and to use these savings to build additional processors, as shown in Figure 15-2. For example, GPU processors may not include sophisticated out-of-order execution capabilities or branch prediction logic used by other types of processors. Due to these tradeoffs, a single data element may be processed on a GPU slower than it would on another processor, but the larger number of processors enables GPUs to process many data elements quickly and efficiently.

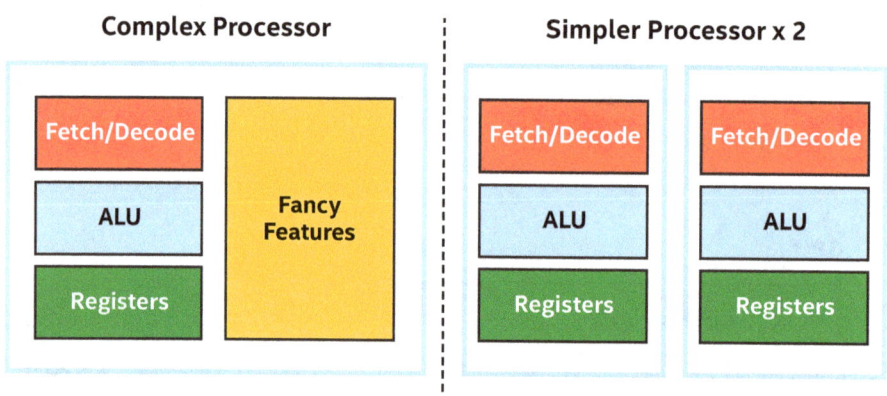

Figure 15-2. *GPU processors are simpler, but there are more of them*

356

CHAPTER 15   PROGRAMMING FOR GPUS

To take advantage of this tradeoff when executing kernels, it is important to give the GPU a sufficiently large range of data elements to process. To demonstrate the importance of offloading a large range of data, consider the matrix multiplication kernel we have been developing and modifying throughout this book.

A REMINDER ABOUT MATRIX MULTIPLICATION

In this book, matrix multiplication kernels are used to demonstrate how changes in a kernel or the way it is dispatched affects performance. Although matrix multiplication performance are significantly improved using the techniques described in this chapter, matrix multiplication is such an important and common operation that many hardware (GPU, CPU, FPGA, DSP, etc.) vendors have implemented highly tuned versions of many routines including matrix multiplication. Such vendors invest significant time and effort implementing and validating functions for specific devices and in some cases may use functionality or techniques that are difficult or impossible to use in standard kernels.

USE VENDOR-PROVIDED LIBRARIES!

When a vendor provides a library implementation of a function, it is almost always beneficial to use it rather than re-implementing the function as a kernel! For matrix multiplication, one can look to oneMKL as part of Intel's oneAPI toolkits for solutions appropriate for DPC++ programmers.

A matrix multiplication kernel may be trivially executed on a GPU by submitting it into a queue as a single task. The body of this matrix multiplication kernel looks exactly like a function that executes on the host CPU and is shown in Figure 15-3.

CHAPTER 15   PROGRAMMING FOR GPUS

```
h.single_task([=]() {
  for (int m = 0; m < M; m++) {
    for (int n = 0; n < N; n++) {
      T sum = 0;
      for (int k = 0; k < K; k++)
        sum += matrixA[m * K + k] * matrixB[k * N + n];
      matrixC[m * N + n] = sum;
    }
  }
});
```

Figure 15-3. A single task matrix multiplication looks a lot like CPU host code

If we try to execute this kernel on a CPU, it will probably perform okay—not great, since it is not expected to utilize any parallel capabilities of the CPU, but potentially good enough for small matrix sizes. As shown in Figure 15-4, if we try to execute this kernel on a GPU, however, it will likely perform very poorly, because the single task will only utilize a single GPU processor.

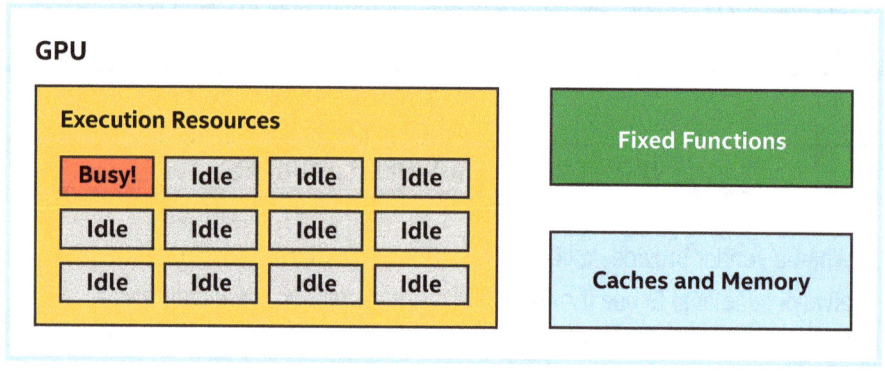

Figure 15-4. A single task kernel on a GPU leaves many execution resources idle

CHAPTER 15 PROGRAMMING FOR GPUS

Expressing Parallelism

To improve the performance of this kernel for both CPUs and GPUs, we can instead submit a range of data elements to process in parallel, by converting one of the loops to a `parallel_for`. For the matrix multiplication kernel, we can choose to submit a range of data elements representing either of the two outermost loops. In Figure 15-5, we've chosen to process rows of the result matrix in parallel.

```
h.parallel_for(range{M}, [=](id<1> idx) {
  int m = idx[0];

  for (int n = 0; n < N; n++) {
    T sum = 0;
    for (int k = 0; k < K; k++)
      sum += matrixA[m * K + k] * matrixB[k * N + n];
    matrixC[m * N + n] = sum;
  }
});
```

Figure 15-5. Somewhat-parallel matrix multiplication

CHOOSING HOW TO PARALLELIZE

Choosing which dimension to parallelize is one very important way to tune an application for both GPUs and other device types. Subsequent sections in this chapter will describe some of the reasons why parallelizing in one dimension may perform better than parallelizing in a different dimension.

Even though the somewhat-parallel kernel is very similar to the single task kernel, it should run better on a CPU and much better on a GPU. As shown in Figure 15-6, the `parallel_for` enables work-items representing rows of the result matrix to be processed on multiple processor resources in parallel, so all execution resources stay busy.

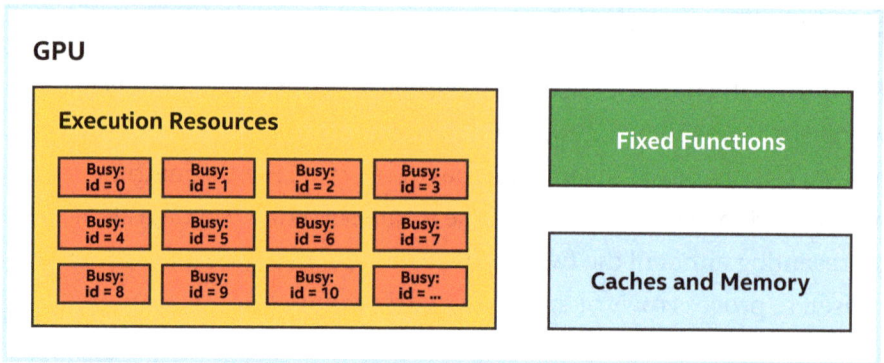

Figure 15-6. Somewhat-parallel kernel keeps more processor resources busy

Note that the exact way that the rows are partitioned and assigned to different processor resources is not specified, giving an implementation flexibility to choose how best to execute the kernel on a device. For example, instead of executing individual rows on a processor, an implementation may choose to execute consecutive rows on the same processor to gain locality benefits.

Expressing More Parallelism

We can parallelize the matrix multiplication kernel even more by choosing to process both outer loops in parallel. Because parallel_for can express parallel loops over up to three dimensions, this is straightforward, as shown in Figure 15-7. In Figure 15-7, note that both the range passed to parallel_for and the item representing the index in the parallel execution space are now two-dimensional.

```
h.parallel_for(range{M, N}, [=](id<2> idx) {
  int m = idx[0];
  int n = idx[1];
  T sum = 0;
  for (int k = 0; k < K; k++)
    sum += matrixA[m * K + k] * matrixB[k * N + n];
  matrixC[m * N + n] = sum;
});
```

Figure 15-7. Even more parallel matrix multiplication

Exposing additional parallelism will likely improve the performance of the matrix multiplication kernel when run on a GPU. This is likely to be true even when the number of matrix rows exceeds the number of GPU processors. The next few sections describe possible reasons why this may be the case.

Simplified Control Logic (SIMD Instructions)

Many GPU processors optimize control logic by leveraging the fact that most data elements tend to take the same control flow path through a kernel. For example, in the matrix multiplication kernel, each data element executes the innermost loop the same number of times since the loop bounds are invariant.

When data elements take the same control flow path through a kernel, a processor may reduce the costs of managing an instruction stream by sharing control logic among multiple data elements and executing them as a group. One way to do this is to implement a *Single Instruction, Multiple Data* or *SIMD* instruction set, where multiple data elements are processed simultaneously by a single instruction.

THREADS VS. INSTRUCTION STREAMS

In many parallel programming contexts and GPU literature, the term "thread" is used to mean an "instruction stream." In these contexts, a "thread" is different than a traditional operating system thread and is typically much more lightweight. This isn't always the case, though, and in some cases, a "thread" is used to describe something completely different.

Since the term "thread" is overloaded and easily misunderstood, this chapter uses the term "instruction stream" instead.

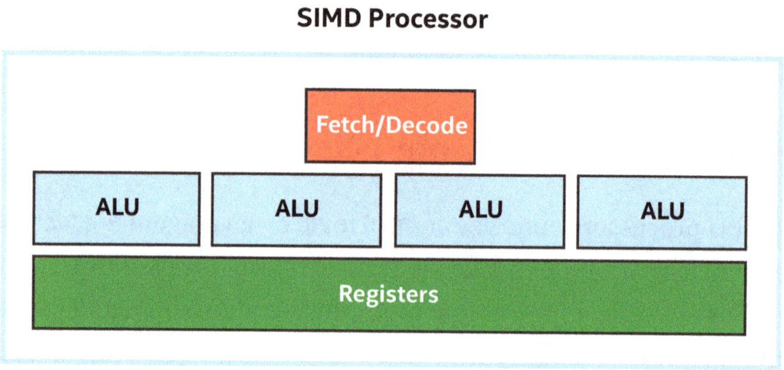

Figure 15-8. Four-wide SIMD processor: The four ALUs share fetch/decode logic

The number of data elements that are processed simultaneously by a single instruction is sometimes referred to as the *SIMD width* of the instruction or the processor executing the instruction. In Figure 15-8, four ALUs share the same control logic, so this may be described as a four-wide SIMD processor.

GPU processors are not the only processors that implement SIMD instruction sets. Other processor types also implement SIMD instruction sets to improve efficiency when processing large sets of data. The main difference between GPU processors and other processor types is that GPU

CHAPTER 15 PROGRAMMING FOR GPUS

processors rely on executing multiple data elements in parallel to achieve good performance and that GPU processors may support wider SIMD widths than other processor types. For example, it is not uncommon for GPU processors to support SIMD widths of 16, 32, or more data elements.

> **PROGRAMMING MODELS: SPMD AND SIMD**
>
> Although GPU processors implement SIMD instruction sets with varying widths, this is usually an implementation detail and is transparent to the application executing data-parallel kernels on the GPU processor. This is because many GPU compilers and runtime APIs implement a *Single Program, Multiple Data* or *SPMD* programming model, where the GPU compiler and runtime API determine the most efficient group of data elements to process with a SIMD instruction stream, rather than expressing the SIMD instructions explicitly. The "Sub-Groups" section of Chapter 9 explores cases where the grouping of data elements is visible to applications.

In Figure 15-9, we have widened each of our execution resources to support four-wide SIMD, allowing us to process four times as many matrix rows in parallel.

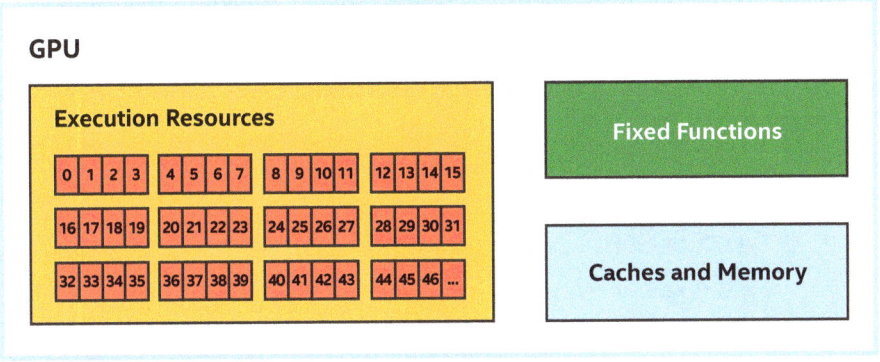

Figure 15-9. *Executing a somewhat-parallel kernel on SIMD processors*

363

The use of SIMD instructions that process multiple data elements in parallel is one of the ways that the performance of the parallel matrix multiplication kernels in Figures 15-5 and 15-7 is able to scale beyond the number of processors alone. The use of SIMD instructions also provides natural locality benefits in many cases, including matrix multiplication, by executing consecutive data elements on the same processor.

Kernels benefit from parallelism across processors and parallelism within processors!

Predication and Masking

Sharing an instruction stream among multiple data elements works well so long as all data elements take the same path through conditional code in a kernel. When data elements take different paths through conditional code, control flow is said to *diverge*. When control flow diverges in a SIMD instruction stream, usually both control flow paths are executed, with some channels masked off or *predicated*. This ensures correct behavior, but the correctness comes at a performance cost since channels that are masked do not perform useful work.

To show how predication and masking works, consider the kernel in Figure 15-10, which multiplies each data element with an "odd" index by two and increments each data element with an "even" index by one.

```
h.parallel_for(array_size, [=](id<1> i) {
  auto condition = i[0] & 1;
  if (condition)
    dataAcc[i] = dataAcc[i] * 2; // odd
  else
    dataAcc[i] = dataAcc[i] + 1; // even
});
```

Figure 15-10. Kernel with divergent control flow

CHAPTER 15 PROGRAMMING FOR GPUS

Let's say that we execute this kernel on the four-wide SIMD processor shown in Figure 15-8 and that we execute the first four data elements in one SIMD instruction stream and the next four data elements in a different SIMD instruction stream and so on. Figure 15-11 shows one of the ways channels may be masked and execution may be predicated to correctly execute this kernel with divergent control flow.

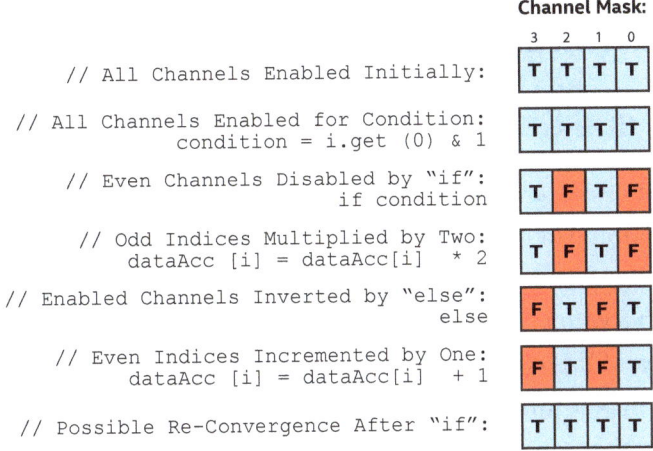

Figure 15-11. Possible channel masks for a divergent kernel

SIMD Efficiency

SIMD efficiency measures how well a SIMD instruction stream performs compared to equivalent scalar instruction streams. In Figure 15-11, since control flow partitioned the channels into two equal groups, each instruction in the divergent control flow executes with half efficiency. In a worst-case scenario, for highly divergent kernels, efficiency may be reduced by a factor of the processor's SIMD width.

365

All processors that implement a SIMD instruction set will suffer from divergence penalties that affect SIMD efficiency, but because GPU processors typically support wider SIMD widths than other processor types, restructuring an algorithm to minimize divergent control flow and maximize converged execution may be especially beneficial when optimizing a kernel for a GPU. This is not always possible, but as an example, choosing to parallelize along a dimension with more converged execution may perform better than parallelizing along a different dimension with highly divergent execution.

SIMD Efficiency and Groups of Items

All kernels in this chapter so far have been basic data-parallel kernels that do not specify any grouping of items in the execution range, which gives an implementation freedom to choose the best grouping for a device. For example, a device with a wider SIMD width may prefer a larger grouping, but a device with a narrower SIMD width may be fine with smaller groupings.

When a kernel is an ND-range kernel with explicit groupings of work-items, care should be taken to choose an ND-range work-group size that maximizes SIMD efficiency. When a work-group size is not evenly divisible by a processor's SIMD width, part of the work-group may execute with channels disabled for the entire duration of the kernel. The kernel preferred_work_group_size_multiple query can be used to choose an efficient work-group size. Please refer to Chapter 12 for more information on how to query properties of a device.

Choosing a work-group size consisting of a single work-item will likely perform very poorly since many GPUs will implement a single-work-item work-group by masking off all SIMD channels except for one. For example, the kernel in Figure 15-12 will likely perform much worse than the very similar kernel in Figure 15-5, even though the only significant difference between the two is a change from a basic data-parallel kernel to an inefficient single-work-item ND-range kernel (nd_range<1>{M, 1}).

```
// A work-group consisting of a single work-item is inefficient!
h.parallel_for(nd_range<1>{M, 1}, [=](nd_item<1> idx) {
  int m = idx.get_global_id(0);

  for (int n = 0; n < N; n++) {
    T sum = 0;
    for (int k = 0; k < K; k++)
      sum += matrixA[m * K + k] * matrixB[k * N + n];
    matrixC[m * N + n] = sum;
  }
});
```

Figure 15-12. Inefficient single-item, somewhat-parallel matrix multiplication

Switching Work to Hide Latency

Many GPUs implement one more technique to simplify control logic, maximize execution resources, and improve performance: instead of executing a single instruction stream on a processor, many GPUs allow multiple instruction streams to be resident on a processor simultaneously.

Having multiple instruction streams resident on a processor is beneficial because it gives each processor a choice of work to execute. If one instruction stream is performing a long-latency operation, such as a read from memory, the processor can switch to a different instruction stream that is ready to run instead of waiting for the operation to complete. With enough instruction streams, by the time that the processor switches back to the original instruction stream, the long-latency operation may have completed without requiring the processor to wait at all.

Figure 15-13 shows how a processor uses multiple simultaneous instruction streams to hide latency and improve performance. Even though the first instruction stream took a little longer to execute with multiple streams, by switching to other instruction streams, the processor was able to find work that was ready to execute and never needed to idly wait for the long operation to complete.

CHAPTER 15 PROGRAMMING FOR GPUS

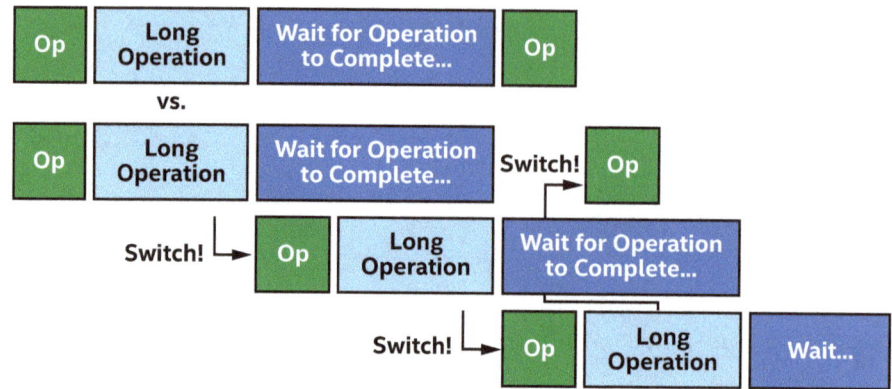

Figure 15-13. Switching instruction streams to hide latency

GPU profiling tools may describe the number of instruction streams that a GPU processor is currently executing vs. the theoretical total number of instruction streams using a term such as *occupancy*.

Low occupancy does not necessarily imply low performance, since it is possible that a small number of instruction streams will keep a processor busy. Likewise, high occupancy does not necessarily imply high performance, since a GPU processor may still need to wait if all instruction streams perform inefficient, long-latency operations. All else being equal though, increasing occupancy maximizes a GPU processor's ability to hide latency and will usually improve performance. Increasing occupancy is another reason why performance may improve with the even more parallel kernel in Figure 15-7.

This technique of switching between multiple instruction streams to hide latency is especially well-suited for GPUs and data-parallel processing. Recall from Figure 15-2 that GPU processors are frequently simpler than other processor types and hence lack complex latency-hiding features. This makes GPU processors more susceptible to latency issues, but because data-parallel programming involves processing a lot of data, GPU processors usually have plenty of instruction streams to execute!

CHAPTER 15   PROGRAMMING FOR GPUS

Offloading Kernels to GPUs

This section describes how an application, the SYCL runtime library, and the GPU software driver work together to offload a kernel on GPU hardware. The diagram in Figure 15-14 shows a typical software stack with these layers of abstraction. In many cases, the existence of these layers is transparent to an application, but it is important to understand and account for them when debugging or profiling our application.

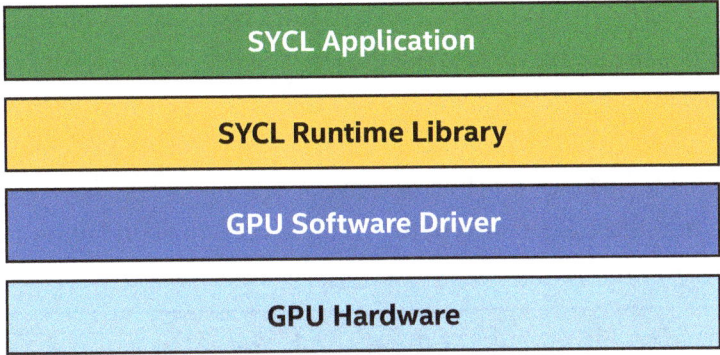

Figure 15-14. *Offloading parallel kernels to GPUs (simplified)*

SYCL Runtime Library

The SYCL runtime library is the primary software library that SYCL applications interface with. The runtime library is responsible for implementing classes such as queues, buffers, and accessors and the member functions of these classes. Parts of the runtime library may be in header files and hence directly compiled into the application executable. Other parts of the runtime library are implemented as library functions, which are linked with the application executable as part of the application build process. The runtime library is usually not device-specific, and the same runtime library may orchestrate offload to CPUs, GPUs, FPGAs, or other devices.

CHAPTER 15   PROGRAMMING FOR GPUS

GPU Software Drivers

Although it is theoretically possible that a SYCL runtime library could offload directly to a GPU, in practice, most SYCL runtime libraries interface with a GPU software driver to submit work to a GPU.

A GPU software driver is typically an implementation of an API, such as OpenCL, Level Zero, or CUDA. Most of a GPU software driver is implemented in a user-mode driver library that the SYCL runtime calls into, and the user-mode driver may call into the operating system or a kernel-mode driver to perform system-level tasks such as allocating memory or submitting work to the device. The user-mode driver may also invoke other user-mode libraries; for example, the GPU driver may invoke a GPU compiler to just-in-time compile a kernel from an intermediate representation to GPU ISA (Instruction Set Architecture). These software modules and the interactions between them are shown in Figure 15-15.

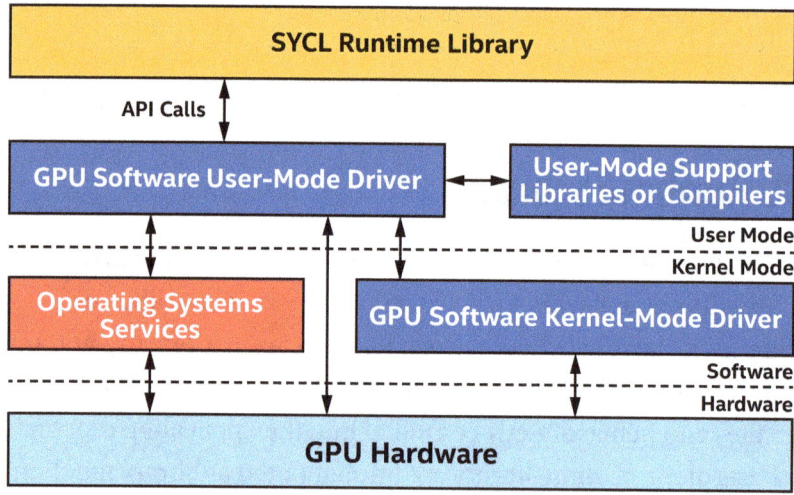

Figure 15-15. Typical GPU software driver modules

GPU Hardware

When the runtime library or the GPU software user-mode driver is explicitly requested to submit work or when the GPU software heuristically determines that work should begin, it will typically call through the operating system or a kernel-mode driver to start executing work on the GPU. In some cases, the GPU software user-mode driver may submit work directly to the GPU, but this is less common and may not be supported by all devices or operating systems.

When the results of work executed on a GPU are consumed by the host processor or another accelerator, the GPU must issue a signal to indicate that work is complete. The steps involved in work completion are very similar to the steps for work submission, executed in reverse: the GPU may signal the operating system or kernel-mode driver that it has finished execution, then the user-mode driver will be informed, and finally the runtime library will observe that work has completed via GPU software API calls.

Each of these steps introduces latency, and in many cases, the runtime library and the GPU software are making a tradeoff between lower latency and higher throughput. For example, submitting work to the GPU more frequently may reduce latency, but submitting frequently may also reduce throughput due to per-submission overheads. Collecting large batches of work increases latency but amortizes submission overheads over more work and introduces more opportunities for parallel execution. The runtime and drivers are tuned to make the right tradeoff and usually do a good job, but if we suspect that driver heuristics are submitting work inefficiently, we should consult documentation to see if there are ways to override the default driver behavior using API-specific or even implementation-specific mechanisms.

Beware the Cost of Offloading!

Although SYCL implementations and GPU vendors are continually innovating and optimizing to reduce the cost of offloading work to a GPU, there will always be overhead involved both when starting work on a GPU and observing results on the host or another device. When choosing where to execute an algorithm, consider both the benefit of executing an algorithm on a device and the cost of moving the algorithm and any data that it requires to the device. In some cases, it may be most efficient to perform a parallel operation using the host processor—or to execute a serial part of an algorithm inefficiently on the GPU—to avoid the overhead of moving an algorithm from one processor to another.

Consider the performance of our algorithm as a whole—it may be most efficient to execute part of an algorithm inefficiently on one device than to transfer execution to another device!

Transfers to and from Device Memory

On GPUs with dedicated memory, be especially aware of transfer costs between dedicated GPU memory and memory on the host or another device. Figure 15-16 shows typical memory bandwidth differences between different memory types in a system.

CHAPTER 15 PROGRAMMING FOR GPUS

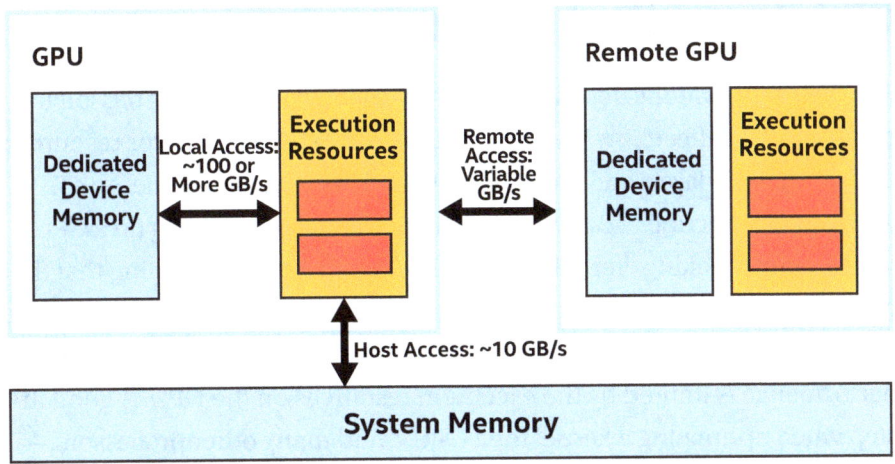

Figure 15-16. Typical differences between device memory, remote memory, and host memory

Recall from Chapter 3 that GPUs prefer to operate on dedicated device memory, which can be faster by an order of magnitude or more, instead of operating on host memory or another device's memory. Even though accesses to dedicated device memory are significantly faster than accesses to remote memory or system memory, if the data is not already in dedicated device memory then it must be copied or migrated.

So long as the data will be accessed frequently, moving it into dedicated device memory is beneficial, especially if the transfer can be performed asynchronously while the GPU execution resources are busy processing another task. When the data is accessed infrequently or unpredictably though, it may preferable to save transfer costs and operate on the data remotely or in system memory, even if per-access costs are higher. Chapter 6 describes ways to control where memory is allocated and different techniques to copy and prefetch data into dedicated device memory. These techniques are important when optimizing program execution for GPUs.

CHAPTER 15 PROGRAMMING FOR GPUS

GPU Kernel Best Practices

The previous sections described how the dispatch parameters passed to a `parallel_for` affect how kernels are assigned to GPU processor resources and the software layers and overheads involved in executing a kernel on a GPU. This section describes best practices when a kernel is executing on a GPU.

Broadly speaking, kernels are either *memory bound*, meaning that their performance is limited by data read and write operations into or out of the execution resources on the GPU, or are *compute bound*, meaning that their performance is limited by the execution resources on the GPU. A good first step when optimizing a kernel for a GPU—and many other processors!—is to determine whether our kernel is memory bound or compute bound, since the techniques to improve a memory-bound kernel frequently will not benefit a compute-bound kernel and vice versa. GPU vendors often provide profiling tools to help make this determination.

Different optimization techniques are needed depending whether our kernel is memory bound or compute bound!

Because GPUs tend to have many processors and wide SIMD widths, kernels tend to be memory bound more often than they are compute bound. If we are unsure where to start, examining how our kernel accesses memory is a good first step.

Accessing Global Memory

Efficiently accessing global memory is critical for optimal application performance, because almost all data that a work-item or work-group operates on originates in global memory. If a kernel operates on global memory inefficiently, it will almost always perform poorly. Even though GPUs often include dedicated hardware *gather* and *scatter* units for

CHAPTER 15 PROGRAMMING FOR GPUS

reading and writing arbitrary locations in memory, the performance of accesses to global memory is usually driven by the *locality* of data accesses. If one work-item in a work-group is accessing an element in memory that is adjacent to an element accessed by another work-item in the work-group, the global memory access performance is likely to be good. If work-items in a work-group instead access memory that is strided or random, the global memory access performance will likely be worse. Some GPU documentation describes operating on nearby memory accesses as *coalesced* memory accesses.

Recall that for our somewhat-parallel matrix multiplication kernel in Figure 15-15, we had a choice whether to process a row or a column of the result matrix in parallel, and we chose to operate on rows of the result matrix in parallel. This turns out to be a poor choice: if one work-item with id equal to m is grouped with a neighboring work-item with id equal to m-1 or m+1, the indices used to access matrixB are the same for each work-item, but the indices used to access matrixA differ by K, meaning the accesses are highly strided. The access pattern for matrixA is shown in Figure 15-17.

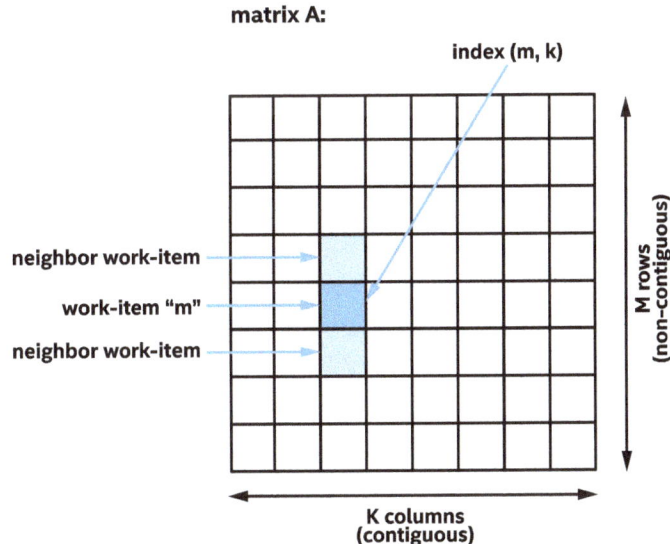

Figure 15-17. *Accesses to* matrixA *are highly strided and inefficient*

CHAPTER 15 PROGRAMMING FOR GPUS

If, instead, we choose to process columns of the result matrix in parallel, the access patterns have much better locality. The kernel in Figure 15-18 is structurally very similar to that in Figure 15-5 with the only difference being that each work-item in Figure 15-18 operates on a column of the result matrix, rather than a row of the result matrix.

```
// This kernel processes columns of the result matrix in parallel.
h.parallel_for(N, [=](item<1> idx) {
  int n = idx[0];

  for (int m = 0; m < M; m++) {
    T sum = 0;
    for (int k = 0; k < K; k++)
      sum += matrixA[m * K + k] * matrixB[k * N + n];
    matrixC[m * N + n] = sum;
  }
});
```

Figure 15-18. *Computing columns of the result matrix in parallel, not rows*

Even though the two kernels are structurally very similar, the kernel that operates on columns of data will significantly outperform the kernel that operates on rows of data on many GPUs, purely due to the more efficient memory accesses: if one work-item with id equal to n is grouped with a neighboring work-item with id equal to n-1 or n+1, the indices used to access matrixA are now the same for each work-item, and the indices used to access matrixB are consecutive. The access pattern for matrixB is shown in Figure 15-19.

CHAPTER 15 PROGRAMMING FOR GPUS

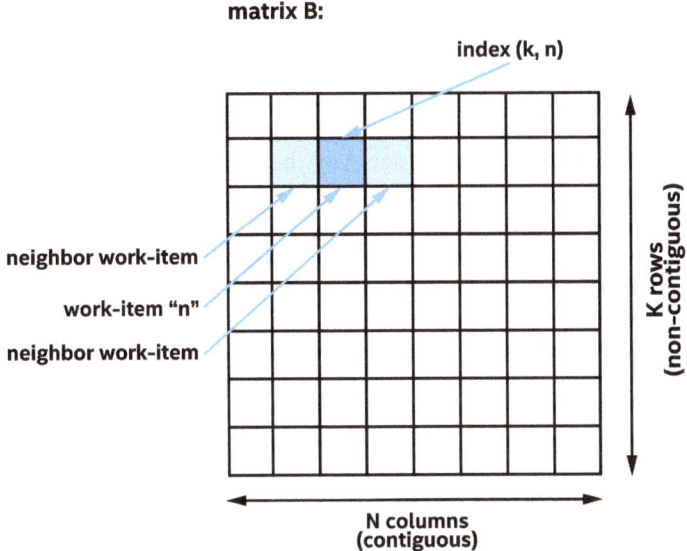

Figure 15-19. Accesses to matrixB are consecutive and efficient

Accesses to consecutive data are usually very efficient. A good rule of thumb is that the performance of accesses to global memory for a group of work-items is a function of the number of GPU cache lines accessed. If all accesses are within a single cache line, the access will execute with peak performance. If an access requires two cache lines, say by accessing every other element or by starting from a cache-misaligned address, the access may operate at half performance. When each work-item in the group accesses a unique cache line, say for a very strided or random accesses, the access is likely to operate at lowest performance.

> **PROFILING KERNEL VARIANTS**
>
> For matrix multiplication, choosing to parallelize along one dimension clearly results in more efficient memory accesses, but for other kernels, the choice may not be as obvious. For kernels where it is important to achieve the best performance, if it is not obvious which dimension to parallelize, it is sometimes worth developing and profiling different kernel variants that parallelize along each dimension to see what works better for a device and data set.

Accessing Work-Group Local Memory

In the previous section, we described how accesses to global memory benefit from *locality*, to maximize cache performance. As we saw, in some cases we can design our algorithm to efficiently access memory, such as by choosing to parallelize in one dimension instead of another. This technique isn't possible in all cases, however. This section describes how we can use work-group local memory to efficiently support more memory access patterns.

Recall from Chapter 9 that work-items in a work-group can cooperate to solve a problem by communicating through work-group local memory and synchronizing using work-group barriers. This technique is especially beneficial for GPUs, since typical GPUs have specialized hardware to implement both barriers and work-group local memory. Different GPU vendors and different products may implement work-group local memory differently, but work-group local memory frequently has two benefits compared to global memory: local memory may support higher bandwidth and lower latency than accesses to global memory, even when the global memory access hits a cache, and local memory is often divided into different memory regions, called *banks*. So long as each work-item in a group accesses a different bank, the local memory access executes with full performance. Banked accesses allow local memory to support far more access patterns with peak performance than global memory.

Many GPU vendors will assign consecutive local memory addresses to different banks. This ensures that consecutive memory accesses always operate at full performance, regardless of the starting address. When memory accesses are strided, though, some work-items in a group may access memory addresses assigned to the same bank. When this occurs, it is considered a *bank conflict* and results in serialized access and lower performance.

For maximum global memory performance, minimize the number of cache lines accessed.

For maximum local memory performance, minimize the number of bank conflicts!

A summary of access patterns and expected performance for global memory and local memory is shown in Figure 15-20. Assume that when `ptr` points to global memory, the pointer is aligned to the size of a GPU cache line. The best performance when accessing global memory can be achieved by accessing memory consecutively starting from a cache-aligned address. Accessing an unaligned address will likely lower global memory performance because the access may require accessing additional cache lines. Because accessing an unaligned local address will not result in additional bank conflicts, the local memory performance is unchanged.

The strided case is worth describing in more detail. Accessing every other element in global memory requires accessing more cache lines and will likely result in lower performance. Accessing every other element in local memory may result in bank conflicts and lower performance, but only if the number of banks is divisible by two. If the number of banks is odd, this case will operate at full performance also.

When the stride between accesses is very large, each work-item accesses a unique cache line, resulting in the worst performance. For local memory though, the performance depends on the stride and the number of banks. When the stride N is equal to the number of banks, each access results in a bank conflict, and all accesses are serialized, resulting in the worst performance. If the stride M and the number of banks share no common factors, however, the accesses will run at full performance. For this reason, many optimized GPU kernels will pad data structures in local memory to choose a stride that reduces or eliminates bank conflicts.

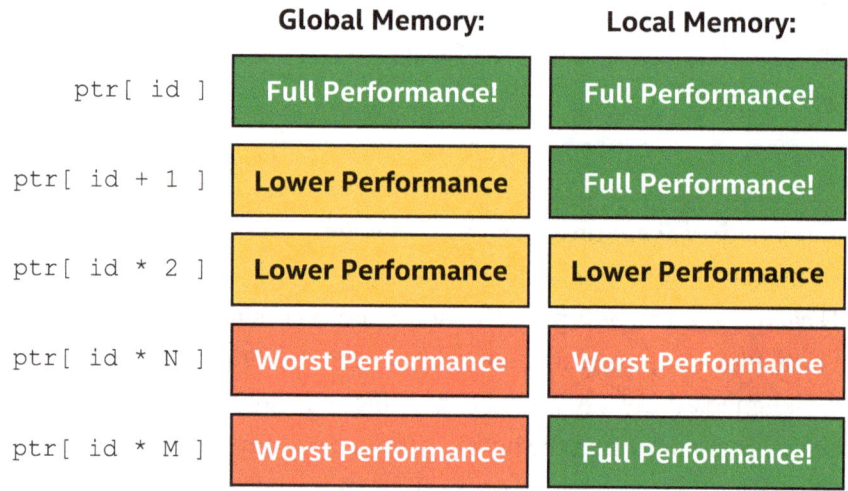

Figure 15-20. Possible performance for different access patterns, for global and local memory

Avoiding Local Memory Entirely with Sub-Groups

As discussed in Chapter 9, sub-group collective functions are an alternative way to exchange data between work-items in a group. For many GPUs, a sub-group represents a collection of work-items processed by a single instruction stream. In these cases, the work-items in the sub-group can inexpensively exchange data and synchronize without using work-group local memory. Many of the best-performing GPU kernels use sub-groups, so for expensive kernels, it is well worth examining if our algorithm can be reformulated to use sub-group collective functions.

Optimizing Computation Using Small Data Types

This section describes techniques to optimize kernels after eliminating or reducing memory access bottlenecks. One very important perspective to keep in mind is that GPUs have traditionally been designed to draw pictures on a screen. Although pure computational capabilities of GPUs have evolved and improved over time, in some areas their graphics heritage is still apparent.

Consider support for kernel data types, for example. Many GPUs are highly optimized for 32-bit floating-point operations, since these operations tend to be common in graphics and games. For algorithms that can cope with lower precision, many GPUs also support a lower-precision 16-bit floating-point type that trades precision for faster processing. Conversely, although many GPUs do support 64-bit double-precision floating-point operations, the extra precision will come at a cost, and 32-bit operations usually perform much better than their 64-bit equivalents.

The same is true for integer data types, where 32-bit integer data types typically perform better than 64-bit integer data types and 16-bit integers may perform even better still. If we can structure our computation to use smaller integers, our kernel may perform faster. One area to pay careful attention to are addressing operations, which typically operate on 64-bit `size_t` data types, but can sometimes be rearranged to perform most of the calculation using 32-bit data types. In some local memory cases, 16 bits of indexing is sufficient, since most local memory allocations are small.

Optimizing Math Functions

Another area where a kernel may trade off accuracy for performance involves SYCL built-in functions. SYCL includes a rich set of math functions with well-defined accuracy across a range of inputs. Most GPUs do not support these functions natively and implement them using a long sequence of other instructions. Although the math function implementations are typically well-optimized for a GPU, if our application can tolerate lower accuracy, we should consider a different implementation with lower accuracy and higher performance instead. Please refer to Chapter 18 for more information about SYCL built-in functions.

For commonly used math functions, the SYCL library includes fast or native function variants with reduced or implementation-defined accuracy requirements. For some GPUs, these functions can be an order of magnitude faster than their precise equivalents, so they are well worth considering if they have enough precision for an algorithm. For example, many image postprocessing algorithms have well-defined inputs and can tolerate lower accuracy and hence are good candidates for using fast or native math functions.

If an algorithm can tolerate lower precision, we can use smaller data types or lower-precision math functions to increase performance!

Specialized Functions and Extensions

One final consideration when optimizing a kernel for a GPU are specialized instructions that are common in many GPUs. As one example, nearly all GPUs support a mad or fma multiply-and-add instruction that performs two operations in a single clock. GPU compilers are generally very good at identifying and optimizing individual multiplies and adds to use a single instruction instead, but SYCL also includes mad and fma functions that can be called explicitly. Of course, if we expect our GPU compiler to optimize multiplies and adds for us, we should be sure that we do not prevent optimizations by disabling floating-point contractions!

Other specialized GPU instructions may only be available via compiler optimizations or extensions to the SYCL language. For example, some GPUs support a specialized dot-product-and-accumulate instruction that compilers will try to identify and optimize for or that can be called directly. Refer to Chapter 12 for more information on how to query the extensions that are supported by a GPU implementation.

Summary

In this chapter, we started by describing how typical GPUs work and how GPUs are different than traditional CPUs. We described how GPUs are optimized for large amounts of data, by trading processor features that accelerate a single instruction stream for additional processors.

We described how GPUs process multiple data elements in parallel using wide SIMD instructions and how GPUs use predication and masking to execute kernels with complex flow control using SIMD instructions. We discussed how predication and masking can reduce SIMD efficiency and decrease performance for kernels that are highly divergent and how choosing to parallelize along one dimension vs. another may reduce SIMD divergence.

Because GPUs have so many processing resources, we discussed how it is important to give GPUs enough work to keep occupancy high. We also described how GPUs use instruction streams to hide latency, making it even more crucial to give GPUs lots of work to execute.

Next, we discussed the software and hardware layers involved in offloading a kernel to a GPU and the costs of offloading. We discussed how it may be more efficient to execute an algorithm on a single device than it is to transfer execution from one device to another.

Finally, we described best practices for kernels once they are executing on a GPU. We described how many kernels start off memory bound and how to access global memory and local memory efficiently or how to avoid local memory entirely by using sub-group operations. When kernels are compute bound instead, we described how to optimize computation by trading lower precision for higher performance or using custom GPU extensions to access specialized instructions.

For More Information

There is much more to learn about GPU programming, and this chapter just scratched the surface!

GPU specifications and white papers are a great way to learn more about specific GPUs and GPU architectures. Many GPU vendors provide very detailed information about their GPUs and how to program them.

At the time of this writing, relevant reading about major GPUs can be found on software.intel.com, devblogs.nvidia.com, and amd.com.

Some GPU vendors have open source drivers or driver components. When available, it can be instructive to inspect or step through driver code, to get a sense for which operations are expensive or where overheads may exist in an application.

This chapter focused entirely on traditional accesses to global memory via buffer accessors or Unified Shared Memory, but most GPUs also include a fixed-function texture sampler that can accelerate operations on images. For more information about images and samplers, please refer to the SYCL specification.

 **Open Access** This chapter is licensed under the terms of the Creative Commons Attribution 4.0 International License (http://creativecommons.org/licenses/by/4.0/), which permits use, sharing, adaptation, distribution and reproduction in any medium or format, as long as you give appropriate credit to the original author(s) and the source, provide a link to the Creative Commons license and indicate if changes were made.

The images or other third party material in this chapter are included in the chapter's Creative Commons license, unless indicated otherwise in a credit line to the material. If material is not included in the chapter's Creative Commons license and your intended use is not permitted by statutory regulation or exceeds the permitted use, you will need to obtain permission directly from the copyright holder.

CHAPTER 16

Programming for CPUs

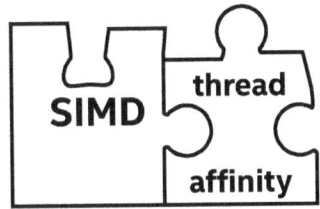

Kernel programming originally became popular as a way to program GPUs. As kernel programming is generalized, it is important to understand how our style of programming affects the mapping of our code to a CPU.

The CPU has evolved over the years. A major shift occurred around 2005 when performance gains from increasing clock speeds diminished. Parallelism arose as the favored solution—instead of increasing clock speeds, CPU producers introduced multicore chips. Computers became more effective in performing multiple tasks at the same time!

While multicore prevailed as the path for increasing hardware performance, releasing that gain in software required non-trivial effort. Multicore processors required developers to come up with different algorithms so the hardware improvements could be noticeable, and this was not always easy. The more cores that we have, the harder it is to keep them efficiently busy. DPC++ is one of the programming languages that address these challenges, with many constructs that help to exploit various forms of parallelism on CPUs (and other architectures).

CHAPTER 16 PROGRAMMING FOR CPUS

This chapter discusses some particulars of CPU architectures, how CPU hardware executes DPC++ applications, and offers best practices when writing a DPC++ code for a CPU platform.

Performance Caveats

DPC++ paves a portable path to parallelize our applications or to develop parallel applications from scratch. The application performance of a program, when run on CPUs, is largely dependent upon the following factors:

- The underlying performance of the single invocation and execution of kernel code

- The percentage of the program that runs in a parallel kernel and its scalability

- CPU utilization, effective data sharing, data locality, and load balancing

- The amount of synchronization and communication between work-items

- The overhead introduced to create, resume, manage, suspend, destroy, and synchronize the threads that work-items execute on, which is made worse by the number of serial-to-parallel or parallel-to-serial transitions

- Memory conflicts caused by shared memory or falsely shared memory

- Performance limitations of shared resources such as memory, write combining buffers, and memory bandwidth

In addition, as with any processor type, CPUs may differ from vendor to vendor or even from product generation to product generation. The best practices for one CPU may not be best practices for a different CPU and configuration.

> To achieve optimal performance on a CPU, understand as many characteristics of the CPU architecture as possible!

The Basics of a General-Purpose CPU

Emergence and rapid advancements in multicore CPUs have driven substantial acceptance of shared memory parallel computing platforms. CPUs offer parallel computing platforms at laptop, desktop, and server levels, making them ubiquitous and exposing performance almost everywhere. The most common form of CPU architecture is cache-coherent Non-Uniform Memory Access (cc-NUMA), which is characterized by access times not being completely uniform. Even many small dual-socket general-purpose CPU systems have this kind of memory system. This architecture has become dominant because the number of cores in a processor, as well as the number of sockets, continues to increase.

In a cc-NUMA CPU system, each socket connects to a subset of the total memory in the system. A cache-coherent interconnect glues all of the sockets together and provides a single system view for programmers. Such a memory system is scalable, because the aggregate memory bandwidth scales with the number of sockets in the system. The benefit of the interconnect is that an application has transparent access to all of the memory in the system, regardless of where the data resides. However, there is a cost: the latency to access data and instructions, from memory is no longer consistent (e.g., fixed access latency). The latency instead depends

CHAPTER 16   PROGRAMMING FOR CPUS

on where that data is stored in the system. In a good case, data comes from memory directly connected to the socket where code runs. In a bad case, data has to come from a memory connected to a socket far away in the system, and that cost of memory access can increase due to the number of hops in the interconnect between sockets on a cc-NUMA CPU system.

In Figure 16-1, a generic CPU architecture with cc-NUMA memory is shown. This is a simplified system architecture containing cores and memory components found in contemporary, general-purpose, multisocket systems today. Throughout the remainder of this chapter, the figure will be used to illustrate the mapping of corresponding code examples.

To achieve optimal performance, we need to be sure to understand the characteristics of the cc-NUMA configuration of a specific system. For example, recent servers from Intel make use of a mesh interconnect architecture. In this configuration, the cores, caches, and memory controllers are organized into rows and columns. Understanding the connectivity of processors with memory can be critical when working to achieve peak performance of the system.

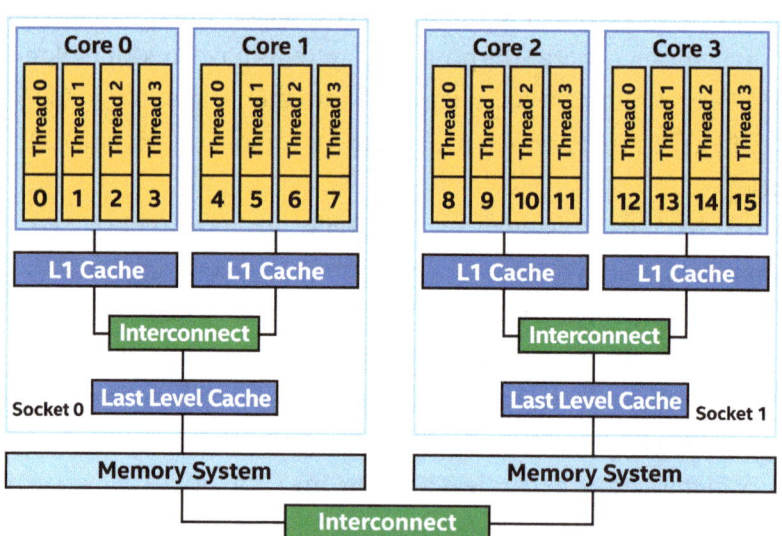

Figure 16-1. *Generic multicore CPU system*

390

The system in Figure 16-1 has two sockets, each of which has two cores with four hardware threads per core. Each core has its own level 1 (L1) cache. L1 caches are connected to a shared last-level cache, which is connected to the memory system on the socket. The memory access latency within a socket is uniform, meaning that it is consistent and can be predicted with accuracy.

The two sockets are connected through a cache-coherent interconnect. Memory is distributed across the system, but all of the memory may be transparently accessed from anywhere in the system. The memory read and write latency is non-uniform when accessing memory that isn't in the socket where code making the access is running, which means it imposes a potentially much longer and inconsistent latency when accessing data from a remote socket. A critical aspect of the interconnect, though, is coherency. We do not need to worry about data becoming inconsistent across the memory system (which would be a functional problem) and instead need to worry only about the performance impact of how we're accessing the distributed memory system.

Hardware threads in CPUs are the execution vehicles. These are the units that execute instruction streams (a thread in CPU terminology). The hardware threads in Figure 16-1 are numbered consecutively from 0 to 15, which is a notation used to simplify discussions on the examples in this chapter. Unless otherwise noted, all references to a CPU system in this chapter are to the reference cc-NUMA system shown in Figure 16-1.

The Basics of SIMD Hardware

In 1996, the first widely deployed SIMD (Single Instruction, Multiple Data according to Flynn's taxonomy) instruction set was MMX extensions on top of the x86 architecture. Many SIMD instruction set extensions have since followed both on Intel architectures and more broadly across the industry. A CPU core carries out its job by executing instructions, and

CHAPTER 16   PROGRAMMING FOR CPUS

the specific instructions that a core knows how to execute are defined by the instruction set (e.g., x86, x86_64, AltiVec, NEON) and instruction set extensions (e.g., SSE, AVX, AVX-512) that it implements. Many of the operations added by instruction set extensions are focused on SIMD instructions.

SIMD instructions allow multiple calculations to be carried out simultaneously on a single core by using a register and hardware that is bigger than the fundamental unit of data being processed. Using 512-bit registers, we can perform eight 64-bit calculations with a single machine instruction.

```
h.parallel_for(1024,[=](id<1> k) {
    z[k] = x[k] + y[k];
});
```

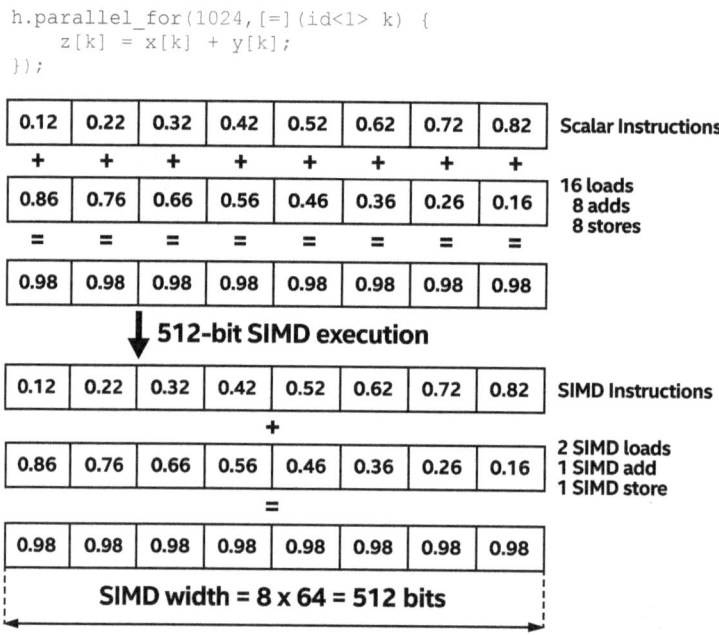

Figure 16-2. SIMD execution in a CPU hardware thread

This example shown in Figure 16-2 could give us up to an eight times speed-up. In reality, it is likely to be somewhat curtailed as a portion of the eight times speed-up serves to remove one bottleneck and expose the next, such as memory throughput. In general, the performance benefit of using SIMD varies depending on the specific scenario, and in a few cases, it can even perform worse than simpler non-SIMD equivalent code. That said, considerable gains are achievable on today's processors when we know when and how to apply (or have the compiler apply) SIMD. As with all performance optimizations, programmers should measure the gains on a typical target machine before putting it into production. There are more details on expected performance gains in following sections of this chapter.

The cc-NUMA CPU architecture with SIMD units forms the foundation of a multicore processor, which can exploit a wide spectrum of parallelism starting from instruction-level parallelism in five different ways as shown in Figure 16-3.

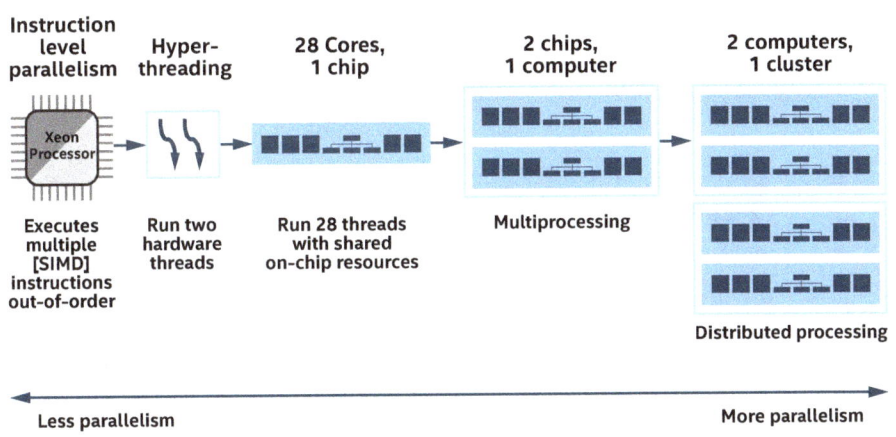

Figure 16-3. Five ways for executing instructions in parallel

In Figure 16-3, instruction-level parallelism can be achieved through both out-of-order execution of scalar instructions and SIMD (Single Instruction, Multiple Data) data parallelism within a single thread. Thread-level parallelism can be achieved through executing multiple threads on the same core or on multiple cores at different scales. More specifically, thread-level parallelism can be exposed from the following:

- Modern CPU architectures allow one core to execute the instructions of two or more threads simultaneously.

- Multicore architectures that contain two or more *brains* within each processor. The operating system perceives each of its execution cores as a discrete processor, with all of the associated execution resources.

- Multiprocessing at the processor (chip) level, which can be accomplished by executing completely separate threads of code. As a result, the processor can have one thread running from an application and another thread running from an operating system, or it can have parallel threads running from within a single application.

- Distributed processing, which can be accomplished by executing processes consisting of multiple threads on a cluster of computers, which typically communicate through message passing frameworks.

In order to fully utilize a multicore processor resource, the software must be written in a way that spreads its workload across multiple cores. This approach is called *exploiting thread-level parallelism* or simply *threading*.

As multiprocessor computers and processors with hyper-threading (HT) technology and multicore technology become more and more common, it is important to use parallel processing techniques as standard

CHAPTER 16 PROGRAMMING FOR CPUS

practice to increase performance. Later sections of this chapter will introduce the coding methods and performance-tuning techniques within DPC++ that allow us to achieve peak performance on multicore CPUs.

Like other parallel processing hardware (e.g., GPUs), it is important to give the CPU a sufficiently large set of data elements to process. To demonstrate the importance of exploiting multilevel parallelism to handle a large set of data, consider a simple C++ STREAM Triad program, as shown in Figure 16-4.

A NOTE ABOUT STREAM TRIAD WORKLOAD

The STREAM Triad workload (www.cs.virginia.edu/stream) is an important and popular benchmark workload that CPU vendors use to demonstrate highly tuned performance. We use the STREAM Triad kernel to demonstrate code generation of a parallel kernel and the way that it is scheduled to achieve significantly improved performance through the techniques described in this chapter. The STREAM Triad is a relatively simple workload, but is sufficient to show many of the optimizations in an understandable way.

USE VENDOR-PROVIDED LIBRARIES!

When a vendor provides a library implementation of a function, it is almost always beneficial to use it rather than re-implementing the function as a parallel kernel!

395

CHAPTER 16 PROGRAMMING FOR CPUS

```
// C++ STREAM Triad workload
// __restrict is used to denote no memory aliasing among arguments
template <typename T>
double triad(T* __restrict VA, T* __restrict VB,
             T* __restrict VC, size_t array_size, const T scalar) {
  double ts = timer_start()
  for (size_t id = 0; id < array_size; id++) {
    VC[id] = VA[id] + scalar * VB[id];
  }
  double te = timer_end();
  return (te - ts);
}
```

Figure 16-4. STREAM Triad C++ loop

The STREAM Triad loop may be trivially executed on a CPU using a single CPU core for serial execution. A good C++ compiler will perform loop vectorization to generate SIMD code for the CPU that has SIMD hardware to exploit instruction-level SIMD parallelism. For example, for an Intel Xeon processor with AVX-512 support, the Intel C++ compiler generates SIMD code as shown in Figure 16-5. Critically, the compiler's transformation of the code reduced the number of loop iterations at execution time, by doing more work (SIMD width and also unrolled iterations) per loop iteration at runtime!

```
// STREAM Triad: SIMD code generated by the compiler, where zmm0, zmm1
// and zmm2 are SIMD vector registers. The vectorized loop is unrolled by 4
// to leverage the out-of-execution of instructions from Xeon CPU and to
// hide memory load and store latency

# %bb.0:                                  # %entry
vbroadcastsd    %xmm0, %zmm0              # broadcast "scalar" to SIMD reg zmm0
movq            $-32, %rax
.p2align        4, 0x90
.LBB0_1:                                  # %loop.19
                                          # =>This Loop Header: Depth=1
vmovupd 256(%rdx,%rax,8), %zmm1           # load 8 elements from memory to zmm1
vfmadd213pd     256(%rsi,%rax,8), %zmm0, %zmm1 # zmm1=(zmm0*zmm1)+mem
                                          # perform SIMD FMA for 8 data elements
                                          # VC[id:8] = scalar*VB[id:8]+VA[id:8]
vmovupd %zmm1, 256(%rdi,%rax,8)           # store 8-element result to mem from zmm1
                                          # This SIMD loop body is unrolled by 4
vmovupd 320(%rdx,%rax,8), %zmm1
vfmadd213pd     320(%rsi,%rax,8), %zmm0, %zmm1 # zmm1=(zmm0*zmm1)+mem
vmovupd %zmm1, 320(%rdi,%rax,8)

vmovupd 384(%rdx,%rax,8), %zmm1
vfmadd213pd     384(%rsi,%rax,8), %zmm0, %zmm1 # zmm1=(zmm0*zmm1)+mem
vmovupd %zmm1, 384(%rdi,%rax,8)

vmovupd 448(%rdx,%rax,8), %zmm1
vfmadd213pd     448(%rsi,%rax,8), %zmm0, %zmm1 # zmm1=(zmm0*zmm1)+mem
vmovupd %zmm1, 448(%rdi,%rax,8)
addq    $32, %rax
cmpq    $134217696, %rax                  # imm = 0x7FFFFE0
jb      .LBB0_1
```

***Figure 16-5.** AVX-512 code for STREAM Triad C++ loop*

As shown in Figure 16-5, the compiler was able to exploit instruction-level parallelism in two ways. First is through the use of SIMD instructions, exploiting instruction-level data parallelism, in which a single instruction can process eight double-precision data elements simultaneously in parallel (per instruction). Second, the compiler applied loop unrolling to get the out-of-order execution effect of these instructions that have no dependences between them, based on hardware multiway instruction scheduling.

If we try to execute this function on a CPU, it will probably run well—not great, though, since it does not utilize any multicore or threading capabilities of the CPU, but good enough for a small array size. If we try to execute this function with a large array size on a CPU, however, it will likely perform very poorly because the single thread will only utilize a single CPU core and will be bottlenecked when it saturates the memory bandwidth of that core.

Exploiting Thread-Level Parallelism

To improve the performance of the STREAM Triad kernel for both CPUs and GPUs, we can compute on a range of data elements that can be processed in parallel, by converting the loop to a `parallel_for` kernel.

A STREAM Triad kernel may be trivially executed on a CPU by submitting it into a queue for a parallel execution. The body of this STREAM Triad DPC++ parallel kernel looks exactly like the body of the STREAM Triad loop that executes in serial C++ on the CPU, as shown in Figure 16-6.

```
constexpr int num_runs = 10;
constexpr size_t scalar = 3;

double triad(
    const std::vector<double>& vecA,
    const std::vector<double>& vecB,
    std::vector<double>& vecC ) {

  assert(vecA.size() == vecB.size() == vecC.size());
  const size_t array_size = vecA.size();
  double min_time_ns = DBL_MAX;

  queue Q{ property::queue::enable_profiling{} };
  std::cout << "Running on device: " <<
    Q.get_device().get_info<info::device::name>() << "\n";

  buffer<double> bufA(vecA);
  buffer<double> bufB(vecB);
  buffer<double> bufC(vecC);

  for (int i = 0; i< num_runs; i++) {
    auto Q_event = Q.submit([&](handler& h) {
      accessor A{ bufA, h };
      accessor B{ bufB, h };
      accessor C{ bufC, h };

      h.parallel_for(array_size, [=](id<1> idx) {
        C[idx] = A[idx] + B[idx] * scalar;
      });
    });

    double exec_time_ns =
      Q_event.get_profiling_info<info::event_profiling::command_end>() -
      Q_event.get_profiling_info<info::event_profiling::command_start>();

    std::cout << "Execution time (iteration " << i << ") [sec]: "
              << (double)exec_time_ns * 1.0E-9 << "\n";
    min_time_ns = std::min(min_time_ns, exec_time_ns);
  }

  return min_time_ns;
}
```

Figure 16-6. *DPC++ STREAM Triad* `parallel_for` *kernel code*

CHAPTER 16   PROGRAMMING FOR CPUS

Even though the parallel kernel is very similar to the STREAM Triad function written as serial C++ with a loop, it runs much faster on a CPU because the `parallel_for` enables different *elements* of the array to be processed on multiple cores in parallel. As shown in Figure 16-7, assume that we have a system with one socket, four cores, and two hyper-threads per core; there are 1024 double-precision data elements to be processed; and in the implementation, data is processed in work-groups containing 32 data elements each. This means that we have 8 threads and 32 work-groups. The work-group scheduling can be done in a round-robin order, that is, *thread-id = work-group-id* mod 8. Essentially, each thread will execute four work-groups. Eight work-groups can be executed in parallel for each round. Note that, in this case, the work-group is a set of work-items that is implicitly formed by the DPC++ compiler and runtime.

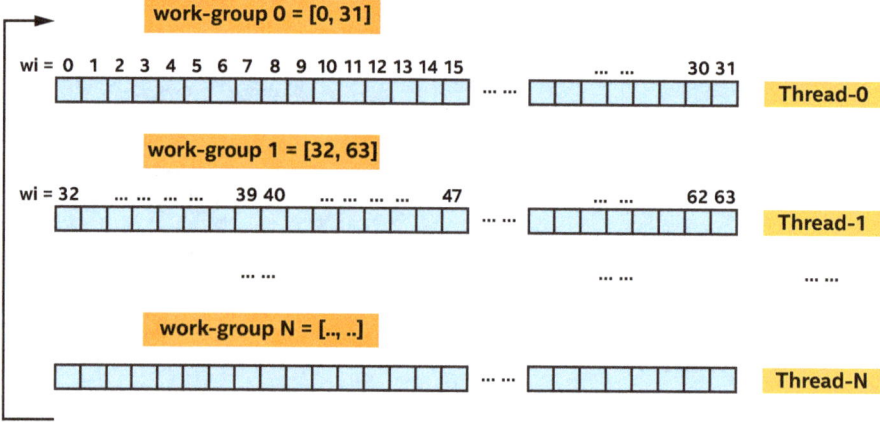

Figure 16-7. *A mapping of a STREAM Triad parallel kernel*

Note that in the DPC++ program, the exact way that data elements are partitioned and assigned to different processor cores (or hyper-threads) is not required to be specified. This gives a DPC++ implementation flexibility to choose how best to execute a parallel kernel on a specific CPU. With that said, an implementation can provide some level of control to programmers to enable performance tuning.

While a CPU may impose a relatively high thread context switch and synchronization overhead, having somewhat more software threads resident on a processor core is beneficial because it gives each processor core a choice of work to execute. If one software thread is waiting for another thread to produce data, the processor core can switch to a different software thread that is ready to run without leaving the processor core idle.

> **CHOOSING HOW TO BIND AND SCHEDULE THREADS**
>
> Choosing an effective scheme to partition and schedule the work among threads is important to tune an application on CPUs and other device types. Subsequent sections will describe some of the techniques.

Thread Affinity Insight

Thread affinity designates the CPU cores on which specific threads execute. Performance can suffer if a thread moves around among cores, for instance, if threads do not execute on the same core, cache locality can become an inefficiency if data ping-pongs between different cores.

The DPC++ runtime library supports several schemes for binding threads to core(s) through environment variables DPCPP_CPU_CU_AFFINITY, DPCPP_CPU_PLACES, DPCPP_CPU_NUM_CUS, and DPCPP_CPU_SCHEDULE, which are not defined by SYCL.

The first of these is the environment variable DPCPP_CPU_CU_AFFINITY. Tuning using these environment variable controls is simple and low cost and can have large impact for many applications. The description of this environment variable is shown in Figure 16-8.

DPCPP_CPU_CU_AFFINITY	Description
spread	Bind successive threads to distinct sockets starting with socket 0 in a round-robin order
close	Bind successive threads to distinct hyper-thread starting with thread 0 in a round-robin order

Figure 16-8. DPCPP_CPU_CU_AFFINITY environment variable

When the environment variable DPCPP_CPU_CU_AFFINITY is specified, a software thread is bound to a hyper-thread through the following formula:

$$spread : boundHT = (tid \bmod numHT) + (tid \bmod numSocket) \times numHT$$

$$close : boundHT = tid \bmod (numSocket \times numHT)$$

where

- `tid` denotes a software thread identifier.
- `boundHT` denotes a hyper-thread (logical core) that thread `tid` is bound to.
- `numHT` denotes the number of hyper-threads per socket.
- `numSocket` denotes the number of sockets in the system.

Assume that we run a program with eight threads on a dual-core dual-socket hyper-threading system—in other words, we have four cores for a total of eight hyper-threads to program. Figure 16-9 shows examples of how threads can map to the hyper-threads and cores for different DPCPP_CPU_CU_AFFINITY settings.

DPCPP_CPU_CU_AFFINITY	socket0		socket1	
	core0	core1	core2	core3
spread	<T0, T4>	<T2, T6>	<T1, T5>	<T3, T7>
close	<T0, T1>	<T2, T3>	<T4, T5>	<T6, T7>

Figure 16-9. Mapping threads to cores with hyper-threads

In conjunction with the environment variable DPCPP_CPU_CU_AFFINITY, there are other environment variables that support CPU performance tuning:

- **DPCPP_CPU_NUM_CUS** = [n], which sets the number of threads used for kernel execution. Its default value is the number of hardware threads in the system.

- **DPCPP_CPU_PLACES** = [sockets | numa_domains | cores | threads], which specifies the places that the affinity will be set similar to OMP_PLACES in OpenMP 5.1. The default setting is cores.

- **DPCPP_CPU_SCHEDULE** = [dynamic | affinity | static], which specifies the algorithm for scheduling work-groups. Its default setting is dynamic.

  - dynamic: Enable the TBB auto_partitioner, which usually performs sufficient splitting to balance the load among worker threads.

  - affinity: Enable the TBB affinity_partitioner, which improves cache affinity and uses proportional splitting when mapping subranges to worker threads.

- static: Enable the TBB `static_partitioner`, which distributes iterations among worker threads as uniformly as possible.

The TBB partitioner uses a grain size to control work splitting, with a default grain size of 1 which indicates that all work-groups can be executed independently. More information can be found at spec.oneapi.com/versions/latest/elements/oneTBB/source/algorithms.html#partitioners.

A lack of thread affinity tuning does not necessarily mean lower performance. Performance often depends more on how many total threads are executing in parallel than on how well the thread and data are related and bound. Testing the application using benchmarks is one way to be certain whether the thread affinity has a performance impact or not. The DPC++ STREAM Triad code, as shown in Figure 16-1, started with a lower performance without thread affinity settings. By controlling the affinity setting and using static scheduling of software threads through the environment variables (exports shown in the following for Linux), performance improved:

```
export DPCPP_CPU_PLACES=numa_domains
export DPCPP_CPU_CU_AFFINITY=close
```

By using `numa_domains` as the places setting for affinity, the TBB task arenas are bound to NUMA nodes or sockets, and the work is uniformly distributed across task arenas. In general, the environment variable `DPCPP_CPU_PLACES` is recommended to be used together with `DPCPP_CPU_CU_AFFINITY`. These environment variable settings help us to achieve a ~30% performance gain on a Skylake server system with 2 sockets and 28 two-way hyper-threading cores per socket, running at 2.5 GHz. However, we can still do better to further improve the performance on this CPU.

Be Mindful of First Touch to Memory

Memory is stored where it is first touched (used). Since the initialization loop in our example is not parallelized, it is executed by the host thread in serial, resulting in all the memory being associated with the socket that the host thread is running on. Subsequent access by other sockets will then access data from memory attached to the initial socket (used for the initialization), which is clearly undesirable for performance. We can achieve a higher performance on the STREAM Triad kernel by parallelizing the initialization loop to control the first touch effect across sockets, as shown in Figure 16-10.

```cpp
template <typename T>
void init(queue &deviceQueue, T* VA, T* VB, T* VC, size_t array_size) {
  range<1> numOfItems{array_size};

  buffer<T, 1> bufferA(VA, numOfItems);
  buffer<T, 1> bufferB(VB, numOfItems);
  buffer<T, 1> bufferC(VC, numOfItems);

  auto queue_event = deviceQueue.submit([&](handler& cgh) {
    auto aA = bufA.template get_access<sycl_write>(cgh);
    auto aB = bufB.template get_access<sycl_write>(cgh);
    auto aC = bufC.template get_access<sycl_write>(cgh);

    cgh.parallel_for<class Init<T>>(numOfItems, [=](id<1> wi) {
      aA[wi] = 2.0; aB[wi] = 1.0; aC[wi] = 0.0;
    });
  });

  queue_event.wait();
}
```

Figure 16-10. STREAM Triad parallel initialization kernel to control first touch effects

Exploiting parallelism in the initialization code improves performance of the kernel when run on a CPU. In this instance, we achieve a ~2x performance gain on an Intel Xeon processor system.

The recent sections of this chapter have shown that by exploiting thread-level parallelism, we can utilize CPU cores and hyper-threads effectively. However, we need to exploit the SIMD vector-level parallelism in the CPU core hardware as well, to achieve peak performance.

> DPC++ parallel kernels benefit from thread-level parallelism across cores and hyper-threads!

SIMD Vectorization on CPU

While a well-written DPC++ kernel without cross-work-item dependences can run in parallel effectively on a CPU, we can also apply vectorization to DPC++ kernels to leverage SIMD hardware, similarly to the GPU support described in Chapter 15. Essentially, CPU processors may optimize memory loads, stores, and operations using SIMD instructions by leveraging the fact that most data elements are often in contiguous memory and take the same control flow paths through a data-parallel kernel. For example, in a kernel with a statement a[i] = a[i] + b[i], each data element executes with same instruction stream *load, load, add,* and *store* by sharing hardware logic among multiple data elements and executing them as a group, which may be mapped naturally onto a hardware's SIMD instruction set. Specifically, multiple data elements can be processed simultaneously by a single instruction.

The number of data elements that are processed simultaneously by a single instruction is sometimes referred to as the vector length (or SIMD width) of the instruction or processor executing it. In Figure 16-11, our instruction stream runs with four-way SIMD execution.

Serial execution				SIMD execution
work-0	work-1	work-2	work 3	vector sub-group
load r0, a[0]	load r0, a[1]	load r0, a[2]	load r0, a[3]	simdload vr0, a[0...3]
load r1, b[0]	load r1, b[1]	load r1, b[2]	load r1, b[3]	simdload vr1, b[0...3]
add r0, r1	add r0, r1	add r0, r1	add r0, r1	simdadd vr0, vr1
store a[0], r0	store a[1], r0	store a[2], r0	store a[3], r0	simdstore a[0...3], vr0

Figure 16-11. Instruction stream for SIMD execution

CPU processors are not the only processors that implement SIMD instruction sets. Other processors such as GPUs implement SIMD instructions to improve efficiency when processing large sets of data. A key difference with Intel Xeon CPU processors, compared with other processor types, is having three fixed-size SIMD register widths 128-bit XMM, 256-bit YMM, and 512-bit ZMM instead of a variable length of SIMD width. When we write DPC++ code with SIMD parallelism using sub-group or vector types, we need to be mindful of SIMD width and the number of SIMD vector registers in the hardware.

Ensure SIMD Execution Legality

Semantically, the DPC++ execution model ensures that SIMD execution can be applied to any kernel, and a set of work-items in each work-group (i.e., a sub-group) may be executed concurrently using SIMD instructions. Some implementations may instead choose to execute loops within a kernel using SIMD instructions, but this is possible if and only if all original data dependences are preserved, or data dependences are resolved by the compiler based on privatization and reduction semantics.

A single DPC++ kernel execution can be transformed from processing of a single work-item to a set of work-items using SIMD instructions within the work-group. Under the ND-range model, the fastest-growing (unit-stride) dimension is selected by the compiler vectorizer on which to generate SIMD code. Essentially, to enable vectorization given an ND-range, there should be no cross-work-item dependences between any two work-items in the same sub-group, or the compiler needs to preserve cross-work-item forward dependences in the same sub-group.

When the kernel execution of work-items is mapped to threads on CPUs, fine-grained synchronization is known to be costly, and the thread context switch overhead is high as well. It is therefore an important performance optimization to eliminate dependences between work-items within a work-group when writing a DPC++ kernel for CPUs. Another effective approach is to restrict such dependences to the work-items within a sub-group, as shown for the read-before-write dependence in Figure 16-12. If the sub-group is executed under a SIMD execution model, the sub-group barrier in the kernel can be treated by the compiler as a no-op, and no real synchronization cost is incurred at runtime.

```
using namespace sycl::intel;

queue Q;
range<2> G = {n, w};
range<2> L = {1, w};

int *a = malloc_shared<int>(n*(n+1), Q);

for (int i = 0; i < n; i++)
  for (int j = 0; j < n+1; j++) a[i*n + j] = i + j;

Q.parallel_for(nd_range<2>{G, L}, [=](nd_item<2> it)
  [[cl::intel_reqd_sub_group_size(w)]] {

  // distribute uniform "i" over the sub-group with 8-way
  // redundant computation
  const int i = it.get_global_id(0);
  sub_group sg = it.get_sub_group();

  for (int j = sg.get_local_id()[0]; j < n; j += w) {
    // load a[i*n+j+1:8] before updating a[i*n+j:8] to preserve
    // loop-carried forward dependence
    auto va = a[i*n + j + 1];
    sg.barrier();
    a[i*n + j] = va + i + 2;
  }
  sg.barrier();

}).wait();
```

Figure 16-12. *Using a sub-group to vectorize a loop with a forward dependence*

The kernel is vectorized (with a vector length of *8*), and its SIMD execution is shown in Figure 16-13. A work-group is formed with a group size of (1, 8), and the loop iterations inside the kernel are distributed over these sub-group work-items and executed with eight-way SIMD parallelism.

In this example, if the loop in the kernel dominates the performance, allowing SIMD vectorization across the sub-group will result in a significant performance improvement.

The use of SIMD instructions that process data elements in parallel is one way to let the performance of the kernel scale beyond the number of CPU cores and hyper-threads.

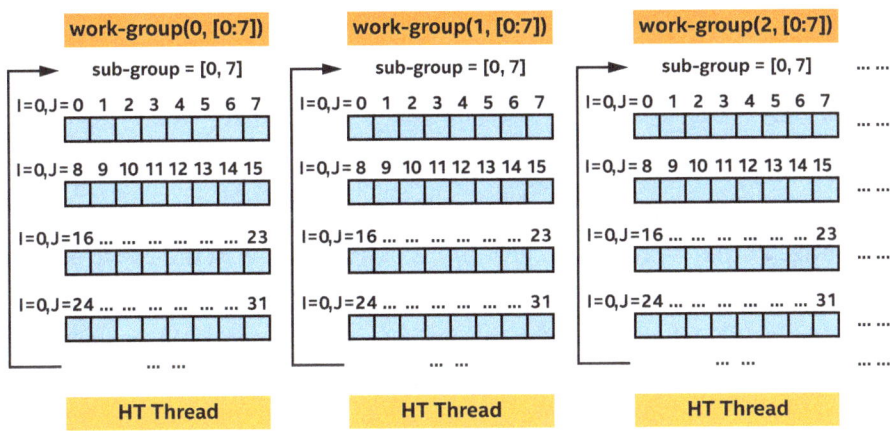

Figure 16-13. *SIMD vectorization for a loop with a forward dependence*

SIMD Masking and Cost

In real applications, we can expect conditional statements such as an `if` statement, conditional expressions such as `a = b > a? a: b`, loops with a variable number of iterations, `switch` statements, and so on. Anything that is conditional may lead to scalar control flows not executing the same code paths and, just like on a GPU (Chapter 15), can lead to decreased performance. A SIMD mask is a set of bits with the value 1 or 0, which is generated from conditional statements in a kernel. Consider an example with A={1, 2, 3, 4}, B={3, 7, 8, 1}, and the comparison expression a < b. The comparison returns a mask with four values {1, 1, 1, 0} that can be stored in a hardware mask register, to dictate which lanes of later SIMD instructions should execute the code that was guarded (enabled) by the comparison.

If a kernel contains conditional code, it is vectorized with masked instructions that are executed based on the mask bits associated with each data element (lane in the SIMD instruction). The mask bit for each data element is the corresponding bit in a mask register.

Using masking may result in lower performance than corresponding non-masked code. This may be caused by

- An additional mask blend operation on each load
- Dependence on the destination

Masking has a cost, so use it only when necessary. When a kernel is an ND-range kernel with explicit groupings of work-items in the execution range, care should be taken when choosing an ND-range work-group size to maximize SIMD efficiency by minimizing masking cost. When a work-group size is not evenly divisible by a processor's SIMD width, part of the work-group may execute with masking for the kernel.

No Masking	Merge Masking	Zero Masking
vmulps zmm0, zmm6, zmm8	vmulps zmm0{k1}, zmm6, zmm8	vmulps zmm0{k1}{z}, zmm6, zmm8
vmulps zmm1, zmm7, zmm8	vmulps zmm1{k1}, zmm7, zmm8	vmulps zmm1{k1}{z}, zmm7, zmm8
Baseline	Slowdown 4x	Slowdown 1x

Figure 16-14. Three masking code generations for masking in kernel

Figure 16-14 shows how using merge masking creates a dependence on the destination register:

- With no masking, the processor executes two multiplies (vmulps) per cycle.

- With merge masking, the processor executes two multiplies every four cycles as the multiply instruction (vmulps) preserves results in the destination register as shown in Figure 16-17.

- Zero masking doesn't have a dependence on the destination register and therefore can execute two multiplies (vmulps) per cycle.

Accessing cache-aligned data gives better performance than accessing non-aligned data. In many cases, the address is not known at compile time or is known and not aligned. In these cases, a peeling on memory accesses may be implemented, to process the first few elements using masked accesses, up to the first aligned address, and then to process unmasked accesses followed by a masked remainder, through multiversioning techniques in the parallel kernel. This method increases code size, but improves data processing overall.

Avoid Array-of-Struct for SIMD Efficiency

AOS (Array-of-Struct) structures lead to gathers and scatters, which can both impact SIMD efficiency and introduce extra bandwidth and latency for memory accesses. The presence of a hardware gather-scatter mechanism does not eliminate the need for this transformation—gather-scatter accesses commonly need significantly higher bandwidth and latency than contiguous loads. Given an AOS data layout of struct {float x; float y; float z; float w;} a[4], consider a kernel operating on it as shown in Figure 16-15.

CHAPTER 16 PROGRAMMING FOR CPUS

```
cgh.parallel_for<class aos<T>>(numOfItems,[=](id<1> wi) {
    x[wi] = a[wi].x;   // lead to gather x0, x1, x2, x3
    y[wi] = a[wi].y;   // lead to gather y0, y1, y2, y3
    z[wi] = a[wi].z;   // lead to gather z0, z1, z2, z3
    w[wi] = a[wi].w;   // lead to gather w0, w1, w2, w3
});
```

Figure 16-15. SIMD gather in a kernel

When the compiler vectorizes the kernel along a set of work-items, it leads to SIMD gather instruction generation due to the need for non-unit-stride memory accesses. For example, the stride of a[0].x, a[1].x, a[2].x and a[3].x is 4, not a more efficient unit-stride of 1.

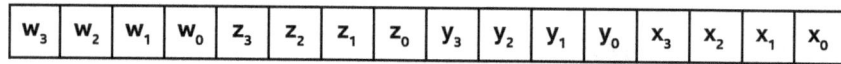

In a kernel, we can often achieve a higher SIMD efficiency by eliminating the use of memory gather-scatter operations. Some code benefits from a data layout change that converts data structures written in an Array-of-Struct (AOS) representation to a Structure of Arrays (SOA) representation, that is, having separate arrays for each structure field to keep memory accesses contiguous when SIMD vectorization is performed. For example, consider a SOA data layout of struct {float x[4]; float y[4]; float z[4]; float w[4];} a; as shown here:

| w_3 | w_2 | w_1 | w_0 | z_3 | z_2 | z_1 | z_0 | y_3 | y_2 | y_1 | y_0 | x_3 | x_2 | x_1 | x_0 |

A kernel can operate on the data with unit-stride (contiguous) vector loads and stores as shown in Figure 16-16, even when vectorized!

```
cgh.parallel_for<class aos<T>>(numOfItems,[=](id<1> wi) {
    x[wi] = a.x[wi]; // lead to unit-stride vector load x[0:4]
    y[wi] = a.y[wi]; // lead to unit-stride vector load y[0:4]
    z[wi] = a.z[wi]; // lead to unit-stride vector load z[0:4]
    w[wi] = a.w[wi]; // lead to unit-stride vector load w[0:4]
});
```

Figure 16-16. SIMD unit-stride vector load in a kernel

The SOA data layout helps prevent gathers when accessing one field of the structure across the array elements and helps the compiler to vectorize kernels over the contiguous array elements associated with work-items. Note that such AOS-to-SOA or AOSOA data layout transformations are expected to be done at the program level (by us) considering all the places where those data structures are used. Doing it at just a loop level will involve costly transformations between the formats before and after the loop. However, we may also rely on the compiler to perform vector-load-and-shuffle optimizations for AOS data layouts with some cost. When a member of SOA (or AOS) data layout has a vector type, the compiler vectorization will perform either horizontal expansion or vertical expansion as described in Chapter 11 based on underlying hardware to generate optimal code.

Data Type Impact on SIMD Efficiency

C++ programmers often use integer data types whenever they know that the data fits into a 32-bit signed type, often leading to code such as

`int id = get_global_id(0); a[id] = b[id] + c[id];`

However, given that the return type of the get_global_id(0) is size_t *(unsigned integer, often 64-bit)*, in some cases, the conversion reduces the optimization that a compiler can legally perform. This can then lead to SIMD gather/scatter instructions when the compiler vectorizes the code in the kernel, for example

- Read of a[get_global_id(0)] leads to a SIMD unit-stride vector load.

- Read of a[(int)get_global_id(0)] leads to a non-unit-stride gather instruction.

This nuanced situation is introduced by the wraparound behavior (unspecified behavior and/or well-defined wraparound behavior in C++ standards) of data type conversion from size_t to int (or uint), which is mostly a historical artifact from the evolution of C-based languages. Specifically, overflow across some conversions is undefined behavior, which actually allows the compiler to assume that such conditions never happen and to optimize more aggressively. Figure 16-17 shows some examples for those wanting to understand the details.

get_global_id(0)	a[(int)get_global_id(0)]	get_globalid(0)	a((uint)get_global_id(0)]
0x7FFFFFFE	a[MAX_INT-1]	0xFFFFFFFE	a[MAX_UINT-1]
0x7FFFFFFF	a[MAX_INT (big positive)]	0xFFFFFFFF	a[MAX_UINT]
0x80000000	a[MIN_INT (big negative)]	0x100000000	a[0]
0x80000001	a[MIN_INT+1]	0x100000001	a[1]

Figure 16-17. *Examples of integer* type *value wraparound*

SIMD gather/scatter instructions are slower than SIMD unit-stride vector load/store operations. In order to achieve an optimal SIMD efficiency, avoiding gathers/scatters can be critical for an application regardless of which programming language is used.

Most SYCL get_*_id() family functions have the same detail, although many cases fit within MAX_INT because the possible return values are bounded (e.g., the maximum id within a work-group). Thus, whenever legal, the DPC++ compiler will assume unit-stride memory addresses across the chunk of neighboring work-items to avoid gather/scatters. For cases that the compiler can't safely generate linear unit-stride vector memory loads/stores because of possible overflow from the value of global IDs and/or derivative value from global IDs, the compiler will generate gathers/scatters.

Under the philosophy of delivering optimal performance for users, the DPC++ compiler assumes no overflow, and captures the realty almost all of the time in practice, so the compiler can generate optimal SIMD code to achieve good performance. However, an overriding compiler macro—D__SYCL_DISABLE_ID_TO_INT_CONV__—is provided by the DPC++ compiler for us to tell the compiler that there will be an overflow and that vectorized accesses derived from the id queries may not be safe. This can have large performance impact and should be used whenever unsafe to assume no overflow.

SIMD Execution Using `single_task`

Under a single task execution model, optimizations related to the vector types and functions depend on the compiler. The compiler and runtime are given a freedom either to enable explicit SIMD execution or to choose scalar execution within the `single_task` kernel, and the result will depend on the compiler implementation. For instance, the DPC++ CPU compiler honors vector types and generates SIMD instructions for CPU SIMD execution. The vec load, store, and swizzle function will perform operations directly on vector variables, informing the compiler that data elements are accessing contiguous data starting from the same (uniform) location in memory and enabling us to request optimized loads/stores of contiguous data.

```
queue Q;
bool *resArray = malloc_shared<bool>(1, Q);
resArray[0] = true;

Q.single_task([=]() {
  sycl::vec<int, 4> old_v = sycl::vec<int, 4>(000, 100, 200, 300);
  sycl::vec<int, 4> new_v = sycl::vec<int, 4>();

  new_v.rgba() = old_v.abgr();
  int vals[] = {300, 200, 100, 000};

  if (new_v.r() != vals[0] || new_v.g() != vals[1] ||
      new_v.b() != vals[2] || new_v.a() != vals[3]) {
    resArray[0] = false;
  }
}).wait();
```

Figure 16-18. Using vector types and swizzle operations in the single_task kernel

In the example as shown in Figure 16-18, under single task execution, a vector with three data elements is declared. A swizzle operation is performed with old_v.abgr(). If a CPU provides SIMD hardware instructions for some swizzle operations, we may achieve some performance benefits of using swizzle operations in applications.

SIMD VECTORIZATION GUIDELINES

CPU processors implement SIMD instruction sets with different SIMD widths. In many cases, this is an implementation detail and is transparent to the application executing kernels on the CPU, as the compiler can determine an efficient group of data elements to process with a specific SIMD size rather than requiring us to use the SIMD instructions explicitly. Sub-groups may be used to more directly express cases where the grouping of data elements should be subject to SIMD execution in kernels.

Given computational complexity, selecting the code and data layouts that are most amenable to vectorization may ultimately result in higher performance. While selecting data structures, try to choose a data layout, alignment, and data width such that the most frequently executed calculation can access memory in a SIMD-friendly manner with maximum parallelism, as described in this chapter.

Summary

To get the most out of thread-level parallelism and SIMD vector-level parallelism on CPUs, we need to keep the following goals in mind:

- Be familiar with all types of DPC++ parallelism and the underlying CPU architectures we wish to target.

- Exploit the right amount of parallelism, not more and not less, at a thread level that best matches hardware resources. Use vendor tooling, such as analyzers and profilers, to help guide our tuning work to achieve this.

- Be mindful of thread affinity and memory first touch impact on program performance.

- Design data structures with a data layout, alignment, and data width such that the most frequently executed calculations can access memory in a SIMD-friendly manner with maximum SIMD parallelism.

- Be mindful of balancing the cost of masking vs. code branches.

- Use a clear programming style that minimizes potential memory aliasing and side effects.

- Be aware of the scalability limitations of using vector types and interfaces. If a compiler implementation maps them to hardware SIMD instructions, a fixed vector size may not match the SIMD width of SIMD registers well across multiple generations of CPUs and CPUs from different vendors.

Open Access This chapter is licensed under the terms of the Creative Commons Attribution 4.0 International License (http://creativecommons.org/licenses/by/4.0/), which permits use, sharing, adaptation, distribution and reproduction in any medium or format, as long as you give appropriate credit to the original author(s) and the source, provide a link to the Creative Commons license and indicate if changes were made.

The images or other third party material in this chapter are included in the chapter's Creative Commons license, unless indicated otherwise in a credit line to the material. If material is not included in the chapter's Creative Commons license and your intended use is not permitted by statutory regulation or exceeds the permitted use, you will need to obtain permission directly from the copyright holder.

CHAPTER 17

Programming for FPGAs

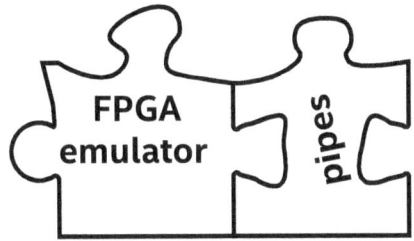

Kernel-based programming originally became popular as a way to access GPUs. Since it has now been generalized across many types of accelerators, it is important to understand how our style of programming affects the mapping of code to an FPGA as well.

Field Programmable Gate Arrays (FPGAs) are unfamiliar to the majority of software developers, in part because most desktop computers don't include an FPGA alongside the typical CPU and GPU. But FPGAs *are* worth knowing about because they offer advantages in many applications. The same questions need to be asked as we would of other accelerators, such as "When should I use an FPGA?", "What parts of my applications should be offloaded to FPGA?", and "How do I write code that performs well on an FPGA?"

This chapter gives us the knowledge to start answering those questions, at least to the point where we can decide whether an FPGA is interesting for our applications, and to know which constructs are commonly used to achieve performance. This chapter is the launching point from which we can then read vendor documentation to fill in details for specific products and toolchains. We begin with an overview of how programs can map to spatial architectures such as FPGAs, followed by discussion of some properties that make FPGAs a good choice as an accelerator, and we finish by introducing the programming constructs used to achieve performance.

The "How to Think About FPGAs" section in this chapter is applicable to thinking about any FPGA. SYCL allows vendors to specify devices beyond CPUs and GPUs, but does not specifically say how to support an FPGA. The specific vendor support for FPGAs is currently unique to DPC++, namely, FPGA selectors and pipes. FPGA selectors and pipes are the only DPC++ extensions used in this chapter. It is hoped that vendors will converge on similar or compatible means of supporting FPGAs, and this is encouraged by DPC++ as an open source project.

Performance Caveats

As with any processor or accelerator, FPGA devices differ from vendor to vendor or even from product generation to product generation; therefore, best practices for one device may not be best practices for a different device. The advice in this chapter is likely to benefit many FPGA devices, both now and in the future, however...

> ...to achieve optimal performance for a particular FPGA, always consult the vendor's documentation!

How to Think About FPGAs

FPGAs are commonly classified as a *spatial* architecture. They benefit from very different coding styles and forms of parallelism than devices that use an Instruction Set Architecture (ISA), including CPUs and GPUs, which are

CHAPTER 17   PROGRAMMING FOR FPGAS

more familiar to most people. To get started forming an understanding of FPGAs, we'll briefly cover some ideas from ISA-based accelerators, so that we can highlight key differences.

For our purposes, an ISA-based accelerator is one where the device can execute many different instructions, one or a few at a time. The instructions are usually relatively primitive such as "load from memory at address A" or "add the following numbers." A chain of operations is strung together to form a program, and the processor conceptually executes one instruction after the other.

In an ISA-based accelerator, a single region of a chip (or the entire chip) executes a different instruction from the program in each clock cycle. The instructions execute on a fixed hardware architecture that can run different instructions at different times, such as shown in Figure 17-1. For example, the memory load unit feeding an addition is probably the same memory load unit used to feed a subtraction. Similarly, the same arithmetic unit is probably used to execute both the addition and subtraction instructions. Hardware on the chip is *reused* by different instructions as the program executes over time.

Simple SA-based Accelerator

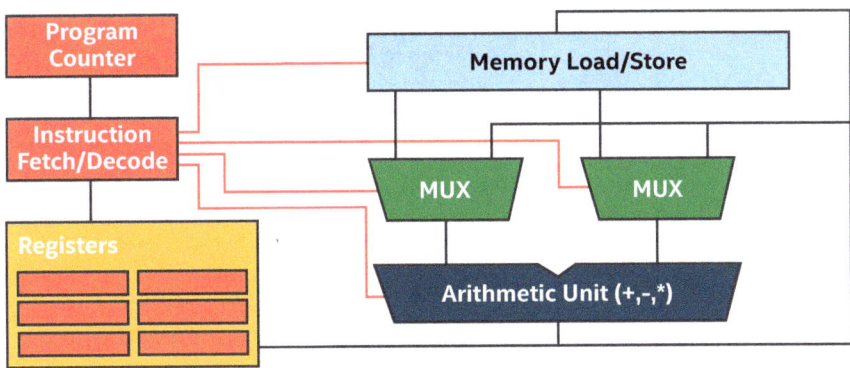

Figure 17-1. Simple ISA-based (temporal) processing: Reuses hardware (regions) over time

421

Spatial architectures are different. Instead of being based around a machine that executes a variety of instructions on shared hardware, they start from the opposite perspective. Spatial implementations of a program conceptually take the entire program as a whole and lay it down *at once* on the device. Different regions of the device implement different instructions in the program. This is in many ways the opposite perspective from sharing hardware between instructions over time (e.g., ISA)—in spatial architectures, each instruction receives its own dedicated hardware that can execute simultaneously (same clock cycle) as the hardware implementing the other instructions. Figure 17-2 shows this idea which is a spatial implementation of an entire program (a very simple program in this example).

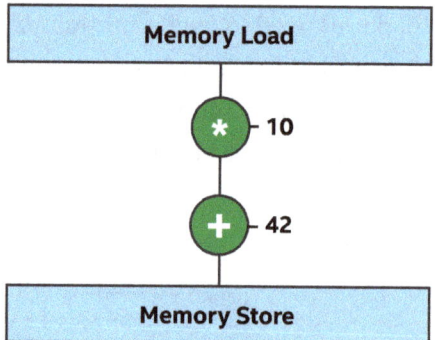

Figure 17-2. Spatial processing: Each operation uses a different region of the device

This description of a spatial implementation of a program is overly simplistic, but it captures the idea that in spatial architectures, different parts of the program execute on *different* parts of the device, as opposed to being issued over time to a shared set of more general-purpose hardware.

CHAPTER 17 PROGRAMMING FOR FPGAS

With different regions of an FPGA programmed to perform distinct operations, some of the hardware typically associated with ISA-based accelerators is unnecessary. For example, Figure 17-2 shows that we no longer need an instruction fetch or decode unit, program counter, or register file. Instead of storing data for future instructions in a register file, spatial architectures connect the output of one instruction to the input of the next, which is why spatial architectures are often called *data flow* architectures.

A few obvious questions arise from the mapping to FPGA that we've introduced. First, since each instruction in the program occupies some percentage of the spatial area of the device, what happens if the program requires more than 100% of the area? Some solutions provide resource sharing mechanisms to enable larger programs to fit at a performance cost, but FPGAs do have the concept of a program *fitting*. This is both an advantage and a disadvantage:

- The benefit: If a program uses most of the area on the FPGA and there is sufficient work to keep all of the hardware busy every clock cycle, then executing a program on the device can be incredibly efficient because of the extreme parallelism. More general architectures may have significant unused hardware per clock cycle, whereas with an FPGA, the use of area can be perfectly tailored to a specific application without waste. This customization can allow applications to run faster through massive parallelism, usually with compelling energy efficiency.

- The downside: Large programs may have to be tuned and restructured to fit on a device. Resource sharing features of compilers can help to address this, but usually with some degradation in performance that reduces the benefit of using an FPGA. ISA-based accelerators are very efficient resource sharing

423

implementations—FPGAs prove most valuable for compute primarily when an application can be architected to utilize most of the available area.

Taken to the extreme, resource sharing solutions on an FPGA lead to an architecture that looks like an ISA-based accelerator, but that is built in reconfigurable logic instead being optimized in fixed silicon. The reconfigurable logic leads to overhead relative to a fixed silicon design—therefore, FPGAs are not typically chosen as ways to implement ISAs. FPGAs are of prime benefit when an application is able to utilize the resources to implement efficient data flow algorithms, which we cover in the coming sections.

Pipeline Parallelism

Another question that often arises from Figure 17-2 is how the spatial implementation of a program relates to a clock frequency and how quickly a program will execute from start to finish. In the example shown, it's easy to believe that data could be loaded from memory, have multiplication and addition operations performed, and have the result stored back into memory, quite quickly. As the program becomes larger, potentially with tens of thousands of operations across the FPGA device, it becomes apparent that for all of the instructions to operate one after the other (operations often depend on results produced by previous operations), it might take significant time given the processing delays introduced by each operation.

Intermediate results between operations are updated (propagated) over time in a spatial architecture as shown in Figure 17-3. For example, the load executes and then passes its result into the multiplier, whose result is then passed into the adder and so on. After some amount of time, the intermediate data has propagated all the way to the end of the chain of operations, and the final result is available or stored to memory.

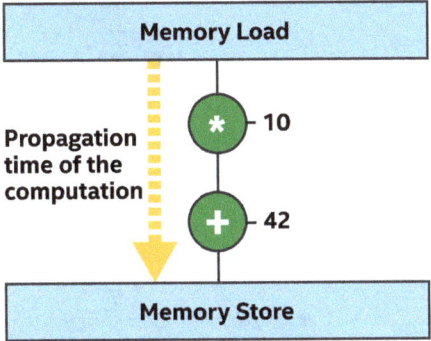

Figure 17-3. Propagation time of a naïve spatial compute implementation

A spatial implementation as shown in Figure 17-3 is quite inefficient, because most of the hardware is only doing useful work a small percentage of the time. Most of the time, an operation such as the multiply is either waiting for new data from the load or holding its output so that operations later in the chain can use its result. Most spatial compilers and implementations address this inefficiency by *pipelining*, which means that execution of a single program is spread across many clock cycles. This is achieved by inserting registers (a data storage primitive in the hardware) between some operations, where each register holds a binary value for the duration of a clock cycle. By holding the result of an operation's output so that the next operation in the chain can see and operate on that held value, the previous operation is free to work on a different computation without impacting the input to following operations.

The goal of algorithmic pipelining is to keep every operation (hardware unit) busy every clock cycle. Figure 17-4 shows a pipelined implementation of the previous simple example. Keep in mind that the compiler does all of the pipelining and balancing for us! We cover this topic so that we can understand how to fill the pipeline with work in the coming sections, not because we need to worry about manually pipelining anything in our code.

CHAPTER 17 PROGRAMMING FOR FPGAS

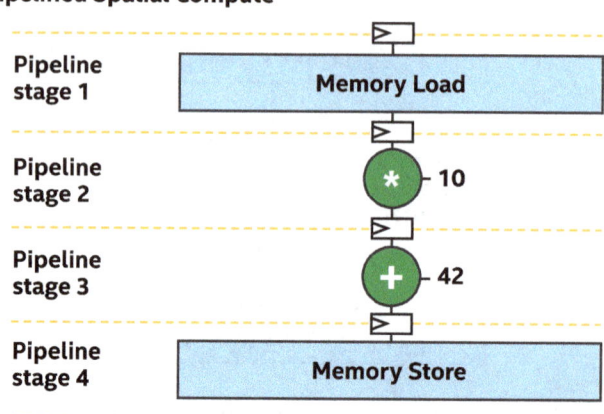

Figure 17-4. Pipelining of a computation: Stages execute in parallel

When a spatial implementation is pipelined, it becomes extremely efficient in the same way as a factory assembly line. Each pipeline stage performs only a small amount of the overall work, but it does so quickly and then begins to work on the next unit of work immediately afterward. It takes many clock cycles for a *single* computation to be processed by the pipeline, from start to finish, but the pipeline can compute *many* different instances of the computation on different data simultaneously.

When enough work starts executing in the pipeline, over enough consecutive clock cycles, then every single pipeline stage and therefore operation in the program can perform useful work during every clock cycle, meaning that the entire spatial device performs work simultaneously. This is one of the powers of spatial architectures—the entire device can execute work in parallel, all of the time. We call this *pipeline parallelism*.

Pipeline parallelism is the primary form of parallelism exploited on FPGAs to achieve performance.

> **PIPELINING IS AUTOMATIC**
>
> In the Intel implementation of DPC++ for FPGAs, and in other high-level programming solutions for FPGAs, the pipelining of an algorithm is performed automatically by the compiler. It is useful to roughly understand the implementation on spatial architectures, as described in this section, because then it becomes easier to structure applications to take advantage of the pipeline parallelism. It should be made clear that pipeline register insertion and balancing is performed by the compiler and not manually by developers.

Real programs and algorithms often have control flow (e.g., if/else structures) that leaves some parts of the program inactive a certain percentage of the clock cycles. FPGA compilers typically combine hardware from both sides of a branch, where possible, to minimize wasted spatial area and to maximize compute efficiency during control flow divergence. This makes control flow divergence much less expensive and less of a development concern than on other, especially vectorized architectures.

Kernels Consume Chip "Area"

In existing implementations, each kernel in a DPC++ application generates a spatial pipeline that consumes some resources of the FPGA (we can think about this as *space* or *area* on the device), which is conceptually shown in Figure 17-5.

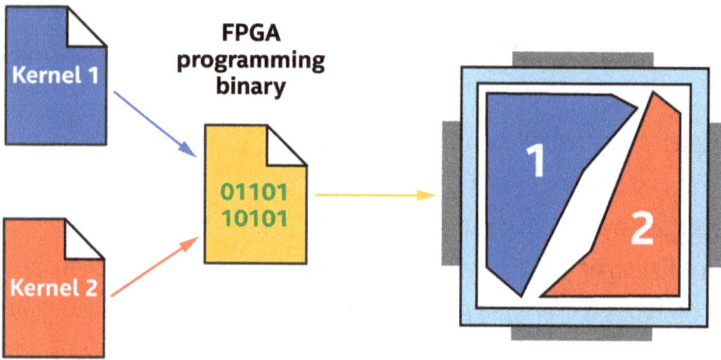

Figure 17-5. Multiple kernels in the same FPGA binary: Kernels can run concurrently

Since a kernel uses its own area on the device, different kernels can execute concurrently. If one kernel is waiting for something such as a memory access, other kernels on the FPGA can continue executing because they are independent pipelines elsewhere on the chip. This idea, formally described as independent forward progress between kernels, is a critical property of FPGA spatial compute.

When to Use an FPGA

Like any accelerator architecture, predicting when an FPGA is the right choice of accelerator vs. an alternative often comes down to knowledge of the architecture, the application characteristics, and the system bottlenecks. This section describes some of the characteristics of an application to consider.

Lots and Lots of Work

Like most modern compute accelerators, achieving good performance requires a large amount of work to be performed. If computing a single result from a single element of data, then it may not be useful to leverage an accelerator at all (of any kind). This is no different with FPGAs. Knowing that FPGA compilers leverage pipeline parallelism makes this more apparent. A pipelined implementation of an algorithm has many stages, often thousands or more, each of which should have different work within it in any clock cycle. If there isn't enough work to occupy most of the pipeline stages most of the time, then efficiency will be low. We'll call the average utilization of pipeline stages over time *occupancy* of the pipeline. This is different from the definition of occupancy used when optimizing other architectures such as GPUs!

There are multiple ways to generate work on an FPGA to fill the pipeline stages, which we'll cover in coming sections.

Custom Operations or Operation Widths

FPGAs were originally designed to perform efficient integer and bitwise operations and to act as glue logic that could adapt interfaces of other chips to work with each other. Although FPGAs have evolved into computational powerhouses instead of just glue logic solutions, they are still very efficient at bitwise operations, integer math operations on custom data widths or types, and operations on arbitrary bit fields in packet headers.

The fine-grained architecture of an FPGA, described at the end of this chapter, means that novel and arbitrary data types can be efficiently implemented. For example, if we need a 33-bit integer multiplier or a 129-bit adder, FPGAs can provide these custom operations with great efficiency. Because of this flexibility, FPGAs are commonly employed in rapidly evolving domains, such as recently in machine learning, where the data widths and operations have been changing faster than can be built into ASICs.

CHAPTER 17 PROGRAMMING FOR FPGAS

Scalar Data Flow

An important aspect of FPGA spatial pipelines, apparent from Figure 17-4, is that the intermediate data between operations not only stays on-chip (is not stored to external memory), but that intermediate data between each pipeline stage has dedicated storage registers. FPGA parallelism comes from pipelining of computation such that many operations are being executed concurrently, each at a different stage of the pipeline. This is different from vector architectures where multiple computations are executed as lanes of a shared vector instruction.

The scalar nature of the parallelism in a spatial pipeline is important for many applications, because it still applies even with tight data dependences across the units of work. These data dependences can be handled without loss of performance, as we will discuss later in this chapter when talking about loop-carried dependences. The result is that spatial pipelines, and therefore FPGAs, are compelling for algorithms where data dependences across units of work (such as work-items) can't be broken and fine-grained communication must occur. Many optimization techniques for other accelerators focus on breaking these dependences though various techniques or managing communication at controlled scales through features such as sub-groups. FPGAs can instead perform well with communication from tight dependences and should be considered for classes of algorithms where such patterns exist.

LOOPS ARE FINE!

A common misconception on data flow architectures is that loops with either fixed or dynamic iteration counts lead to poor data flow performance, because they aren't simple feed-forward pipelines. At least with the Intel DPC++ and FPGA toolchains, this is not true. Loop iterations can instead be a good way to produce high occupancy within the pipeline, and the compilers are built around the concept of allowing multiple loop iterations to execute in an overlapped way. Loops provide an easy mechanism to keep the pipeline busy with work!

CHAPTER 17 PROGRAMMING FOR FPGAS

Low Latency and Rich Connectivity

More conventional uses of FPGAs which take advantage of the rich input and output transceivers on the devices apply equally well for developers using DPC++. For example, as shown in Figure 17-6, some FPGA accelerator cards have network interfaces that make it possible to stream data directly into the device, process it, and then stream the result directly back to the network. Such systems are often sought when processing latency needs to be minimized and where processing through operating system network stacks is too slow or needs to be offloaded.

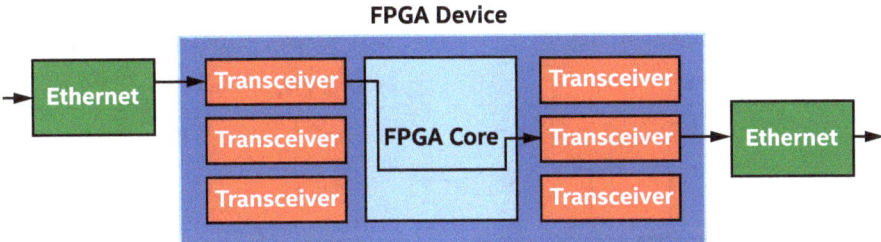

Figure 17-6. Low-latency I/O streaming: FPGA connects network data and computation tightly

The opportunities are almost limitless when considering direct input/output through FPGA transceivers, but the options do come down to what is available on the circuit board that forms an accelerator. Because of the dependence on a specific accelerator card and variety of such uses, aside from describing the pipe language constructs in a coming section, this chapter doesn't dive into these applications. We should instead read the vendor documentation associated with a specific accelerator card or search for an accelerator card that matches our specific interface needs.

431

CHAPTER 17　PROGRAMMING FOR FPGAS

Customized Memory Systems

Memory systems on an FPGA, such as function private memory or workgroup local memory, are built out of small blocks of on-chip memory. This is important because each memory system is custom built for the specific portion of an algorithm or kernel using it. FPGAs have significant on-chip memory bandwidth, and combined with the formation of custom memory systems, they can perform very well on applications that have atypical memory access patterns and structures. Figure 17-7 shows some of the optimizations that can be performed by the compiler when a memory system is implemented on an FPGA.

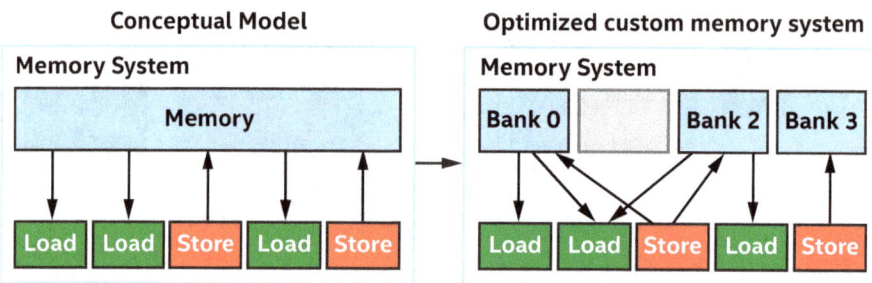

Figure 17-7. FPGA memory systems are customized by the compiler for our specific code

Other architectures such as GPUs have fixed memory structures that are easy to reason about by experienced developers, but that can also be hard to optimize around in many cases. Many optimizations on other accelerators are focused around memory pattern modification to avoid bank conflicts, for example. If we have algorithms that would benefit from a custom memory structure, such as a different number of access ports per bank or an unusual number of banks, then FPGAs can offer immediate advantages. Conceptually, the difference is between writing code to use a fixed memory system efficiently (most other accelerators) and having the memory system custom designed by the compiler to be efficient with our specific code (FPGA).

Running on an FPGA

There are two steps to run a kernel on an FPGA (as with any ahead-of-time compilation accelerator):

1. Compiling the source to a binary which can be run on our hardware of interest

2. Selecting the correct accelerator that we are interested in at runtime

To compile kernels so that they can run on FPGA hardware, we can use the command line:

```
dpcpp -fintelfpga my_source_code.cpp -Xshardware
```

This command tells the compiler to turn all kernels in my_source_code.cpp into binaries that can run on an Intel FPGA accelerator and then to package them within the host binary that is generated. When we execute the host binary (e.g., by running ./a.out on Linux), the runtime will automatically program any attached FPGA as required, before executing the submitted kernels, as shown in Figure 17-8.

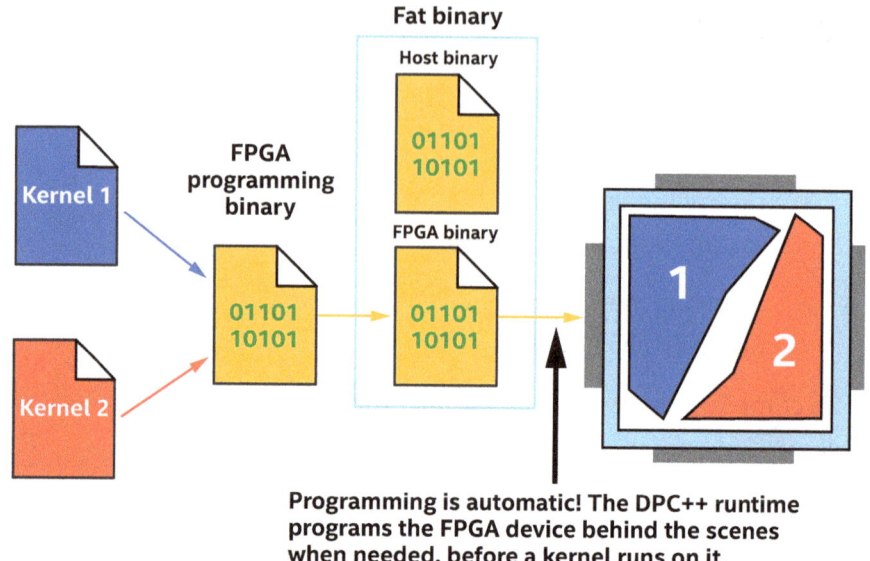

Figure 17-8. FPGA programmed automatically at runtime

FPGA programming binaries are embedded within the compiled DPC++ executable that we run on the host. The FPGA is automatically configured behind the scenes for us.

When we run a host program and submit the first kernel for execution on an FPGA, there might be a slight delay before the kernel begins executing, while the FPGA is programmed. Resubmitting kernels for additional executions won't see the same delay because the kernel is already programmed to the device and ready to run.

Selection of an FPGA device at runtime was covered in Chapter 2. We need to tell the host program where we want kernels to run because there are typically multiple accelerator options available, such as a CPU and GPU, in addition to the FPGA. To quickly recap one method to select an FPGA during program execution, we can use code like that in Figure 17-9.

```cpp
#include <CL/sycl.hpp>
#include <CL/sycl/intel/fpga_extensions.hpp> // For fpga_selector
using namespace sycl;

void say_device (const queue& Q) {
  std::cout << "Device : "
            << Q.get_device().get_info<info::device::name>()
            << "\n";
}

int main() {
  queue Q{ INTEL::fpga_selector{} };
  say_device(Q);

  Q.submit([&](handler &h){
    h.parallel_for(1024, [=](auto idx) {
      // ...
    });
  });

  return 0;
}
```

Figure 17-9. Choosing an FPGA device at runtime using the fpga_selector

Compile Times

Rumors abound that compiling designs for an FPGA can take a long time, much longer than compiling for ISA-based accelerators. The rumors are true! The end of this chapter overviews the fine-grained architectural elements of an FPGA that lead to both the advantages of an FPGA and the computationally intensive compilation (place-and-route optimizations) that can take hours in some cases.

The compile time from source code to FPGA hardware execution is long enough that we don't want to develop and iterate on our code exclusively in hardware. FPGA development flows offer several stages that minimize the number of hardware compilations, to make us productive despite the hardware compile times. Figure 17-10 shows the typical stages, where most of our time is spent on the early steps that provide fast turnaround and rapid iteration.

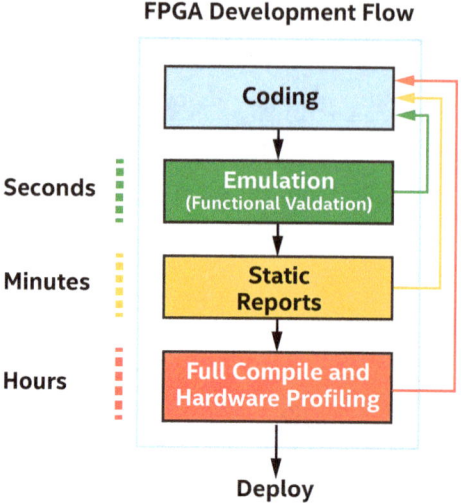

Figure 17-10. Most verification and optimization occurs prior to lengthy hardware compilation

Emulation and static reports from the compiler are the cornerstones of FPGA code development in DPC++. The emulator acts as if it was an FPGA, including supporting relevant extensions and emulating the execution model, but runs on the host processor. Compilation time is therefore the same as we would expect from compilation to a CPU device, although we won't see the performance boost that we would from execution on actual FPGA hardware. The emulator is great for establishing and testing functional correctness in an application.

Static reports, like emulation, are generated quickly by the toolchain. They report on the FPGA structures created by the compiler and on bottlenecks identified by the compiler. Both of these can be used to predict whether our design will achieve good performance when run on FPGA hardware and are used to optimize our code. Please read the vendor's documentation for information on the reports, which are often improved from release to release of a toolchain (see documentation for the latest and greatest features!). Extensive documentation is provided by vendors on how to interpret and optimize based on the reports. This information would be the topic of another book, so we can't dive into details in this single chapter.

The FPGA Emulator

Emulation is primarily used to functionally debug our application, to make sure that it behaves as expected and produces correct results. There is no reason to do this level of development on actual FPGA hardware where compile times are longer. The emulation flow is activated by removing the -Xshardware flag from the dpcpp compilation command and at the same time using the INTEL::fpga_emulator_selector instead of the INTEL::fpga_selector in our host code. We would compile using a command like

```
dpcpp -fintelfpga my_source_code.cpp
```

Simultaneously, we would choose the FPGA emulator at runtime using code such as in Figure 17-11. By using fpga_emulator_selector, which uses the host processor to emulate an FPGA, we maintain a rapid development and debugging process before we have to commit to the lengthier compile for actual FPGA hardware.

```
#include <CL/sycl.hpp>
#include <CL/sycl/intel/fpga_extensions.hpp> // For fpga_selector
using namespace sycl;

void say_device (const queue& Q) {
  std::cout << "Device : "
    << Q.get_device().get_info<info::device::name>() << "\n";
}

int main() {
  queue Q{ INTEL::fpga_emulator_selector{} };
  say_device(Q);

  Q.submit([&](handler &h){
      h.parallel_for(1024, [=](auto idx) {
          // ...
          });
      });

  return 0;
}
```

Figure 17-11. Using fpga_emulator_selector for rapid development and debugging

If we are switching between hardware and the emulator frequently, it can make sense to use a macro within our program to flip between device selectors from the command line. Check the vendor's documentation and online FPGA DPC++ code examples for examples of this, if needed.

FPGA Hardware Compilation Occurs "Ahead-of-Time"

The *Full Compile and Hardware Profiling* stage in Figure 17-10 is an *ahead-of-time* compile in SYCL terminology. This means that the compilation of the kernel to a device binary occurs when we initially compile our program and not when the program is submitted to a device to be run. On an FPGA, this is particularly important because

CHAPTER 17 PROGRAMMING FOR FPGAS

1. Compilation takes a length of time that we don't normally want to incur when running an application.

2. DPC++ programs may be executed on systems that don't have a capable host processor. The compilation process to an FPGA binary benefits from a fast processor with a good amount of attached memory. Ahead-of-time compilation lets us easily choose where the compile occurs, rather than having it run on systems where the program is deployed.

A LOT HAPPENS BEHIND THE SCENES WITH DPC++ ON AN FPGA!

Conventional FPGA design (not using a high-level language) can be very complicated. There are many steps beyond just writing our kernel, such as building and configuring the interfaces that communicate with off-chip memories and *closing timing* by inserting registers needed to make the compiled design run fast enough to communicate with certain peripherals. DPC++ solves all of this for us, so that we don't need to know anything about the details of conventional FPGA design to achieve working applications! The tooling treats our kernels as code to optimize and make efficient on the device and then automatically handles all of the details of talking to off-chip peripherals, closing timing, and setting up drivers for us.

Achieving peak performance on an FPGA still requires detailed knowledge of the architecture, just like any other accelerator, but the steps to move from code to a working design are much simpler and more productive with DPC++ than in traditional FPGA flows.

CHAPTER 17 PROGRAMMING FOR FPGAS

Writing Kernels for FPGAs

Once we have decided to use an FPGA for our application or even just decided to try one out, having an idea of how to write code to see good performance is important. This section describes topics that highlight important concepts and covers a few topics that often cause confusion, to make getting started faster.

Exposing Parallelism

We have already looked at how pipeline parallelism is used to efficiently perform work on an FPGA. Another simple pipeline example is shown in Figure 17-12.

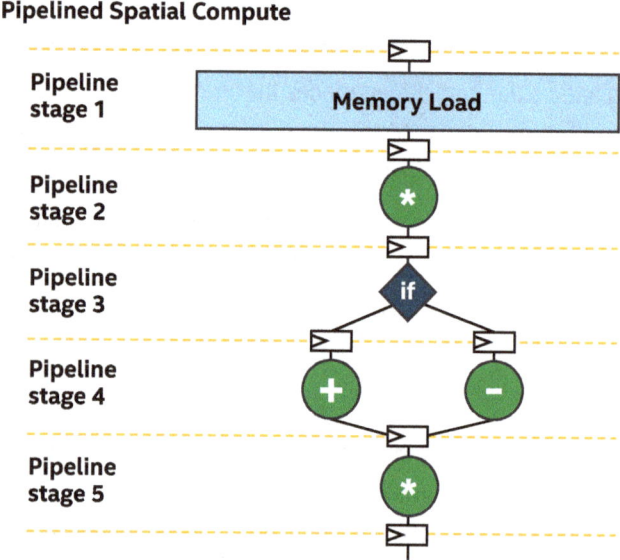

Figure 17-12. Simple pipeline with five stages: Six clock cycles to process an element of data

CHAPTER 17 PROGRAMMING FOR FPGAS

In this pipeline, there are five stages. Data moves from one stage to the next once per clock cycle, so in this very simple example, it takes six clock cycles from when data enters into stage 1 until it exits from stage 5.

A major goal of pipelining is to enable multiple elements of data to be processed at different stages of the pipeline, simultaneously. To be sure that this is clear, Figure 17-13 shows a pipeline where there is not enough work (only one element of data in this case), which causes each pipeline stage to be unused during most of the clock cycles. This is an inefficient use of the FPGA resources because most of the hardware is idle most of the time.

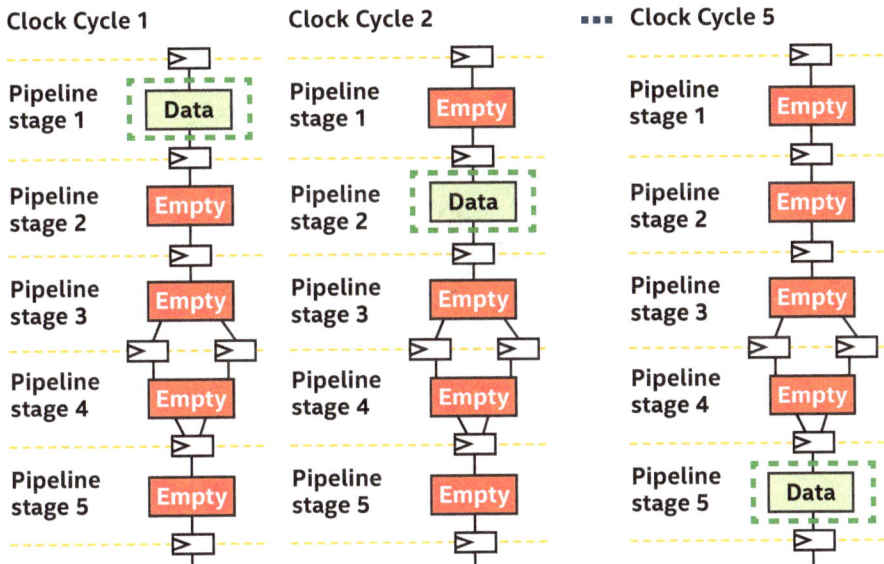

Figure 17-13. *Pipeline stages are mostly unused if processing only a single element of work*

441

CHAPTER 17 PROGRAMMING FOR FPGAS

To keep the pipeline stages better occupied, it is useful to imagine a queue of un-started work waiting before the first stage, which *feeds* the pipeline. Each clock cycle, the pipeline can consume and start one more element of work from the queue, as shown in Figure 17-14. After some initial startup cycles, each stage of the pipeline is occupied and doing useful work every clock cycle, leading to efficient utilization of the FPGA resources.

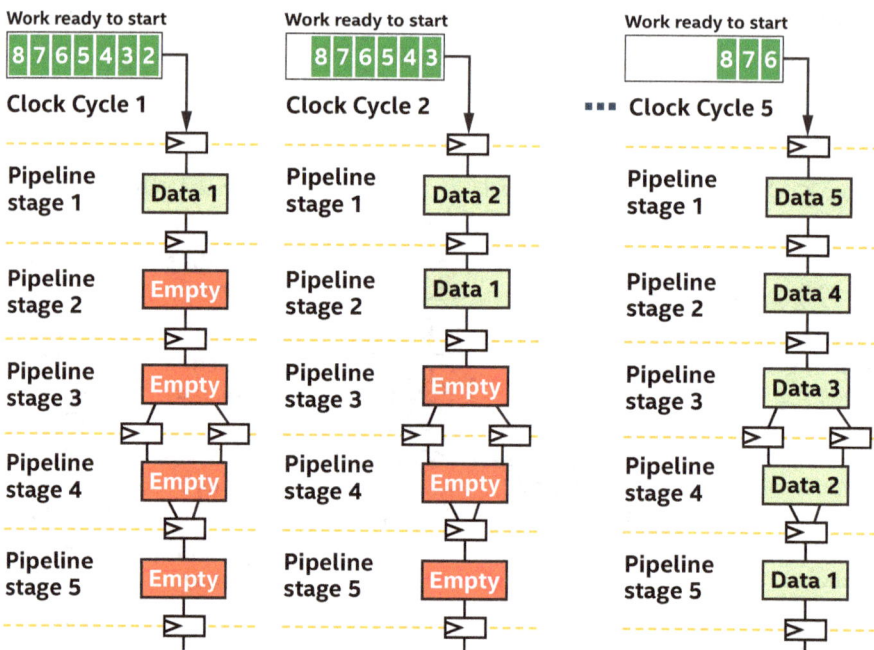

Figure 17-14. Efficient utilization comes when each pipeline stage is kept busy

The following two sections cover methods to keep the queue feeding the pipeline filled with work that is ready to start. We'll look at

1. ND-range kernels
2. Loops

CHAPTER 17   PROGRAMMING FOR FPGAS

Choosing between these options impacts how kernels that run on an FPGA should be fundamentally architected. In some cases, algorithms lend themselves well to one style or the other, and in other cases programmer preference and experience inform which method should be chosen.

Keeping the Pipeline Busy Using ND-Ranges

The ND-range hierarchical execution model was described in Chapter 4. Figure 17-15 illustrates the key concepts: an ND-range execution model where there is a hierarchical grouping of work-items, and where a work-item is the primitive unit of work that a kernel defines. This model was originally developed to enable efficient programming of GPUs where work-items may execute concurrently at various levels of the execution model hierarchy. To match the type of work that GPU hardware is efficient at, ND-range work-items do not frequently communicate with each other in most applications.

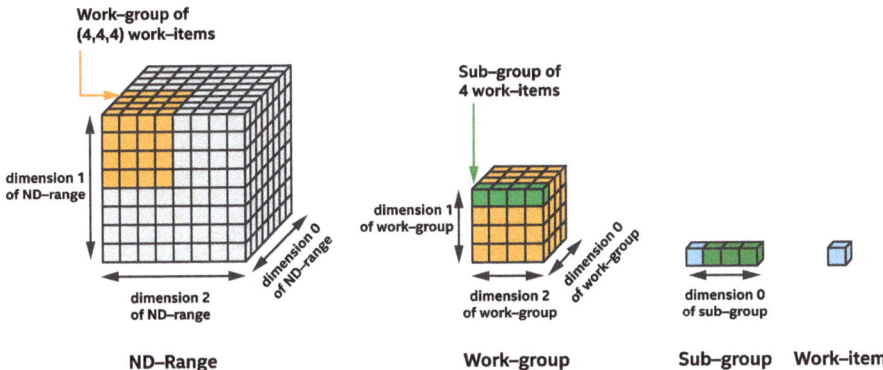

Figure 17-15. ND-range execution model: A hierarchical grouping of work-items

443

The FPGA spatial pipeline can be very efficiently filled with work using an ND-range. This programming style is fully supported on FPGA, and we can think of it as depicted in Figure 17-16 where on each clock cycle, a different work-item enters the first stage of the pipeline.

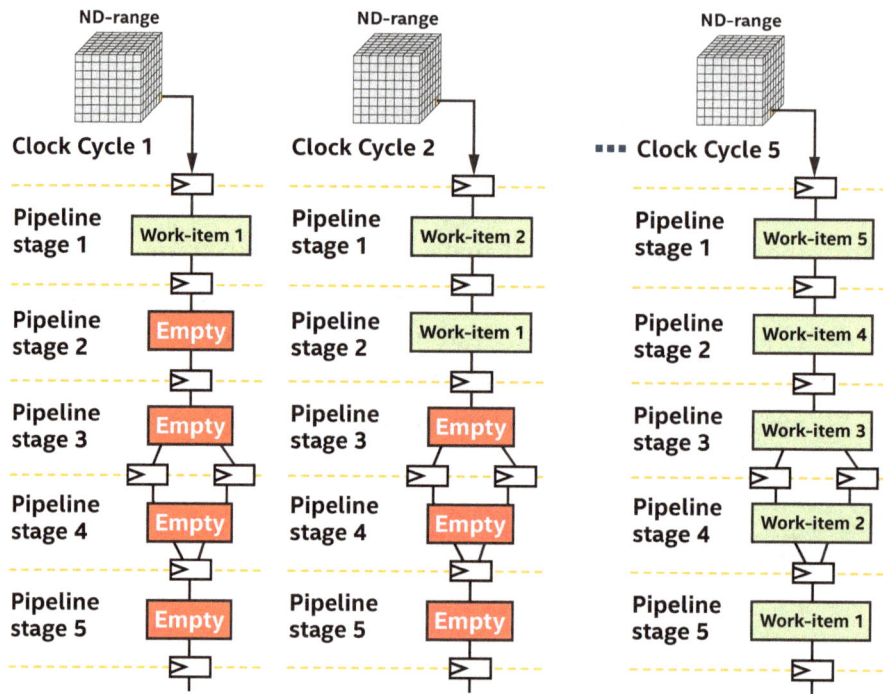

Figure 17-16. ND-range feeding a spatial pipeline

When should we create an ND-range kernel on an FPGA using work-items to keep the pipeline occupied? It's simple. Whenever we can structure our algorithm or application as independent work-items that don't need to communicate often (or ideally at all), we should use ND-range! If work-items do need to communicate often or if we don't naturally think in terms of ND-ranges, then loops (described in the next section) provide an efficient way to express our algorithm as well.

If we can structure our algorithm so that work-items don't need to communicate much (or at all), then ND-range is a great way to generate work to keep the spatial pipeline full!

A good example of a kernel that is efficient with an ND-range feeding the pipeline is a random number generator, where creation of numbers in the sequence is independent of the previous numbers generated.

Figure 17-17 shows an ND-range kernel that will call the random number generation function once for each work-item in the 16 × 16 × 16 range. Note how the random number generation function takes the work-item id as input.

```
h.parallel_for({16,16,16}, [=](auto I) {
  output[I] = generate_random_number_from_ID(I);
});
```

Figure 17-17. *Multiple work-item (16 × 16 × 16) invocation of a random number generator*

The example shows a `parallel_for` invocation that uses a `range`, with only a global size specified. We can alternately use the `parallel_for` invocation style that takes an nd_range, where both the global work size and local work-group sizes are specified. FPGAs can very efficiently implement work-group local memory from on-chip resources, so feel free to use work-groups whenever they make sense, either because we want work-group local memory or because having work-group IDs available simplifies our code.

CHAPTER 17 PROGRAMMING FOR FPGAS

PARALLEL RANDOM NUMBER GENERATORS

The example in Figure 17-17 assumes that `generate_random_number_from_ID(I)` is a random number generator which has been written to be safe and correct when invoked in a parallel way. For example, if different work-items in the `parallel_for` range execute the function, we expect different sequences to be created by each work-item, with each sequence adhering to whatever distribution is expected from the generator. Parallel random number generators are themselves a complex topic, so it is a good idea to use libraries or to learn about the topic through techniques such as block skip-ahead algorithms.

Pipelines Do Not Mind Data Dependences!

One of the challenges when programming vector architectures (e.g., GPUs) where some work-items execute together as lanes of vector instructions is structuring an algorithm to be efficient without extensive communication between work-items. Some algorithms and applications lend themselves well to vector hardware, and some don't. A common cause of a poor mapping is an algorithmic need for extensive sharing of data, due to data dependences with other computations that are in some sense neighbors. Sub-groups address some of this challenge on vector architectures by providing efficient communication between work-items in the same subgroup, as described in Chapter 14.

FPGAs play an important role for algorithms that can't be decomposed into independent work. FPGA spatial pipelines are not vectorized across work-items, but instead execute consecutive work-items across pipeline stages. This implementation of the parallelism means that fine-grained communication between work-items (even those in different work-groups) *can* be implemented easily and efficiently within the spatial pipeline!

CHAPTER 17 PROGRAMMING FOR FPGAS

One example is a random number generator where output N+1 depends on knowing what output N was. This creates a data dependence between two outputs, and if each output is generated by a work-item in an ND-range, then there is a data dependence between work-items that can require complex and often costly synchronization on some architectures. When coding such algorithms serially, one would typically write a loop, where iteration N+1 uses the computation from iteration N, such as shown in Figure 17-18. Each iteration depends on the state computed by the previous iteration. This is a very common pattern.

```
int state = 0;
for (int i=0; i < size; i++) {
  state = generate_random_number(state);
  output[i] = state;
}
```

Figure 17-18. *Loop-carried data dependence (state)*

Spatial implementations can very efficiently communicate results backward in the pipeline to work that started in a later cycle (i.e., to work at an earlier stage in the pipeline), and spatial compilers implement many optimizations around this pattern. Figure 17-19 shows the idea of backward communication of data, from stage 5 to stage 4. Spatial pipelines are not vectorized across work-items. This enables efficient data dependence communication by passing results backward in the pipeline!

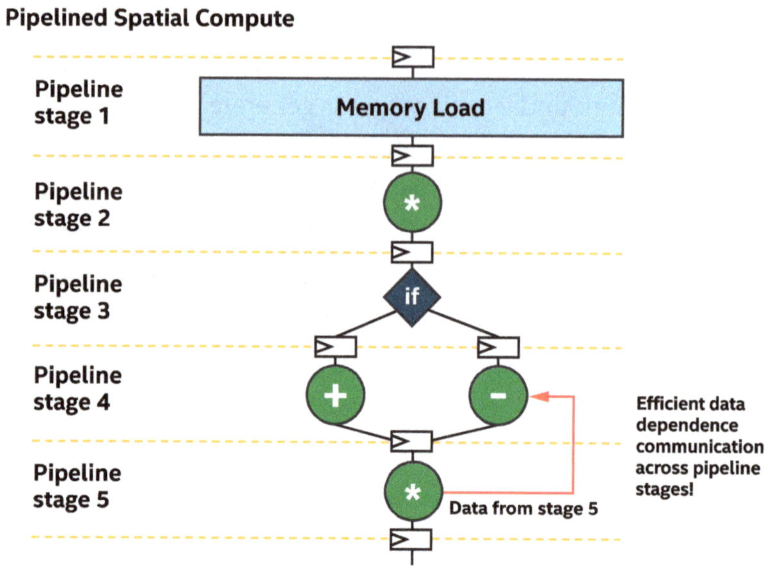

CHAPTER 17 PROGRAMMING FOR FPGAS

Pipelined Spatial Compute

Figure 17-19. Backward communication enables efficient data dependence communication

The ability to pass data backward (to an earlier stage in the pipeline) is key to spatial architectures, but it isn't obvious how to write code that takes advantage of it. There are two approaches that make expressing this pattern easy:

1. Loops
2. Intra-kernel pipes with ND-range kernels

The second option is based on pipes that we describe later in this chapter, but it isn't nearly as common as loops so we mention it for completeness, but don't detail it here. Vendor documentation provides more details on the pipe approach, but it's easier to stick to loops which are described next unless there is a reason to do otherwise.

CHAPTER 17 PROGRAMMING FOR FPGAS

Spatial Pipeline Implementation of a Loop

A loop is a natural fit when programming an algorithm that has data dependences. Loops frequently express dependences across iterations, even in the most basic loop examples where the counter that determines when the loop should exit is carried across iterations (variable i in Figure 17-20).

```
int a = 0;
for (int i=0; i < size; i++) {
  a = a + i;
}
```

Figure 17-20. Loop with two loop-carried dependences (i.e., i and a)

In the simple loop of Figure 17-20, it is understood that the value of a which is on the right-hand side of a= a + i reflects the value stored by the previous loop iteration or the initial value if it's the first iteration of the loop. When a spatial compiler implements a loop, iterations of the loop can be used to fill the stages of the pipeline as shown in Figure 17-21. Notice that the queue of work which is ready to start now contains loop iterations, not work-items!

CHAPTER 17 PROGRAMMING FOR FPGAS

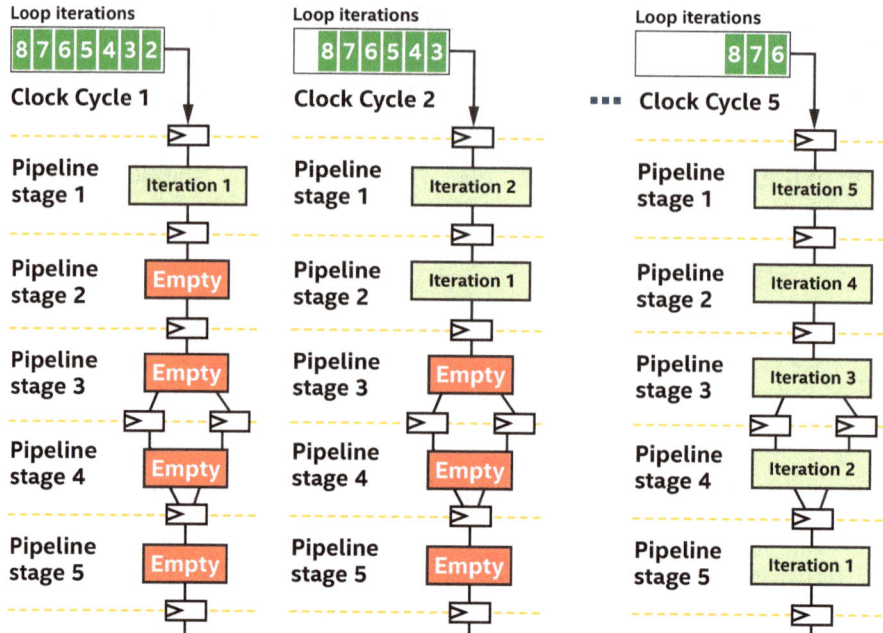

Figure 17-21. Pipelines stages fed by successive iterations of a loop

A modified random number generator example is shown in Figure 17-22. In this case, instead of generating a number based on the id of a work-item, as in Figure 17-17, the generator takes the previously computed value as an argument.

```
h.single_task([=]() {
  int state = seed;
  for (int i=0; i < size; i++) {
    state = generate_incremental_random_number(state);
    output[i] = state;
  }
});
```

Figure 17-22. Random number generator that depends on previous value generated

The example uses `single_task` instead of `parallel_for` because the repeated work is expressed by a loop within the single task, so there isn't a reason to also include multiple work-items in this code (via `parallel_for`). The loop inside the `single_task` makes it much easier to express (programming convenience) that the previously computed value of `temp` is passed to each invocation of the random number generation function.

In cases such as Figure 17-22, the FPGA can implement the loop efficiently. It can maintain a fully occupied pipeline in many cases or can at least tell us through reports what to change to increase occupancy. With this in mind, it becomes clear that this same algorithm would be much more difficult to describe if loop iterations were replaced with work-items, where the value generated by one work-item would need to be communicated to another work-item to be used in the incremental computation. The code complexity would rapidly increase, particularly if the work couldn't be batched so that each work-item was actually computing its own independent random number sequence.

Loop Initiation Interval

Conceptually, we probably think of iterations of a loop in C++ as executing one after another, as shown in Figure 17-23. That's the programming model and is the right way to think about loops. In implementation, though, compilers are free to perform many optimizations as long as most behavior (i.e., defined and race-free behavior) of the program doesn't observably change. Regardless of compiler optimizations, what matters is that the loop appears to execute *as if* Figure 17-23 is how it happened.

CHAPTER 17 PROGRAMMING FOR FPGAS

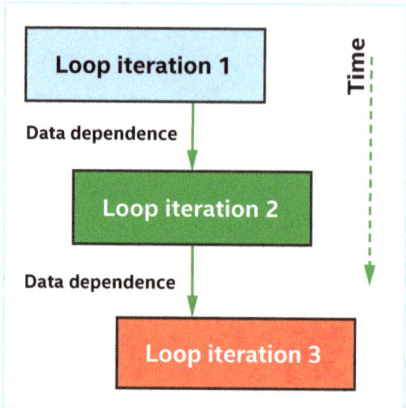

Figure 17-23. Conceptually, loop iterations execute one after another

Moving into the spatial compiler perspective, Figure 17-24 shows a loop pipelining optimization where the execution of iterations of a loop are overlapped in time. Different iterations will be executing different stages of the spatial pipeline from each other, and data dependences across stages of the pipeline can be managed by the compiler to ensure that the program appears to execute as if the iterations were sequential (except that the loop will finish executing sooner!).

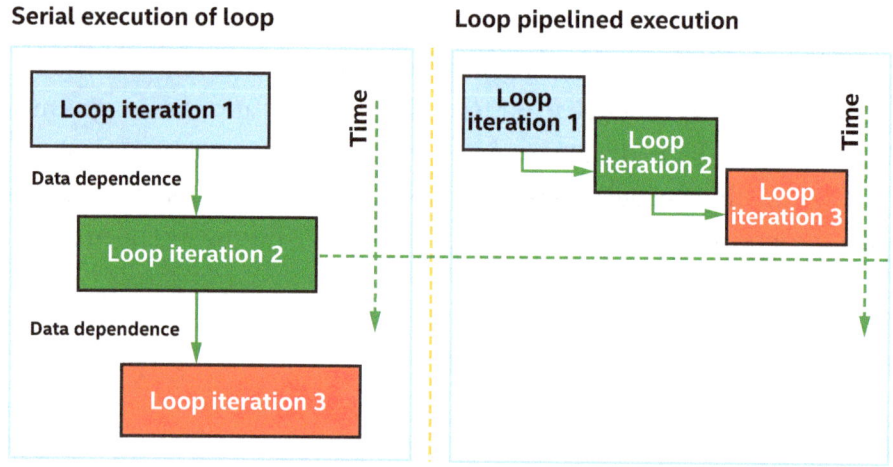

Figure 17-24. Loop pipelining allows iterations of the loop to be overlapped across pipeline stages

CHAPTER 17 PROGRAMMING FOR FPGAS

Loop pipelining is easy to understand with the realization that *many* results within a loop iteration may finish computation well before the loop iteration finishes *all* of its work and that, in a spatial pipeline, results can be passed to an earlier pipeline stage when the compiler decides to do so. Figure 17-25 shows this idea where the results of stage 1 are fed backward in the pipeline, allowing a future loop iteration to use the result early, before the previous iteration has completed.

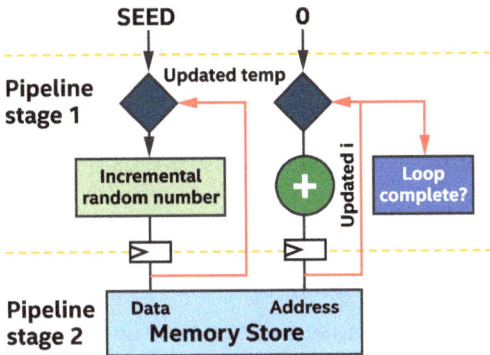

Figure 17-25. *A pipelined implementation of the incremental random number generator*

With loop pipelining, it is possible for the execution of many iterations of a loop to overlap. The overlap means that even with loop-carried data dependences, loop iterations can still be used to fill the pipeline with work, leading to efficient utilization. Figure 17-26 shows how loop iterations might overlap their executions, even with loop-carried data dependences, within the same simple pipeline as was shown in Figure 17-25.

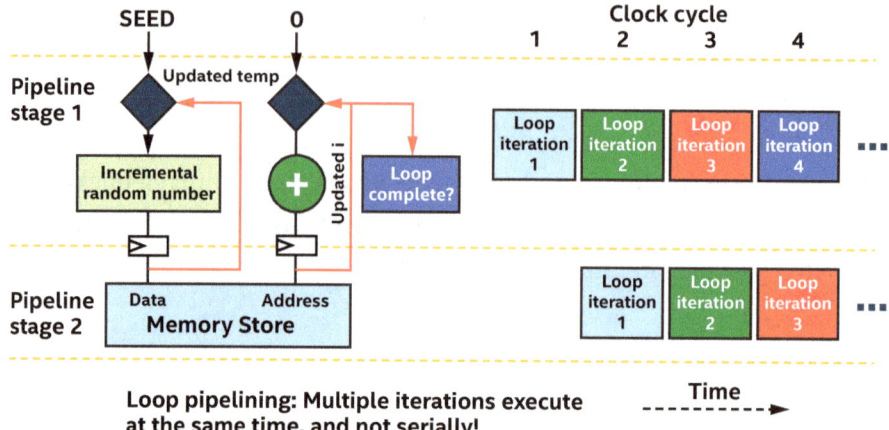

Figure 17-26. Loop pipelining simultaneously processes parts of multiple loop iterations

In real algorithms, it is often not possible to launch a new loop iteration every single clock cycle, because a data dependence may take multiple clock cycles to compute. This often arises if memory lookups, particularly from off-chip memories, are on the critical path of the computation of a dependence. The result is a pipeline that can only initiate a new loop iteration every N clock cycles, and we refer to this as an *initiation interval* (II) of N cycles. An example is shown in Figure 17-27. A loop initiation interval (II) of two means that a new loop iteration can begin every second cycle, which results in sub-optimal occupancy of the pipeline stages.

CHAPTER 17 PROGRAMMING FOR FPGAS

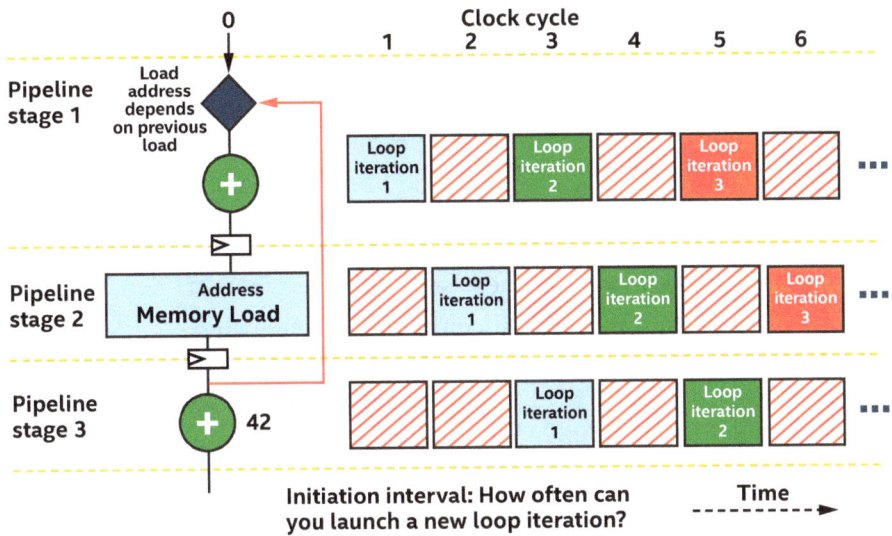

Figure 17-27. Sub-optimal occupancy of pipeline stages

An II larger than one can lead to inefficiency in the pipeline because the average occupancy of each stage is reduced. This is apparent from Figure 17-27 where II=2 and pipeline stages are unused a large percentage (50%!) of the time. There are multiple ways to improve this situation.

The compiler performs extensive optimization to reduce II whenever possible, so its reports will also tell us what the initiation interval of each loop is and give us information on why it is larger than one, if that occurs. Restructuring the compute in a loop based on the reports can often reduce the II, particularly because as developers, we can make loop structural changes that the compiler isn't allowed to (because they would be observable). Read the compiler reports to learn how to reduce the II in specific cases.

An alternative way to reduce inefficiency from an II that is larger than one is through nested loops, which can fill all pipeline stages through interleaving of outer loop iterations with those of an inner loop that has II>1. Check vendor documentation and the compiler reports for details on using this technique.

455

CHAPTER 17 PROGRAMMING FOR FPGAS

Pipes

An important concept in spatial and other architectures is a first-in first-out (FIFO) buffer. There are many reasons that FIFOs are important, but two properties are especially useful when thinking about programming:

1. There is **implicit control information carried alongside the data**. These signals tell us whether the FIFO is empty or full and can be useful when decomposing a problem into independent pieces.

2. FIFOs have **storage capacity**. This can make it easier to achieve performance in the presence of dynamic behaviors such as highly variable latencies when accessing memory.

Figure 17-28 shows a simple example of a FIFO's operation.

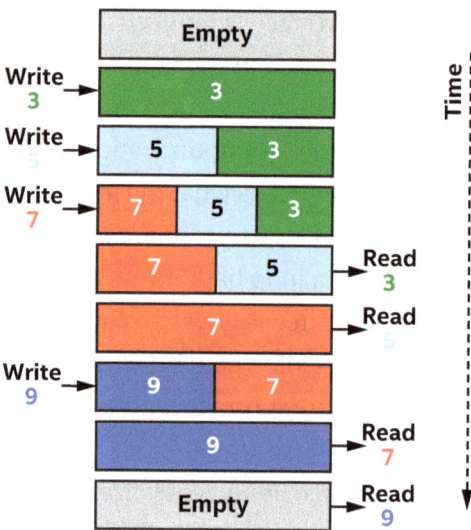

Figure 17-28. Example operation of a FIFO over time

456

CHAPTER 17 PROGRAMMING FOR FPGAS

FIFOs are exposed in DPC++ through a feature called *pipes*. The main reason that we should care about pipes when writing FPGA programs is that they allow us to decompose a problem into smaller pieces to focus on development and optimizations in a more modular way. They also allow the rich communication features of the FPGA to be harnessed. Figure 17-29 shows both of these graphically.

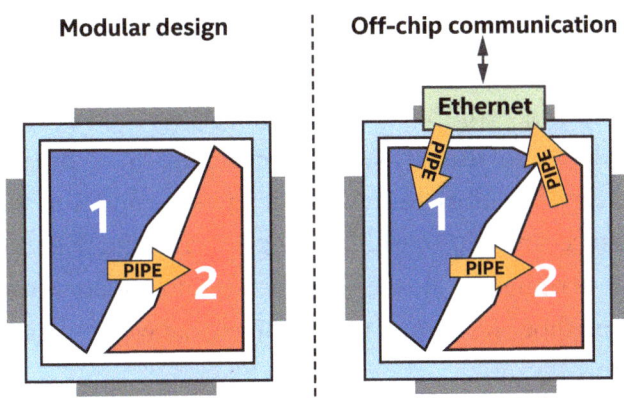

Figure 17-29. *Pipes simplify modular design and access to hardware peripherals*

Remember that FPGA kernels can exist on the device simultaneously (in different areas of the chip) and that in an efficient design, all parts of the kernels are active all the time, every clock cycle. This means that optimizing an FPGA application involves considering how kernels or parts of kernels interact with one another, and pipes provide an abstraction to make this easy.

Pipes are FIFOs that are implemented using on-chip memories on an FPGA, so they allow us to communicate between and within running kernels without the cost of moving data to off-chip memory. This provides inexpensive communication, and the control information that is coupled with a pipe (empty/full signals) provides a lightweight synchronization mechanism.

CHAPTER 17 PROGRAMMING FOR FPGAS

> **DO WE NEED PIPES?**
>
> No. It is possible to write efficient kernels without using pipes. We can use all of the FPGA resources and achieve maximum performance using conventional programming styles without pipes. But it is easier for most developers to program and optimize more modular spatial designs, and pipes are a great way to achieve this.

As shown in Figure 17-30, there are four general types of pipes available. In the rest of this section, we'll cover the first type (inter-kernel pipes), because they suffice to show what pipes are and how they are used. Pipes can also communicate within a single kernel and with the host or input/output peripherals. Please check vendor documentation for more information on those forms and uses of pipes that we don't have room to dive into here.

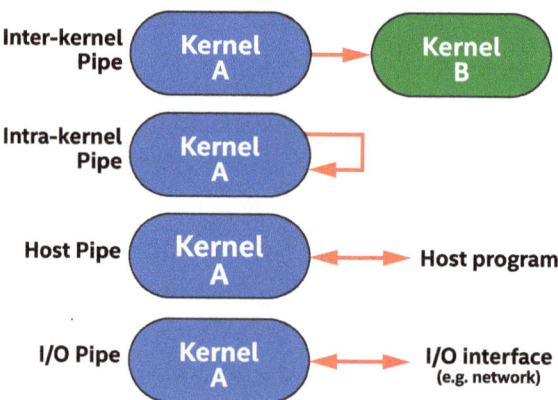

Figure 17-30. Types of pipe connectivity in DPC++

A simple example is shown in Figure 17-31. In this case, there are two kernels that communicate through a pipe, with each read or write operating on a unit of an int.

```
// Create alias for pipe type so that consistent across uses
using my_pipe = pipe<class some_pipe, int>;

// ND-range kernel
Q.submit([&](handler& h) {
  auto A = accessor(B_in, h);

  h.parallel_for(count, [=](auto idx) {
    my_pipe::write( A[idx] );
  });
});

// Single_task kernel
Q.submit([&](handler& h) {
  auto A = accessor(B_out, h);

  h.single_task([=]() {
    for (int i=0; i < count; i++) {
      A[i] = my_pipe::read();
    }
  });
});
```

Figure 17-31. Pipe between two kernels: (1) ND-range and (2) single task with a loop

There are a few points to observe from Figure 17-31. First, two kernels are communicating with each other using a pipe. If there are no accessor or event dependences between the kernels, the DPC++ runtime will execute both *at the same time*, allowing them to communicate through the pipe instead of full SYCL memory buffers or USM.

Pipes are identified using a type-based approach, where each is identified using a parameterization of the pipe type which is shown in Figure 17-32. The parameterization of the pipe type identifies a specific pipe. Reads or writes on the same pipe type are to the same FIFO. There are three template parameters that together define the type and therefore identity of a pipe.

```
template <typename name,
          typename dataT,
          size_t min_capacity = 0>
class pipe;
```

Figure 17-32. *Parameterization of the pipe type*

It is recommended to use type aliases to define our pipe types, as shown in the first line of code in Figure 17-31, to reduce programming errors and improve code readability.

Use type aliases to identify pipes. This simplifies code and prevents accidental creation of unexpected pipes.

Pipes have a `min_capacity` parameter. It defaults to 0 which is *automatic selection*, but if specified, it guarantees that at least that number of words can be written to the pipe without any being read out. This parameter is useful when

1. Two kernels communicating with a pipe do *not* run at the same time, and we need enough capacity in the pipe for a first kernel to write all of its outputs before a second kernel starts to run and reads from the pipe.

2. If kernels generate or consume data in bursts, then adding capacity to a pipe can provide isolation between the kernels, decoupling their performance from each other. For example, a kernel producing

data can continue to write (until the pipe capacity becomes full), even if a kernel consuming that data is busy and not ready to consume anything yet. This provides flexibility in execution of kernels relative to each other, at the cost only of some memory resources on the FPGA.

Blocking and Non-blocking Pipe Accesses

Like most FIFO interfaces, pipes have two styles of interface: *blocking* and *non-blocking*. Blocking accesses wait (block/pause execution!) for the operation to succeed, while non-blocking accesses return immediately and set a Boolean value indicating whether the operation succeeded.

The definition of success is simple: If we are reading from a pipe and there was data available to read (the pipe wasn't empty), then the read succeeds. If we are writing and the pipe wasn't already full, then the write succeeds. Figure 17-33 shows both forms of access member functions of the pipe class. We see the member functions of a pipe that allow it to be written to or read from. Recall that accesses to pipes can be blocking or non-blocking.

```
// Blocking
T read();
void write( const T &data );

// Non-blocking
T read( bool &success_code );
void write( const T &data, bool &success_code );
```

Figure 17-33. Member functions of a pipe that allow it to be written to or read from

Both blocking and non-blocking accesses have their uses depending on what our application is trying to achieve. If a kernel can't do any more work until it reads data from the pipe, then it probably makes sense to use a blocking read. If instead a kernel wants to read data from any one of a set of pipes and it is not sure which one might have data available, then reading from pipes with a non-blocking call makes more sense. In that case, the kernel can read from a pipe and process the data if there was any, but if the pipe was empty, it can instead move on and try reading from the next pipe that potentially has data available.

For More Information on Pipes

We could only scratch the surface of pipes in this chapter, but we should now have an idea of what they are and the basics of how to use them. FPGA vendor documentation has a lot more information and many examples of their use in different types of applications, so we should look there if we think that pipes are relevant for our particular needs.

Custom Memory Systems

When programming for most accelerators, much of the optimization effort tends to be spent making memory accesses more efficient. The same is true of FPGA designs, particularly when input and output data pass through off-chip memory.

There are two main reasons that memory accesses on an FPGA can be worth optimizing:

1. To reduce required bandwidth, particularly if some of that bandwidth is used inefficiently

2. To modify access patterns on a memory that is leading to unnecessary stalls in the spatial pipeline

CHAPTER 17 PROGRAMMING FOR FPGAS

It is worth talking briefly about *stalls* in the spatial pipeline. The compiler builds in assumptions about how long it will take to read from or write to specific types of memories, and it optimizes and balances the pipeline accordingly, hiding memory latencies in the process. But if we access memory in an inefficient way, we can introduce longer latencies and as a by-product stalls in the pipeline, where earlier stages cannot make progress executing because they're blocked by a pipeline stage that is waiting for something (e.g., a memory access). Figure 17-34 shows such a situation, where the pipeline above the load is stalled and unable to make forward progress.

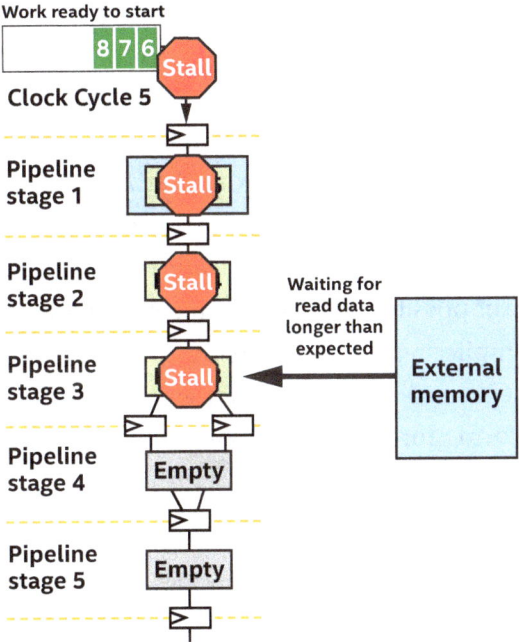

Figure 17-34. *How a memory stall can cause earlier pipeline stages to stall as well*

There are a few fronts on which memory system optimizations can be performed. As usual, the compiler reports are our primary guide to what the compiler has implemented for us and what might be worth tweaking or improving. We list a few optimization topics here to highlight some of the degrees of freedom available to us. Optimization is typically available both through explicit controls and by modifying code to allow the compiler to infer the structures that we intend. The compiler static reports and vendor documentation are key parts of memory system optimization, sometimes combined with profiling tools during hardware executions to capture actual memory behavior for validation or for the final stages of tuning.

1. **Static coalescing**: The compiler will combine memory accesses into a smaller number of wider accesses, where it can. This reduces the complexity of a memory system in terms of numbers of load or store units in the pipeline, ports on the memory system, the size and complexity of arbitration networks, and other memory system details.
   In general, we want to enable static coalescing wherever possible, which we can confirm through the compiler reports. Simplifying addressing logic in a kernel can sometimes be enough for the compiler to perform more aggressive static coalescing, so always check in the reports that the compiler has inferred what we expect!

2. **Memory access style**: The compiler creates load or store units for memory accesses, and these are tailored to both the memory technology being accessed (e.g., on-chip vs. DDR vs. HBM) and the access pattern inferred from the source code (e.g., streaming, dynamically coalesced/widened, or

likely to benefit from a cache of a specific size).
The compiler reports tell us what the compiler has
inferred and allow us to modify or add controls to
our code, where relevant, to improve performance.

3. **Memory system structure**: Memory systems (both
on- and off-chip) can have banked structures
and numerous optimizations implemented by
the compiler. There are many controls and mode
modifications that can be used to control these
structures and to tune specific aspects of the spatial
implementation.

Some Closing Topics

When talking with developers who are getting started with FPGAs, we find that it often helps to understand at a high level the components that make up the device and also to mention clock frequency which seems to be a point of confusion. We close this chapter with these topics.

FPGA Building Blocks

To help with an understanding of the tool flows (particularly compile time), it is worth mentioning the building blocks that make up an FPGA. These building blocks are abstracted away through DPC++ and SYCL, and knowledge of them plays no part in typical application development (at least in the sense of making code functional). Their existence does, however, factor into development of an intuition for spatial architecture optimization and tool flows, and occasionally in advanced optimizations when choosing the ideal data type for our application, for example.

CHAPTER 17 PROGRAMMING FOR FPGAS

A very simplified modern FPGA device consists of five basic elements.

1. **Look-up tables**: Fundamental blocks that have a few binary input wires and produce a binary output. The output relative to the inputs is defined through the entries programmed into a look-up table. These are extremely primitive blocks, but there are many of them (millions) on a typical modern FPGA used for compute. These are the basis on which much of our design is implemented!

2. **Math engines**: For common math operations such as addition or multiplication of single-precision floating-point numbers, FPGAs have specialized hardware to make those operations very efficient. A modern FPGA has thousands of these blocks—some devices have more than 8000—such that at least these many floating-point primitive operations can be performed in parallel *every clock cycle*! Most FPGAs name these math engines *Digital Signal Processors* (DSPs).

3. **On-chip memory**: This is a distinguishing aspect of FPGAs vs. other accelerators, and memories come in two flavors (more actually, but we won't get into those here): (1) registers that are used to pipeline between operations and some other purposes and (2) block memories that provide small random-access memories spread across the device. A modern FPGA can have on the order of millions of register bits and more than 10,000 20 Kbit RAM memory blocks. Since each of those can be active every clock cycle, the result is significant on-chip memory capacity and bandwidth, when used efficiently.

4. **Interfaces to off-chip hardware**: FPGAs have evolved in part because of their very flexible transceivers and input/output connectivity that allows communications with almost anything ranging from off-chip memories to network interfaces and beyond.

5. **Routing fabric between all of the other elements**: There are many of each element mentioned in the preceding text on a typical FPGA, and the connectivity between them is not fixed. A complex programmable routing fabric allows signals to pass between the fine-grained elements that make up an FPGA.

Given the numbers of blocks on an FPGA of each specific type (some blocks are counted in the millions) and the fine granularity of those blocks such as look-up tables, the compile times seen when generating FPGA configuration bitstreams may make more sense. Not only does functionality need to be assigned to each fine-grained resource but routing needs to be configured between them. Much of the compile time comes from finding a first legal mapping of our design to the FPGA fabric, before optimizations even start!

Clock Frequency

FPGAs are extremely flexible and configurable, and that configurability comes with some cost to the frequency that an FPGA runs at compared with an equivalent design hardened into a CPU or any other fixed compute architecture. But this is not a problem! The spatial architecture of an FPGA more than makes up for the clock frequency because there are so many independent operations occurring simultaneously, spread across the area of the FPGA. Simply put, the frequency of an FPGA is lower than other architectures because of the configurable design, but more happens per clock cycle which balances out the frequency. We should compare compute throughput (e.g., in operations per second) and not raw frequency when benchmarking and comparing accelerators.

This said, as we approach 100% utilization of the resources on an FPGA, operating frequency may start to decrease. This is primarily a result of signal routing resources on the device becoming overused. There are ways to remedy this, typically at the cost of increased compile time. But it's best to avoid using more than 80-90% of the resources on an FPGA for most applications unless we are willing to dive into details to counteract frequency decrease.

Rule of thumb Try not to exceed 90% of any resources on an FPGA and certainly not more than 90% of multiple resources. Exceeding may lead to exhaustion of routing resources which leads to lower operating frequencies, unless we are willing to dive into lower-level FPGA details to counteract this.

Summary

In this chapter, we have introduced how pipelining maps an algorithm to the FPGA's spatial architecture. We have also covered concepts that can help us to decide whether an FPGA is useful for our applications and that can help us get up and running developing code faster. From this starting point, we should be in good shape to browse vendor programming and optimization manuals and to start writing FPGA code! FPGAs provide performance and enable applications that wouldn't make sense on other accelerators, so we should keep them near the front of our mental toolbox!

 **Open Access** This chapter is licensed under the terms of the Creative Commons Attribution 4.0 International License (http://creativecommons.org/licenses/by/4.0/), which permits use, sharing, adaptation, distribution and reproduction in any medium or format, as long as you give appropriate credit to the original author(s) and the source, provide a link to the Creative Commons license and indicate if changes were made.

The images or other third party material in this chapter are included in the chapter's Creative Commons license, unless indicated otherwise in a credit line to the material. If material is not included in the chapter's Creative Commons license and your intended use is not permitted by statutory regulation or exceeds the permitted use, you will need to obtain permission directly from the copyright holder.

CHAPTER 18

Libraries

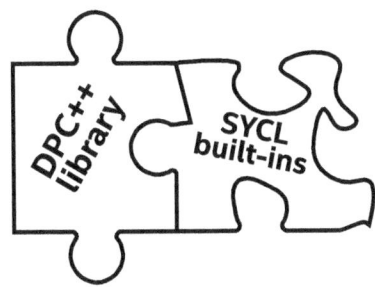

We have spent the entire book promoting the art of *writing our own code*. Now we finally acknowledge that some great programmers have already written code that we can just use. Libraries are the best way to get our work done. This is not a case of being lazy—it is a case of having better things to do than reinvent the work of others. This is a puzzle piece worth having.

The open source DPC++ project includes some libraries. These libraries can help us continue to use libstdc++, libc++, and MSVC library functions even within our kernel code. The libraries are included as part of DPC++ and the oneAPI products from Intel. These libraries are not tied to the DPC++ compiler so they can be used with any SYCL compiler.

The DPC++ library provides an alternative for programmers who create heterogeneous applications and solutions. Its APIs are based on familiar standards—C++ STL, Parallel STL (PSTL), and SYCL—to provide high-productivity APIs to programmers. This can minimize programming effort across CPUs, GPUs, and FPGAs while leading to high-performance parallel applications that are portable.

CHAPTER 18   LIBRARIES

The SYCL standard defines a rich set of built-in functions that provide functionality, for host and device code, worth considering as well. DPC++ and many SYCL implementations implement key math built-ins with math libraries.

The libraries and built-ins discussed within this chapter are compiler agnostic. In other words, they are equally applicable to DPC++ compilers or SYCL compilers. The `fpga_device_policy` class is a DPC++ feature for FPGA support.

Since there is overlap in naming and functionality, this chapter will start with a brief introduction to the SYCL built-in functions.

Built-In Functions

DPC++ provides a rich set of SYCL built-in functions with respect to various data types. These built-in functions are available in the `sycl` namespace on host and device with low-, medium-, and high-precision support for the target devices based on compiler options, for example, the `-mfma`, `-ffast-math`, and `-ffp-contract=fast` provided by the DPC++ compiler. These built-in functions on host and device can be classified as in the following:

- Floating-point math functions: asin, `acos`, `log`, `sqrt`, `floor`, etc. listed in Figure 18-2.

- Integer functions: `abs`, `max`, `min`, etc. listed in Figure 18-3.

- Common functions: `clamp`, `smoothstep`, etc. listed in Figure 18-4.

- Geometric functions: `cross`, `dot`, `distance`, etc. listed in Figure 18-5.

- Relational functions: `isequal`, `isless`, `isfinite`, etc. listed in Figure 18-6.

CHAPTER 18 LIBRARIES

If a function is provided by the C++ std library, as listed in Figure 18-8, as well as a SYCL built-in function, then DPC++ programmers are allowed to use either. Figure 18-1 demonstrates the C++ `std::log` function and SYCL built-in `sycl::log` function for host and device, and both functions produce the same numeric results. In the example, the built-in relational function `sycl::isequal` is used to compare the results of `std:log` and `sycl:log`.

```cpp
constexpr int size = 9;
std::array<double, size> A;
std::array<double, size> B;

bool pass = true;

for (int i = 0; i < size; ++i) { A[i] = i; B[i] = i; }

queue Q;
range sz{size};

buffer<double> bufA(A);
buffer<double> bufB(B);
buffer<bool>   bufP(&pass, 1);

Q.submit([&](handler &h) {
  accessor accA{ bufA, h};
  accessor accB{ bufB, h};
  accessor accP{ bufP, h};

  h.parallel_for(size, [=](id<1> idx) {
    accA[idx] = std::log(accA[idx]);
    accB[idx] = sycl::log(accB[idx]);
    if (!sycl::isequal( accA[idx], accB[idx]) ) {
      accP[0] = false;
    }
  });
});
```

Figure 18-1. *Using* `std::log` *and* `sycl::log`

In addition to the data types supported in SYCL, the DPC++ device library provides support for `std:complex` as a data type and the corresponding math functions defined in the C++ std library.

Use the `sycl::` Prefix with Built-In Functions

The SYCL built-in functions should be invoked with an explicit `sycl::` prepended to the name. With the current SYCL specification, calling just `sqrt()` is not guaranteed to invoke the SYCL built-in on all implementations even if "`using namespace sycl;`" has been used.

SYCL built-in functions should always be invoked with an explicit `sycl::` in front of the built-in name. Failure to follow this advice may result in strange and non-portable results.

If a built-in function name conflicts with a non-templated function in our application, in many implementations (including DPC++), our function will prevail, thanks to C++ overload resolution rules that prefer a non-templated function over a templated one. However, if our code has a function name that is the same as a built-in name, the most portable thing to do is either avoid `using namespace sycl;` or make sure no actual conflict happens. Otherwise, some SYCL compilers will refuse to compile the code due to an unresolvable conflict within their implementation. Such a conflict will not be silent. Therefore, if our code compiles today, we can safely ignore the possibility of future problems.

CHAPTER 18 LIBRARIES

Function			Description
Tf **acos**(Tf x)			Arc cosine
Tf **acosh**(Tf x)			Inverse hyperbolic cosine
Tf **acospi**(Tf x)			acos(x) / π
Tf **asin**(Tf x)			Arc sine
Tf **asinh**(Tf x)			Inverse hyperbolic sine
Tf **asinpi**(Tf x)			asin(x) / π
Tf **atan**(Tf y_over_x)			Arc tangent
Tf **atan2**(Tf y,Tf x)			Arc tangent of y / x
Tf **atanh**(Tf x)			Hyperbolic arc tangent
Tf **atanpi**(Tf x)			atan(x) / π
Tf **atan2pi**(Tf x,Tf y)			atan2(y,x) / π
Tf **cbrt**(Tf x)			Cube root
Tf **ceil**(Tf x)			Round to integer toward + infinity
Tf **copysign**(Tf x,Tf y)			x with sign changed to sign of y
Tf **cos**(Tf x)		H	Cosine
Tf **cosh**(Tf x)	N		Hyperbolic cosine
Tf **cospi**(Tf x)			cos(π x)
Tf **divide**(Tf x,Tf y)	*N		x / y
Tf **erfc**(Tf x)			Complementary error function
Tf **erf**(Tf x)			Calculates error function
Tf **exp**(Tf x)	N	H	Exponential base e
Tf **exp2**(Tf x)	N	H	Exponential base 2
Tf **exp10**(Tf x)	N	H	Exponential base 10
Tf **expm1**(Tf x)	N	H	ex -1.0
Tf **fabs**(Tf x)			Absolute value
Tf **fdim**(Tf x,Tf y)			Positive difference between x and y
Tf **floor**(Tf x)			Round to integer toward infinity
Tf **fma**(Tf a,Tf b,Tf c)			Multiply and add, then round
Tf **fmax**(Tf x,Tf y)			Return y if x < y, otherwise it returns x
Tf **fmin**(Tf x,Tf y)			
Tf **fmod**(Tf x,Tf y)			Modulus. Returns x − y trunc(x/y)
floatn **fract**(floatn x, intn *iptr)			Fractional value in x
float **fract**(float x, int *iptr)			
doublen **frexp**(doublen x, intn *exp)			Extract mantissa and exponent
double **frexp**(double x, int *exp)			
Tf **hypot**(Tf x,Tf y)			Square root of x2 + y2
int **logb**(float x)			Return exponent as an integer value
intn **ilogb**(Tf x)			
int **logb**(double x)			
intn **logb**(doublen x)			

Function			Description
Tf **ldexp**(Tf x,Ti k)			x * 2^n
floatn **ldexp**(floatn x, int k)			
doublen **ldexp**(doublen x , int k)			
Tf **lgamma**(Tf x)			Log gamma function.
Tf **lgamma_r**(Tf x,Ti*signp)			
Tf **log**(Tf)	N	H	Natural logarithm
Tf **log2**(Tf)	N	H	Base 2 logarithm
Tf **log10**(Tf)	N	H	Base 10 logarithm
Tf **log1p**(Tf x)			ln(1.0 + x)
Tf **logb**(Tf x)			Exponent of x
Tf **mad**(Tf a,Tf b,Tf c)			Approximates a * b + c
Tf **maxmag**(Tf x,Tf y)			Maximum magnitude of x and y
Tf **minmag**(Tf x,Tf y)			Minimum magnitude of x and y
Tf **modf**(Tf x,Tf *iptr)			Decompose floating-point number
floatn **nan**(uintn nancode)			Quiet NaN (Return is scalar when nancode is scalar)
float **nan**(unsigned int nancode)			
doublen **nan**(ulonglongn nancode)			
double **nan**(longlong int nancode)			
Tf **nextafter**(Tf x,Tf y)			Next representable floating-point value after x in the direction of y
Tf **pow**(Tf x,Tf y)			Compute x to the power of y
Tf **pown**(Tf x,Ti y)			Compute x y, where y is an integer
Tf **powr**(Tf x,Tf y)		N	Compute x y, where x is >= 0
Tf **recip**(Tf x)		*N H	1 / x
Tf **remainder**(Tf x,Tf y)			Floating point remainder
Tf **remquo**(Tf x,Tf y,Ti *q)			Remainder and quotient
Tf **rint**(Tf)			Round to nearest even integer
Tf **rootn**(Tf x,Ti y)			Compute x to the power of 1/y
Tf **round**(Tf x)			Integral value nearest to x rounding
Tf **rsqrt**(Tf x)	N	H	Inverse square root
Tf **sin**(Tf)	N	H	Sine
Tf **sincos**(Tf x,Tf *cosval)			Sine and cosine of x
Tf **sinh**(Tf x)			Hyperbolic sine
Tf **sinpi**(Tf x)			sin(π x)
Tf **sqrt**(Tf x)	N	H	Square root
Tf **tan**(Tf x)	N	H	Tangent
Tf **tanh**(Tf x)			Hyperbolic tangent
Tf **tanpi**(Tf x)			tan(π x)
Tf **tgamma**(Tf x)			Gamma function
Tf **trunc**(Tf x)			Round to integer toward zero

For floatn, doublen, and intn: n is 2, 3, 4, 8, or 16.
Tf (genfloat in the spec) is type float, floatn, double, or doublen.
sTf (sgenfloat in the spec) is type float or double.
Ti (genint in the spec) is type int or intn.
N indicates that native variants are available.
*N indicates availability only in native forms.
H indicates availability in half-precision for devices with fp16 extension available.

Figure 18-2. Built-in math functions

Tui **abs**(Ti x)	| x |
Tui **abs_diff**(Ti x,Ti y)	| x - y | without modulo overflow
Ti **add_sat** (Ti x,Ti y)	x + y and saturates the result
Ti **hadd**(Ti x,Ti y)	(x + y) >> 1 without mod. overflow
Ti **rhadd**(Ti x,Ti y)	(x + y + 1) >> 1
Ti **clamp**(Ti x,Ti min,Ti max)	min(max(x,min),max)
Ti **clamp**(Ti x,Tsi min,Tsi max)	min(max(x,min),max)
Ti **clz**(Ti x)	number of leading zero-bits in x; special case for x == 0: returns the size in bits of the type of x, or the component type of x if x is a vector type.
Ti **ctz**(Ti x)	Same as clz() but for *trailing* zero-bits
Ti **mad_hi**(Ti a,Ti b,Ti c)	mul_hi(a,b) + c
Ti **mad_sat** (Ti a,Ti b,Ti c)	a * b + c and saturates the result
Ti **max**(Ti x,Ti y)	y if x < y,otherwise it returns x
Ti **max**(Ti x,Tsi y)	y if x < y,otherwise it returns x
Ti **min**(Ti x,Ti y)	y if y < x,otherwise it returns x
Ti **min**(Ti x,Tsi y)	y if y < x,otherwise it returns x
Ti **mul_hi**(Ti x,Ti y)	high half of the product of x and y
Ti **popcount** (Ti x)	Number of non-zero bits in x
Ti **rotate**(Ti v,Ti i)	result[indx] = v[indx] << i[indx]
Ti **sub_sat**(Ti x,Ti y)	x - y and saturates the result
T popcount(T x)	Number of non-zero bits in x
shortn **upsample**(charn hi,ucharn lo)	result[i]=((short)hi[i]<< 8)|lo[i]
ushortn **upsample**(ucharn hi,ucharn lo)	result[i]=((ushort)hi[i]<< 8)|lo[i]
intn **upsample**(shortn hi,ushortn lo)	result[i]=((int)hi[i]<< 16)|lo[i]
uintn **upsample**(ushortn hi,ushortn lo)	result[i]=((uint)hi[i]<< 16)|lo[i]
longlongn **upsample**(intn hi,uintn lo)	result[i]=((long)hi[i]<< 32)|lo[i]
ulonglongn **upsample**(uintn hi,uintn lo)	result[i]=((ulong)hi[i]<< 32)|lo[i]
intn **mad24**(intn x,intn y,intn z)	Multiply 24-bit integer values x,y,add 32-bit int. result to 32-bit integer z
uintn **mad24**(uintn x,uintn y,uintn z)	Multiply 24-bit integer values x,y,add 32-bit int. result to 32-bit integer z
intn **mul24**(intn x,intn y)	Multiply 24-bit integer values x and y
uintn **mul24**(uintn x,uintn y)	Multiply 24-bit integer values x and y

T (gentype in the spec) is all integer and float types.
Ti (geninteger in spec) is all signed and unsigned integer types.
Tsi (sgeninteger in the spec) is all scalar integer types.
Tui (ugeninteger in the spec) is all unsigned integer types.

Figure 18-3. Built-in integer functions

Tf **clamp**(Tf x,Tf minval,Tf maxval) floatn **clamp** (floatn x,float minval,float maxval) doublen **clamp** (doublen x,double minval,double maxval)	Clamp x to range given by minval,maxval
Tf **degrees**(Tf radians)	radians to degrees
Tf **max**(Tf x,Tf y) Tff **max**(Tff x,float y) Tfd **max**(Tfd x,double y)	Max of x and y
Tf **min**(Tf x,Tf y) Tff **min**(Tff x,float y) Tfd **min**(Tfd x,double y)	Min of x and y
Tf **mix**(Tf x,Tf y,Tf a) Tff **mix**(Tff x,Tff y,float a) Tfd **mix**(Tfd x,Tfd y,double a)	Linear blend of x and y
Tf **radians**(Tf degrees)	degrees to radians
Tf **step**(Tf edge,Tf x) Tff **step**(float edge,Tff x) Tfd **step**(double edge,Tfd x)	0.0 if x < edge,else 1.0
Tf **smoothstep** (Tf edge0,Tf edge1,Tf x) Tff **smoothstep**(float edge0,float edge1,Tff x); Tfd **smoothstep**(double edge0,double edge1,Tfd x)	Step and interpolate
Tf **sign**(Tf x)	Sign of x

For floatn and doublen: n is 2, 3, 4, 8, or 16.
Tf (genfloat in the spec) is float, floatn, double, or doublen types.
Tff (genfloatf in the spec) is float or floatn types.
Tfd (genfloatd in the spec) is double or doublen types.

Figure 18-4. Built-in common functions

T34 cross (T34 p0,T34 p1)	Cross product
T distance(Tn p0,Tn p1)	Vector distance
T dot(Tn p0,Tn p1)	Dot product
T length(Tn p)	Vector length
Tn normalize(Tn p)	Normal vector length 1
float fast_distance(floatn p0,floatn p1)	Vector distance
float fast_length(floatn p)	Vector length
floatn fast_normalize(floatn p)	Normal vector length 1

For Tn: n is 2, 3, 4, 8, or 16.
T34 means either T3 or T4.
T is type float, floatn, double, or doublen, consistently applied per function.

Figure 18-5. Built-in geometric functions

CHAPTER 18 LIBRARIES

Functions F(...) can be: isequal isnotequal isgreater isgreaterequal isless islessequal islessgreater isordered isunordered	int F(float x,float y) intn F(floatn x,floatn y) long long F(double x,double y) long longn F(doublen x,doublen y)
Functions F(...) can be: isfinite isinf isnan isnormal signbit	int F(float) intn F(floatn) long long F(double) long longn F(doublen)
int **any**(Ti x)	1 if MSB in component of x is set; else 0
int **all**(Ti x)	1 if MSB in all components of x are set else 0
T **bitselect** (T a,T b,T c)	Each bit of result is corresponding bit of a if corresponding bit of c is 0
T **select** (T a,T b,Ti c)	For each component of a vector type,result[i] = if MSB of c[i] is set ? b[i] : a[i] For scalar type,result = c ? b : a

For intn and longn: n is 2, 3, 4, 8, or 16.
T (gentype in the spec) is all signed , unsigned, float, double, scalar and vector types.
Ti (geninteger in spec) is signed and unsigned integer types.
Tui (ugeninteger in the spec) is all unsigned integer types.

Figure 18-6. Built-in relational functions

DPC++ Library

The DPC++ library consists of the following components:

- A set of tested C++ standard APIs—we simply need to include the corresponding C++ standard header files and use the `std` namespace.

- Parallel STL that includes corresponding header files. We simply use `#include <dpstd/...>` to include them. The DPC++ library uses namespace `dpstd` for the extended API classes and functions.

CHAPTER 18 LIBRARIES

Standard C++ APIs in DPC++

The DPC++ library contains a set of tested standard C++ APIs. The basic functionality for a number of C++ standard APIs has been developed so that these APIs can be employed in device kernels similar to how they are employed in code for a typical C++ host application. Figure 18-7 shows an example of how to use `std::swap` in device code.

```cpp
class KernelSwap;
std::array <int,2> arr{8,9};
buffer<int> buf{arr};

{
  host_accessor host_A(buf);
  std::cout << "Before: " << host_A[0] << ", " << host_A[1] << "\n";
} // End scope of host_A so that upcoming kernel can operate on buf

queue Q;
Q.submit([&](handler &h) {
  accessor A{buf, h};
  h.single_task([=]() {
  // Call std::swap!
  std::swap(A[0], A[1]);
  });
});

host_accessor host_B(buf);
std::cout << "After:  " << host_B[0] << ", " << host_B[1] << "\n";
```

Figure 18-7. Using `std::swap` in device code

We can use the following command to build and run the program (assuming it resides in the stdswap.cpp file):

```
dpcpp -std=c++17 stdswap.cpp -o stdswap.exe
./stdswap.exe
```

The printed result is:

8, 9
9, 8

Figure 18-8 lists C++ standard APIs with "*Y*" to indicate those that have been tested for use in DPC++ kernels for CPU, GPU, *and* FPGA devices, at the time of this writing. A blank indicates incomplete coverage (not all three device types) at the time of publication for this book. A table is also included as part of the online DPC++ language reference guide and will be updated over time—the library support in DPC++ will continue to expand its support.

In the DPC++ library, some C++ std functions are implemented based on their corresponding built-in functions on the device to achieve the same level of performance as the SYCL versions of these functions.

CHAPTER 18 LIBRARIES

C++ standard API	libstdc++	libc++	MSVS
std::acos	Y		
std::acosh	Y		
std::add_const	Y	Y	Y
std::add_cv	Y	Y	Y
std::add_volatile	Y	Y	Y
std::alignment_of	Y	Y	Y
std::array	Y	Y	Y
std::asin	Y		
std::is_fundamental	Y	Y	Y
std::is_literal_type	Y	Y	Y
std::is_member_pointer	Y	Y	Y
std::is_move_assignable	Y	Y	Y
std::is_move_constructible	Y	Y	Y
std::is_object	Y	Y	Y
std::is_pod	Y	Y	Y
std::is_reference	Y	Y	Y
std::is_fundamental	Y	Y	Y
std::is_literal_type	Y	Y	Y
std::is_member_pointer	Y	Y	Y
std::is_move_assignable	Y	Y	Y
std::is_move_constructible	Y	Y	Y
std::is_object	Y	Y	Y
std::is_pod	Y	Y	Y
std::asinh	Y		
std::assert	Y		Y
std::atan	Y		
std::atan2	Y		
std::atanh	Y		
std::binary_negate	Y	Y	Y
std::binary_search	Y	Y	Y
std::bit_and	Y	Y	Y
std::bit_not	Y	Y	Y
std::bit_or	Y	Y	Y
std::bit_xor	Y	Y	Y
std::cbrt	Y		
std::common_type	Y	Y	Y
std::complex	Y		
std::conditional	Y	Y	Y
std::cos	Y		
std::cosh	Y		
std::decay	Y	Y	Y
std::declval	Y	Y	Y
std::divides	Y	Y	Y
std::enable_if	Y	Y	Y
std::equal_range	Y	Y	Y
std::equal_to	Y	Y	Y
std::erf	Y		
std::erfc	Y		
std::exp	Y		
std::exp2	Y		
std::expm1	Y		
std::extent	Y	Y	Y
std::fdim	Y		
std::fmod	Y		
std::forward	Y	Y	Y
std::frexp	Y		
std::greater	Y	Y	Y
std::greater_equal	Y	Y	Y
std::hypot	Y		
std::ilogb	Y		
std::initializer_list	Y	Y	Y
std::integral_constant	Y	Y	Y
std::is_arithmetic	Y	Y	Y
std::is_assignable	Y	Y	Y
std::is_base_of	Y	Y	Y
std::is_base_of_union	Y	Y	Y
std::is_compound	Y	Y	Y
std::is_const	Y	Y	Y
std::is_constructible	Y	Y	Y
std::is_convertible	Y	Y	Y
std::is_copy_assignable	Y	Y	Y
std::is_copy_constructible	Y	Y	Y
std::is_default_constructible	Y	Y	Y
std::is_destructible	Y	Y	Y
std::is_empty	Y	Y	Y
std::is_same	Y	Y	Y
std::is_scalar	Y	Y	Y
std::is_signed	Y	Y	Y
std::is_standard_layout	Y	Y	Y
std::is_trivial	Y	Y	Y
std::is_trivially_assignable	Y	Y	Y
std::is_trivially_constructible	Y	Y	Y
std::is_trivially_copyable	Y	Y	Y
std::is_unsigned	Y	Y	Y
std::is_volatile	Y	Y	Y
std::ldexp	Y		
std::less	Y	Y	Y
std::less_equal	Y	Y	Y
std::lgamma	Y		
std::log	Y		
std::log10	Y		
std::log1p	Y		
std::log2	Y		
std::logb	Y		
std::logical_and	Y	Y	Y
std::logical_not	Y	Y	Y
std::logical_or	Y	Y	Y
std::lower_bound	Y	Y	Y
std::minus	Y	Y	Y
std::modf	Y		
std::modulus	Y	Y	Y
std::move	Y	Y	Y

Figure 18-8. *Library support with CPU/GPU/FPGA coverage (at time of book publication)*

std::move if noexcept	Y	Y	Y
std::multiplies	Y	Y	Y
std::negate	Y	Y	Y
std::nextafter	Y		
std::not equal to	Y	Y	Y
std::not1/2	Y	Y	Y
std::numeric limits	Y	Y	Y
std::pair	Y	Y	Y
std::plus	Y	Y	Y
std::pow	Y		
std::rank	Y	Y	Y
std::ratio	Y	Y	Y
std::ref/cref	Y	Y	Y

std::reference wrapper	Y	Y	Y
std::remainder	Y		
std::remove all extents	Y	Y	Y
std::remove const	Y	Y	Y
std::remove cv	Y	Y	Y
std::remove extent	Y	Y	Y
std::remove volatile	Y	Y	Y
std::remquo	Y		
std::sin	Y		
std::sinh	Y		
std::sqrt	Y		
std::swap	Y	Y	Y

Figure 18.8. (*continued*)

The tested standard C++ APIs are supported in libstdc++ (GNU) with gcc 7.4.0 and libc++ (LLVM) with clang 10.0 and MSVC Standard C++ Library with Microsoft Visual Studio 2017 for the host CPU as well.

On Linux, GNU libstdc++ is the default C++ standard library for the DPC++ compiler, so no compilation or linking option is required. If we want to use libc++, use the compile options -stdlib=libc++ -nostdinc++ to leverage libc++ and to not include C++ std headers from the system. The DPC++ compiler has been verified using libc++ in DPC++ kernels on Linux, but the DPC++ runtime needs to be rebuilt with libc++ instead of libstdc++. Details are in https://intel.github.io/llvm-docs/GetStartedGuide.html#build-dpc-toolchain-with-libc-library. Because of these extra steps, libc++ is not the recommended C++ standard library for us to use in general.

On FreeBSD, libc++ is the default standard library, and the -stdlib=libc++ option is not required. More details are in https://libcxx.llvm.org/docs/UsingLibcxx.html. On Windows, only the MSVC C++ library can be used.

To achieve cross-architecture portability, if a std function is not marked with "Y" in Figure 18-8, we need to keep portability in mind when we write device functions!

DPC++ Parallel STL

Parallel STL is an implementation of the C++ standard library algorithms with support for execution policies, as specified in the ISO/IEC 14882:2017 standard, commonly called C++17. The existing implementation also supports the unsequenced execution policy specified in Parallelism TS version 2 and proposed for the next version of the C++ standard in the C++ working group paper P1001R1.

When using algorithms and execution policies, specify the namespace std::execution if there is no vendor-specific implementation of the C++17 standard library or pstl::execution otherwise.

For any of the implemented algorithms, we can pass one of the values seq, unseq, par, or par_unseq as the first parameter in a call to the algorithm to specify the desired execution policy. The policies have the following meanings:

Execution Policy	Meaning
seq	Sequential execution.
unseq	Unsequenced SIMD execution. This policy requires that all functions provided are safe to execute in SIMD.
par	Parallel execution by multiple threads.
par_unseq	Combined effect of unseq and par.

Parallel STL for DPC++ is extended with support for DPC++ devices using special execution policies. The DPC++ execution policy specifies where and how a Parallel STL algorithm runs. It inherits a standard C++ execution policy, encapsulates a SYCL device or queue, and allows us to set an optional kernel name. DPC++ execution policies can be used with all standard C++ algorithms that support execution policies according to the C++17 standard.

CHAPTER 18 LIBRARIES

DPC++ Execution Policy

Currently, only the parallel unsequenced policy (par_unseq) is supported by the DPC++ library. In order to use the DPC++ execution policy, there are three steps:

1. Add #include <dpstd/execution> into our code.

2. Create a policy object by providing a standard policy type, a class type for a unique kernel name as a template argument (optional), and one of the following constructor arguments:

    - A SYCL queue
    - A SYCL device
    - A SYCL device selector
    - An existing policy object with a different kernel name

3. Pass the created policy object to a Parallel STL algorithm.

A dpstd::execution::default_policy object is a predefined device_policy created with a default kernel name and default queue. This can be used to create custom policy objects or passed directly when invoking an algorithm if the default choices are sufficient.

Figure 18-9 shows examples that assume use of the using namespace dpstd::execution; directive when referring to policy classes and functions.

```
auto policy_b =
  device_policy<parallel_unsequenced_policy, class PolicyB>
    {sycl::device{sycl::gpu_selector{}}};
std::for_each(policy_b, …);

auto policy_c =
  device_policy<parallel_unsequenced_policy, class PolicyC>
    {sycl::default_selector{}};
std::for_each(policy_c, …);

auto policy_d = make_device_policy<class PolicyD>(default_policy);
std::for_each(policy_d, …);

auto policy_e = make_device_policy<class PolicyE>(sycl::queue{});
std::for_each(policy_e, …);
```

Figure 18-9. Creating execution policies

FPGA Execution Policy

The `fpga_device_policy` class is a DPC++ policy tailored to achieve better performance of parallel algorithms on FPGA hardware devices. Use the policy when running the application on FPGA hardware or an FPGA emulation device:

1. Define the _PSTL_FPGA_DEVICE macro to run on FPGA devices and additionally _PSTL_FPGA_EMU to run on an FPGA emulation device.

2. Add #include <dpstd/execution> to our code.

3. Create a policy object by providing a class type for a unique kernel name and an unroll factor (see Chapter 17) as template arguments (both optional) and one of the following constructor arguments:

    - A SYCL queue constructed for the FPGA selector (the behavior is undefined with any other device type)

    - An existing FPGA policy object with a different kernel name and/or unroll factor

4. Pass the created policy object to a Parallel STL algorithm.

The default constructor of fpga_device_policy creates an object with a SYCL queue constructed for fpga_selector, or for fpga_emulator_selector if _PSTL_FPGA_EMU is defined.

dpstd::execution::fpga_policy is a predefined object of the fpga_device_policy class created with a default kernel name and default unroll factor. Use it to create customized policy objects or pass it directly when invoking an algorithm.

Code in Figure 18-10 assumes using namespace dpstd::execution; for policies and using namespace sycl; for queues and device selectors.

Specifying an unroll factor for a policy enables loop unrolling in the implementation of algorithms. The default value is 1. To find out how to choose a better value, see Chapter 17.

```
auto fpga_policy_a = fpga_device_policy<class FPGAPolicyA>{};
auto fpga_policy_b = make_fpga_policy(queue{intel::fpga_selector{}});
constexpr auto unroll_factor = 8;
auto fpga_policy_c =
  make_fpga_policy<class FPGAPolicyC, unroll_factor>(fpga_policy);
```

Figure 18-10. Using FPGA policy

Using DPC++ Parallel STL

In order to use the DPC++ Parallel STL, we need to include Parallel STL header files by adding a subset of the following set of lines. These lines are dependent on the algorithms we intend to use:

- #include <dpstd/algorithm>
- #include <dpstd/numeric>
- #include <dpstd/memory>

dpstd::begin and dpstd::end are special helper functions that allow us to pass SYCL buffers to Parallel STL algorithms. These functions accept a SYCL buffer and return an object of an unspecified type that satisfies the following requirements:

- Is CopyConstructible, CopyAssignable, and comparable with operators == and !=.

- The following expressions are valid: a + n, a - n, and a - b, where a and b are objects of the type and n is an integer value.

- Has a get_buffer method with no arguments. The method returns the SYCL buffer passed to dpstd::begin and dpstd::end functions.

To use these helper functions, add #include <dpstd/iterators> to our code. See the code in Figures 18-11 and 18-12 using the std::fill function as examples that use the begin/end helpers.

```
#include <dpstd/execution>
#include <dpstd/algorithm>
#include <dpstd/iterators>

sycl::queue Q;
sycl::buffer<int> buf { 1000 };

auto buf_begin = dpstd::begin(buf);
auto buf_end   = dpstd::end(buf);

auto policy = dpstd::execution::make_device_policy<class fill>( Q );
std::fill(policy, buf_begin, buf_end, 42);
// each element of vec equals to 42
```

Figure 18-11. Using std::fill

REDUCE DATA COPYING BETWEEN THE HOST AND DEVICE

Parallel STL algorithms can be called with ordinary (host-side) iterators, as seen in the code example in Figure 18-11.

In this case, a temporary SYCL buffer is created, and the data is copied to this buffer. After processing of the temporary buffer on a device is complete, the data is copied back to the host. Working directly with existing SYCL buffers, where possible, is recommended to reduce data movement between the host and device and any unnecessary overhead of buffer creations and destructions.

```
#include <dpstd/execution>
#include <dpstd/algorithm>

std::vector<int> v( 1000000 );
std::fill(dpstd::execution::default_policy, v.begin(), v.end(), 42);
// each element of vec equals to 42
```

Figure 18-12. Using `std::fill` *with default policy*

Figure 18-13 shows an example which performs a binary search of the input sequence for each of the values in the search sequence provided. As the result of a search for the ith element of the search sequence, a Boolean value indicating whether the search value was found in the input sequence is assigned to the ith element of the result sequence. The algorithm returns an iterator that points to one past the last element of the result sequence that was assigned a result. The algorithm assumes that the input sequence has been sorted by the comparator provided. If no comparator is provided, then a function object that uses `operator<` to compare the elements will be used.

The complexity of the preceding description highlights that we should leverage library functions where possible, instead of writing our own implementations of similar algorithms which may take significant debugging and tuning time. Authors of the libraries that we can take advantage of are often experts in the internals of the device architectures to which they are coding, and may have access to information that we do not, so we should always leverage optimized libraries when they are available.

The code example shown in Figure 18-13 demonstrates the three typical steps when using a DPC++ Parallel STL algorithm:

- Create DPC++ iterators.

- Create a named policy from an existing policy.

- Invoke the parallel algorithm.

The example in Figure 18-13 uses the `dpstd::binary_search` algorithm to perform binary search on a CPU, GPU, or FPGA, based on our device selection.

CHAPTER 18 LIBRARIES

```cpp
#include <dpstd/execution>
#include <dpstd/algorithm>
#include <dpstd/iterator>

buffer<uint64_t, 1> kB{ range<1>(10) };
buffer<uint64_t, 1> vB{ range<1>(5) };
buffer<uint64_t, 1> rB{ range<1>(5) };

accessor k{kB};
accessor v{vB};

// create dpc++ iterators
auto k_beg = dpstd::begin(kB);
auto k_end = dpstd::end(kB);
auto v_beg = dpstd::begin(vB);
auto v_end = dpstd::end(vB);
auto r_beg = dpstd::begin(rB);

// create named policy from existing one
auto policy = dpstd::execution::make_device_policy<class bSearch>
  (dpstd::execution::default_policy);

// call algorithm
dpstd::binary_search(policy, k_beg, k_end, v_beg, v_end, r_beg);

// check data
accessor r{rB};
if ((r[0] == false) && (r[1] == true) &&
    (r[2] == false) && (r[3] == true) && (r[4] == true)) {
  std::cout << "Passed.\nRun on "
            << policy.queue().get_device().get_info<info::device::name>()
            << "\n";
} else
  std::cout << "failed: values do not match.\n";
```

Figure 18-13. Using binary_search

Using Parallel STL with USM

The following examples describe two ways to use the Parallel STL algorithms in combination with USM:

- Through USM pointers
- Through USM allocators

If we have a USM allocation, we can pass the pointers to the start and (one past the) end of the allocation to a parallel algorithm. It is important to be sure that the execution policy and the allocation itself were created for the same queue or context, to avoid undefined behavior at runtime.

If the same allocation is to be processed by several algorithms, either use an in-order queue or explicitly wait for completion of each algorithm before using the same allocation in the next one (this is typical operation ordering when using USM). Also wait for completion before accessing the data on the host, as shown in Figure 18-14.

Alternatively, we can use `std::vector` with a USM allocator as shown in Figure 18-15.

```
#include <dpstd/execution>
#include <dpstd/algorithm>

sycl::queue q;
const int n = 10;
int* d_head = static_cast<int*>(
  sycl::malloc_device(n * sizeof(int),
                      q.get_device(),
                      q.get_context()));

std::fill(dpstd::execution::make_device_policy(q),
          d_head, d_head + n, 78);
q.wait();

sycl::free(d_head, q.get_context());
```

Figure 18-14. Using Parallel STL with a USM pointer

```
#include <dpstd/execution>
#include <dpstd/algorithm>

sycl::queue Q;
const int n = 10;
sycl::usm_allocator<int, sycl::usm::alloc::shared>
                    alloc(Q.get_context(), Q.get_device());
std::vector<int, decltype(alloc)> vec(n, alloc);

std::fill(dpstd::execution::make_device_policy(Q),
                           vec.begin(), vec.end(), 78);
Q.wait();
```

Figure 18-15. Using Parallel STL with a USM allocator

CHAPTER 18 LIBRARIES

Error Handling with DPC++ Execution Policies

As detailed in Chapter 5, the DPC++ error handling model supports two types of errors. With *synchronous* errors, the runtime throws exceptions, while *asynchronous* errors are only processed in a user-supplied error handler at specified times during program execution.

For Parallel STL algorithms executed with DPC++ policies, handling of all errors, synchronous or asynchronous, is a responsibility of the caller. Specifically

- No exceptions are thrown explicitly by algorithms.

- Exceptions thrown by the runtime on the host CPU, including DPC++ synchronous exceptions, are passed through to the caller.

- DPC++ asynchronous errors are not handled by the Parallel STL, so must be handled (if any handling is desired) by the calling application.

To process DPC++ asynchronous errors, the queue associated with a DPC++ policy must be created with an error handler object. The predefined policy objects (default_policy and others) have no error handlers, so we should create our own policies if we need to process asynchronous errors.

Summary

The DPC++ library is a companion to the DPC++ compiler. It helps us with solutions for portions of our heterogeneous applications, using pre-built and tuned libraries for common functions and parallel patterns. The DPC++ library allows explicit use of the C++ STL API within kernels, it streamlines cross-architecture programming with Parallel STL algorithm extensions, and it increases the successful application of parallel

CHAPTER 18 LIBRARIES

algorithms with custom iterators. In addition to support for familiar libraries (libstdc++, libc++, MSVS), DPC++ also provides full support for SYCL built-in functions. This chapter overviewed options for leveraging the work of others instead of having to write everything ourselves, and we should use that approach wherever practical to simplify application development and often to realize superior performance.

 **Open Access** This chapter is licensed under the terms of the Creative Commons Attribution 4.0 International License (http://creativecommons.org/licenses/by/4.0/), which permits use, sharing, adaptation, distribution and reproduction in any medium or format, as long as you give appropriate credit to the original author(s) and the source, provide a link to the Creative Commons license and indicate if changes were made.

The images or other third party material in this chapter are included in the chapter's Creative Commons license, unless indicated otherwise in a credit line to the material. If material is not included in the chapter's Creative Commons license and your intended use is not permitted by statutory regulation or exceeds the permitted use, you will need to obtain permission directly from the copyright holder.

CHAPTER 19

Memory Model and Atomics

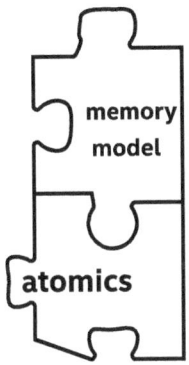

Memory consistency is not an esoteric concept if we want to be good parallel programmers. It is a critical piece of our puzzle, helping us to ensure that data is where we need it when we need it and that its values are what we are expecting. This chapter brings to light key things we need to master in order to ensure our program hums along correctly. This topic is not unique to SYCL or to DPC++.

Having a basic understanding of the memory (consistency) model of a programming language is necessary for *any* programmer who wants to allow concurrent updates to memory (whether those updates originate from multiple work-items in the same kernel, multiple devices, or both). This is true regardless of how memory is allocated, and the content of this chapter is equally important to us whether we choose to use buffers or USM allocations.

CHAPTER 19   MEMORY MODEL AND ATOMICS

In previous chapters, we have focused on the development of simple kernels, where program instances either operate on completely independent data or share data using structured communication patterns that can be expressed directly using language and/or library features. As we move toward writing more complex and realistic kernels, we are likely to encounter situations where program instances may need to communicate in less structured ways—understanding how the memory model relates to DPC++ language features and the capabilities of the hardware we are targeting is a necessary precondition for designing correct, portable, and efficient programs.

The memory consistency model of standard C++ is sufficient for writing applications that execute entirely on the host device, but is modified by DPC++ in order to address complexities that may arise when programming heterogeneous systems and when talking about program instances that do not map cleanly to the concept of C++ threads. Specifically, we need to be able to

- Reason about which types of memory allocation can be accessed by which devices in the system: using buffers and USM.

- Prevent unsafe concurrent memory accesses (data races) during the execution of our kernels: using barriers and atomics.

- Enable safe communication between program instances executing the same kernel and safe communication between different devices: using barriers, fences, atomics, memory orders, and memory scopes.

- Prevent optimizations that may alter the behavior of parallel applications in ways that are incompatible with our expectations: using barriers, fences, atomics, memory orders, and memory scopes.

CHAPTER 19 MEMORY MODEL AND ATOMICS

- Enable optimizations that depend on knowledge of programmer intent: using memory orders and memory scopes.

Memory models are a complex topic, but for a good reason—processor architects care about making processors and accelerators execute our codes as efficiently as possible! We have worked hard in this chapter to break down this complexity and highlight the most critical concepts and language features. This chapter starts us down the path of not only knowing the memory model inside and out but also enjoying an important aspect of parallel programming that many people don't know exists. If questions remain after reading the descriptions and example codes here, we highly recommend visiting the websites listed at the end of this chapter or referring to the C++, SYCL, and DPC++ language specifications.

What Is in a Memory Model?

This section expands upon the motivation for programming languages to contain a memory model and introduces a few core concepts that parallel programmers should familiarize themselves with:

- Data races and synchronization
- Barriers and fences
- Atomic operations
- Memory ordering

Understanding these concepts at a high level is necessary to appreciate their expression and usage in C++, SYCL, and DPC++. Readers with extensive experience in parallel programming, especially using C++, may wish to skip ahead.

497

Data Races and Synchronization

The *operations* that we write in our programs typically do not map directly to a single hardware instruction or micro-operation. A simple addition operation such as data[i] += x may be broken down into a sequence of several instructions or micro-operations:

1. Load data[i] from memory into a temporary (register).
2. Compute the result of adding x to data[i].
3. Store the result back to data[i].

This is not something that we need to worry about when developing sequential applications—the three stages of the addition will be executed in the order that we expect, as depicted in Figure 19-1.

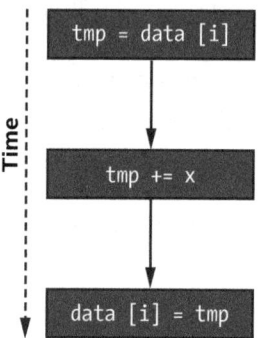

Figure 19-1. *Sequential execution of data[i] += x broken into three separate operations*

Switching to parallel application development introduces an extra level of complexity: if we have multiple operations being applied to the same data concurrently, how can we be certain that their view of that data is consistent? Consider the situation shown in Figure 19-2, where two executions of data[i] += x have been interleaved. If the two executions use different values of i, the application will execute correctly. If they use the same value of i, both load the same value from memory, and one of the results is overwritten by the other! This is just one of many possible ways in which their operations could be scheduled, and the behavior of our application depends on which program instance gets to which data first—our application contains a *data race*.

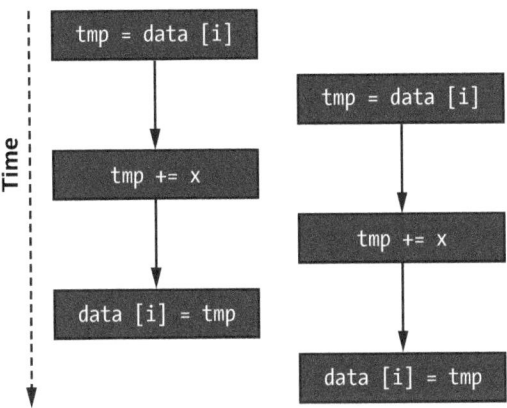

Figure 19-2. *One possible interleaving of* data[i] += x *executed concurrently*

The code in Figure 19-3 and its output in Figure 19-4 show how easily this can happen in practice. If M is greater than or equal to N, the value of j in each program instance is unique; if it isn't, values of j will conflict, and updates may be lost. We say *may* be lost because a program containing a data race could still produce the correct answer some or all of the time (depending on how work is scheduled by the implementation and hardware). Neither the compiler nor the hardware can possibly know what this program is *intended* to do or what the values of N and M may be at runtime—it is our responsibility as programmers to understand whether our programs may contain data races and whether they are sensitive to execution order.

CHAPTER 19   MEMORY MODEL AND ATOMICS

```
int* data = malloc_shared<int>(N, Q);
std::fill(data, data + N, 0);

Q.parallel_for(N, [=](id<1> i) {
   int j = i % M;
   data[j] += 1;
}).wait();

for (int i = 0; i < N; ++i) {
   std::cout << "data [" << i << "] = " << data[i] << "\n";
}
```

Figure 19-3. Kernel containing a data race

```
N = 2, M = 2:
data [0] = 1
data [1] = 1

N = 2, M = 1:
data [0] = 1
data [1] = 0
```

Figure 19-4. Sample output of the code in Figure 19-3 for small values of N and M

In general, when developing massively parallel applications, we should not concern ourselves with the exact order in which individual work-items execute—there are hopefully hundreds (or thousands!) of work-items executing concurrently, and trying to impose a specific ordering upon them will negatively impact both scalability and performance. Rather, our focus should be on developing portable applications that execute correctly, which we can achieve by providing the compiler (and hardware) with information about when program instances share data, what guarantees are needed when sharing occurs, and which execution orderings are legal.

CHAPTER 19 MEMORY MODEL AND ATOMICS

Massively parallel applications should not be concerned with the exact order in which individual work-items execute!

Barriers and Fences

One way to prevent data races between work-items in the same group is to introduce synchronization across different program instances using work-group barriers and appropriate memory fences. We could use a work-group barrier to order our updates of data[i] as shown in Figure 19-5, and an updated version of our example kernel is given in Figure 19-6. Note that because a work-group barrier does not synchronize work-items in different groups, our simple example is only guaranteed to execute correctly if we limit ourselves to a single work-group!

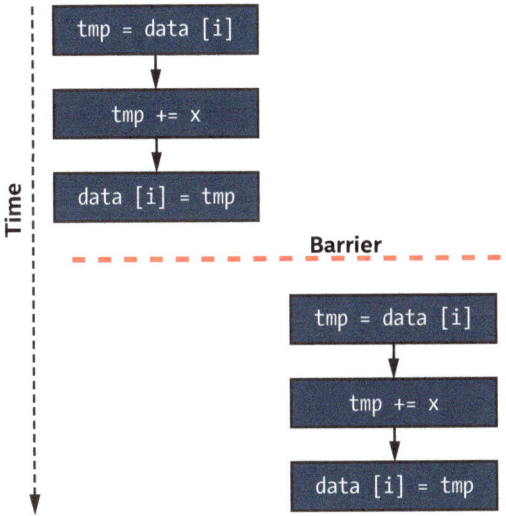

Figure 19-5. *Two instances of* data[i] += x *separated by a barrier*

501

```
int* data = malloc_shared<int>(N, Q);
std::fill(data, data + N, 0);

// Launch exactly one work-group
// Number of work-groups = global / local
range<1> global{N};
range<1> local{N};

Q.parallel_for(nd_range<1>{global, local}, [=](nd_item<1> it) {
   int i = it.get_global_id(0);
   int j = i % M;
   for (int round = 0; round < N; ++round) {
     // Allow exactly one work-item update per round
     if (i == round) {
       data[j] += 1;
     }
     it.barrier();
   }
}).wait();

for (int i = 0; i < N; ++i) {
  std::cout << "data [" << i << "] = " << data[i] << "\n";
}
```

Figure 19-6. Avoiding a data race using a barrier

Although using a barrier to implement this pattern is possible, it is not typically encouraged—it forces the work-items in a group to execute sequentially and in a specific order, which may lead to long periods of inactivity in the presence of load imbalance. It may also introduce more synchronization than is strictly necessary—if the different program instances happen to use different values of i, they will still be forced to synchronize at the barrier.

Barrier synchronization is a useful tool for ensuring that all work-items in a work-group or sub-group complete some stage of a kernel before proceeding to the next stage, but is too heavy-handed for fine-grained (and potentially data-dependent) synchronization. For more general synchronization patterns, we must look to *atomic* operations.

CHAPTER 19 MEMORY MODEL AND ATOMICS

Atomic Operations

Atomic operations enable concurrent access to a memory location without introducing a data race. When multiple atomic operations access the same memory, they are guaranteed not to overlap. Note that this guarantee does not apply if only some of the accesses use atomics and that it is our responsibility as programmers to ensure that we do not concurrently access the same data using operations with different atomicity guarantees.

> Mixing atomic and non-atomic operations on the same memory location(s) at the same time results in undefined behavior!

If our simple addition is expressed using atomic operations, the result may look like Figure 19-8—each update is now an indivisible chunk of work, and our application will always produce the correct result. The corresponding code is shown in Figure 19-7—we will revisit the atomic_ref class and the meaning of its template arguments later in the chapter.

```
int* data = malloc_shared<int>(N, Q);
std::fill(data, data + N, 0);

Q.parallel_for(N, [=](id<1> i) {
   int j = i % M;
   atomic_ref<int, memory_order::relaxed, memory_scope::system,
              access::address_space::global_space> atomic_data(data[j]);
   atomic_data += 1;
}).wait();

for (int i = 0; i < N; ++i) {
   std::cout << "data [" << i << "] = " << data[i] << "\n";
}
```

Figure 19-7. Avoiding a data race using atomic operations

503

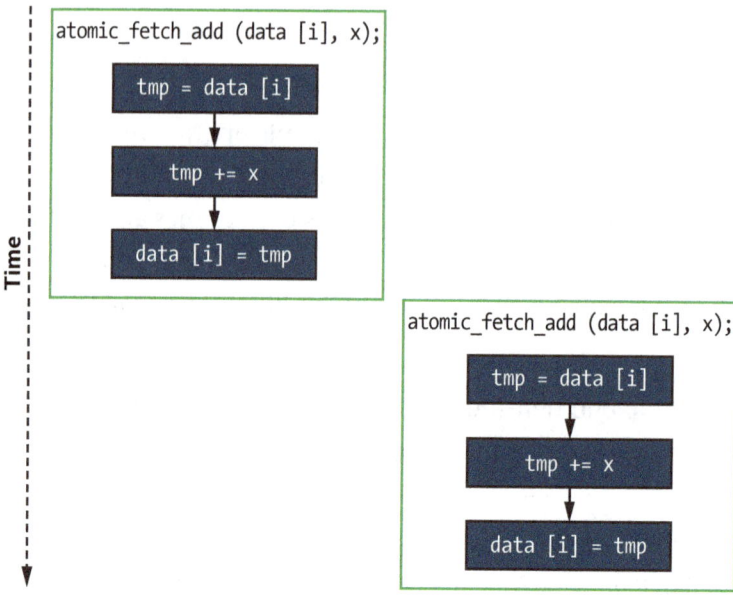

Figure 19-8. *An interleaving of* data[i] += x *executed concurrently with atomic operations*

However, it is important to note that this is still only one possible execution order. Using atomic operations guarantees that the two updates do not overlap (if both instances use the same value of i), but there is still no guarantee as to which of the two instances will execute first. Even more importantly, there are no guarantees about how these atomic operations are ordered with respect to any *non-atomic* operations in different program instances.

Memory Ordering

Even within a sequential application, optimizing compilers and the hardware are free to re-order operations if they do not change the observable behavior of an application. In other words, the application must behave *as if* it ran exactly as it was written by the programmer.

Unfortunately, this as-if guarantee is not strong enough to help us reason about the execution of parallel programs. We now have two sources of re-ordering to worry about: the compiler and hardware may re-order the execution of statements within each sequential program instance, and the program instances themselves may be executed in any (possibly interleaved) order. In order to design and implement safe communication protocols between program instances, we need to be able to constrain this re-ordering. By providing the compiler with information about our desired *memory order*, we can prevent re-ordering optimizations that are incompatible with the intended behavior of our applications.

Three commonly available memory orderings are

1. A *relaxed* memory ordering
2. An *acquire-release* or *release-acquire* memory ordering
3. A *sequentially consistent* memory ordering

Under a relaxed memory ordering, memory operations can be re-ordered without any restrictions. The most common usage of a relaxed memory model is incrementing shared variables (e.g., a single counter, an array of values during a histogram computation).

Under an acquire-release memory ordering, one program instance *releasing* an atomic variable and another program instance *acquiring* the same atomic variable acts as a synchronization point between those two program instances and guarantees that any prior writes to memory issued by the releasing instance are visible to the acquiring instance. Informally, we can think of atomic operations releasing side effects from other memory operations to other program instances or acquiring the side effects of memory operations on other program instances. Such a memory model is required if we want to communicate values between pairs of program instances via memory, which may be more common than we would think. When a program *acquires* a lock, it typically goes on to perform some additional calculations and modify some memory before eventually *releasing* the lock—only the lock variable is ever updated atomically, but we expect memory updates guarded by the lock to be protected from data races. This behavior relies on an acquire-release memory ordering for correctness, and attempting to use a relaxed memory ordering to implement a lock will not work.

Under a sequentially consistent memory ordering, the guarantees of acquire-release ordering still hold, but there additionally exists a single global order of all atomic operations. The behavior of this memory ordering is the most intuitive of the three and the closest that we can get to the original as-if guarantee we are used to relying upon when developing sequential applications. With sequential consistency, it becomes significantly easier to reason about communication between groups (rather than pairs) of program instances, since all program instances must agree on the global ordering of all atomic operations.

Understanding which memory orders are supported by a combination of programming model and device is a necessary part of designing portable parallel applications. Being explicit in describing the memory order required by our applications ensures that they fail predictably (e.g., at compile time) when the behavior we require is unsupported and prevents us from making unsafe assumptions.

The Memory Model

The chapter so far has introduced the concepts required to understand the memory model. The remainder of the chapter explains the memory model in detail, including

- How to express the memory ordering requirements of our kernels

CHAPTER 19 MEMORY MODEL AND ATOMICS

- How to query the memory orders supported by a specific device

- How the memory model behaves with respect to disjoint address spaces and multiple devices

- How the memory model interacts with barriers, fences, and atomics

- How using atomic operations differs between buffers and USM

The memory model is based on the memory model of standard C++ but differs in some important ways. These differences reflect our long-term vision that DPC++ and SYCL should help inform future C++ standards: the default behaviors and naming of classes are closely aligned with the C++ standard library and are intended to extend standard C++ functionality rather than to restrict it.

The table in Figure 19-9 summarizes how different memory model concepts are exposed as language features in standard C++ (C++11, C++14, C++17, C++20) vs. SYCL and DPC++. The C++14, C++17, and C++20 standards additionally include some clarifications that impact implementations of C++. These clarifications should not affect the application code that we write, so we do not cover them here.

Feature	Standard C++	SYCL / DPC++
Atomic Objects	`std::atomic`	Not available.
Atomic References	`std::atomic_ref` (C++20 onwards)	`sycl::atomic_ref`
Memory Orders	relaxed consume acquire release scq_rel seq_cst	relaxed acquire release scq_rel seq_cst
Memory Scopes	Not available. Behavior of atomics and fences matches DPC++ system scope.	work_item sub_group work_group device system
Fences	`std::atomic_thread_fence`	`sycl::atomic_fence`
Barriers	`std::barrier` (C++20 onwards)	`nd_item::barrier` `sub_group::barrier`
Address Spaces	All memory is in a single (host) address space.	Host Device (Global) Device (Local) Device (Private) Shared (USM)

Figure 19-9. Comparing standard C++ and SYCL/DPC++ memory models

The `memory_order` Enumeration Class

The memory model exposes different memory orders through six values of the memory_order enumeration class, which can be supplied as arguments to fences and atomic operations. Supplying a memory order argument to an operation tells the compiler what memory ordering guarantees are required for all other memory operations (to any address) *relative to that operation*, as explained in the following:

CHAPTER 19   MEMORY MODEL AND ATOMICS

- `memory_order::relaxed`

    Read and write operations can be re-ordered before or after the operation with no restrictions. There are no ordering guarantees.

- `memory_order::acquire`

    Read and write operations appearing after the operation in the program must occur after it (i.e., they cannot be re-ordered before the operation).

- `memory_order::release`

    Read and write operations appearing before the operation in the program must occur before it (i.e., they cannot be re-ordered after the operation), and preceding write operations are guaranteed to be visible to other program instances which have been synchronized by a corresponding acquire operation (i.e., an atomic operation using the same variable and `memory_order::acquire` or a barrier function).

- `memory_order::acq_rel`

    The operation acts as both an acquire and a release. Read and write operations cannot be re-ordered around the operation, and preceding writes must be made visible as previously described for `memory_order::release`.

- `memory_order::seq_cst`

    The operation acts as an acquire, release, or both depending on whether it is a read, write, or read-modify-write operation, respectively. All operations with this memory order are observed in a sequentially consistent order.

509

There are several restrictions on which memory orders are supported by each operation. The table in Figure 19-10 summarizes which combinations are valid.

Functions	Supported memory_order Values				
	relaxed	acquire	release	acq_rel	seq_cst
load	✓	✓	✗	✗	✓
store	✓	✗	✓	✗	✓
exchange compare_exchange_* fetch_*	✓	✓	✓	✓	✓
fence	✓	✓	✓	✓	✓

Figure 19-10. Supporting atomic operations with memory_order

Load operations do not write values to memory and are therefore incompatible with release semantics. Similarly, store operations do not read values from memory and are therefore incompatible with acquire semantics. The remaining read-modify-write atomic operations and fences are compatible with all memory orderings.

MEMORY ORDER IN C++

The C++ memory model additionally includes memory_order::consume, with similar behavior to memory_order::acquire. However, the C++17 standard discourages its use, noting that its definition is being revised. Its inclusion in DPC++ has therefore been postponed to a future version.

The `memory_scope` Enumeration Class

The standard C++ memory model assumes that applications execute on a single device with a single address space. Neither of these assumptions holds for DPC++ applications: different parts of the application execute on different devices (i.e., a host device and one or more accelerator devices); each device has multiple address spaces (i.e., private, local, and global); and the global address space of each device may or may not be disjoint (depending on USM support).

In order to address this, DPC++ extends the C++ notion of memory order to include the *scope* of an atomic operation, denoting the minimum set of work-items to which a given memory ordering constraint applies. The set of scopes are defined by way of a `memory_scope` enumeration class:

- `memory_scope::work_item`

    The memory ordering constraint applies only to the calling work-item. This scope is only useful for image operations, as all other operations within a work-item are already guaranteed to execute in program order.

- `memory_scope::sub_group`, `memory_scope::work_group`

    The memory ordering constraint applies only to work-items in the same sub-group or work-group as the calling work-item.

- `memory_scope::device`

    The memory ordering constraint applies only to work-items executing on the same device as the calling work-item.

CHAPTER 19   MEMORY MODEL AND ATOMICS

- `memory_scope::system`

   The memory ordering constraint applies to all work-items in the system.

Barring restrictions imposed by the capabilities of a device, all memory scopes are valid arguments to all atomic and fence operations. However, a scope argument may be automatically demoted to a narrower scope in one of three situations:

1. If an atomic operation updates a value in work-group local memory, any scope broader than `memory_scope::work_group` is narrowed (because local memory is only visible to work-items in the same work-group).

2. If a device does not support USM, specifying `memory_scope::system` is always equivalent to `memory_scope::device` (because buffers cannot be accessed concurrently by multiple devices).

3. If an atomic operation uses `memory_order::relaxed`, there are no ordering guarantees, and the memory scope argument is effectively ignored.

Querying Device Capabilities

To ensure compatibility with devices supported by previous versions of SYCL and to maximize portability, DPC++ supports OpenCL 1.2 devices and other hardware that may not be capable of supporting the full C++ memory model (e.g., certain classes of embedded devices). DPC++ provides device queries to help us reason about the memory order(s) and memory scope(s) supported by the devices available in a system:

- `atomic_memory_order_capabilities`

  `atomic_fence_order_capabilities`

  Return a list of all memory orderings supported by atomic and fence operations on a specific device. All devices are required to support at least `memory_order::relaxed`, and the host device is required to support all memory orderings.

- `atomic_memory_scope_capabilities`

  `atomic_fence_scope_capabilities`

  Return a list of all memory scopes supported by atomic and fence operations on a specific device. All devices are required to support at least `memory_order::work_group`, and the host device is required to support all memory scopes.

It may be difficult at first to remember which memory orders and scopes are supported for which combinations of function and device capability. In practice, we can avoid much of this complexity by following one of the two development approaches outlined in the following:

1. Develop applications with sequential consistency and system fences.

   Only consider adopting less strict memory orders during performance tuning.

2. Develop applications with relaxed consistency and work-group fences.

   Only consider adopting more strict memory orders and broader memory scopes where required for correctness.

The first approach ensures that the semantics of all atomic operations and fences match the default behavior of standard C++. This is the simplest and least error-prone option, but has the worst performance and portability characteristics.

The second approach is more aligned with the default behavior of previous versions of SYCL and languages like OpenCL. Although more complicated—since it requires that we become more familiar with the different memory orders and scopes—it ensures that the majority of the DPC++ code we write will work on any device without performance penalties.

Barriers and Fences

All previous usages of barriers and fences in the book so far have ignored the issue of memory order and scope, by relying on default behavior.

Every group barrier in DPC++ acts as an acquire-release fence to all address spaces accessible by the calling work-item and makes preceding writes visible to at least all other work-items in the same group. This ensures memory consistency within a group of work-items after a barrier, in line with our intuition of what it means to synchronize (and the definition of the *synchronizes-with* relation in C++).

The `atomic_fence` function gives us more fine-grained control than this, allowing work-items to execute fences with a specified memory order and scope. Group barriers in future versions of DPC++ may similarly accept an optional argument to adjust the memory scope of the acquire-release fences associated with a barrier.

CHAPTER 19   MEMORY MODEL AND ATOMICS

Atomic Operations in DPC++

DPC++ provides support for many kinds of atomic operations on a variety of data types. All devices are guaranteed to support atomic versions of common operations (e.g., loads, stores, arithmetic operators), as well as the atomic *compare-and-swap* operations required to implement lock-free algorithms. The language defines these operations for all fundamental integer, floating-point, and pointer types—all devices must support these operations for 32-bit types, but 64-bit-type support is optional.

The `atomic` Class

The `std::atomic` class from C++11 provides an interface for creating and operating on atomic variables. Instances of the atomic class own their data, cannot be moved or copied, and can only be updated using atomic operations. These restrictions significantly reduce the chances of using the class incorrectly and introducing undefined behavior. Unfortunately, they also prevent the class from being used in DPC++ kernels—it is impossible to create atomic objects on the host and transfer them to the device! We are free to continue using `std::atomic` in our host code, but attempting to use it inside of device kernels will result in a compiler error.

> **ATOMIC CLASS DEPRECATED IN SYCL 2020 AND DPC++**
>
> The SYCL 1.2.1 specification included a `cl::sycl::atomic` class that is loosely based on the `std::atomic` class from C++11. We say *loosely* because there are some differences between the interfaces of the two classes, most notably that the SYCL 1.2.1 version does not own its data and defaults to a relaxed memory ordering.
>
> The `cl::sycl::atomic` class is fully supported by DPC++, but its use is discouraged to avoid confusion. We recommend that the `atomic_ref` class (covered in the next section) be used in its place.

The `atomic_ref` Class

The `std::atomic_ref` class from C++20 provides an alternative interface for atomic operations which provides greater flexibility than `std::atomic`. The biggest difference between the two classes is that instances of `std::atomic_ref` do not own their data but are instead constructed from an existing non-atomic variable. Creating an atomic reference effectively acts as a promise that the referenced variable will only be accessed atomically for the lifetime of the reference. These are exactly the semantics needed by DPC++, since they allow us to create non-atomic data on the host, transfer that data to the device, and treat it as atomic data only after it has been transferred. The `atomic_ref` class used in DPC++ kernels is therefore based on `std::atomic_ref`.

We say *based on* because the DPC++ version of the class includes three additional template arguments as shown in Figure 19-11.

```
template <typename T,
          memory_order DefaultOrder,
          memory_scope DefaultScope,
          access::address_space AddressSpace>
class atomic_ref {
 public:
  using value_type = T;
  static constexpr size_t required_alignment =
    /* implementation-defined */;
  static constexpr bool is_always_lock_free =
    /* implementation-defined */;
  static constexpr memory_order default_read_order =
    memory_order_traits<DefaultOrder>::read_order;
  static constexpr memory_order default_write_order =
    memory_order_traits<DefaultOrder>::write_order;
  static constexpr memory_order default_read_modify_write_order =
    DefaultOrder;
  static constexpr memory_scope default_scope = DefaultScope;

  explicit atomic_ref(T& obj);
  atomic_ref(const atomic_ref& ref) noexcept;
};
```

Figure 19-11. Constructors and static members of the `atomic_ref` class

As discussed previously, the capabilities of different DPC++ devices are varied. Selecting a default behavior for the atomic classes of DPC++ is a difficult proposition: defaulting to standard C++ behavior (i.e., memory_order::seq_cst, memory_scope::system) limits code to executing only on the most capable of devices; on the other hand, breaking with C++ conventions and defaulting to the lowest common denominator (i.e., memory_order::relaxed, memory_scope::work_group) could lead to unexpected behavior when migrating existing C++ code. The design adopted by DPC++ offers a compromise, allowing us to define our desired default behavior as part of an object's type (using the DefaultOrder and DefaultScope template arguments). Other orderings and scopes can be provided as runtime arguments to specific atomic operations as we see fit—the DefaultOrder and DefaultScope only impact operations where we do not or cannot override the default behavior (e.g., when using a shorthand operator like +=). The final template argument denotes the address space in which the referenced object is allocated.

An atomic reference provides support for different operations depending on the type of object that it references. The basic operations supported by all types are shown in Figure 19-12, providing the ability to atomically move data to and from memory.

CHAPTER 19 MEMORY MODEL AND ATOMICS

```
void store(T operand,
  memory_order order = default_write_order,
  memory_scope scope = default_scope) const noexcept;
T operator=(T desired) const noexcept; // equivalent to store

T load(memory_order order = default_read_order,
       memory_scope scope = default_scope) const noexcept;
operator T() const noexcept; // equivalent to load

T exchange(T operand,
  memory_order order = default_read_modify_write_order,
  memory_scope scope = default_scope) const noexcept;

bool compare_exchange_weak(T &expected, T desired,
  memory_order success,
  memory_order failure,
  memory_scope scope = default_scope) const noexcept;

bool compare_exchange_weak(T &expected, T desired,
  memory_order order = default_read_modify_write_order,
  memory_scope scope = default_scope) const noexcept;

bool compare_exchange_strong(T &expected, T desired,
  memory_order success,
  memory_order failure,
  memory_scope scope = default_scope) const noexcept;

bool compare_exchange_strong(T &expected, T desired,
  memory_order order = default_read_modify_write_order,
  memory_scope scope = default_scope) const noexcept;
```

Figure 19-12. Basic operations with atomic_ref for all types

Atomic references to objects of integral and floating-point types extend the set of available atomic operations to include arithmetic operations, as shown in Figures 19-13 and 19-14. Devices are required to support atomic floating-point types irrespective of whether they feature native support for floating-point atomics in hardware, and many devices are expected to emulate atomic floating-point addition using an atomic compare exchange. This emulation is an important part of providing performance and portability in DPC++, and we should feel free to use floating-point atomics anywhere that an algorithm requires them—the resulting code will work correctly everywhere and will benefit from future improvements in floating-point atomic hardware without any modification!

```
Integral fetch_add(Integral operand,
  memory_order order = default_read_modify_write_order,
  memory_scope scope = default_scope) const noexcept;

Integral fetch_sub(Integral operand,
  memory_order order = default_read_modify_write_order,
  memory_scope scope = default_scope) const noexcept;

Integral fetch_and(Integral operand,
  memory_order order = default_read_modify_write_order,
  memory_scope scope = default_scope) const noexcept;

Integral fetch_or(Integral operand,
  memory_order order = default_read_modify_write_order,
  memory_scope scope = default_scope) const noexcept;

Integral fetch_min(Integral operand,
  memory_order order = default_read_modify_write_order,
  memory_scope scope = default_scope) const noexcept;

Integral fetch_max(Integral operand,
  memory_order order = default_read_modify_write_order,
  memory_scope scope = default_scope) const noexcept;

Integral operator++(int) const noexcept;
Integral operator--(int) const noexcept;
Integral operator++() const noexcept;
Integral operator--() const noexcept;
Integral operator+=(Integral) const noexcept;
Integral operator-=(Integral) const noexcept;
Integral operator&=(Integral) const noexcept;
Integral operator|=(Integral) const noexcept;
Integral operator^=(Integral) const noexcept;
```

Figure 19-13. Additional operations with `atomic_ref` *only for integral types*

```
Floating fetch_add(Floating operand,
  memory_order order = default_read_modify_write_order,
  memory_scope scope = default_scope) const noexcept;

Floating fetch_sub(Floating operand,
  memory_order order = default_read_modify_write_order,
  memory_scope scope = default_scope) const noexcept;

Floating fetch_min(Floating operand,
  memory_order order = default_read_modify_write_order,
  memory_scope scope = default_scope) const noexcept;

Floating fetch_max(Floating operand,
  memory_order order = default_read_modify_write_order,
  memory_scope scope = default_scope) const noexcept;

Floating operator+=(Floating) const noexcept;
Floating operator-=(Floating) const noexcept;
```

Figure 19-14. Additional operations with atomic_ref only for floating-point types

Using Atomics with Buffers

As discussed in the previous section, there is no way in DPC++ to allocate atomic data and move it between the host and device. To use atomic operations in conjunction with buffers, we must create a buffer of non-atomic data to be transferred to the device and then access that data through an atomic reference.

```
Q.submit([&](handler& h) {
  accessor acc{buf, h};
  h.parallel_for(N, [=](id<1> i) {
    int j = i % M;
    atomic_ref<int, memory_order::relaxed, memory_scope::system,
               access::address_space::global_space> atomic_acc(acc[j]);
    atomic_acc += 1;
  });
});
```

Figure 19-15. Accessing a buffer via an explicitly created atomic_ref

The code in Figure 19-15 is an example of expressing atomicity in DPC++ using an explicitly created atomic reference object. The buffer stores normal integers, and we require an accessor with both read and write permissions. We can then create an instance of atomic_ref for each data access, using the += operator as a shorthand alternative for the fetch_add member function.

This pattern is useful if we want to mix atomic and non-atomic accesses to a buffer within the same kernel, to avoid paying the performance overheads of atomic operations when they are not required. If we know that only a subset of the memory locations in the buffer will be accessed concurrently by multiple work-items, we only need to use atomic references when accessing that subset. Or, if we know that work-items in the same work-group only concurrently access local memory during one stage of a kernel (i.e., between two work-group barriers), we only need to use atomic references during that stage.

Sometimes we are happy to pay the overhead of atomicity for every access, either because every access must be atomic for correctness or because we're more interested in productivity than performance. For such cases, DPC++ provides a shorthand for declaring that an accessor must always use atomic operations, as shown in Figure 19-16.

```
buffer buf(data);

Q.submit([&](handler& h) {
  atomic_accessor acc(buf, h, relaxed_order, system_scope);
  h.parallel_for(N, [=](id<1> i) {
    int j = i % M;
    acc[j] += 1;
  });
});
```

Figure 19-16. Accessing a buffer via an atomic_ref implicitly created by an atomic accessor

The buffer stores normal integers as before, but we replace the regular accessor with a special `atomic_accessor` type. Using such an atomic accessor automatically wraps each member of the buffer using an atomic reference, thereby simplifying the kernel code.

Whether it is best to use the atomic reference class directly or via an accessor depends on our use case. Our recommendation is to start with the accessor for simplicity during prototyping and initial development, only moving to the more explicit syntax if necessary during performance tuning (i.e., if profiling reveals atomic operations to be a performance bottleneck) or if atomicity is known to be required only during a well-defined phase of a kernel (e.g., as in the histogram code later in the chapter).

Using Atomics with Unified Shared Memory

As shown in Figure 19-17 (reproduced from Figure 19-7), we can construct atomic references from data stored in USM in exactly the same way as we could for buffers. Indeed, the only difference between this code and the code shown in Figure 19-15 is that the USM code does not require buffers or accessors.

```
q.parallel_for(range<1>(N), [=](size_t i) {
  int j = i % M;
  atomic_ref<int, memory_order::relaxed, memory_scope::system,
             access::address_space::global_space> atomic_data(data[j]);
  atomic_data += 1;
}).wait();
```

Figure 19-17. Accessing a USM allocation via an explicitly created `atomic_ref`

There is no way of using only standard DPC++ features to mimic the shorthand syntax provided by atomic accessors for USM pointers. However, we expect that a future version of DPC++ will provide a shorthand built on top of the `mdspan` class that has been proposed for C++23.

Using Atomics in Real Life

The potential usages of atomics are so broad and varied that it would be impossible for us to provide an example of each usage in this book. We have included two representative examples, with broad applicability across domains:

1. Computing a histogram
2. Implementing device-wide synchronization

Computing a Histogram

The code in Figure 19-18 demonstrates how to use relaxed atomics in conjunction with work-group barriers to compute a histogram. The kernel is split by the barriers into three phases, each with their own atomicity requirements. Remember that the barrier acts both as a synchronization point and an acquire-release fence—this ensures that any reads and writes in one phase are visible to all work-items in the work-group in later phases.

The first phase sets the contents of some work-group local memory to zero. The work-items in each work-group update independent locations in work-group local memory by design—race conditions cannot occur, and no atomicity is required.

The second phase accumulates partial histogram results in local memory. Work-items in the same work-group may update the same locations in work-group local memory, but synchronization can be deferred until the end of the phase—we can satisfy the atomicity requirements using memory_order::relaxed and memory_scope::work_group.

The third phase contributes the partial histogram results to the total stored in global memory. Work-items in the same work-group are guaranteed to read from independent locations in work-group local memory, but may update the same locations in global memory—we

CHAPTER 19 MEMORY MODEL AND ATOMICS

no longer require atomicity for the work-group local memory and can satisfy the atomicity requirements for global memory using memory_order::relaxed and memory_scope::system as before.

```
// Define shorthand aliases for the types of atomic needed by this kernel
template <typename T>
using local_atomic_ref = atomic_ref<
  T,
  memory_order::relaxed,
  memory_scope::work_group,
  access::address_space::local_space>;

template <typename T>
using global_atomic_ref = atomic_ref<
  T,
  memory_order::relaxed,
  memory_scope::system,
  access::address_space::global_space>;

Q.submit([&](handler& h) {
   auto local = local_accessor<uint32_t, 1>{B, h};
   h.parallel_for(
     nd_range<1>{num_groups * num_items, num_items}, [=](nd_item<1> it){
      // Phase 1: Work-items co-operate to zero local memory
      for (int32_t b = it.get_local_id(0); b < B;
           b += it.get_local_range(0)) {
        local[b] = 0;
      }
      it.barrier(); // Wait for all to be zeroed

      // Phase 2: Work-groups each compute a chunk of the input
      // Work-items co-operate to compute histogram in local memory
      auto grp = it.get_group();
      const auto [group_start, group_end] = distribute_range(grp, N);
      for (int i = group_start + it.get_local_id(0); i < group_end;
           i += it.get_local_range(0)) {
        int32_t b = input[i] % B;
        local_atomic_ref<uint32_t>(local[b])++;
      }
      it.barrier(); // Wait for all local histogram updates to complete

      // Phase 3: Work-items co-operate to update global memory
      for (int32_t b = it.get_local_id(0); b < B;
           b += it.get_local_range(0)) {
        global_atomic_ref<uint32_t>(histogram[b]) += local[b];
      }
   });
}).wait();
```

Figure 19-18. Computing a histogram using atomic references in different memory spaces

CHAPTER 19 MEMORY MODEL AND ATOMICS

Implementing Device-Wide Synchronization

Back in Chapter 4, we warned against writing kernels that attempt to synchronize work-items across work-groups. However, we fully expect several readers of this chapter will be itching to implement their own device-wide synchronization routines atop of atomic operations and that our warnings will be ignored.

Device-wide synchronization is currently not portable and is best left to expert programmers. Future versions of the language will address this.

The code discussed in this section is dangerous and should not be expected to work on all devices, because of potential differences in scheduling and concurrency guarantees. The memory ordering guarantees provided by atomics are orthogonal to forward progress guarantees; and, at the time of writing, work-group scheduling in SYCL and DPC++ is completely implementation-defined. Formalizing the concepts and terminology required to discuss execution models and scheduling guarantees is currently an area of active academic research, and future versions of DPC++ are expected to build on this work to provide additional scheduling queries and controls. For now, these topics should be considered expert-only.

Figure 19-19 shows a simple implementation of a device-wide latch (a single-use barrier), and Figure 19-20 shows a simple example of its usage. Each work-group elects a single work-item to signal arrival of the group at the latch and await the arrival of other groups using a naïve spin-loop, while the other work-items wait for the elected work-item using a work-group barrier. It is this spin-loop that makes device-wide synchronization unsafe; if any work-groups have not yet begun executing or the currently executing work-groups are not scheduled fairly, the code may deadlock.

> Relying on memory order alone to implement synchronization primitives may lead to deadlocks in the absence of independent forward progress guarantees!

For the code to work correctly, the following three conditions must hold:

1. The atomic operations must use memory orders at least as strict as those shown, in order to guarantee that the correct fences are generated.

2. Each work-group in the ND-range must be capable of making forward progress, in order to avoid a single work-group spinning in the loop from starving a work-group that has yet to increment the counter.

3. The device must be capable of executing all work-groups in the ND-range concurrently, in order to ensure that all work-groups in the ND-range eventually reach the latch.

CHAPTER 19 MEMORY MODEL AND ATOMICS

```
struct device_latch {
  using memory_order = intel::memory_order;
  using memory_scope = intel::memory_scope;

  explicit device_latch(size_t num_groups) :
          counter(0), expected(num_groups) {}

  template <int Dimensions>
  void arrive_and_wait(nd_item<Dimensions>& it) {
    it.barrier();
    // Elect one work-item per work-group to be involved
    // in the synchronization
    // All other work-items wait at the barrier after the branch
    if (it.get_local_linear_id() == 0) {
      atomic_ref<
          size_t,
          memory_order::acq_rel,
          memory_scope::device,
          access::address_space::global_space> atomic_counter(counter);

      // Signal arrival at the barrier
      // Previous writes should be visible to
      // all work-items on the device
      atomic_counter++;

      // Wait for all work-groups to arrive
      // Synchronize with previous releases by
      // all work-items on the device
      while (atomic_counter.load() != expected) {}
    }
    it.barrier();
  }
  size_t counter;
  size_t expected;
};
```

Figure 19-19. *Building a simple device-wide latch on top of atomic references*

```cpp
// Allocate a one-time-use device_latch in USM
void* ptr = sycl::malloc_shared(sizeof(device_latch), Q);
device_latch* latch = new (ptr) device_latch(num_groups);
Q.submit([&](handler& h) {
  h.parallel_for(R, [=](nd_item<1> it) {
    // Every work-item writes a 1 to its location
    data[it.get_global_linear_id()] = 1;

    // Every work-item waits for all writes
    latch->arrive_and_wait(it);

    // Every work-item sums the values it can see
    size_t sum = 0;
    for (int i = 0; i < num_groups * items_per_group; ++i) {
      sum += data[i];
    }
    sums[it.get_global_linear_id()] = sum;
  });
}).wait();
free(ptr, Q);
```

Figure 19-20. Using the device-wide latch from Figure 19-19

Although this code is not guaranteed to be portable, we have included it here to highlight two key points: 1) DPC++ is expressive enough to enable device-specific tuning, sometimes at the expense of portability; and 2) DPC++ already contains the building blocks necessary to implement higher-level synchronization routines, which may be included in a future version of the language.

Summary

This chapter provided a high-level introduction to memory model and atomic classes. Understanding how to use (and how not to use!) these classes is key to developing correct, portable, and efficient parallel programs.

Memory models are an overwhelmingly complex topic, and our focus here has been on establishing a base for writing real applications. If more information is desired, there are several websites, books, and talks dedicated to memory models referenced in the following.

For More Information

- A. Williams, *C++ Concurrency in Action: Practical Multithreading*, Manning, 2012, 978-1933988771

- H. Sutter, "atomic<> Weapons: The C++ Memory Model and Modern Hardware", https://herbsutter.com/2013/02/11/atomic-weapons-the-c-memory-model-and-modern-hardware/

- H-J. Boehm, "Temporarily discourage memory_order_consume," http://wg21.link/p0371

- C++ Reference, "std::atomic,"

    https://en.cppreference.com/w/cpp/atomic/atomic

- C++ Reference, "std::atomic_ref,"

    https://en.cppreference.com/w/cpp/atomic/atomic_ref

CHAPTER 19 MEMORY MODEL AND ATOMICS

 **Open Access** This chapter is licensed under the terms of the Creative Commons Attribution 4.0 International License (http://creativecommons.org/licenses/by/4.0/), which permits use, sharing, adaptation, distribution and reproduction in any medium or format, as long as you give appropriate credit to the original author(s) and the source, provide a link to the Creative Commons license and indicate if changes were made.

The images or other third party material in this chapter are included in the chapter's Creative Commons license, unless indicated otherwise in a credit line to the material. If material is not included in the chapter's Creative Commons license and your intended use is not permitted by statutory regulation or exceeds the permitted use, you will need to obtain permission directly from the copyright holder.

EPILOGUE

Future Direction of DPC++

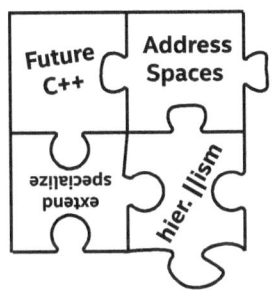

Take a moment now to feel the peace and calm of knowing that we finally understand everything about programming using SYCL and DPC++. All the puzzle pieces have fallen into place.

Before we get too comfortable, let's note that this book was written at an exciting time for SYCL and DPC++. It has been a period of rapid development that coincided with the release of the first DPC++ specification and the SYCL 2020 provisional specification. We've endeavored to ensure that the code samples, in all previous chapters, compile with the open source DPC++ compiler at the time that this book was sent to publication (Q3 2020) and execute on a wide range of hardware. However, the future-looking code shown in this epilogue does not compile with any compiler as of mid-2020.

EPILOGUE FUTURE DIRECTION OF DPC++

In this epilogue, we speculate on the future. Our crystal ball can be a bit difficult to read—this epilogue comes without any warranty.

The vast majority of what this book covers and teaches will endure for a long time. That said, it is too hot of an area for it to remain at rest, and changes are occurring that may disrupt some of the details we have covered. This includes several items that appeared first as vendor extensions and have since been welcomed into the specification (such as sub-groups and USM). That so many new features are on track to become part of the next SYCL standard is fantastic, but it has made talking about them complicated: should we refer to such features as vendor extensions, experimental/provisional features of SYCL, or part of SYCL?

This epilogue provides a sneak peek of upcoming DPC++ features that we are very excited about, which were unfortunately not quite finished at the time we sent the book to be published. We offer no guarantees that the code samples printed in this epilogue compile: some may already be compatible with a SYCL or DPC++ compiler released after the book, while others may compile only after some massaging of syntax. Some features may be released as extensions or incorporated into future standards, while others may remain experimental features indefinitely. The code samples in the GitHub repository associated with this book may be updated to use new syntax as it evolves. Likewise, we will have an erratum for the book, which may get additions made from time to time. We recommend checking for updates in these two places (code repository and book errata—links can be found early in Chapter 1).

Alignment with C++20 and C++23

Maintaining close alignment between SYCL, DPC++, and ISO C++ has two advantages. First, it enables SYCL and DPC++ to leverage the newest and greatest features of standard C++ to improve developer productivity. Second, it increases the chances of heterogeneous programming features introduced in SYCL or DPC++ successfully influencing the future direction of standard C++ (e.g., executors).

SYCL 1.2.1 was based on C++11, and many of the biggest improvements to the interfaces of SYCL 2020 and DPC++ are only possible because of language features introduced in C++14 (e.g., generic lambdas) and C++17 (e.g., class template argument deduction—CTAD).

The C++20 specification was ratified in 2020 (while we were writing this book!). It includes a number of features (e.g., std::atomic_ref, std::bit_cast) that have already been *pre-adopted* by DPC++ and SYCL—as we move toward the next official release of SYCL (after 2020 provisional) and the next version of DPC++, we expect to more closely align with C++20 and incorporate the most useful parts of it. For example, C++20 introduced some additional thread synchronization routines in the form of std::latch and std::barrier; we already explored in Chapter 19 how similar interfaces could be used to define device-wide barriers, and it may make sense to reexamine sub-group and work-group barriers in the context of the new C++20 syntax as well.

Work for any standard committee is never done, and work has already begun on C++23. Since the specification is not finalized yet, adopting any of these features into a SYCL or DPC++ specification would be a mistake—the features may change significantly before making it into C++23, resulting in incompatibilities that may prove hard to fix. However, there are many features under discussion that may change the way that future SYCL and DPC++ programs look and behave. One of the most exciting proposed features is mdspan, a non-owning view of data that provides both multidimensional array syntax for pointers and an AccessorPolicy as an extension point for controlling access to the underlying data. These semantics are very similar to those of SYCL accessors, and mdspan would enable accessor-like syntax to be used for both buffers and USM allocations, as shown in Figure EP-1.

EPILOGUE   FUTURE DIRECTION OF DPC++

```
queue Q;
constexpr int N = 4;
constexpr int M = 2;
int* data = malloc_shared<int>(N * M, Q);
stdex::mdspan<int, N, M> view{data};
Q.parallel_for(range<2>{N, M}, [=](id<2> idx) {
  int i = idx[0];
  int j = idx[1];
  view(i, j) = i * M + j;
}).wait();
```

Figure EP-1. *Attaching accessor-like indexing to a USM pointer using* mdspan

Hopefully it is only a matter of time until mdspan becomes standard C++. In the meantime, we recommend that interested readers experiment with the open source production-quality reference implementation available as part of the Kokkos project.

Another exciting proposed feature is the std::simd class template, which seeks to provide a portable interface for explicit vector parallelism in C++. Adopting this interface would provide a clear distinction between the two different uses of vector types described in Chapter 11: uses of vector types for programmer convenience and uses of vector types by ninja programmers for low-level performance tuning. The presence of support for both SPMD and SIMD programming styles within the same language also raises some interesting questions: how should we declare which style a kernel uses, and should we be able to mix and match styles within the same kernel? We expect future vendor extensions to explore these questions, as vendors experiment with the possibilities in this space ahead of standardization.

Address Spaces

As we have seen in earlier chapters, there are some cases in which otherwise simple codes are complicated by the existence of memory spaces. We are free to use regular C++ pointers in most places, but at other times are required to use the multi_ptr class and explicitly specify which address space(s) their code is expected to support.

Many modern architectures solve this problem by providing hardware support for a so-called *generic* address space; pointers may point to any allocation in any memory space, so that we (and compilers!) can leverage runtime queries to specialize code in situations where different memory spaces require different handling (e.g., accessing work-group local memory may use different instructions). Support for a generic address space is already available in other programming languages, such as OpenCL, and it is expected that a future version of SYCL will adopt generic-by-default in place of inference rules.

This change would greatly simplify many codes and make usage of the `multi_ptr` class an optional performance-tuning feature instead of one that is required for correctness. Figure EP-2 shows a simple class written using the existing address spaces, and Figures EP-3 and EP-4 show two alternative designs that would be enabled by the introduction of a generic address space.

```
// Pointers in structs must be explicitly decorated with address space
// Supporting both address spaces requires a template parameter
template <access::address_space AddressSpace>
struct Particles {
  multi_ptr<float, AddressSpace> x;
  multi_ptr<float, AddressSpace> y;
  multi_ptr<float, AddressSpace> z;
};
```

Figure EP-2. Storing pointers to a specific address space in a class

```
// Pointers in structs default to the generic address space
struct Particles {
  float* x;
  float* y;
  float* z;
};
```

Figure EP-3. Storing pointers to the generic address space in a class

```
// Template parameter defaults to generic address space
// User of class can override address space for performance tuning
template <access::address_space AddressSpace =
    access::address_space::generic_space>

struct Particles {
 multi_ptr<float, AddressSpace> x;
 multi_ptr<float, AddressSpace> y;
 multi_ptr<float, AddressSpace> z;
};
```

Figure EP-4. Storing pointers with an optional address space in a class

Extension and Specialization Mechanism

Chapter 12 introduced an expressive set of queries enabling the host to extract information about a device at runtime. These queries enable runtime parameters such as work-group size to be tuned for a specific device and for different kernels implementing different algorithms to be dispatched to different types of device.

Future versions are expected to augment these runtime queries with compile-time queries, allowing code to be specialized based on whether an implementation understands a vendor extension. Figure EP-5 shows how the preprocessor could be used to detect whether the compiler supports a specific vendor extension.

```
#ifdef SYCL_EXT_INTEL_SUB_GROUPS
sycl::ext::intel::sub_group sg = it.get_sub_group();
#endif
```

Figure EP-5. Checking for Intel sub-group extension compiler support with #ifdef

EPILOGUE FUTURE DIRECTION OF DPC++

There are also plans to introduce compile-time queries enabling kernels to be specialized based on properties (which we call *aspects*) of the targeted device (e.g., the device type, support for a specific extension, the size of work-group local memory, the sub-group size selected by the compiler). These aspects represent a special kind of constant expression not currently present in C++—they are not necessarily `constexpr` when the host code is compiled but become `constexpr` when the target device becomes known. The exact mechanism used to expose this device `constexpr` concept is still being designed. We expect it to build on the specialization constants feature introduced in the SYCL 2020 provisional and to look and behave similarly to the code shown in Figure EP-6.

```
h.parallel_for(..., [=](item<1> it) {
 if devconstexpr (this_device().has<aspect::cpu>()) {
  /* Code specialized for CPUs */
 }
 else if devconstexpr (this_device().has<aspect::gpu>()) {
  /* Code specialized for GPUs */
 }
});
```

Figure EP-6. *Specializing kernel code based on device aspects at kernel compile time*

Hierarchical Parallelism

As we noted back in Chapter 4, we consider the hierarchical parallelism in older versions of SYCL to be an experimental feature and expect it to be slower than basic data-parallel and ND-range kernels in its adoption of new language features.

There are a *lot* of new language features in DPC++ and SYCL 2020, and several of them are currently incompatible with hierarchical parallelism (e.g., sub-groups, group algorithms, reductions). Closing this gap would help to improve programmer productivity and would enable more compact syntax for some simple cases. The code in Figure EP-7 shows a possible route for extending reduction support to hierarchical parallelism, enabling a hierarchical reduction: each work-group computes a sum, and the kernel as a whole computes the maximum of all sums across all workgroups.

```
h.parallel_for_work_group(N, reduction(max, maximum<>()),
  [=](group<1> g, auto& max) {
  float sum = 0.0f;
  g.parallel_for_work_item(M, reduction(sum, plus<>()),
    [=](h_item<1> it, auto& sum) {
    sum += data[it.get_global_id()];
  });
  max.combine(sum);
});
```

***Figure EP-7.** Using hierarchical parallelism for a hierarchical reduction*

The other aspect of hierarchical parallelism that was briefly touched on in Chapter 4 is its implementation complexity. Mapping nested parallelism to accelerators is a challenge that is not unique to SYCL or DPC++, and this topic is the subject of much interest and research. As implementers gain experience with the implementation of hierarchical parallelism and the capabilities of different devices, we expect syntax in SYCL and DPC++ to evolve in alignment with standard practice.

Summary

There is already a lot of excitement around SYCL and DPC++, and this is just the beginning! We (as a community) have a long path ahead of us, and it will take significant continued effort to distil the best practices for heterogeneous programming and to design new language features that strike the desired balance between performance, portability, and productivity.

EPILOGUE   FUTURE DIRECTION OF DPC++

We need your help! If your favorite feature of C++ (or any other programming language) is missing from SYCL or DPC++, please reach out to us. Together, we can shape the future direction of SYCL, DPC++, and ISO C++.

For More Information

- Khronos SYCL Registry, www.khronos.org/registry/SYCL/
- J. Hoberock et al., "A Unified Executors Proposal for C++," http://wg21.link/p0443
- H. Carter Edwards et al., "mdspan: A Non-Owning Multidimensional Array Reference," http://wg21.link/p0009
- D. Hollman et al., "Production-Quality mdspan Implementation," https://github.com/kokkos/mdspan

Index

A

accelerator_selector, 39
Accessors, *see* Buffers, accessors
Actions, 53–54
Address spaces, 534–536
Ahead-of-time (AOT)
  compilation, 301
  vs. just-in-time (JIT), 301
all_of function, 235
Amdahl's Law, 9
Anonymous function objects, *see*
  Lambda function
any_of function, 235
Asynchronous errors, 136–142
Asynchronous Task Graphs, 15
atomic_fence function, 514
Atomic operations
  atomic_fence, 513
  atomic_ref class, 503
  data race, 17, 305, 498–500
  device-wide synchronization,
    525–528
  std:atomic class, 515
  std:atomic_ref class, 516–520
  Unified Shared Memory, 522

B

Barrier function, 215, 509
  in ND-range kernels, 223
  in hierarchical kernels, 226
Broadcast function, 234
Buffers, 66
  access modes, 74
  accessors, 72–74
  context_bound, 181
  host memory, 182
  use_host_ptr, 180, 181
  use_mutex, 180–181
build_with_kernel_type, 256
Built-in functions, 472–478

C

Central Processing Unit (CPU,
  46–48, 387–417
Choosing devices, 29
Collective functions, 217, 234
  broadcast, 234
  load and store, 238, 239
  shuffles, 235–238
  vote, 235

INDEX

Command group (CG)
  actions, 198
  event-based
    dependences, 198, 199
  execution, 206
Communication
  work-group local memory,
    217–219, 378–380
  work-items, 214–215
Compilation model, 300–303
Concurrency, 22
Concurrent Execution, 214–215
copy method, 207
CPU execution, 47
cpu_selector, 40
CUDA code, 321, 322
Custom device selector, 45, 281–284

D

Data management
  buffers, 66
  explicit, 64, 65
  images, 66
  implicit, 65
  strategy selection, 66, 86, 87
  USM, 66, 149–171, 522
    advantage of, 66
    allocations, 67, 68
    explicit data
      movement, 68, 69
    implicit data
      movement, 70, 71

    malloc, 67
    unified virtual address, 67
Data movement
  explicit, 161–163, 207
  implicit
    graph scheduling, 208, 209
    memcpy, 163
    migration, 165–166
Data parallelism
  basic data-parallel kernels
    id class, 104, 105
    item class, 105, 106
    parallel_for function, 100, 101
    range class, 103, 104
  hierarchical kernels, 118
    h_item class, 122
    parallel_for_work_group
      function, 119–121
    parallel_for_work_item
      function, 119–122
    private_memory
      class, 123, 124
  loops *vs.* kernels, 95, 96
  multidimensional kernels,
    93–95
  ND-range kernels, 106
    group class, 116, 117
    local accessors, 112, 223
    nd_item class, 114, 115
    nd_range class, 113, 114
    sub_group class, 117, 118
    sub-groups, 110–112
    work-groups, 108–110
    work-items, 108

INDEX

Data-parallel programming, 11, 12
Debugging
    kernel code, 306, 307
    parallel programming errors, 305
    runtime error, 307–310
default_selector, 39
depends_on(), 79
Device code, 28
Device information
    custom device selectors, 281–284
    device queries, 290–292
    kernel queries, 292
Device selection, 25–58, 277–294
Directed acyclic graph (DAG), 75
Direct Programming, 21
Download code, 4

E

Error handling, 131–146
Event, 78, 198
Extension and specialization mechanism, 536–537

F

Fallback, 56–58
Fences, 496
Fencing memory, 215
Field Programmable Gate Arrays (FPGAs), 43–44, 419–469

ahead-of-time compilation, 438, 439
building blocks, 465
    look-up tables, 466
    math engines, 466
    off-chip hardware, 467
    on-chip memory, 466
    Routing fabric, 467
compilation time, 435–437
customized memory systems, 432
custom memory systems, 465
    memory access, 462, 464, 465
    optimization, 464
    stages, 463
    static coalescing, 464
custom operations/operation widths, 429
emulation, 437, 438
pipes, 456–461
First-in first-out (FIFO), 456, 457
fpga_selector, 39
FPGA emulation, 436
Functions, built-in, 472–478
functors, *see* Named function objects

G

get_access, 185
get_global_id(), 115
get_info, 285
get_local_id(), 115

543

get_pointer_type, 168
GitHub, 4
gpu_selector, 39
Graphics Processing Units (GPUs), 353–384
  building blocks
    caches and memory, 355
    execution resources, 354
    fixed functions, 355
  device_selector, 39–43
  fp16, 381
  fast math functions, 382
  half-precision
    floating-point, 382
  predication, 364
  masking, 364
  offloading kernels
    abstraction, 369
    cost of, 372, 373
    software drivers, 370
    SYCL runtime library, 369
  profiling kernels, 378
Graph scheduling
  command group
    actions, 198
    event-based dependences, 198, 199
  host synchronization, 209–211
GPU, *see* Graphics Processing Units
Graph scheduling, 196
group class, 116–117
Group functions, 340, 341
Gustafson, 9

H

Handler class, 50–51, 87–89
Heterogeneous Systems, 10–11
Hierarchical parallelism, 118–124, 537, 538
Host code, 27
Host device, 48
  development and debugging, 35–38
  fallback queue, 56–58
host_selector, 39

I

id class, 103
In-order queues, 77
Initializing data, 310, 311, 313, 315–318
Initiation interval, 451
Intermediate representation (IR), 252, 253
Interoperability, 241, 251–254
item class, 105

J

Just-in-time (JIT), 301
  vs. ahead-of-time (AOT), 301

K

Kernels, 241–257
  advantages and disadvantages, 242

interoperability
    API-defined objects, 253, 254
    API-defined source, 252, 253
    functionality, 251
    implementation, 251
lambda functions
    definition, 244
    elements, 244–247
    name template parameter, 247, 248
named function objects
    definition, 248, 249
    elements, 249–251
in program objects, 255–257

L

Lambda function, 18–21, 244–248
Latency and Throughput, 7–8
Libraries
    built-in functions, 472–474
        common functions, 477
        geometric functions, 477
        host and device, 472
        integer functions, 476
        math functions, 475
        relational functions, 478
load() member function, 268
Local Accessor, 223
Local Memory, 217–219
    in ND-Range kernels, 223
    in hierarchical kernels, 226
Loop initiation interval, 451
Loop pipelining, 449

M

malloc functions, 154, 155
Map pattern, 325, 326, 341, 342
mem_advise(), 168
memcpy, 151, 163, 208
Memory allocation, 61–89
Memory consistency, 215, 496–506
Memory Fence, 226
Memory model, 224, 497, 506, 507
    barriers and fences, 501, 502, 514
    C++ and SYCL/DPC++, 508
    data races and synchronization, 498–500
    definition, 497
    memory consistency, 495, 496
    memory_order enumeration class, 508–510
    memory_scope enumeration class, 511, 512
    ordering, 504–506
    querying device capabilities, 512–514
memory_order enumeration class, 508–510
memory_scope enumeration class, 511, 512
memset function, 161
Multiarchitecture binaries, 300
Multidimensional Kernels, 93–95
Multiple translation units, 319, 320

INDEX

N

Named function objects, 248–251
ND-range kernels, 106–107, 113
    example, 225–226

O

oneAPI DPC++ Library
    (oneDPL), 339
Out-of-order (OoO) queues, 78

P

Pack, 332, 333, 348, 349
parallel_for, 118
parallel_for_work_group
    function, 227
parallel_for_work_item function, 227
Parallel patterns, 323–351
    map, 325, 326
    pack, 332, 333
    properties, 324
    reduction, 328–330
    scan, 330, 331
    stencil, 326–328
    unpack, 333
Parallel STL (PSTL)
    algorithms, 486
    DPC++ execution policy, 484, 485
    dpstd :binary_search algorithm,
        489, 490
    FPGA execution policy, 485, 486
    requirements, 487
    std:fill function, 487, 488

USM, 490, 491
Pipes, 456
Pipeline parallelism, 424
Platform model
    compilation model, 300–303
    host device, 299
    multiarchitecture binary, 300
    SYCL and DPC++, 298
Portability, 21
prefetch (), 167
Program build options, 256

Q

Queries
    device information, 290–292
    kernel information, 292, 294
    local memory type, 217
    memory model, 506–507
    unified shared memory, 168–170
Queues
    binding to a device, 34
    definition, 31, 32
    device_selector class, 34, 39, 40
    multiple queues, 33, 34

R

Race Condition, 16
Reduction library, 334–337
Reduction patterns, 328–330,
    344, 345
Run time type information
    (RTTI), 29

S

Sample code download, 3
Scaling, 9–10
Scan patterns, 330, 331, 345–348
Selecting devices, 29–30
set_final_data, 182
set_write_back, 182
shared allocation, 151
Shuffle functions, 235–238
Single Program, Multiple Data (SPMD), 99
Single-Source, 12, 26–27
Standard Template Library (STL), 339
std::function, 142
Stencil pattern, 326–328, 342, 344
store() member function, 268
Sub-Groups, 110–112, 230
    compiler optimizations, 238
    loads and stores, 238
    sub_group class, 117–118
SYCL versions, 3
Synchronous errors, 135, 136, 140, 141

T

Task graph, 48–49, 82–85, 196–211
    DAG, 75
    disjoint dependence, 76, 77
    execution, 75
    explicit dependences, 78, 79
    implicit dependences, 80–85
    in-order queue object, 77
    OoO queues, 78
    simple task graph, 75
Throughput and Latency, 7–8
throw_asynchronous(), 145
Translation units, 319–320
try-catch structure, 140

U

Unified shared memory (USM), 67, 149–170, 522
    aligned_malloc functions, 159
    allocations, 67, 68
    data initialization, 160, 161
    data movement, *see* Data movement
    definition, 150
    device allocation, 151
    explicit data movement, 68, 69
    host allocation, 151
    implicit data movement, 70, 71
    malloc, 67
    unified virtual address, 67
    memory allocation
        C++ allocator-style, 154, 157, 158
        C++-style, 154, 156, 157
        C-style, 154, 155
        deallocation, 159, 160
        new, malloc, or allocators, 153
    queries, 168–170
    shared allocation, 151, 152

Unnamed function objects, *see* Lambda function
Unpack patterns, 333, 350, 351
update_host method, 207

V

vec class, 263, 264
Vectors, 259–275
    explicit vector code, 262, 263
    features and hardware, 261
    load and store operations, 267, 268
    swizzle operations, 269, 270
vote functions, 235
    any_of function, 235
    all_of function, 235

W, X, Y, Z

wait(), 78
wait_and_throw(), 145
Work Groups, 108–110, 214–215
Work-group local memory, 217–222, 378–380
Work-Item, 107, 214–215

CPSIA information can be obtained
at www.ICGtesting.com
Printed in the USA
LVHW080454060421
683530LV00001B/12